STRANGE COMPANY
MILITARY ENCOUNTERS WITH UFOs IN WORLD WAR II

KEITH CHESTER

San Antonio • New York

An Original Publication of Anomalist Books

Strange Company
ISBN: 978-1-933665-20-7
ISBN 10: 1-933665-20-3

Cover image: An artist's interpretation based on Leonard Stringfield's original sketch of the foo fighters he witnessed in August of 1945.

Back cover auhor photo by Nancy Chester and Richard Callan.

Book design by Seale Studios

For information about Anomalist Books, go to anomalistbooks.com or write to:

Anomalist Books   Anomalist Books
5150 Broadway #108   PO Box 577
San Antonio, TX 78209   Jefferson Valley, NY 10535

CONTENTS

This book is dedicated to my friend and mentor:
Mr. Leonard H. Stringfield

Sergeant Leonard H. Stringfield.
November 1945. (Courtesy Mrs. Dell Stringfield)

Foreword

In this eye-opening, thoroughly researched book, bristling with surprising revelations, Keith Chester challenges decades of conventional wisdom about the UFO phenomenon.

UFO history is ordinarily judged to date from Kenneth Arnold's exhaustingly chronicled June 24, 1947, sighting over Mount Rainier, Washington, which was followed by the first of many waves that continue to this day. Nobody asserts, of course, that UFOs actually *begin* on that legendary Tuesday afternoon; sightings of aerial anomalies are known to have been reported decades – some claim centuries – earlier. But it is assumed that the phenomenon as a more or less constant presence among the world's enigmas dates to the post-war period. *Strange Company* shows how wrong this standard view is.

Chester does not make the point explicitly, so I will do so here:

The persistent (as opposed to occasional) UFO phenomenon, in just about all of its varieties, arrived during World War II, not in 1947. Ufologists have been aware of "foo fighters" – indeed, newspaper accounts in the summer of 1947 mention them as predating flying saucers – but this book documents just how remarkably frequent and ubiquitous encounters with them were.

It also demonstrates that foo fighters were an inclusive phrase, which did not refer simply to nebulous lights, but to structured craft-like objects as well. Witnesses, pilots and aircrews prominent among them, were convinced that the phenomena were under intelligent control. In common with untold numbers of observers in later years, they were baffled by the objects' extraordinary performance characteristics. Only the huge distraction of global conflict – not to mention the demands of military secrecy – kept this curious development from rising to the level of widespread popular attention.

Having written about it extensively, I know something about UFO history, but I knew only a fraction of the story Keith Chester tells here. I am certain that whether you are a novice or a veteran of ufology, just about every page here will supply you with new information and fresh insight. Filling a huge gap in both the literature and our understanding, *Strange Company* will be an indispensable UFO book.

Jerome Clark
April 16, 2007

Introduction

It was a time when Buck Rogers and Flash Gordon, characters who appeared in the pages of science fiction, lived in a world of astonishing inventions: rocket ships, space travel, and powerful weapons. These fictional heroes represented the future, and that future was taking shape on Earth.

Mankind had reached a threshold in the forth decade of the twentieth century. There were unprecedented scientific and technological achievements, but despite such progress, humanity was entering one of its darkest chapters. By 1933, a gathering storm threatened the entire civilized world. It finally struck on September 1, 1939, as the German war machine crossed into Poland unleashing newly developed blitzkrieg tactics and lethal firepower. World War II gripped the world with terror for the next six years.

Both civilians and military personnel saw numerous highly unconventional aircraft around the world prior to and during World War II. From the war's outbreak in 1939, these unconventional aircraft were observed in all theaters of operation in a variety of shapes, sizes, and colors. They had extraordinary flight performance capabilities, were able to travel at phenomenal speeds, and could avoid radar detection. These remarkable objects seemed to come straight from the pages of science fiction.

Confusing the issue, these unconventional aircraft were sighted along with enemy weaponry and pyrotechnic activity: there were antiaircraft artillery rounds (commonly referred to as flak); an assortment of flares, some designed to psychologically spook the airmen; rockets and missiles of all sizes; and jet and rocket-propelled aircraft. All these sightings were listed under the heading of "phenomena" or "phenomenon" in military intelligence memoranda. With each passing year, though unconventional aircraft sightings defied explanation, they were usually lumped together with flares, rockets, and experimental aircraft.

During World War II, the term Unidentified Flying Object (UFO) did not exist. Instead, these strange and mysterious aircraft or objects were labeled with whatever term the observer felt like using at the time. Air crews called them "meteors," "freaks," and "balls of fire." Those names were entered in the crew's mission report, and from there, if the name stuck, it would be used in later reports to describe the same phenomenon. It was not until 1945 that these objects became known as "Foo Fighters."

At this point, I would like to provide the reader with some background regarding how this book came about. It all started in May of 1989. During my first UFO investigation, I was preparing to inteview a witness with second-hand knowledge of a UFO allegedly recovered by the United States government.[1] Having no experience with this kind of interview, I knew a game plan of sorts was needed. Understanding the importance of obtaining accurate and untainted information, I wanted to speak with someone in the field who might be able to provide some advice.

My first step was placing an impromptu telephone call to Leonard Stringfield, a well-known and well-respected UFO author and researcher. Stringfield had already dedicated nearly forty years to the subject, focusing the last ten years on what he called "UFO Crash and Retrievals." Introducing myself, I explained why I had called, and asked if he would be interested in offering his advice and guidance. To my surprise, he was very receptive to helping me.

As a result, Stringfield and I became fast friends and continued communicating with each other long after my investigation was closed. During one of our telephone conversations, we discussed Stringfield's personal wartime foo fighter observation. His sighting occurred during the late summer of 1945. At that time, he was flying into mainland Japan, assigned to an intelligence unit with the Fifth Air Force. In broad daylight, he observed a formation of three circular, wingless aircraft, apparently under intelligent control.

Having read about the foo fighters in earlier intelligence reports, Stringfield was certain he had seen the same things. Strangely, though, the war was over, and the Allied Air Forces had complete air supremacy, so he was convinced that what he had seen were not enemy aircraft. Moreover, as far as he was concerned, the objects were nothing like any aircraft he had ever seen prior to, during, or after the war.

I barraged Stringfield with question after question, asking about the size, shape, color, and speed of the objects. I asked about what he thought while watching the objects. We discussed theories surrounding the event, trying to determine if the foo fighters were misidentified enemy secret weapons, or meteorological or celestial phenomena. But no matter how hard we tried piecing together a conventional explanation, it fell apart. The bottom line: he was sure he had observed something truly fantastic. In fact, after decades of postwar research, Stringfield was convinced he had seen an extraterrestrial spacecraft.[2]

I found Stringfield's story absolutely fascinating. I knew UFO sightings were reported throughout the war and around the world, but his sighting was the most detailed I had ever heard. I realized that Stringfield's encounter was probably not a unique event and wondered just how many other amazing wartime sightings there were out there. In any event, hearing Stringfield's account was spellbinding. I was hooked.

I began my research by reading all the available UFO literature I could get my hands on. Since the early 1950s, much had been written about the subject. But after reading literally dozens of books, I soon learned that very little had been written about UFOs during World War II; usually this time period was just mentioned in a paragraph, maybe on a page or two, and rarely in a whole chapter.

By 1999, almost ten years after my first venture into the subject, I had the time to seriously delve into the mystery of what exactly was seen during World War II. Accumulating information from a variety of sources, I began building my own database. The respected UFO historians Barry Greenwood and Jan Aldrich proved invaluable as resources. Their generosity in supplying me with some of the best wartime documentation available quickly brought me up to speed.

I soon realized that there existed very little military documentation about the so-called foo fighters. Already having an interest in the war's history, I decided to narrow my search to military sightings, primarily focusing on those reported by British and American airmen.

Now armed with a game plan, I was off and running. For my own satisfaction, I felt it was important to have at least one official document that indicated the UFO phenomenon was real and had existed during the war. Though not well known except by UFO historians and researchers, and a small public following, I knew of one such document: The "Report of Meetings of the Scientific Advisory Panel on Unidentified Flying Objects Convened by [the] Office of Scientific Intelligence, CIA, January 14-18, 1953, The Robertson Panel Report."[3] This document revealed that for several days the CIA hosted a meeting, consisting of a small group of eminent scientists, to review the unprecedented amount of UFO sightings that had taken place from 1947 through 1952. These sightings had caused quite a stir within the U.S. government and military hierarchies. The CIA had asked the scientists to determine if UFOs posed a national security threat.

Of significance in the Robertson Panel report is the section titled "On Lack of Danger," which mentions foo fighters: "The panel concluded unanimously that there was no evidence of a direct threat to national security in the objects sighted. Instances of 'Foo fighters' were cited. These were unexplained phenomena sighted by aircraft pilots during World

War II in European and Far East theaters of operation wherein 'balls of light' would fly near or with the aircraft and maneuver rapidly. They were believed to be electrostatic (similar to St. Elmo's fire) or electromagnetic phenomena or possibly light reflections from light crystals in the air, but their exact cause or nature was never defined."

But the most startling statement in the Robertson Panel document appears in the next paragraph: "If the term 'flying saucers' had been popular in 1943-1945, these objects would have been so labeled." Not only did the Robertson Panel report affirm the reality of the wartime UFO phenomenon, it admitted that the phenomenon greatly challenged conventional wisdom.

Just as startling perhaps is the fact that many of the eminent scientists on the Robertson Panel report had been actively involved with investigating the foo fighters and other unconventional objects during the war. One of those scientists was California Institute of Technology physicist Howard P. Robertson, the same Robertson who chaired the 1953 CIA UFO panel. Another was physicist Luis W. Alvarez, at the University of California. But most importantly, the Robertson Report names David T. Griggs, a professor of geophysics at the University of California at Los Angeles, as being "the most knowledgeable person" regarding the foo fighters.

These men had been aware of, and studying, this phenomenon longer than anyone else, years before the well-publicized, "first" flying saucer sighting reported by Kenneth Arnold in 1947. I thought that surely a record of their investigations must exist. Surely they must have known more than the conclusion offered in the Robertson Panel Report, that the "exact cause or nature" of this phenomenon "was never defined." And so began my quest.

After four years of research at the National Archives and Records Administration (NARA), located in College Park, Maryland, I wrote *Strange Company*, the first in-depth account of unconventional aircraft observed and reported by the military during World War II. It begins in the early 1930s with the rise of Nazi Germany and continues right through the end of the war in 1945. Instead of following battles and campaigns, it chronicles unconventional aircraft sightings, month-by-month and year-by-year. In some instances, several of the sightings were so remarkable they left an indelible mark in the witnesses' memories, keeping them hunting for answers long after the war's end.

Strange Company includes the reactions by military commands, their viewpoints, and theories as they struggled to make sense of the observations. It also examines the Allied intelligence gathering missions created for fact finding and exploitation in Germany and Japan. These intelligence missions are important because they were a perfect apparatus to help learn the truth about the foo fighters, if indeed the technology was of German or Japanese origin.

Strange Company presents one of the greatest wartime mysteries, one that has been shrouded in ignorance for more than sixty years. And it suggests that while an immense twentieth century war was raging on Earth, there appeared to be someone, or something, from somewhere else, watching us.

Chapter One

Among The War Clouds

In the early 1930s a new Germany was on the rise, funneling its available funds into building a military juggernaut. Throughout Europe tension mounted as political unrest signaled an inevitable conflict. Though Germany was getting stronger, several years remained before its aviation industry could rule the skies. Until then, like most air forces around the world, its aircraft designs consisted of two and three winged aircraft, still a rare sight over most nations.[4]

Commonly referred to as aeroplanes, these aircraft were identified by their looks, sounds, and flight capabilities. But soon things began to change. According to witness accounts, a few aeroplanes were flying much greater distances, at night, and in extremely harsh weather conditions. Confusing many in authority, it appeared someone or some nation had accomplished a tremendous leap in aviation technology. Questions poured forth, but there were no answers, nor did anyone claim responsibility for the flights. Reports of strange and unidentifiable aircraft began peppering the newspapers.

According to the *New York Times*, on the night of October 11, 1931 a "flaming, one hundred foot blimp" crashed near the Ohio River. Gallipolis Ferry, West Virginia residents told the police they were positive they saw a "crashed blimp" or dirigible. Speaking with all dirigible companies in the area, the police learned that none of the companies had lost a dirigible, and they had not launched any in the West Virginia area. After conducting an extensive all-day foot and air search, the sighting could not be confirmed; authorities found no wreckage or signs of a crash site.

On December 29, 1932, the New Jersey Police were contacted that an aircraft had crashed. Though the witness heard no plane engines, he saw the blinking lights of an "airplane" dropping behind the tress. Immediately a search and rescue operation was formed but after an exhaustive effort, the rescue party found no bodies or wreckage.[5]

The following summer, a strange sighting occurred over Sussex, England on the evening of July 5. Four Royal Air Force (RAF) Hawker Fury I biplane fighters flying on a cross-country training exercise encountered a gigantic "light" that shone directly down into the center of their formation from a higher altitude. Experiencing mechanical trouble, the two Hawkers were unable to remain in formation and separated from the group. Captain Nigel Tompkins and Lt. Bruce H. Thomas were forced to make an emergency landing when both their planes' engines quit running. On his way down, Thomas passed so close to the intense "light" that it caused burns on his face and hands.[6]

A few months later a mysterious aircraft was seen, and sometimes heard, nightly for two weeks, flying with its lights on over Britain and the East Coast of the United States. The sightings, while never explained, were relatively few in number as compared to the flurry of mysterious aerial activity reported over Scandinavia.

For ten days in late December 1933, the Swedish Air Force searched in vain, hunting for an aerial intruder operating unchallenged in northern Norway and northern Sweden. Authorities believed the aircraft was flying out of a secret mountain base located near Westerbotten.[7] Oddly, no weather condition was severe enough to keep the "mysterious airplane" grounded and, on one occasion, was even heard flying towards Norway during a snowstorm.[8] Not only was the "mysterious airplane" flying in weather that greatly challenged then current conventional aircraft capabilities, but it "frequently circled low, projecting powerful searchlights on the ground." Reports of engine noise accompanied some sightings, while other witnesses "sometimes described low-level maneuvers in complete silence."[9]

Around 6 p.m. on December 24, witnesses in the town of Kalix, Sweden saw "beams of light" coming from a "machine" that searched the ground below. The "beams of light" were described as "blinding," creating illumination compared to daylight.[10]

On December 30, two highway motorists watched a "low-flying aeroplane" pass over them at an estimated altitude of 150 feet. According to the Swedish press, authorities said "no ambulance planes or military aircraft were in the area at that time."

The Swedish military became concerned about the "mysterious airplanes" flying in Sweden's restricted airspace. On December 31, the Fourth Swedish Flying Corps issued orders instructing their army aviators to "chase" the unknown aircraft.[11] In an attempt to discover whether the intruders were flying out of a mountain base, two Swedish airplanes carried out aerial reconnaissance. Their attempt failed. Both planes were lost in the search, but fortunately, the crews survived. On Christmas day, a second effort was initiated by Lt. Wanberg, who conducted a lone scouting expedition on foot, but he never returned. In an effort to locate him, three skiers embarked on a rescue mission. Sadly, they too, disappeared. The treacherous weather and rough terrain had proven absolutely brutal, and as of January 9, 1934, the military failed in their attempt to find all four men.[12]

By January 28, the loss of life and two military aircraft had cast a dark shadow over the entire affair. In response, the Swedish Air Force conducted an official investigation of the "phantom fliers." The sightings became more than a Swedish problem, since many of the Swiss sighting reports indicated the phantom fliers had crossed over neighboring Norway's airspace. Both countries were alarmed by the mysterious aircraft, which were "obviously locating and circling forts, military and railway installations, and were boldly buzzing restricted areas of strategic importance."[13]

On February 3, 1934, Finnish authorities began reporting that they, too, were receiving reports of an aeroplane flying in their airspace. Picked up by the newspapers, the story made headlines. "Continued night flights over Northern Finland, Sweden and Norway by so-called 'ghost aviators,' which have caused such apprehension here as to prompt the general staff to organize reconnoitering on a wide scale by army planes all over Northern Finland, still remain a deep mystery," reported the *New York Times*. "Many eyewitnesses have been unable to identify the planes." Aviation experts called in to investigate the sightings determined that whoever was flying the aeroplanes had "exceptional skill" and were "undoubtedly superior to that of Northern European aviators."

Intrigue surrounded the sightings, grabbing the attention of many and fueling political and military theories by experts who were following the mystery. One expert suggested the sightings were Japanese aircraft conducting a scouting mission of the Arctic Ocean, and in response, the Soviets sent up an aircraft. Finnish authorities, echoing a similar scenario, were compelled to believe that the "mystery planes" constituted "an extensive scheme to explore aviation possibilities for a future war."[14]

Meanwhile, over Oslo, Norway, a very unusual sighting was reported on April 1, 1934, in the newspaper *Tidens-Tegn*. According to the story, five witnesses observed "a very large aeroplane over Sandnessjoen." One witness, a sixteen-year old boy, said "he saw the machine in the brilliant moonlight," and the object had eight propellers. As the large aeroplane descended, it did not land, but began to move in wide circles over the water. From his vantage point, the boy was able to clearly observe the object, noting that there were "cabin windows" and they were all alit.[15]

By the spring, Sweden, Norway, and Finland were inundated with sighting reports. Despite focused military investigations and attempts to capture one of the "mystery planes," the issue remained both convoluted and confusing. This was abundantly clear from the mixed signals the authorities were presenting to the public. As if aimed to demystify the event or to calm any war nerves, on March 3 Swiss newspaper, *Dagens Nyheter*, issued a very odd statement declaring, "there had never been any ghost-fliers at all!" The investigation was called off because the search for "mysterious aeroplanes and other strange objects" had proven "futile."

The Swedish and Finnish Air Forces discontinued their investigations but not the Norwegians.[16] On March 10, General Henriek Johannessen of the Norwegian Air Force told the press that since the newspapers were continuing to receive sighting reports, the military could not discount "all" the "observations as illusions"; the military were treating these sightings as real threats.

On April 30, to avoid alarm but to keep the public somewhat informed, Major General Reutersward, commanding general of upper Norrland, told the newspapers that authorities were entertaining the possibility that the mystery airplanes were conducting reconnaissance exercises over very sensitive military areas. General Reutersward further stated that, although highly reliable witnesses made many close-up observations, "no identifying insignia or identifying marks were visible on the machines," and he added that "it was impossible to explain away the whole thing as mere imagination. The question is: Who or Whom are they, and why have they been invading our air territory?"[17]

Nightly sightings of the "mystery planes" continued through 1934, many times being reported as large and grey in color and sometimes flying in "formation of threes," and on into 1935.[18]

On January 14, the *New York Times* ran the story "Mysterious Planes Soviet's, Oslo Hears." In an attempt to answer the mystery, *Tidens Tegn*, a Norwegian newspaper, working on its own initiative, set up listening posts along the Finland-Russian border. Over several months, the posts monitored strange radio signals, which were thought to work in conjunction with the mystery planes flying on reconnaissance missions. "This is undoubtedly the real background and purpose of the mysterious airplanes and radio signals," reported the *Tidens-Tegn*. Another Norwegian newspaper, however, challenged the findings, calling them "not conclusive, since they were stopped by the Norwegian military authorities, who themselves are conducting an investigation."[19]

The 1933-1935 Scandinavian "mystery planes," "phantom fliers," or "ghost aviators" defy what history tells us regarding the state of aviation during the early to mid-1930s. Researcher John Keel suggests that pointing a finger at Russia has its merits but lacks proof; the country was nearly economically and militarily dead. To assume the Soviets had sent aircraft on pre-war reconnaissance missions over Finland is logical since unprecedented Soviet troop movement was occurring close to their border, but a Russian invasion was five years away. Even if the Soviets tried to obtain valuable route information, Finnish defensive positions, and geographical mapping, a mission of this complexity was too costly for the Soviets. Furthermore, the Russian air force was very weak. They had no exceptional pilots, and its aviation industry was nearly inoperable.

Keel points out that Great Britain and the United States were hit so hard by the depression they had no reason to allocate valuable funds for an aerial survey of Finland, Sweden, or Norway. If the United States was responsible, an aircraft carrier capable of operating in the Arctic Ocean was needed. But the Arctic Sea was far too rough for an aircraft carrier built in the 1930s. Assuming the ship managed to cope with such violent conditions, the ship's aircraft were short-ranged biplanes incapable of long-range missions. Japan, another nation capable of mounting a large-scale aerial mission, was engulfed in a war with China and had no reason to mount such an operation thousands of miles away. This left Germany as a possible culprit. Hitler was ignoring the Versailles Treaty of 1919. He was determined to build a powerful Luftwaffe, Germany's air force. His air armada, however, like Russia's, was not substantial in the early 1930s.

Assuming any of these nations were able to financially support the Scandinavian over-flights, then further funds were needed for building landing fields throughout Sweden, Finland, and Norway to support the operation, as long range flying was unknown at the time.[20]

In 1935, the "mystery plane" over-flights continued on the other side of the Atlantic. On November 24, just outside Palestine, Texas, witnesses were amazed to see a "bright shaft of light" suspended vertically to the ground and remain motionless high in the evening sky. Twice during the month of December, South Americans witnessed something similar in the night skies over Brazil: "Snake-like shafts of light" hanging motionless at great altitudes.[21]

Back in the U.S., Howard S. Behr was bringing in the New Year of 1937, spending some of his time that day flying to North Carolina in his Curtis-Wright Sedan. At 3,000 feet, Behr's visibility was good, as long as he stayed below the overcast. Around noon while over Virginia, he had no trouble identifying the shape of an aircraft about 1,000 feet below him and moving across his flight path. He watched as the 30-to-40-foot object passed by, noting there were no signs of windows or propellers. He said it "looked like a gondola, gun metal in color, with both of its ends turned up." Traveling some 60 mph faster than his Curtis, Behr estimated that the object reached a speed of 150 mph.[22]

Over Norway, on February 11, 1937, the crew of the fishing vessel named Fram spotted something that night while departing Kvalsik. Around 9:00 p.m., as they motored out from a cape and passed a secluded area between some hills and the mainland, they noticed a "large aeroplane" with red and green glowing lights resting on top of the water. The Fram's captain turned his boat around to offer his assistance, but as he approached, almost immediately the aeroplane's lights were extinguished; it was cloaked within a "cloud of smoke" before vanishing.

The "mystery planes" also returned to Sweden that year and were seen everywhere around the country, notably making their presence known over sensitive military positions. Despite calls for a new investigation of the "phantom fliers," the Swedish Minister of Defense would not authorize one, pointing out that despite a previous investigation, and searchlights and listening posts placed in the sighting areas, they had uncovered nothing.[23]

During the summer of 1937, another notable sighting occurred on July 20 over London. This time the aeroplane nicknamed the "ghost flier" made a nightly visit. Only observed as a light, it behaved so oddly that its actions gave the Air Ministry no choice but to investigate the matter. Officials were dumbfounded, but they too were unable to provide the public with any explanation.

Two days later, the crew of the British ship *Ranee* reported spotting an "aircraft" some 500 miles off the U.S. coast. The *New York Times* reported that lights were visible, but the object itself was not. The alleged aircraft was so far out over the Atlantic that its flight was considered a major undertaking. The press wanted to know who this "daredevil" was; for 1937, executing such a risky "trans-Atlantic flight" was an impressive feat. Contact was made with "American and Canadian seaboard facilities" and wealthy aviators such as Howard Hughes in hopes of learning who was flying the dangerous stunt. No one who was capable of such a flight knew anything about it, or anyone else who was capable of pulling it off.

By the end of 1937 witnesses near the German-Polish border described objects in the sky like "swords" and "coffins," reminiscent of those observed over North and South America in years prior.

On February 8, 1938, *The Daily Telegraph*, an English newspaper, carried a story based on letters to its editor. Written accounts were received from four witnesses, two of which were from scientists who said they had observed "'things like glowing spheres' that were 'floating in the

British sky.'" In another letter, Mr. H. Bond described an object he and his friend witnessed that "resembled an enormous shield of brass lighted by a searchlight."[24]

During the summer of 1938, Somerville, Massachusetts resident Malcolm B. Perry was walking home under the visible moon just after midnight. The rain had stopped and the sky had nearly cleared. Much to Perry's surprise, for close to a minute he saw not far above him, a "silvery" object that passed by silently. It was the size of "a twelve inch ruler at arm's length." At first, Perry thought it was a Navy blimp but soon realized that it was shaped differently, having no crew cabin below or propellers attached to the object.

Upon further observation, Perry was able to determine that the "silvery" object was "slimmer than a conventional blimp." It had tapered ends coming to sharp points, and there were "four rectangular portholes on one side" that emitted an "orange hue" from within. But more curious were the silhouettes of people "looking down" at him. Unsure of how to respond, he looked around to see if others were also watching the strange object. There was no one in sight, and the aircraft continued on, disappearing among low clouds.[25]

There were five years of incredible worldwide aerial sightings, representing a perplexing and confusing mystery to police, military, and scientific authorities. Official investigations conducted by Sweden, Norway, and Finland fell short, offering no concrete answers, while press coverage was alive with theories of everything from drug smuggling to secret air reconnaissance by Russia, Japan, and Germany. All explanations had their logic and plausibility problems, however.

One thing was certain: as of 1938, strange aircraft sightings were part of a phenomenon that was not going to fade away.

Chapter Two

From War of the Worlds, To a World at War

In 1938, only those with imaginative minds openly entertained the possibility that reconnaissance spacecraft from another world were monitoring the Earth's civilizations. This concept was not beyond plausibility; rocketry was progressing at an accelerated pace and space travel was not that far away. For years science fiction writers fueled the public's imagination, offering tales of space travel and extraterrestrial encounters with the adventures of Buck Rogers and Flash Gordon. With the increased interest in Earth's celestial neighbors, technological progress, and reports of worldwide aerial phenomena, many were convinced that life existed elsewhere in outer space, even as close as Mars.

On the evening of October 30, 1938, families settled in for the night and tuned into their favorite radio programs on one of the affiliate stations of the Columbia Broadcasting System (CBS). Suddenly, the music was interrupted by a commanding voice informing them that astronomers at a Chicago observatory had reported seeing several strange explosions of incandescent gas on Mars that were heading towards Earth. Radio listeners riveted by the breaking bulletins soon learned that a large fireball or meteorite had fallen on a farm in New Jersey. Reporters at the scene described a metallic "cylinder" buried deep within the impact crater. Horrified, listeners stared at their radios in disbelief as they were told the object was no meteor; it was aliens invading Earth from another world.[26]

Soon after the panic subsided, citizens learned the gripping news was nothing more than Orson Well's dramatic radio presentation of *War of the Worlds* by H.G. Wells.

The planet Mars had now captured everyone's attention. The following summer, on the evening of July 27, 1939, radio WOR Special Features Division was broadcasting live from the Haydn Planetarium of the American Museum of Natural History in New York City. The planet Mars and Earth were at their closest since 1924. WOR engineers and Clyde Fisher, curator of the Haydn Planetarium, had collaborated on the project and were sending the first radio communication to Mars.[27]

Anxiously awaiting a return call from the red planet, they received nothing but radio static. The Martians had not called back. Despite the lack of response, many continued to scan the skies, watching, waiting, and wondering if intelligent life existed in space, and if so, was there a chance that one day Earth would be invaded?

Meanwhile, sightings reminiscent of 1935's "shafts of light" were reported in the U.S. Around 9:30 p.m., one day in July, Pittsburg, Pennsylvania residents Mr. and Mrs. J.M. Williams sat on their front porch. A slight breeze blew as scattered clouds slowly passed overhead, exposing the brightest of stars. Mrs. Williams saw, hanging motionless about forty-five degrees above the horizon, a different light, one that was not a star. Soon, her husband, a fifteen-year Navy veteran, looked on in amazement. The light was sword-shaped and hung in the air, tilted at an angle. They watched for some time, noticing the object was solid and surrounded by a "weird glow" as compared to car's fog light. Mr. Williams heard no sound and said it "resembled a modern-day jet airliner without its wings."[28] He stated that "It seemed slightly tapered and the smaller end displayed a fin-like protrusion on each side similar to stabilizers on conventional aircraft." And "assuming that the end containing and protruding devices were a tail end, the front end pointed toward the ground at a 45 degree angle."

The couple watched the object for some time, until a cloud passed in front of it, momentarily obstructing their view, and when the cloud moved, the object was gone.[29]

It was nearly a year since the frightening "War of the Worlds" radio broadcast. Earth survived the fictional attack. There were no spaceships. There were no monsters. But there was an invasion, and it was not by aliens from the planet Mars. It was real and from a place called Germany. And the monster's name was Adolph Hitler.

Beginning on September 1, 1939, Hitler set his war machine in motion, unveiling its new Blitzkrieg tactics that pounced upon its prey. His troops and panzers flooded the landscape, and his mighty Luftwaffe bombed from above, simultaneously unleashing a dreadful reign of destruction against Poland.[30]

As Hitler's armies marched onward, Reginald V. Jones reported to his new job as scientific officer on the staff of Britain's Air Ministry. Because of his background in infrared radar experimentation, Jones was asked by Sir Henry Tizard, committee leader for the Survey of Air Defense, to learn "what the Germans were doing in applying science to air warfare."

The committee felt that since British Air Intelligence had found no answers to that question, they wanted Jones to learn why there was a lack of information on the subject and to recommend how to improve the situation. Reporting to the Directorate of Scientific Research, Jones was placed under the command of Wing Commander F.W. Winterbotham, head of the Air Intelligence Branch, AII(c), a section belonging to the Secret Intelligence Service (SIS), better known as MI6. Within days of his assignment, Jones was in the town of Bletchley Park, at an estate referred to as "Station X," the place where MI6 stored all its pre-war files. It was here that Jones combed the files for hints of what Hitler's Luftwaffe was capable of, and what secret weapon(s) were at its disposal.

The files were a fantastic read, a real gold mine loaded with alleged true stories, filled with wild reports of earthquake machines, engine-stopping rays, pilotless aircraft, atomic energy, bacteriological warfare.[31] Since British MI6 monitored fantastic weapon ideas, it's a good bet that reports of the 1930s "mystery planes" were among the SIS files Jones examined.

In the meantime, Britain faced an immediate threat from Germany. During May and June, the Royal Air Force (RAF) Bomber Command accumulated nearly one hundred accounts of enemy engagements while aiding neighboring countries to counter the German onslaught. Responding to reports of unidentifiable aircraft, Bomber Command interviewed returning crews and acknowledged something odd had been observed. They continued monitoring the developing situation, funneling copies of their operational reports to the Air Ministry.

On August 11, 1940, British Bomber Command released its report of the sightings: "Phenomena Connected With Enemy Night Tactics." The report detailed engagements with enemy aircraft, primarily over the coast of Holland and the Ruhr Valley area in Germany. In response to conflicting reports, Bomber Command stated: "It is difficult to assess the degree of accuracy of some of the reports, where enemy aircraft have not attacked, or have not approached close enough to be identified with certainty, and where the reports have not been substantiated by more than one crew."

Mystified by accounts of alleged enemy aircraft, and unable to accurately define them, Bomber Command tried to explain them away: "The strain upon a member of the crew maintaining a vigilant lookout for long periods of time is intense. Under such conditions, the stories of 'shadowing' are apt to stimulate the very natural tendency to think that any unidentified shape seen, or imagined in the sky, is an enemy aircraft. In this connection it is interesting to note that, except on occasions when fire ensued, only one report of the 92 considered can be definitely confirmed by more than one member of the crew. It is appreciated that the reason for this is probably the limited view from crew positions, but is, nevertheless, not without interest."

Continuing with their assessment, Bomber Command further stated: "...It is quite a well known practice for the Germans to test experimental apparatus under active service conditions and it appears highly probable that some of the peculiar incidents reported by pilots have been due to some new detection device or searchlight installed for experimental purposes."[32]

Bomber Command's so-called "peculiar incidents" are strangely reminiscent of the 1930s "mystery planes." It is not known what more was learned during the RAF crew interrogations. Without seeing the crew's original reports, three questions come to mind: (1) Why would an enemy aircraft bring attention to itself with a light, especially in a situation that offered no real combat value? (2) Were these sightings too unbelievable for Bomber Command to accept as German aircraft carrying experimental devices? (3) And, if so, how much information was not included in the Bomber Command report?

The August 11 report suggests that higher authorities, probably the Air Ministry, knew more than they were saying and instructed Bomber Command to take an official stance – that anything unusual observed, no matter how strange, was due to either experimental aircraft, misidentifications, or hallucinations resulting from stress during combat. Furthermore, since copies of Bomber Command's operational reports were funneled to the Air Ministry, they were probably sent to the Assistant Director of Intelligence (Science), R.V. Jones.[33]

As the Battle of Britain raged above England, a very special group of men had crossed the Atlantic. Led by Sir Henry Tizard, scientific advisor to the Air Ministry and Ministry of Aircraft Production, a group of fellow scientists and military representatives had come to the United States on an extremely important mission: to create an exchange program between the two nations regarding military weaponry and its use.[34]

Meeting in Washington, the British team carried with them "a black deed box" filled with films, manuals, and blueprints representing Britain's most valuable technological developments, regarding jets and other weapons to ward off Germany's onslaught. But the most important content of the box was a sample of a magnetron, an instrument affording astonishing new advances in ground, airborne, and on-ship radar applications. Tizard was given the authority to hand over this information in exchange for information about America's top technological developments.[35]

Responding to Britain's plight, by March 1941, elements of the newly formed American National Research Defense Council (NRDC) had set up shop in London.[36] It seems that the newly created London mission gave the Royal Air Force a great scientific opportunity to query U.S. officials about mysterious aircraft reported by the Navy and Army Air Force fliers, including those by private commercial aircraft over the U.S. and abroad.

Desiring an intelligence organization to handle national secrets without compartmentalization, President Franklin D. Roosevelt appointed William J. Donovan as the Coordinator of Information (COI) in July of 1941, to "collect and analyze all information and data" affecting national security.[37] Two months later, in September of 1941, a Royal Navy crewman observed something over the Indian Ocean. The *SS Pulaski*, a converted Polish ship used to ferry troops, had set sail from Durban, South Africa on a long journey to Suez.

That night, somewhere between the African mainland of Mozambique and the island of Madagascar, seaman Mar Doroba stood watch under a star-filled, moonless sky when he observed a "strange globe glowing with greenish light, about half the size of the full moon." Another of the ship's gunners, also watching the object, yelled to Doroba, wanting to know what they were observing. Stunned by the object's appearance, Doroba had no clue. Both men continued watching the eerie sight for more than an hour before it "disappeared." Not wanting to be ridiculed, Doroba kept quiet about the incident.[38] Apparently, the other witnesses did the same.

In a little over twenty-four months, the Nazis conquered Poland, Finland, Holland, Norway and France; Yugoslavia and Greece were dominated, and Crete fell. War found North Africa, and Russia struggled against annihilation. Germany and her allies, Italy and Japan, were giving Hitler great confidence in his quest for world domination. Americans feared for the Europeans, but were determined to remain a neutral country. However, President Roosevelt understood his nation could not ignore the war drums forever; important allies were suffering.

On the morning of December 7, 1941, the Japanese attacked the islands of Hawaii, Guam, Wake, and Midway. Within days, Japan's destructive path extended throughout the South China Sea and Pacific Ocean. And on December 11, Hitler declared war against the United States. The United States had no choice but to join the global conflict; both coasts of the U.S. were now possible battlegrounds.[39] Fueled by war nerves, U.S. military and civil defense units kept a close vigil on the skies and oceans.

During the first two weeks of December 1941, three military officers, including Lt. Walter Hanson and his wife, were stranded in the Georgia countryside. The Hanson's waited behind while their friend departed with a passing motorist to retrieve gas. Gazing up at the night sky, Mrs. Hanson saw it first: one of the stars began to move. It made no sense. According to Mrs. Hanson, the light "went in circles counter-clock wise, which was especially baffling. It made these circles so quickly it was hard to believe our own eyes. Suddenly, it stopped dead again and just as quickly took off obliquely, upward and out of sight."[40]

Later that month, on December 22, Utica, New York resident George Bogner, an electrical engineer, stopped his car at the corner of St. Agnes Avenue and Pleasant Street to watch "a round, sharply outlined object" speed silently across the sky. The sun reflected off its "bright aluminum or chrome finish." Not more than 1,000 feet away, Bogner estimated the "disc-shaped object" had a diameter of 100 feet, flew no more than 400 feet off the ground at around 300 miles per hour, and made no sound. Completely puzzled, Bogner raced home to tell his wife, only to find that she, too, had witnessed an "immense, perfectly round, shiny object streak over the city." They contacted the media to share their sighting.[41]

Meanwhile Japanese aircraft and submarines were sighted repeatedly along the Pacific Coast of the U.S.; in one instance, a Japanese submarine fired several shells against a California oil refinery. U.S. Naval Intelligence in California received information that more attacks were imminent.

Chapter Three

Over Coasts and Valleys

I t was a bit chilly on the night of February 24, 1942. The crisp air added beauty to another California evening, punctuated by the circadian sound of ocean waves breaking, crashing, and flowing ashore.[42] Suddenly, around 1900 hours, alarms pierced the night's serenity, sending a shrill call of danger to inhabitants of the Los Angeles area. Naval Intelligence received word from the 37th Coastal Artillery Brigade Headquarters that a high number of "flares and blinking lights" were observed near the defense plants.[43] A Yellow Alert was issued from the Mexican border to the coast of Monterey. Home defense units scanned the skies and sea for signs of danger. By 2223 hours, no attack had come; it was a false alarm.[44]

The all-clear siren was sounded, giving the Pacific-coast citizens a chance to relax and calm their nerves. But that was short lived. A few hours later, around 0144 hours, radar units again picked up an "unidentifiable aerial target." At 0200 hours, First Lt. Kenneth R. Martin, of the 4th Interceptor Command, confirmed the "well tracked" target.[45] Fifteen minutes later, antiaircraft units were ordered to "Green Alert." An unidentified target was a little more than one hundred miles away and heading towards Los Angeles. Until an attack was confirmed, the Army Air Force held what few fighters they had on the ground. At 0221 hours the unidentified target "came within a few miles of the coast," so the regional controller issued a blackout.

"Enemy planes" were reported everywhere, though they had "vanished" off the radar screens. A few minutes later, at 0243 hours, antiaircraft batteries in the vicinity saw something in the sky. Responding with gunfire, they sparked a chain reaction, and the night sky erupted into a frenzy of pyrotechnics.[46] All hell had broken loose; forty searchlights danced over the city, their cones of light stretching deep into the night sky. Flares hung pulsating in the air, and tracer rounds, followed by deadly antiaircraft munitions, streaked upwards in all directions. Confused, most citizens remained in their shelters while some ventured outside to watch. Though several units with the Army said a balloon caused them to open fire, many eyewitnesses said they saw something else flying over the area: a "triangular grouping" of "glowing objects" was heading inland over the coast, near defense factories in the area.

Air raid warden Raymond Angier, an employee with the Douglas Aircraft Company, witnessed the "unidentified aircraft" approaching Los Angeles: "When I went running outside to make sure people had doused their lights and were heading for shelters, I saw what had triggered the alarm: a formation of six to nine luminous white dots, in triangular formation, visible in the northwest. The formation moved painfully slowly — you might call it leisurely, as if it were oblivious to the whole stampede it had created..." Commenting further, he said: "You'll never know what it was like. One minute the city was bedded down for the night; the next thing you know, the streets were swarming with air raid wardens, people going in both directions and a lot of talk about enemy overhead..."

Running back inside and up to the roof of his home, Angier got a better look. The formation of "luminous white dots" was flying in a triangular formation, moving very slowly at about 20,000 feet. Returning to the street, he saw the triangle of lights were "almost at zenith, possibly slightly past." Angier heard sporadic antiaircraft fire but, in between bursts of fire, no sound came from the objects.

Angier talked with air raid wardens for about thirty minutes and then returned to the rooftop. From there he observed that the triangle of "dots" no longer showed individual round lights but a single "faint light" – "probably the luminous triangle of dots seen on edge." The triangle brought anti-aircraft fire, but its altitude was too high for the rounds to reach.[47]

Another witness, Paul T. Collins, was heading home. An air raid warden signaled him to pull off the road and turn off his headlights until further notice. Looking towards the horizon, Collins saw "bright red spots of light...moving in a strange manner." The light's altitude was approximately ten thousand feet and had appeared out of nowhere, "zigzagging from side to side".

Collins and others watched and listened as the antiaircraft shells exploded around the objects. Some of the lights disappeared, blinking out, "vanishing into the night." Remarkably, several searchlights had caught one of the objects in their crossbeams. It was completely illuminated and remained motionless while several antiaircraft shells appeared to explode right against the object's surface. According to a *Herald Express* reporter witnessing the event, the antiaircraft shells hit the object, but had no apparent damage or effect.[48]

An object sustaining antiaircraft fire without affect was captured on film and printed in the newspapers. Close examination of the picture reveals the classic shape of a flying saucer, not a conventional fighter, bomber, hovering dirigible, or balloon.[49]

Collins watched guns of an anti-aircraft battery near the Douglas Aircraft Company, also his place of employment, fire at the red objects. "Taking into account our distance from Long Beach," said Collins, "the extensive pattern of firing from widely separated antiaircraft batteries, and the movement of the unidentified red objects among 'and around' the bursting shells in wide orbits, we estimated their top speed conservatively to be five miles per second..." Collins added that he did not see the huge object that thousands had witnessed closer to the coast, stating the object was further up the coast.[50]

Observations by military witnesses also varied. Colonel Henry C. Davis, executive officer and acting commander of the 37th Coastal Artillery Brigade said that at first he thought there were up to fifteen planes flying overhead. But then he decided that smoke caused the confusion and there were no planes at all. Posted on a rooftop in downtown Los Angeles, another witness, Lt. Buchanen, saw and heard up to "thirty planes" caught in the searchlights, but looking through his binoculars, he saw nothing.[51]

Correspondent Rodney L. Brink with the *Christian Science Monitor* reported that men firing anti-aircraft guns witnessed targets illuminated by searchlights that looked "like a silver dot" or "like a moving star." Other men said they observed a "big object, too big to be an airplane."

In southeast Los Angeles, Lieutenant Miles reported seeing three planes flying at 9,000 feet in a "V" formation, even though his radar showed nothing on its screen, Lt. Bendixon "counted fourteen planes flying high and slowly." Colonel Watson of the 203rd Coast Artillery and Captain Cohen of the 214th Coast Artillery both saw a meteorological balloon flying at 8,000 to 9,000 feet; even the searchlights captured it in their beams. Strangely enough, Sergeant Bowman, also with the 214th, saw "five planes" flying in a "wedge formation that changed to a 'T' formation." Lt. Anderson, with the 78th Coast Artillery stationed at the Douglas Aircraft Factory in Long Beach, saw a single aircraft through his field glasses and confirmed on radar, flying at 20,000 feet.[52]

By dawn, people saw for themselves the aftermath of a battle that never came. Debris from antiaircraft shell casings, unexploded rounds, and rubble from damaged streets and buildings littered the area.[53]

Within twenty-four hours, the "Battle of Los Angeles" had expanded into a full-scale mystery. In addition to conflicting testimonies, the event turned more puzzling when separate branches of the armed forces disagreed on the incident. On February 25, Secretary of the Navy Frank Knox declared the raid nothing more than a false alarm, with no evidence of any aircraft; the Fourth Army Air Force was also convinced that no planes were present.[54]

But Army authorities disagreed. After waiting a day to get their facts straight, Secretary of War Henry L. Stimson announced that the War Department indicated that possibly fifteen enemy-operated "unidentified airplanes" were involved.[55] Stimson determined that there were two possibilities: the aircraft were either Japanese planes launched from a submarine sitting offshore, or commercial planes flown by enemy agents from "secret fields in California and Mexico."[56] Stimson based his findings from information in a report received from his Army Chief of Staff, General George C. Marshall,[57] who received the details from military commands on the West Coast.

Marshall immediately sent a report to President Roosevelt: "The following is the information we have from HQ at this moment regarding the air alarm over Los Angeles of yesterday morning:

"From details at this hour:

"1. Unidentified airplanes, other than American Army or Navy planes, were probably over Los Angeles, and were fired on by elements of the 37th CA Brigade (AA) between 3:12 and 4:15 a.m. These units expended 1430 rounds of ammunition.

"2. As many as fifteen airplanes may have been involved, flying at various speeds from what is officially reported as being 'very slow' to as much as 200 MPH and at elevations from 9000 to 18000 feet."

General Marshall stated that neither the Army nor the Navy were responsible for sending any United States aircraft into action, that no casualties were reported among the ground troops, and that an investigation into the matter was ongoing.

"Investigation continuing," the report continued. "It seems reasonable to conclude, that if unidentified airplanes were involved they may have been from commercial sources, operated by enemy agents for purposes of spreading alarm, disclosing location of antiaircraft positions, and slowing production through blackout. Such conclusion is supported by varying speed of operation and the fact that no bombs were dropped."[58]

Press coverage continued for days and debates over the situation flourished. Confusion over why the authorities contradicted one another had escalated public and congressional concern. Many criticized the military for being unsure and misleading. A real enemy threat faced the American people and they wanted assurance from their government that they would be kept informed and that war games would not be played at the expense of their fraying nerves.[59]

On February 26, the same day that General Marshall informed President Roosevelt that California was under attack, another highly unusual object was observed in another part of the world. The Dutch Cruiser *Tromp* was sailing in the Timor Sea, a part of the Indian Ocean between the island of Timor and India. The *Tromp* crewmen were puzzled by "a large, illuminated disc approaching at terrific speed." For almost four hours, they watched in amazement as the wingless object circled above their ship. Finally, the "disc" departed the area at an estimated 3,500 miles per hour.[60]

Following the Battle of Los Angeles, unidentified aircraft activity continued in the U.S. but remained obscure at best. In Kentucky, Bill Iversole, Charles, Furnash, and R.N. Danner were train operators running a line in the Licking River Valley one evening when they saw a "powerful searchlight" that seemed about 300 feet above them, illuminating a hillside below. They were unable to distinguish the shape of the object; it at times remained stationary, but moved on as the light shone down.

Over Evanston, Illinois, Reverend Robert H. Moore and six others attending the Seabury-Western Theological Seminary were witness to something very peculiar. According to Reverend Moore: "It was straight up from the northern section of Evanston, very small, or very high as it occupied less than 5° of angle-sight in length. It was a sharply defined rectangle, about 3 times as long as it was wide. Color: an even light gray, much lighter and brighter than the surrounding sky. No perceptible shading, indicating a flat surface rather than a cylinder viewed 90° to its axis. No apparent motion for about ten minutes."

Unfortunately, none of the witnesses saw the object leave; they just noticed it had disappeared. Thinking the device was "attached to a weather balloon" or some kind of an Army experimental device, they soon discounted that notion as no balloons were observed in the vicinity, and there was no visible means to support the object.[61]

On June 13, Coordinator of Information William J. Donovan, now General, took charge of the Office of Strategic Services (OSS), the forerunner of the CIA. Under the umbrella of the Joint Chiefs of Staff, Donovan was pleased the reorganized OSS reflected the "'strategic' importance of intelligence and clandestine operations in modern war."[62]

By mid-1942, German experimental rockets had been tested, but it is very doubtful they had achieved the level of sophistication observed in this June 25, 1942, sighting.[63] Returning from their successful mission against targets in Germany's Ruhr Valley area, a group of RAF Wellington Bombers headed home. Weather was clear as the bombers crossed over

Holland. Flight Lieutenant Roman (Ray) Sabinski, piloting one of the bombers assigned to the 301 Squadron, was part of a Polish division attached to the Royal Air Force.

Breaking in over Sabinski's headset, the rear gunner informed him that "an aircraft was approaching the rear" of their bomber. Sabinski immediately gave the controls over to his co-pilot and climbed into position for a better look. Unable to determine its exact distance, possibly a couple miles away, Sabinski saw "a very bright light" heading towards his aircraft. Sabinski told the rear gunner that if the "object" came any closer, "open fire on it." As the object steadily gained on his aircraft, Lt. Sabinski thought it was a German fighter equipped with a searchlight attached to the nose; he had seen German fighter aircraft with lights on their wings but never in the nose.

The object was the size of the moon, possibly a little bigger, and was visible high in the sky. Sabinski was able to discern the object's true color since it was well within firing range: not white but a shinning copper, sort of dull like a setting sun, yet not very intense. The object's edges were not well defined but rather fuzzy in appearance. Approaching dangerously close to his aircraft, the "object" was approximately two hundred yards away. "Give him a blast!" Sabinski ordered. The rear gunner, blazing away with all four machineguns, sent a hail of lead and tracer rounds towards the intruder.

Something did not make sense. The tracer rounds, used to direct the line of fire to the object, were hitting their mark. To the crew's surprise, the rounds were simply entering the object and not coming out the other side. The bullets were neither falling towards the ground, nor were they passing through the object; they simply entered the ball of light and disappeared. Remarkably, with so many apparent hits on the object, the crew could see no visible damage, no affect whatsoever.

The mystifying occurrence lasted about two minutes, and then the shiny object "suddenly changed position and at a terrific speed moved over to port side, almost at the same distance, about 200 yards from the wing." Sabinski gave the order to fire. Both the rear and front gunner blasted away. Seeing the tracers enter the target at two angles, Sabinski was now sure the object was around two hundred yards away from his aircraft, receiving the full firepower of two machine guns.

Unable to make sense of what he was seeing, Sabinski recalled: "I moved over to my seat in the cockpit and I took the controls myself and I did an evasive action because I was quite concerned with this object, which I did not know what it was. And while I was doing quite violent maneuvers, moving the wings up and down, uh, this object stayed exactly at the extension of the wing, which means you would have to, at that distance, would develop tremendous speed to catch up and keep formation with my aircraft."

It was useless. No matter what Lt. Sabinski tried, the object was there like a shadow. Pulling out of his evasive maneuvers, the machine gunners resumed their assault. Their gunfire was dead on the object, and the tracer rounds still disappeared within its light. A moment later, the object moved to the front of his aircraft, stayed in that position for a short period, then, moving in an upward direction, "took off at a fantastic speed, at least a forty-five degree angle and just disappeared between the stars."

Back at base, Lt. Sabinski proceeded directly to the unit's intelligence office, armed with one hell of a sighting to report and many questions to ask. Sabinski told his story. The intelligence officer, not believing a word of his account, joked about the incident and wanted to know how many beers Lt. Sabinski had been drinking. Sabinski told the intelligence officer to forget he had ever said anything about it. Sabinski left the debriefing with the understanding that, officially, his encounter did not happen; end of story.

Frustrated over the ordeal, Lt. Sabinski carried out his own low-key inquiry. Speaking in private with the captain of another Wellington bomber crew, Sabinski discovered his crew was not the only witness; just minutes after their encounter, the other Wellington Bomber crew, traveling not too far behind Sabinski's aircraft, had encountered the same phenomenon. The only difference was that the other captain and crew chose not to report the strange event to avoid ridicule and humiliation.[64]

Bomber Command's "Phenomena" report, issued in August 1940, is very relevant to Lt. Sabinski's sighting. The report states that the enemy was known to have "searchlights installed for experimental purposes." I suspect that Sabinski's sighting was sent to Bomber Command Headquarters and the Air Ministry, where such a report, citing the appearance of new enemy secret weaponry, no matter how crazy it sounded, certainly came to the attention of Reginald Jones at the Air Ministry. Sabinski's report referenced a wingless, circular aircraft, with astounding maneuvers and speed, and the ability to absorb machine gun and tracer rounds without damage. In addition the men flying British bombers were well trained, had excellent eyesight, and were able to discern lights on an aircraft far better than the average observer. Reginald Jones was also in the position to personally brief the new American air staff. One person having an immediate need to know was the overall Commander of the U.S. Army Air Forces in Great Britain, General Carl A. Spaatz. Arriving at his new post in London on June 18,[65] it is likely that the topic of aerial phenomena and unconventional aircraft was discussed with General Spaatz, his intelligence staff, the Air Ministry, and Bomber Command.

If General Spaatz was not informed on the subject by Reginald Jones, his information may have come via his close affiliation with one of the most important U.S. scientists working in the London mission: physicist Howard P. Robertson.[66]

Chapter Four

What Phenomenon Is It?

B etween the Coral Sea and the southwest Pacific Ocean sit the Solomons, a cluster of islands that were targeted for the first Allied counter-offensive in retaliation for Japan's surprise attack on Pearl Harbor. Under the codename Operation Watchtower, a U.S. Pacific fleet task force patiently awaited their August 7, 1942, assault of Florida, Gavutu, Tulgi, Tanambogo, and Guadacanal.[67] The United States Naval task force was poised, ready to unleash its immense firepower, softening the beaches for troops waiting to flood ashore.

Early on the morning of August 5, as the sun greeted a clear and cloudless sky, an aircraft approached the *USS Helm*, sharply defined against the blue backdrop. Considered an enemy aircraft, a full alert was sounded; there was no chance of it striking first. As the aircraft approached, three cruisers and seven destroyers executed a pre-emptive strike; a full-fledge Navy welcome. Through a dense wall of lead, the aircraft continued unscathed, getting closer to the *Helm*. When the "aircraft" reached within 3,000 yards, it executed a sharp turn, increased its speed, and proceeded to circle once around the entire fleet. By now, the entire task force zeroed their guns in on the unknown intruder. According to one witness: "... directional control released all guns and said for the gun captains to go local control. Although the director could keep up with him, they weren't able to take enough lead out of their machines to allow us to swing far enough ahead to hit him. So we just swung wild and just started throwing shells in and firing with the 50's and whatever else available to try and get at least one hit. With so many explosions near we couldn't tell where we were shooting, or anybody else, so there was just no way really of getting a crack at him."

Keeping its distance, and circling the ship for a second time, the "aircraft" seemed unaffected by the ship's concentrated firepower. The witness, who was assigned a security detail, observed the "aircraft" through a pair of 750-power field binoculars, noting it did not appear to be any known U.S. or Japanese aircraft. It was approximately ninety feet in diameter, and looked like a silver-colored, cigar-shaped object. At times, the "aircraft" had an "oval and flat" shape to it, with a "round dome" on top. Both the captain and the executive officer had a good look, and they confirmed it had the appearance of a "streamlined" cigar. Though unable to identify it as a Japanese fighter or bomber, they "assumed it was an enemy aircraft."

Understandably, the gunfire blocked out any noise from the aircraft's engines, and there was no visible exhaust. Another detail throwing a wrench in conventional thought was the "the director control insisted" that the object "had reached speeds of 10,000 mph."

The aircraft's ability to execute incredible speeds and maneuvers left the *Helm*'s crew shaken. At the time, there was very little the task force commanders could do since radio silence was enforced between ships to conceal the invasion. The *Helm*'s captain promised that once the radio transmission blackout was lifted he would look into the matter. Until then, he said the *Helm* could relay the information to passing planes, but it would be several hours before an allied plane flew by the fleet. Waiting for word about their sighting to reach headquarters, the men discussed the sighting among themselves, trying to figure out what the "aircraft" was and whether it would make a return visit; it did not. Finally, several days later, with communication traffic back to normal, the *USS Helm*'s captain told his crew he had received confirmation from command headquarters that the aircraft was not a German or Japanese aircraft.[68]

By mid-August, the campaign for retaking the Solomon Islands was in full swing. On Tulagi Island, during a lull in the fighting, Marine Sergeant Stephen J. Brickner sat perched on the edge of his foxhole, cleaning his rifle. He had endured five days of serious combat with the 1st Marine Division. It was August 12. According to Sergeant Brickner, he witnessed the most "awe-inspiring and yet frightening spectacle" of his life: "Suddenly, the air raid warning was sounded. There had been no 'Condition Red.' I immediately dove into my foxhole, with my back to the ground and my face turned up to the sky. I heard the formation before I saw it. Even then, I was puzzled by the sound. It was a mighty roaring sound that seemed to echo gloriously in the heavens. It didn't sound at all like the high-pitched 'sewing-machine' drone of the Jap formations. A few seconds later, I saw the formation of silvery objects directly overhead."

Eventually able to see what was making all the noise, Brickner observed the objects flying at an altitude too high for a bombing raid against the small island. Close-by, another Marine, also taking cover in a foxhole, yelled that the aircraft were probably searching for the United States Naval fleet. This made sense to Brickner, but he was still puzzled.

"First, the formation was huge," Brickner added. "I would say over a hundred and fifty objects were in it. Instead of the usual tight V of the twenty-five planes, this formation was in straight, majestic lines of ten to twelve objects, each behind the other. The speed was a little faster than Jap planes, and they were soon out of sight. A few other things that puzzled me: I couldn't seem to make out any wings or tails. They seemed to wobble slightly, and every time they wobbled, they would shimmer brightly from the sun. Their color was like highly polished silver."[69]

Another summer of 1942 sighting occurred farther south in the Pacific, near the island of Tasmania, which sits off the coast of Australia. Connecting the two is the Bass Strait, over which members of the Australian Royal Air Force were flying one evening. They were assigned the task of checking out the location "where fishermen had reported seeing mysterious lights on the sea at night." Major Brennan and his crew then spotted an object in the clouds. "At 5:50 P.M., of a lovely sunny evening, we were flying some miles east of the Tasman Peninsula when, [all of] a sudden, there came out of a cloud bank, a singular airfoil of glistening bronze color," the Major recalled. "I'd say it was around 150 feet long, and around fifty feet in diameter. It had a sort of beak at its prow, and the surface seemed buried, or rippled or fluted. On its upper surface was a dome, or cupola, from which I seemed to see reflected flashes as the Sun struck something, which might or might not have been a helmet, worn by something inside. The other end of the airfoil thinned out into a sort of fin. Every now and again, there came from its keel greenish-blue flashes. It turned at a small angle towards us and I was amazed to see, framed in a white circle on the front of the dome, an image of a large, grinning Cheshire cat! The damn thing flew parallel to us for some minutes, and then it abruptly turned away and, as it did so, it showed four things like fins on its belly-side. It went off at a hell of a pace, turned and dived straight down into the Pacific, and went under, throwing up a regular whirlpool of waves! Just as if it had been a submarine. No, the Japs had nothing in the amphibious line like that mysterious bird."

Knowing exactly what their story sounded like, Major Brennan and his crew kept their mouths shut. Commenting on why they chose silence, the Major said, "If we reported to intelligence what we'd seen, we should likely have been grounded as suffering from nerve strain. So we did not report it!"[70]

Meanwhile, there had been a dramatic shift in the European theater. On July 4, 1942, six American bombers accompanied the Royal Air Force to bomb targets in Holland. This was the first time British and American planes had collaborated, sending a huge statement to Hitler's Germany: the American Air Forces were on the way.[71]

A month later, on the evening of August 11/12, British bomber crews, flying in the neighborhood of Aachen observed "a phenomenon described as a bright white light" rising from the ground. Reaching approximately 8,000 feet, it "flew on a more or less level course for about two minutes." It was brilliant white in color, and several of the crews stated they witnessed the so-called rockets "zig-zag along the ground before taking off in a climbing turn."

Further information revealed that "brilliant white periodic bursts occurred which may have caused a change of course; some crews thought that the light sub-divided when the bursts took place, others that it flew in a circular course, the radius which was about one mile. The phenomenon shed burning pieces 'like a meteor.' The colour eventually faded to an orange and the object was last seen heading towards the ground. This display lasted about five minutes. All crews taking part in the raid contributed to the account of this phenomenon, which was probably seen on four separate occasions."

A week later, on August 17/18, another RAF bomber crew, flying at 15,000 feet, near the town of Osnabruk, reported observing "a rocket with a long white tail of light on the same altitude of their aircraft." Three other crews reported the same thing. All crews saw no explosive bursts.[72]

Air intelligence was skeptical of these reports, calling them a "phenomenon" and "so-called rockets." Even Fighter Command used the word "phenomenon" in their report, revealing there was a real hesitancy in accepting rockets as the culprit of the sightings. Reviewing the Fighter Command report today, these anti-aircraft rockets were well in advance of German technology at that time. The so-called rockets displayed a propulsion system capable of a five-minute engine burn time, and they had the ability to fly on a parallel course with allied aircraft. This was pretty remarkable for 1942 and is highly suspect. But one cannot entirely rule out the possibility that the Germans had been experimenting with some pretty advanced designs at this early date.[73]

By mid-August 1942, German infantry had experienced serious fighting on the Russian front. In the Tula region near Moscow, it was an exercise in fight, retreat, and dig in; a scenario that took place almost weekly.

It was a late summer day, around 2:00 p.m. The air was warm. A slight breeze carried a mist from the broken cloud cover parked high above. Twenty-one German infantrymen were going about their tasks. Then, according to one infantryman: "I saw the most baffling object...in my life. Out of a cloudy sky appeared slowly a huge cigar-shaped object, something like a Zeppelin, but much bulkier and rounder at the front." Its size was tremendous, "approximately 300 yards long and 100 yards high at the thickest part..." He could see "no markings," it was an "aluminum-hued colour," and it was "very smooth" looking.

Moving out of the clouds, the object's "snout" pointed "downwards," remaining stationary for at least a minute, giving the infantryman time to see there were "no visible windows or any sign of a gondola." The object leveled out and then turned its nose upward in slow and direct movements, in contrast to the surprising outburst of energy when it suddenly began climbing "at a terrific speed," disappearing within seconds, and leaving no vapor trail. The witness was especially amazed at hearing no sound when the object shot upwards out of sight.

The German soldiers thought the object was some kind of new Russian secret weapon, but eventually decided it was a "mirage."[74]

With major air war campaigns about to unfold in the European, Mediterranean, and Pacific theaters of operation, reporting any and all unknown operational "aircraft" was a necessity, no matter how unbelievable they seemed. A mocking attitude would lead witnesses to suppress information about their sightings. Hearing airmen describe something unusual, unconventional, and able to avoid radar, Air Intelligence personnel had every reason to pay close attention to eyewitness reports.

Meeting the challenge of radar and anti-radar technology was imperative. In response, radar experts were employed in all allied theaters of operation. Aiding the U.S. Army Air Force's efforts was one of the America's leading authorities on the subject: David T. Griggs.

On August 18, 1942, Edward Bowles, expert consultant to the U.S. Secretary of War, informed Griggs, who was already part of his personal staff, to concern himself "primarily with the airborne application of radar and all related devices." It was Griggs's job to keep Bowles advised of "progress in introducing various new devices and in bringing them actively to bear against the enemy." Furthermore, Griggs was to familiarize himself with "all electrical and related devices" and "all airborne applications of radar such as ASV [air-to-surface vessel], AI [air intercept], and AGL [above ground level], radar altimeters, radar aids to bombing, guided missiles, and the like," and to coordinate with the "Directors of Technical Services and Military Requirements, Headquarters Army Air Forces and, where necessary, with Chief Signal Officer and such other offices as may be concerned." Griggs was headquartered in Bowles office.[75]

Bowles's explicit letter made abundantly clear that Griggs was the War

Department's leading authority on radar. Therefore, it can be surmised that if unconventional objects were being tracked on radar, could avoid radar, or be clocked traveling several thousand miles per hour, Griggs would have been briefed on the subject.

Furthermore, Griggs probably had access to other scientists working with U.S. and British forces, including Howard Robertson of the London mission and Reginald Jones of the British Air Ministry.

While Griggs, Robertson, and Jones remained active behind the scenes, the war front continually presented challenge after challenge to the British Air Ministry. With nearly three years of combat experience, the Royal Air Force had assembled a sightings database containing several categories of aerial phenomena.

On September 25, Bomber Command's Operational Research Section (ORS) released a report called, "A Note On Pyrotechnic Activity Over Germany." To get a better understanding of the observed phenomena, "an investigation covering No.3 and No.5 Groups was undertaken in collaboration with the Flak Liaison Officer of No. 5 Group, in an endeavor to determine the probable purpose of these devices." Conflicting reports revealed there appeared "to be at least two different phenomena which unfortunately seem often to have been reported by the same name 'Chandelier Flares.'"

The ORS report listed the flare sightings as "Phenomenon 1" and "Phenomenon 2."

"Phenomenon 1" was described as being shot from the ground, having no visible trail, becoming a "ball of fire" that was 50 to 60 feet in diameter and dripping "muiti-coloured fragments." Aircraft that had spotted the Chandelier Flares at close distances said they resembled "aircraft falling in flames." It was felt this was a psychological ploy designed to spook the airmen into thinking many of their bombers were being blasted out of the sky, something the Germans were known to do.

"Phenomenon 2" described flares seen over friendly and enemy territory, "probably" dropped by aircraft. The flares were seen in multiples, apparently employed to provide a large amount of light, possibly attached to parachutes to sustain their altitudes longer.

In addition to Phenomena 1 and 2, another type of flare phenomenon reported were "small coloured balls" that climbed up to around seven thousand feet; considered a track indicating flare. The report suggested "that suitable names should be bestowed on 'Phenomena 1 and 2' to facilitate reporting and an attempt to do this will be made in a report shortly to be published jointly by MI14(E) and this section."[76]

The use of "flare" terminology goes back to the August 11, 1940, "Enemy Night Tactics" report. Now two years later, in addition to the "Chandelier," new names like "Scarecrow" and "Balls of fire" were added to the list. This very important report shows the difficulty the Allies had in identifying ordnance and reveals how the sighting of an unconventional craft could have been easily misidentified and categorized as a flare.

Chapter Five

"Neither a Dream, Nor a Buck Rogers Invention"

On October 12, 1942, Bomber Command sent a memorandum entitled "Enemy Defenses — Phenomenon," with an attached copy of the ORS "Pyrotechnic" Report to the headquarters of eight bomb groups. It read in part:"The Operational Research Station at this Headquarters has carried out an investigation into enemy pyrotechnic activity which has recently been experienced over Germany. The AOC in C has issued instructions that the information contained in this report be brought to the notice of all crews. We would remind you that Consolidated FLO Reports issued by MI14(E)refer to Phenomenon, when reported, and give possible explanations."[77]

The ORS report was cited in various U.S. and British intelligence memoranda,[78] as MI14(E) and Bomber Command's No. 3 Group and No. 5 Group continued investigating rocket phenomena. MI14(E) was the British War Office's flak intelligence branch.

Less than two months later No. 5 Group received a sighting report of something that in no way could be categorized as a flare.

On December 2, Headquarters of RAF Station, Syerston, sent a "Secret" memo to Major Mullock, Flight Liaison Officer, at the Headquarters of No. 5 Group. The memo was in reference to an object sighted by a crew flying aircraft 'J,' commanded by Captain Lever of the 61 Squadron during their raid on Turin, Italy, on the night of November 28/29.

"The object referred to above was seen by the entire crew of the above aircraft. They believe it to have been 200-300 feet in length and its width is estimated at 1/5th or 1/6th of its length. The speed was estimated at 500 m.p.h., and it had four pairs of red lights spaced at equal distances along its body. These lights did not appear in any way like exhaust flames; no trace was seen. The object kept a level course.

"The crew saw the object twice during the raid, and brief details are given below:-

"(i) After bombing, time 2240 hours, a/c height 11,000 feet. The aircraft was some 10/15 miles South-West of Turin traveling in a north-westerly direction. The object was traveling South-East at the same height or slightly below the aircraft.

"(ii) After bombing, time 2245 hours, a/c height 14,000 feet. The aircraft was approaching the Alps when the object was seen again travelling West-South-West up a valley in the Alps below the level of the peaks. The lights appeared to go out and the object disappeared from view.

"The Captain of the aircraft also reports that he has seen a similar object about three months ago North of Amsterdam. In this instance, it appeared to be on the ground, and later traveling at high speed at a lower level than the heights given above along the coast for about two seconds; the lights then went out for the same period of time and came on again, and the object was still seen to be traveling in the same direction."[79]

The following day, December 3, the "Turin" report arrived at the headquarters of Bomber Command, sent by the Air Vice-Marshal commanding No. 5 Group. On the report's cover sheet, entitled "Enemy Defenses-Phenomenon," he wrote: "Herewith a copy of a report received from a crew of a Lancaster after raid on TURIN. The crew refuses to be shaken in their story in the face of the usual banter and ridicule."[80]

The Turin sighting must have sent shock waves through the Allied Air Force commands. Evidently, the Turin sighting was purposely kept out of mainstream military channels. There was absolutely no mention of Captain Lever's extraordinary sighting in the Flak Liaison Officer's December 14 report of the mission. The report was shared with the Americans; six copies were issued to the U.S. Army Air Force and six copies went to the Office of Naval Intelligence.[81]

To date, most the unconventional airborne objects had been observed over Germany and Holland, but now things began to change. Around the same time that Captain Lever and his crew witnessed their highly unusual object, another sighting occurred over the Bay of Biscay, England. Though this sighting also does not appear in official records, it is very significant. C.J.J. and his mates were part of an anti-submarine squadron that was patrolling the coast of England. While making their rounds, the tail gunner reported observing a strange craft that had no wings.

Other crewmen on board also witnessed the object. According to the assistant engineer, the intercom began malfunctioning, becoming "a jumbled mess of incoherent squawks" while the object was in sight. Unable to see the object for himself, the pilot was kept informed by other crewman who relayed details to him about what they were witnessing.[82]

"C.J.J.," who was a ball gunner on the aircraft's underbelly, left his position to make contact with the other crewmembers, who were observing what he called the "thing," which was "massive" in size. It was flying behind them at an undeterminable distance in the five o'clock position. Gaining altitude, it remained in view for about fifteen minutes before it executed "a 180 degree angle turn and disappeared." The crew saw no visible means of propulsion associated with the object.

Fortunately, during the sighting Technical Sergeant F.M.B. was busy photographing the thing with a K-20 camera. Most of the photographs, according to C.J.J., were not clear, showing little detail, except one that was taken with a filter.[83]

In all probability, the photographs were sent to an RAF photo-intelligence section for review. Huge amounts of aerial photographs and motion pictures were taken during the war, as most fighters and bombers had gun cameras to validate their combat kills of targets hit both in the air and on the ground. The crews also sometimes carried hand-held cameras.[84]

Sometime during the month of December, B. C. Lumsden was piloting his Hurricane fighter at approximately 7,000 feet. While flying over the French coast near the mouth of the Somme River, he noticed something suddenly climbing towards him from below. Approaching were two lights, amber and orange colored, slowly making their way to his altitude. At first, he assumed they were tracer-flak of some kind, but then realized they were traveling too slowly for such ordnance. The lights had by then reached his altitude and were maintaining a level course with his aircraft. Lumsden watched as the lights grew larger in size and brighter in luminance.

Unable to identify what they were, Lumsden felt something was simply not right and out of place. Concerned for his safety, he dropped his extra fuel tanks and began evasive action, diving several thousand feet before leveling out and accelerating up to 260 mph. In unison, the two lights descended with him, actually dropping to a lower altitude before ascending again, and then continued their pursuit. Lumsden noticed that the lights maintained a relatively constant distance from each other, only varying in height at times. He was sure they were not aircraft wingtip lights due to their flying angle. During the episode, he noticed no enemy flak or searchlights. Able to out distance the lights, Lumsden fled the scene.

Once back at base, he faced the usual ridicule. "I found it hard to make other members of the squadron believe me when I told my story," Lumsden remarked, "but the following night one of the squadron flight commanders, in the same area, had a similar experience with a green light.[85]

On December 18, 1942, MI14(E) presented their latest findings regarding the aerial pyrotechnic phenomena. It is interesting to note that while ordnance related objects were discussed, the report was quick to point out some unaccountable discrepancies: "Reports of various types of phenomenon are frequently received from aircrews operating over enemy territory. Many are only reported on isolated occasions and, in default of satisfactory confirmation, have to be discounted as 'freaks.'"

Just as Bomber Command's Operational Research Section had done previously, MI14(E) was now listing the sightings under separate categories. There were "Scarecrow" flares, "Chandelier" flares, and Track-indicating Flares. Joining the list of oddities, a newer category labeled "Meteor projectiles" was added in response to the strange sighting reported on August 11/12 by a number of British aircrews flying over Aachen, Germany. So far, the "meteor" projectile had only been seen once, and it, too, was quickly "classified as an isolated 'freak' incident."

Identifying these sightings was proving difficult for many, including MI14(E): "Owing to the scarcity of information about this phenomenon, which may well have been in the nature of an experiment, it is difficult to submit an explanation. It is possibly a miniature aircraft structure carrying a number of rockets and explosive charges. Its changes of course are probably predetermined, radio control being thought improbable owing to the cost of production, the small chance of directing such a projectile on to a bomber and the fact that it would be virtually impossible to bring it in to land intact by night."[86]

There is no doubt the MI14(E) staff were doing their best to reasonably assess the situation, but even for them, it seems their logic surrounding German capabilities was proving illogical for the times. In general, flak phenomena were now on the minds of Air Intelligence staff personnel throughout the RAF and USAAF Headquarters.[87] The appearance of "meteor projectiles" created yet another category that further complicated matters as it too included possible unconventional aircraft sightings.

By January, ORS's September 25, 1942, "Pyrotechnic" phenomena report was well known among intelligence officers in all the Air Divisions, Wings, Bomb Groups, and Squadrons of the U.S. Army Air Forces. The ORS report had also circulated throughout the highest level U.S. military intelligence channels, including the War Department where it was reprinted in their Command Information Intelligence Summary: "Several pyrotechnic phenomena, as yet insufficiently explained, have been observed during recent months by RAF crews over Germany. Information at present available on these is here briefly summarized. It is desired that any information resulting from further observations be forwarded to the

Director of Intelligence Service, with care to distinguish between the several varieties."[88]

Other types of pyrotechnic phenomena began showing up in 1943. On January 11, twenty-two B-17 bombers with the U.S. Army Air Force 384th Bomb Group were heading towards Halberstadt, Germany.[89] Flying in formation at 21,000 feet, pilot G.W. Stier's crew observed a "smoke ball floating and swirling" in the air of "burning particles." Stier's tail gunner said it looked like "a big swarm of bees milling around."[90] The term "swarm of bees" would continue to be used for months in discussions of the phenomenon.

Another odd sighting occurred on January 15. During a U.S. raid over Cherbourg, France, several crews saw "large numbers of projectiles (estimated at between 50 and 100 feet at a time) resembling 'schools of flying fish,' about a foot long and similar to incendiary bombs, coming up from a direction of the town." According to a British flak liaison officer flying with the group, the objects "might possibly have been some kind of rockets, but this suggestion must be treated with reserve pending further confirmation."[91]

Then during a cloudless, moonlit night over Milan, Italy, on the evening of February 14, RAF crews reported observing something else new. According to MI14(E): "In addition to 'chandelier flares' and 'incandescent bursts' many crews described another type of phenomenon not hitherto reported. The projectiles involved, which possibly constitute a variation of the more normal 'incandescent burst,' were said to have no visible trace before bursting, when 8-12 'fingers' were thrown out horizontally, apparently forwards; the 'fingers,' which had a considerable trace, appeared to continue on a horizontal course for a few seconds and then to fall away in a gentle curve. No more than two or three such projectiles were seen at the same time."[92]

British crews observed the so-called "fingers" for several weeks. They were then called "simulation of burning aircraft" sightings because they were thought to give the appearance of destroyed bombers going down in flames, causing fear and lower morale among the Allied bomber crews.

On March 13, over Naples, Italy, the U.S. Ninth Air Force's 376th Bomb Group twice sighted "Roman Candle" lights. The first sighting "came up from the water and glowed in the sky for a few seconds." About thirty minutes after leaving Naples, the second sighting, a "bright very large red light" appeared at the aircraft's altitude (17,000 feet). The crew said "it looked like a huge irregular mass of neon, and was a steady light, not a reflection." Turning away from the light, the crew said it "remained motionless in the place where first seen."[93]

The so-called "Roman Candle" sighting was a new American term used in describing unusual lights. Unfortunately, the War Department's intelligence summary on the episode offers no further information; it remains unknown if the second light came up from the water and whether it disappeared, dissipated, or remained in view until the American aircraft traveled beyond visual range.

By now, U.S. Army Air Forces were involved in all theaters of operation: European, Pacific, Mediterranean, and China-Burma-India. The Allied air forces were bombing day and night. Sightings of pyrotechnic phenomena were at an all-time high, as were standard enemy flak and fighters that increasingly challenged the airmen's nerves.

During the month of May, "freak" sightings were back, and RAF crews were the first to report them. It was a cloudless, moonlit evening with good visibility. The bombers were flying at 24,000 to 27,000 feet, heading towards targets in the town of Duisburg, Germany. According to the flak liaison officer: "On 12/13 May one aircrew reported that when flying at 20,000 feet just after leaving Duisburg they saw a 'meteor' traveling from North of the target in a southerly direction at about 16,000 feet. The object was reddish-orange in colour, and three times during the observation, it was said to have emitted a burst giving off a green star. It disappeared from view when it had lost height to about 12,000 feet."

On May 13/14, a similar incident was reported during an operation against Pilson, Germany. According to the flak liaison officer: "It was described as giving off a sequence of sparks and as having a definite tail leaving a trail of smoke; it was seen to travel about ten miles before falling to the ground, where it burnt out after a minute. The crew who made this report said they had seen similar phenomena on previous occasions in approximately the same area, and also in the neighborhood of KIEL. These descriptions bear a strong resemblance to the 'meteor' projectile reported by a number of aircrews in the area AACHEN/VERVIERS – 12 miles SW of SPA-AACHEN on 11/12 Aug 42 and subsequently only once reported again. It was thought at the time to have been in the nature of an experiment, but there is still no information to suggest whether it is intended primarily as a deterrent device or whether the enemy considers it may have some lethal value, perhaps against considerable concentrations of aircraft."[94]

Just over a week later (23/24), Bomber Command was conducting a raid on Dortmund, Germany: "During this operation a large number of reports were received of so-called 'rockets' which were observed not only in the approaches to the Ruhr and the target area, but also over HOLLAND. In general these phenomena appear to have been similar to the 'meteor' projectiles recently cited in Consolidated FLO Report No. 159, except that on this occasion many were said to have been seen flying at lower altitudes (some quite close to the ground) and mainly in a horizontal direction."[95]

Word games continued to play out in the intelligence memoranda. Some reports used the term "meteor," while others used the term "rocket" and both were considered "freak" sightings. But the next sighting was in a league of its own, coming straight from the pages of science fiction.

According to RAF co-pilot Sergeant Gordon N. Cockcroft, on the evening of May 27/28 he was flying with pilot Captain Ray Smith at 18,000 feet in a four-engine Halifax Bomber. Crossing over the coast of Holland and then over the Ruhr Valley, they were heading towards Essen, Germany. Their target was clearly visible; it had just suffered a previous attack by another wave of bombers.

Zeroing in on their drop zone, Captain Smith was the first to see the strange looking object in front and slightly portside of their aircraft. The object was "silvery-gold in color," larger than their aircraft, and sharply defined. Its shape was "cylindrical" and had several "portholes" evenly spaced along its side. Captain Smith noticed the object was not in motion, just suspended in the air at a 45-degree angle.

Cockcroft said that most of the crew witnessed the object except the two who were busy watching for enemy fighters and making sure their aircraft stayed on course. The object remained in position for about twenty or thirty seconds before it climbed abruptly at an incredible speed, possibly several thousand miles per hour, and vanished from sight.

Upon returning to base, they were debriefed by their unit's intelligence officer. Strangely, their observation made no impression on him, leaving Sergeant Cockcroft puzzled by the lack of concern. Not pressing the issue, and since the object showed no signs of aggression, Cockcroft dropped the subject; he was personally more concerned by greater threats: flak and fighters.[96]

Were Air Intelligence debriefing officers instructed to show little interest in strange sightings and then immediately funnel the reports directly to Bomber Command? We don't know. But Sergeant Cockcroft's sighting further corroborates the suspicion that measures were taken to downplay such sightings. We know from official records that an RAF raid was flown against Essen, Germany, on the night of May 27/28, but no mention is made of Cockcroft's sighting in the flak liaison officer's report: "Moderate to intense heavy Flak fire was encountered, crews reporting mainly barrage fire between 14,000 and 19,000 feet, particularly in the vicinity of release point flares, as well as predictor control 'unseen'; some bursts were observed up to 24,000 feet. It appears that searchlights also attempted at times to illuminate the flares, and that a considerable amount of Flak was fired into the resultant 'cones.'"

Another interesting detail of the flak liaison officer's report is that there is no "Phenomena" category listed for the Essen raid, though there was a "Phenomena" listing included in the report for the prior night: "It is noteworthy that on this occasion only one 'meteor' projectile was reported (near S'HERTOGENBOSCH), compared with the prolific reports of such phenomena on the operation against DORTMUND (23/24 May), when weather conditions were more favourable."[97]

Since the Essen raid was included in the consolidated report, it is a little strange that a "silvery-gold," "cylindrical" shaped object with "portholes" along its side, hanging motionless in the sky until it departed at a speed of approximately "several thousand miles per hour" is not included in the report!

Another RAF sighting took place in May during the return leg of a mission over Germany. Captain Gordon W. Cammell was piloting his Lancaster bomber back over the English Channel when he and his entire crew "saw what appeared to be a huge orange ball on or near the sea, seven or eight thousand feet" below them. Over the next ten minutes, the crew watched the stationary illuminated object, projecting a "bright" and "constant" light.

The captain and his crew determined that the shining object "was not an aircraft or ship on fire," since there were "no flames or reflections on the water." Upon returning to the RAF base at East Wretham in Suffolk, England, the Lancaster crew reported their sighting to their intelligence officer, who was at a loss for explanations.[98]

On June 11, a couple of weeks after Sergeant Cockcroft's remarkable sighting, geophysicist David Griggs accompanied Robert A. Lovett, the U.S. Assistant Secretary of War for Air, on a special visit to the United Kingdom. Griggs had come along to "look over the radar needs of the Eighth Air Force."[99] His visit to England was timely and necessary. Unbeknownst to the public, the British homeland was facing a danger that loomed silently on the horizon. Prime Minister Winston S. Churchill now had confirmation that Germany's operational long-range rockets were ready for action, and England was its primary prey. He was also there at a time when sightings of "a swarm of bees" and "confetti flak," and objects "fluttering down like leaves" were on the increase. These were considered to be anti-radar defensive measures, but according to a U.S. VIII Bomber Command report, "Until captured documents or enemy ammunition reveal the nature of the above phenomena only 'learned guesses' can be made as to their nature."[100]

The Griggs visit was of utmost importance. The German long-range rocket was no joke, and new ways of countering radar was no joke either. Also, an issue for a radar expert such as Griggs and the entire Allied air staff were unconventional aircraft, especially those that did not fit into any "phenomena" categories or apparent German capabilities.

On August 25, 1943, Germany's new glider-bombs, the Hs-293s, attacked British ships sailing in the Bay of Biscay.[101] Though not very accurate, Allied intelligence knew it was only a matter of time before new variants arrived on the scene. Following up on the Hs-293 story, the Eighth Air Force issued a report in their September 5 *Weekly Intelligence Digest* article entitled "The Enemy's Air Weapons – Some of the Reasons He's Experimenting – And Some of The Results of His Labor." The report pointed out Germany's need to introduce a large variety of new devices to combat the Allied effort. These new weapons included rocket guns, aircraft rockets, and the new Hs-293. In reference to radio controlled weapons, the report stated: "These weapons were neither a dream nor a Buck Rogers invention as long ago as of the end of the last war, but had been actually tested by reputable scientists."

The Allied Command understood the importance of weapons that could correct their flight after launch, and they realized that Germany was fine-tuning these weapons. But the Hs-293 had made an unsuccessful debut, and from its poor performance the U.S. Eighth Air Force concluded, "it is one thing to correct them against a still target and quite another against a fast, maneuverable target, such as a plane." The report ended by stating: "The poor results shown against such relatively slow and un-maneuverable targets as surface ships indicate what may be expected if similar tactics are employed against aircraft."[102]

Apparently, the Hs-293 was no great threat. The V-1 and more sophisticated V-2 were far more worrisome, but they, too, were inaccurate. They all, however, had one common factor: they were inflicting a psychological toll. While these were no "Buck Rogers invention," there were unconventional aircraft sightings plaguing Air Intelligence that certainly fit the bill.

Chapter Six

Silvery-Discs,
Pie-Plates, and the Light

On September 6, 1943, at 0950 hours, the U.S. First and Third Bombardment Divisions, comprised of 338 flying fortresses, 176 Thunderbolt fighters, and 161 British Spitfires, approached Stuttgart, Germany.[103]

Stuttgart, a highly industrialized city of great importance, was heavily defended. Aircrews were advised to expect intense flak and a large quantity of enemy fighters, some donning rocket cannons.[104]

Captain Raymond P. Ketelson was the 384th Bomb Group's Leader that day.[105] His bombers were nearing the target area at 22,000 to 24,000 feet when the flak erupted.[106] Once over Stuttgart, enemy fighters pounced upon the bombers. It was during the heated air battle that two of Captain Ketelson's crews witnessed "objects resembling silver discs about the size of half-dollars" floating downward.[107]

News of the "silver discs" spread fast. Later that day an update, "Additional Information On The Observation Of Silvery Colored Discs On Mission To Stuttgart, 6 Sept. 1943," was sent to 1st Bombardment Wing: "This observation was made by two crews of the 384th Group and was the only place it was noted. At this time from 2 to 4 FW 190's or ME 109's and 1 JU 88 were flying 2 to 3000 feet above and a little ahead of our formation. These E/A were not seen to drop the material out. It came from above our A/C/. As to its shape, it was a mass of material, kept a good pattern, did not dissipate as it streamed down and fell comparatively slow. In one instance, the cluster appeared to be about 8 ft. in length and about 4 feet wide as it streaked down. Another observation stated it was about 75 feet long and 20 feet wide. These dimensions in length being the size from top to bottom as it fell. The cluster was composed of small round objects, silvery in color. In all instances, the objects fell in the path of our A/C. Some was observed to fall on the wing of a B-17 belonging to our group. The wing immediately started to burn. This a/c did not return. No further information available."[108]

It is interesting to note the different terminology used to describe the objects. Initially called "discs," they were then cited as "balls" within the same paragraph. Size and shape was not the issue, though. The apparent downing of the B-17 by the new "silver–disc" ordnance, with some type of incendiary capabilities, caused heads to turn in bomber division commands.

On September 11, the British followed with another Hs-293 report stating there were actually two new forms of remote controlled bombs currently being utilized by the Nazis: the Hs-293 glider bomb and a remote-controlled bomb. Both were carried by German aircraft, the mothership being the Do-217. Information gleaned from an enemy prisoner of war, revealed the remote control bomb, about six feet long, was connected to a wire. There was no kind of propulsion, just an electrical frequency used by the operator guiding the bomb in towards its target with a joy-stick. During the day a "blue rocket trail" is used to follow its path and at night, a blue light. The Hs-293 glider-bomb was about eight feet long, radio-controlled, rocket- or jet-propelled, and also steered by an operator in the releasing aircraft. It made little noise and was very maneuverable in flight. Supposedly, there were green lights in its tail, allowing more visibility for control by the operator. The limiting feature of both weapons was that they were guided by direct eye contact. Countermeasures were relatively easy: fighter aircraft, antiaircraft, and bright lights could confuse or distract the operator.[109]

Allied air intelligence now had two additional concerns, but as information came in regarding their operational use, and any type of light associated with them, it was surely becoming apparent that Germany had nothing in their arsenal to account for the remarkable unconventional aircraft being reported by air crews.

On September 13, General Ira C. Eaker, commanding officer of the VIII Bomber Command, sent a copy of the "silvery colored discs" supplemental report to General Henry "Hap" Arnold, commanding General of the entire U.S. Army Air Forces.[110] Eaker's communication with General Arnold set the wheels in motion. There was no time to lose. They wanted answers.

Three days later, in response, "Major Bauman, Chemical Warfare Officer, War Plans, and Theater Division, Intelligence Branch, Gravelly Point" had supplied the Allied air staff with some ideas to consider about what the discs might be. In a memorandum dated September 16 and entitled "Possible Explanation of Silvery-Colored Discs Used On Stuttgart Mission, 6 September 1943," he postulated that the "silvery-colored discs" were composed of (1) "white phosphorous and a sticky substance which would cause it to cling to the plane…";(2) "Thermite with some sort of igniting compound inherent in a sticky substance…"; or (3)"Flat round glass containers loaded with either of the above incendiary compounds."

According the memorandum's author, Major W.W. Spencer, Chief, Tactical Section: "The substance dropped by the enemy planes was reported to fall comparatively slowly which would seem to preclude the use of glass discs which would be heavier and fall more rapidly."[111]

The Schweinfurt incident was making its rounds. By September 22, Colonel W. M Burgess, chief of the Informational Division of the Office of Assistant Chief of Air Staff, Intelligence, responded to General Eaker's A-2, Colonel Lucius Ordway; a copy also went to Colonel Bunker in the European theater of operations. Responding to the proposed idea that "silvery-colored discs"were incendiary devices,Colonel Burgess emphasized that, "while this explanation is believed to be largely speculative, it is passed along for what it is worth. Further details relative to the substance and employment are requested by cable as soon as available."[112]

By September 24, the British Anti-Aircraft (AA) Command was also reporting on "slivery-disc" sightings by Americans. The report, which commented about the air incendiaries on two fronts without offering any observations by British planes, or presenting any of their own input, stated: "It is reported, in *American Weekly Air Intelligence Digest*, that silver-coloured-discs, about the size of a five-shilling piece, were dropped on Fortresses in the attack on STUTTGART on 6 Sept."

The report noted that while there were five enemy aircraft present in the area, "these aircraft were not seen to drop the material, but it came from somewhere above."[113]

The British report was a reprint of the Eighth Air Force information, most likely targeted for lower echelon intelligence staff. It is doubtful that U.S. Air Intelligence had not immediately contacted high level intelligence staff with the RAF, requesting their knowledge of the subject.

The Stuttgart "silvery-discs"were a major concern for Allied Air Force intelligence due to their incendiary properties. But apparently, they were not the first disc-shaped objects reported by the Eighth Air Force; in fact, disc-shaped objects had been reported several months prior to the Stuttgart mission. And there was a difference between the different sightings; the earlier objects appeared to be more explosive than incendiary. This was revealed in a follow-up report released in the *US Eight Air Force Weekly Digest* on September 26, "More On Enemy Weapons-New Reports on Some Old Phenomena: Parachute and 'Pie-Plate' Projectiles": "Several new aerial weapons developed by the enemy have been inspected and reported upon during recent weeks. Past week has brought additional information along these lines, together with more reports from USAAF crews in this and the Mediterranean Theater on phenomena on which few details are yet known…

"'Pie –Plate' Projectiles were reported several months ago by Eighth Air Force crews. These were disc-shaped projectiles apparently lobbed into formations from enemy aircraft on their stern. One B-17 returned from a mission on 28 July after being hit by such a projectile, which exploded against the cockpit just above the co-pilot's window. Only damage was a dent in the skin and some cracked, but not broken plexiglass."

Also included was a brief summary of "doughnut shaped projectiles." In a final comment, the report stated: "On basis of the interrogation of Eighth Air Force crews who have seen similar projectiles, it is thought that they are not launched directly from a projector on the attacking enemy aircraft. Rather, it seems likely that a container holding a number of such projectiles is fired or dropped from the enemy plane, and that this container later bursts (probably as the result of an explosive charge), hurling the projectiles from it. The enemy's hope in such a case would probably be that the container exploded in the midst of a formation, where a number of our planes might be in range of the 'pie-plates' or 'doughnuts.' So far, this appears to be mostly a hope."[114]

Correspondence between U.S. Army Air Force commands started reflecting the same dialogue as their British counterparts. The AAF was using terms "phenomenon" and "phenomena" to describe confusing observations; further confirming information about the subject was poor, misidentified, and conflicting. The issue was far from over. The "discs" over Stuttgart had garnered unprecedented attention. Every available resource was used to help answer the question: what exactly were the "silvery"-colored discs?

On October 14, three U.S. Bombardment Wings roared towards the city of Schweinfurt. It was a deep run into Germany for the American bombers, especially without fighter support. The crews were told the bold mission was dangerous, but its importance was of vital importance to the European campaign.[115]

Piloting the 546th Heavy Bomb Squadron's lead plane was Major G.W. Harris and his co-pilot, Captain P. M. Algar. Nearing the target, both Harris and Algar observed "silver-colored discs," one to three inches in diameter, gliding "slowly down in a very uniform cluster." Unable to avoid their path, the aircraft's "right wing went directly through a cluster" sustaining no damage to the engines or plane's surface. They could hear them striking the plane's tail section, fortunately without explosions. Like the Stuttgart mission, the crew observed a "mass of black debris of varying sizes" about twenty feet from the "discs." On two other occasions they observed the "discs" and debris, and each time they were unable to identify the source from which they came.[116]

Flying directly behind Major Harris was First Lt. Edmund Goulder and his co-pilot, Second Lt. Ernest Boyce. Their B-17 was shot up pretty badly, but they were able to make it back to England before bailing out. At their debriefing with RAF Intelligence Officers, Lt. Goulder was able to offer additional information, stating that the "fighters were dropping pie-plates" on them.[117]

The Stuttgart and Schweinfurt "discs" of 1943 are a very important element in the story of wartime unconventional aircraft sightings. As the months progressed, the so-called "silvery-discs" were possibly confused with larger disc-shaped aircraft flying or hovering in the distance. Under combat stress, it can be understood how each time a disc-shaped object was observed and reported, Squadron Intelligence personnel (S-2s) interrogating the crews may have filed the sighting away as German ordnance. To further illustrate how sightings in general were possibly confused, the following U.S. report is worth mentioning.

By late 1943, American flyers were experiencing the horror of air combat firsthand. Already their losses were mounting and the high number of casualties was shocking. Morale among the airmen plummeted. Many missions were aborted under the guise of aircraft failure, weather, etc. Addressing the issue, a late summer report was most timely. Entitled "Defense Against the Fortress," it was released by the U.S. Eighth Air Force. This lengthy document assessed the Luftwaffe's efforts in destroying American bombers and offered comments about human observation during a wartime experience.

The report's section, "Rocket or Bomb," states: "Most of our crews were at best relatively inexperienced. They early learned to identify the most obvious forms of conventional flak and cannon bursts but many of them from the first insisted they had seen multi-colored explosions of one kind and another. These observations were greeted with skepticism if not derision at first. It is likely that many valuable reports were lost by the crewmember's reluctance to report such strange things as they knew they had seen. These men had little general knowledge of ordnance and usually their observations were only fleeting glimpses caught in the heat of battle. 'Pink Flak' became a joke long before it was a well-understood phenomenon.

"To compound the difficulty interrogating intelligence officers were new to their business and no better acquainted with the galaxy of ordnance devices than the crews. At first, they had no personal estimate of the relative reliability of individual crew members. And finally all crew interrogation was performed against an arbitrarily set time limit.

"Experience has slowly clarified much of the mystery overhanging these phenomena but the question: Rocket or Bomb? remains unanswered in many cases despite the testimony of reliable observers. Rockets and bombs are often used against the same formations; some crew members see one thing and the others see the other and the most conscientious effort to get at the truth often produces little certainty.

"There have by now been positive identifications of both but mistakes and uncertainties still make it impossible to be sure of every identification and therefore to measure the relative incidence and effectiveness of the two accurately."

The report further stated: "Under such conditions, it will remain a debatable question, Rocket or Bomb, until clear camera shots or sufficient fragments of the object are brought back for technical experts to give indisputable answers."

The Eighth Air Force report indicated that much change was needed during interrogation. "Particular attention must be paid to the crew interrogation for the purpose of extracting information that may seem irrelevant in itself but is possibly the missing link in a general pattern of correlated study," the report stated. If needed, a subsequent interrogation would be necessary.[118]

Due to the large amounts of conflicting information, accurate assessments were nearly impossible. Airmen returning to base after a harrowing mission, fatigued or pumped up on adrenaline, and riddled with nervous exhaustion brought about by fear were apt to provide sketchy details for accurate identification. Herein, the Eighth Air Force report had made clear the difficulty air intelligence personnel faced in carrying out their job, especially when presented with encounter reports of the unknown: experimental weaponry and experimental aircraft, and possibly something else entirely.

Though intrigued by these reports, nothing matched the Allied air force's concern over another development: Germany's jet-propelled aircraft progress. Allied intelligence knew of three jets in experimental stages. The three known designs were: the Heinkel "T," an improved version of a pre-war Italian design known as the Campini, capable of reaching 500 miles per hour; the He-280, a two engine design, also capable of reaching 500 mph; and the Me-262, another two engine type, but capable of 520 mph. It was felt some might see flight before the end of 1943.[119]

New jet information filtered in on a daily basis. One alarming report came via a German Prisoner of War (POW). General Jacob L. Devers, commanding general of the European Theater of Operations Command, received word from General George V. Strong, Army G-2 (Intelligence), indicating the Germans were experimenting with a jet-propelled stratospheric bomber able to reach altitudes of 60,000 feet. The British felt their POW source had proven somewhat reliable.[120]

In late September, concerned over the influx of rocket intelligence, Prime Minister Winston Churchill was briefed by Reginald Jones of the Air Ministry. Within weeks, Churchill revealed his anxiety over the impending threat to President Roosevelt and asked Sir Stafford Cripps, Britain's Minister of Aircraft Production, to conduct an in-depth study.[121] The long-range rocket issue was especially troubling. Though Churchill's staff worked feverishly on the issue, a complete picture of what to expect was greatly lacking. Joining the concentrated effort, U.S. Secretary of War Henry L. Stimson established the New Developments Division, an organization charged with overseeing "innovation, development, and application of new weapons, devices, and techniques of military value."[122]

Apparently, the influx of Germany's advanced weaponry was becoming an unsettling affair for the Allied aircrews flying over enemy occupied territory. Responding to the uneasy situation, the U.S. Assistant Chief of Air Staff, Intelligence, offered a little reassurance in his article entitled "ENEMY Rockets, Glider Bombs & Flying Doughnuts."

"Some of them hiss through space," it stated. "Some have blue or green lights flashing in their tails. Some seem to shudder in mid-air as if they were 'frantic'. Some are shaped like flying doughnuts. These reports of different types of German projectiles indicate that they are enjoying a big success, at least by the standards of Flash Gordon or H.G. Wells. Actually, Germany's new weapons are still in an experimental stage. And despite some success with rocket projectiles in attacking U.S. bombers over Schweinfurt, their bark is worse than their bite. With almost no data to go on, our newspapers have played up German rocket and glider bomb stories whenever possible. It is advisable, then, that U.S. airmen should be set straight on the main types of these new projectiles, radio controlled and otherwise."

The report described the various attempts by Germany to destroy Allied planes, including the "doughnut or pie-plate" discs with a "hole in the center" seen by the Northwest African Air Force. "This variety of weapons testifies to German ingenuity, and to the German willingness to experiment with new ideas," the report stated in closing. "As a potential threat, of course, that should not be minimized. But they also testify to Germany's desperate efforts to defend herself. They are a compliment to our increasing air strength."[123]

The Allied Air Intelligence staff was specifically addressing nothing but the ordnance related matters within their memoranda. The war took precedence over all else. Until there was aggression shown, and bombers were shot down from the sky, unconventional aircraft, the type that were beyond known enemy capabilities, remained either a closely guarded secret or a haunting worry.

In late 1943, the town of Bari was a key operating center for the Psychological Warfare Branch (PWB) of British Intelligence. As the "real capital" of southern Italy, Bari was the heart of anti-fascist Italy, pumping out a propaganda war designed to manipulate the nation's political and cultural arenas. The PWB controlled the newspapers, selecting stories for print and creating motion pictures designed to influence Italian soldiers not allied with anti-fascists. For anyone hungry and in need of money, the PWB was a perfect opportunity for those willing to work for the cause.[124]

One such man had become an operative and sent on a mission to Termoli, where he met Captain James Cameron, a member of the British Special Air Service (SAS). A relationship between both men developed and while working together, the operative learned of Cameron's involvement with very unconventional aircraft during his missions in northern Italy.

Amazed by Cameron's stories of SAS pilots who witnessed strange aircraft, the operative learned that aircraft were caught "many times" on film during the making of propaganda films. The footage was cut from the film's final edit, but remained in the original negatives. Captain Cameron informed the operative that the negative film stock was stored in Rome at the United Nations News (UNN); the main distributor for PWB operations.

Months later, the operative landed a job as an editor working undercover for the PWB. His credentials allowed him access to the UNN in Rome where he became acquainted with the individual who was in charge of storing the 35mm films. The operative watched the films. They were so clear he "could perfectly see the movement of the objects beside the bomber formations." In fact, the footage was so amazing the operative was repeatedly startled each time the aircraft appeared on screen. Unable to obtain copies of the films, the operative managed to convince the UNN man to give him a few copies of photographs, which are allegedly still in his possession today.[125]

The PWB was very relevant to the intelligence gathering missions gearing up for an upcoming Allied invasion of Italy.

Back in England, another intelligence operation important to the British homeland was underway.[126] Designated the "Crossbow Committee," this group was formed by Prime Minister Churchill, who felt the subject was of such critical importance that he decided to personally direct the project. Crossbow was the codename issued "to designate Anglo-American operations against all phases of the German long-range weapons program—operations against German research, experimentation, manufacture, construction of launching sites, and the transportation and firing of finished missiles, and also against missiles in flight, once they had been fired."[127]

Before continuing with the front-line action, a 1943 stateside sighting is relevant to the "rocket" phenomena sightings that were causing so much confusion over Europe. The exact month and day is unknown. A flying instructor with the 6th Ferry Group of the Air Transport Command and his student were flying one morning over Long Beach, California. Their BT-13A type trainer was above the fog, overcast at 5,000 feet, when an object made a dramatic approach.

The flight instructor was heading southwest when the "object appeared from the northeast on a level flight path and turned while decelerating from a great speed to fly parallel" to their aircraft. It was "international orange in color, had an elliptical or rounded forward structure," and "was proportioned in a manner as a conventional aircraft's fuselage." When the object decelerated, it wobbled in "an unstable manner." The pilot saw no wings, propellers, jet exhaust, smoke, or vapor trails.

For the next thirty seconds the object remained on a steady course right with the BT trainer. Then it sped up, passing in front of them at a speed of between "2,000 to 5,000 miles per hour" and disappeared from sight.[128]

For the time being, rockets remained top priority for many Allied air force staffers who tried to decipher incoming reports. On December 11, U.S. bombers conducted a daylight raid over Edmen, Germany. The weather was in favor of an accurate bombing run; there were no clouds with good visibility. German ground units had employed a defensive smokescreen and moderate to intense flak was nailing the lower formations of bombers approaching between 21,000 and 24,000 feet. Over the target area, crews observed an "unidentified object."

According to the crew's report, "It was described as being about the size of a Thunderbolt aircraft and passed 50-75 yards beneath the formation, flying straight and level at a 'terrific speed.' It left a streak like a vapour trail, which was all white and which remained visible for a very long time. The object passed so quickly that its observers could not describe it more completely."

Assessing the available information, technical authorities investigated the sighting and suggested that the object "was probably a jet-propelled fighter."[129] Operational jet-propelled aircraft showing up on the scene was not the kind of news British or U.S. Air Force Commands wanted; German jet aircraft were expected, but not that soon.

On December 14, 1943, British 255 Night Fighter Squadron leader, P.H.V. Wells was piloting his Bristol Beaufighter during a night patrol mission around Naples, Italy. His navigator-radio man (NAVRAD) was First Sergeant Izowsky, who stood behind him, as he had done on so many other missions. During the flight, Squadron Leader Wells noticed a small round bright "light." It was clearly defined, behind them at the same altitude and same speed, possibly a little faster. The light stayed right on their tail, but occasionally moved from side to side of their Beaufighter. Though the light displayed no aggressive behavior, Wells tried to maneuver his fighter around to the object's rear to get off a shot but failed. His opportunity to engage the light in combat was short lived, as it only lasted one or two minutes before disappearing in another direction.[130]

By the end of December, an RAF unit had something to say about the Emden "Thunderbolt" sighting. The 115 Squadron had just issued its first newsletter, put together for both information and amusement. A section of its new publication was devoted to "Phenomena": "Under this heading there occur from time to time reports of weird and wonderful apparitions seen during our (and the American) attacks on Germany. We have asked our local Inner Circle bloke to comment on the latest species of wizardry. Here is his story...believe it or not."

After quoting from the U.S. mission report, a little editorial humor was added: "It flew STRAIGHT AND LEVEL. No chaps, it was not a Lanc. Gone mad... at a terrific speed, leaving a streak like a vapor trail which was all white and which remained visible for a long time. The object passed so quickly that the observer could not determine it more accurately...

"Suggestions will be welcome...serious ones...as to what this Loch Ness Monster of Emden might have been."[131]

Despite months of unusual sighting reports, the 115 Squadron's article is another example reflecting the general attitude by intelligence personnel, which was subtly becoming problematic for those airmen who witnessed strange aerial objects not yet recognized or acknowledged as new weaponry.

By early winter 1943, a "monster" traversing the sky was no laughing matter among those commanding the Allied Forces. There were monsters to fear. Churchill's Crossbow operation was hunting the long-range sea serpents, V-weapons, soon expected to scream across the sky, spitting fire in their wake. Fierce birds of prey, German jet-propelled aircraft, were blazing the skies, preparing for their swift attack. These "monsters" were real. And the war was far from over.

Chapter Seven

Rockets, Airships, and Balloons

As the war entered its fifth year, January of 1944 began with renewed hope for Europe. The Allies had achieved three successful amphibious landings: North Africa, Sicily, and Italy.[132] Setting up shop in London, the newly formed Supreme Headquarters Allied Expeditionary Force (SHAEF) prepared for the Allied invasion of France. Taking charge of this behemoth effort was the commander in chief, General Dwight D. Eisenhower, who immediately began developing and coordinating the pre–invasion details.[133] Many factors were potentially disastrous for the invasion, including rockets, jets, and a potential German atomic bomb. Throw in unconventional aircraft – so far harmless, but nonetheless unpredictable – and there was much for Eisenhower's staff to consider.

One of the year's first sightings of unconventional craft occurred during the late hours of January 2/3. An RAF 463 Squadron Mosquito pilot, Flight Lieutenant Mortimer, reported: "Engaged by two rockets in the vicinity of HALBERSTADT and later near HANNOVER, 90 degrees alteration of course made and definitely established that rockets altered course. Overtook us slowly, appearing with a fiery head and blazing stern on a parallel course. Initial velocity seemed to be fairly great. Duration: approximately one minute; Disappeared without explosion."[134]

A second interrogation of the crew revealed additional details: "The only amplification of the details already given is the way in which the rear gunner established that the rockets followed the aircraft on the 90° alterations of course. He is sure of this because he had his guns trained on the rockets dead astern throughout and when the aircraft turned 90° he did not have to move his guns more than 10° from dead astern in each case. He estimates that one of them was at range of approximately 200 yards at its closest and kept pace at this range with M/463 for 30/40 seconds. He did not fire, in case a hit might detonate it, causing damage to the aircraft at that range."[135]

Lt. Mortimer's pesky "rockets" were defied Allied intelligence assessments that remote-control rockets were not in operation, especially those capable of effectively stalking aircraft.

In the meantime, newer aerial ordnance appeared on the scene. On January 5, targets in Kiel, Germany were attacked for the second day in a row. As usual, the bomber crews had plenty to keep them alert. They were met with aerial rockets and air-to-air bombings.[136] Air Intelligence officers recorded more incidents of aerial ordnance phenomena in their reports. One crew with the U.S. 303rd Group stated that "red flak opened like tulips into red balls."[137] Some of the 40th Combat Wing's 306th Group crews reported witnessing a flak burst, "quite like a regular one, then 'red things would come out like Fourth of July night fireworks."'Three of these unusual flak bursts were seen in the area, but it was felt there was no relation to enemy fighters or to the standard flak bursts being employed. One crew witnessed a very odd display, reporting "six bursts, about 100 feet in diameter, red in color, forming a circle which seemed to float in the air and drift." Not long after departing the target area, several crews observed "black plate sized discs, leaving a smoke trail, which did not explode."[138]

The new commanding general of the Eighth Air Force, James H. Doolittle, was informed that "a number of white balls, described as tennis balls made of cotton wool, were observed floating through the air in the target area." According to the Tactical Report of the mission, "they were moving along in lines of 8 to 10 balls with a gap of approximately 5 feet between each ball," appeared not to be connected, "and no enemy fighters were observed at the time."[139]

At 1050 hours on January 6, twenty-eight B-26s took to the sky. Captain L.C. Richter, formation commander, and First Lt. L.H. Carlson were leading elements of the U.S. 17th Bomb Group towards their target of the Pontedera Marshalling Yards in Italy. It was their turn to observe something unusual. Near their drop zone one of the crews reported flak bursts "emitting 15-20 streaks 18 inches long." The tail gunner of the same aircraft said that after the flak burst he saw "silver colored squares fluttering down."[140]

Early January presented a host of new observations for the squadron level S-2s to sort out. Some sightings were already frequently reported phenomena, but the descriptions were slightly different. In any case, they needed to send the ordnance phenomena reports up the chain of command as soon as possible.

Churchill's "Crossbow" Campaign was a priority, one of many, but nonetheless exceedingly important. Now that Operation Overlord was moving full steam ahead, anxiety was building, especially as the French coast invasion was scheduled for less than six months away. The invasion of Europe was the single most important Allied campaign; the war's longevity was riding on its outcome. The Crossbow staff was worried. They had not obtained any reliable information about the operational status of Hitler's terror weapons. SHAEF was worried too, asking countless times: Would the Allied troops meet disaster at the staging areas or on the beaches of France as Hitler's V rockets devastated them while wading ashore?[141]

In the U.S., on January 6, the long-range rocket dilemma was addressed.[142] By the following day the American Crossbow operation had begun. Major General S. G. Henry officially established the Committee on Counter-measures Against German Secret Weapons. Their mandate was determining the "nature and capabilities of the secret weapons" and "counter-measures to nullify the use of such weapons." A scientific and technical group was set up within the committee composed of the three civilian scientists: Howard P. Robertson, A.L. Loomis, and Roger Adams. They were "assisted by any other officers and scientists they required as consultants..."[143] It is of particular importance to note Robertson's growing affiliation with key committees, agencies, and organizations.

On the night of January 28, a British Mosquito night fighter crew belonging to the No. 23 Squadron was flying somewhere over France. According to a report from the Mediterranean Allied Coastal Air Force, the crew observed: "Airborne red light seen dead astern. Mosquito orbited, but made no contact. Continued on course and was seen again astern, and was seen several times, but the Mosquito was unable to trace any aircraft."[144]

This sighting had the earmarks of an unconventional aircraft, possibly the same type of object Squadron Leader Wells reported on December 14, 1943, when he described a "screaming dog-fight with the light." On this occasion, the light was red, and from all indications, it operated in an intelligent manner, playing a sort of cat and mouse game with the Mosquito.

The next night, RAF pilot Simpson of the 49 Squadron had an encounter at 20,500 feet with something that displayed more surprising rocketry characteristics; the "rockets" were having no trouble following aircraft.

"A red ball leaving a trail of yellow/red flames and black smoke, approximately 1,000 feet away at the same height and dead astern," states Simpson's raid report. "It was closing in. I dived to starboard and the object followed, appearing to fizzle out and then immediately to reappear. I turned hard to port and it followed us round in a tighter turn than we were in. When within 100 yards or less of the aircraft, it fizzled out."[145]

These two "rocket" sightings were too important to discount as misidentifications or dismiss as inaccurate observer details. It appeared conventional rocketry had advanced to the next level. In response, the RAF launched a group level investigation. No. 5 Group's air intelligence team had assembled the facts, and interrogated and re-interrogated crews. The two primary cases explored – those causing the most confusion – were Flight Lt. Mortimer's January 2/3 and pilot Simpson's January 27/28 sightings. Though the sightings were listed as "Rocket Phenomena" in their raid reports, the No. 5 Group's Air Vice-Marshall (AVM) wrote that the sightings struck him as "being highly improbable." Perplexed by the alleged rocket's flight performance, the AVM wanted information concerning performance capabilities of all German rockets. He wrote: "The straightforward rocket has I believe a velocity in the region of 3,000 ft. per second, so that there can be no question of its turning."

In reference to the Hs-293, he wrote: "The rocket propelled aeroplane used for the attacks against shipping would also seem likely to have a speed considerably higher than a Lancaster and although it can be maneuvered by its parent aircraft it would be extremely difficult at night to make it follow another aircraft which was maneuvering in the manner referred to..."[146]

On February 4, a Flak Liaison Officer (FLO), Major [name illegible], who was very involved with the No. 5 Group's "Rocket Phenomena" investigation, attended a conference at the British War Office with "representatives of Bomber Command Headquarters, the American Air Forces, and RAF, Medmenham." Greenhalsh brought up the alleged German rocket sightings and the confusion surrounding them. He informed the attendees that "all crews were 'rocket conscious,'" but there was limited rocket information available.

Two days later, the FLO provided an assessment to the Air Officer in Charge (AOC) of No. 5 Group, regarding information received from Bomber Command at the War Office meeting. Dismissing the probability of rockets, Bomber Command said they had yet to receive any damage to aircraft from rockets. No ground projectors were photographed, and only an estimated twenty percent of German night fighters were equipped with the ability to fire rockets. Even if the crews had seen rockets, "there can be no question of their turning in flight." The FLO was of the opinion "that what crews are now reporting as rockets is nothing more or less than light flak tracer over 10/10ths cloud base". Hand written at the bottom of FLO's comments, another officer wrote: "Draft a letter to Bases and Stations summing up information on rockets explained..." and "say no evidence whatever of any rocket capable of following an a/c [aircraft]."[147]

By February 9, No. 5 Group's Senior Air Staff Officer issued a two-page report of their investigation. Entitled "Rocket Phenomena," it was basically a reiteration of No. 5 Group's FLO's own thoughts and information provided from Bomber Command. "Reports by air crews suggesting the use by the enemy of some form of anti-aircraft rocket projectile have been received many times during the past year, and with increasing frequency during recent months. Observations have often been characterized by a visible trace and many of the reports have referred to changes of course enabling the rocket to follow in the path of the aircraft under attack."

Even though there was "no confirmation from independent sources of the development of such weapons," the senior FLO for the No. 5 Group felt it was "possible" that rockets were "used in some target areas, albeit in an experimental stage." In addition, he wrote: "It is considered, however, that the time has now arrived when all the available information on this subject should be summarized for the information of all concerned."

The report's conclusion indicated the crews were seeing either rockets fired from aircraft, parachute rockets, or High Explosive (HE) projectiles at maximum altitudes of 18,000 feet. Regarding rockets changing their course in flight, there were two proposed explanations: rocket defects caused their erratic behavior, or that they were actually light flak tracers observed reaching their highest trajectory point and then beginning to fall.[148]

On January 31, around the time No. 5 Group's investigation began, the U.S. War Department's Crossbow Committee met in Washington to discuss countermeasures in the event that Hitler's long-range rockets brought devastation to London and other areas. Briefing the committee was Edward Bowles, expert consultant to the Secretary of War. Bowles proposed that General Spaatz, commanding general of the newly formed United States Strategic Air Forces in Europe (USSTAF), coordinate the effort, and that Howard Robertson become General Spaatz's consultant.[149]

The Crossbow Committee was quick to agree with Bowles's choice of Spaatz and Robertson, and was anxious to learn if Robertson had contacted Reginald Jones during his recent trip to England. They were unable to meet, however. Bowles further emphasized that civilian specialists were an important commodity and their assistance was needed within military headquarters as advisors to SHAEF commanders on a host of subject matter.[150]

Since unconventional aircraft sightings were being continually reported, especially during the pre-invasion months, was the Crossbow operation also monitoring the unconventional aircraft sightings as part of a larger investigation emanating from President Roosevelt's and Prime Minister Winston Churchill's inner circle? Certainly if the rockets were of concern, so were the unconventional objects.

On February 4, while No. 5 Group's FLO attended the War Office meeting, U.S. Eighth Air Force bombers were conducting a massive raid on Frankfurt, Germany.[151] Observations reported on this mission included numerous sightings of alleged balloons. One sighting, reported by a crew with the 303rd Bomb Group, was a "stationary object of tear drop shape, resembling a balloon just above the cloud tops at 16,000–17,000 ft."[152]

Another "balloon" was seen at 22,000 feet by a crew with the 92nd Bomb Group, about ten miles from their aircraft. It "appeared to be a shiny silver ball of several feet in diameter and shining by its own incandescence." Looking like a "very bright weather balloon with a metal sheen," the witnesses watched as the "stationary ball" hung below the aircraft's altitude for approximately five minutes; the witness saw no cable or attachment.[153] More curiously, just after crossing the Dutch coast at 23,000 feet, a crewman with the 482nd Bomb Group looked below and observed "one long black stationary object similar to a small flak burst floating at 18,000 feet to 20,000 feet."[154]

Things were no different four days later during a second Frankfurt mission. Lt. Robinson and his crew with the 384th Bomb Group watched a silver-colored, "ball-like object" hang stationary in the sky for close to fifteen minutes. Once back home, they reported the sighting to their S-2 (Squadron Intelligence), Major Dolan, who in turn reported to his superiors that the object was "something they could not identify."[155] In Dolan's memorandum to A-2 with the 41st Combat Wing, he pointed out that the stationary silver object had no chute attached, nor did the crew see the object fired from the ground.[156]

Why some crews quickly identified the Frankfurt sightings as balloons, while others used phrases like "appear" or "resembling a balloon," and in two cases made no mention of balloons at all, just "objects," is unknown. The Frankfurt "balloon" sightings are included here to show that there was yet another variable involved in the aerial phenomena sightings. Another variable that air intelligence personnel had to contend with. Another variable that the unnerved airmen had to worry about: was it an ordinary balloon, a weapon, or something unknown?[157]

On the night of February 19/20, 1944, Bomber Command was hitting targets all over Germany. Small groups of bombers hit Aachen, Munich, Stuttgart, Duisburg, and Dusseldorf. A much larger force was approaching targets in Leipzig.

Catching intelligence officers by surprise were the "many reports of unusual phenomena" reported that night. According to the flak liaison officer's consolidated report: "1. Two aircrews provided remarkably similar reports of 'rocket phenomena' in the Leipzig-Berlin area. In each case the projectile was observed flying on a horizontal course and was first seen as a pinpoint of light which rapidly grew into a 'glowing ball' trailing sparks behind it. It appeared to be spinning relatively slowly and very unsteadily, a fact which lends colour to previous reports of similar projectiles having a 'snake-like' motion. The projectiles probably did not approach nearer than a half a mile to the observing aircraft; they did not terminate in an explosion, but merely lost height and fizzled out. The only difference between the two reports was that in one case the object was described as orange-red and in the other as white. It is unlikely, though this is not established, that both crews observed the same specific occurrence, nor is it known whether the phenomena originated from the ground or the air.

"2. Two observations were reported, one near COBLENZ and the other a few miles SW of AACHEN, of a 'silver cigar-shaped object like an airship', which in the first case was seen at a distance of about 2-3,000 yards from the aircraft, flying on a parallel course at the same height and gradually dropping astern; it appeared to turn in towards the aircraft, passing from starboard to port well astern. In the second case, it was stated that there appeared to be a line of windows along the bottom of the object.

"No explanation of these observations can be offered at present, but it is interesting to recall that it was in the neighborhood of Aachen that the phenomenon, which was christened a 'meteor' projectile, was reported in August 1942 (Consolidated FLO Report No. 115.) The 'meteor' projectile was not reliably reported again and is thought to have been some kind of experiment. It is possible that the present phenomenon falls into the same category."[158]

Within days another airship-like sighting occurred during a night operation on February 24/25 against targets in Schweinfurt, Germany. The following account appeared under the "Phenomena" section of the mission report: "Southwest of St. Quentin, three silver objects about 30 ft. long were seen 1,000 ft. below and 600 yards astern of the observers. They were described as resembling Zeppelins and, although moving in unison independently of the wind, were apparently not interconnected. Similar phenomena were described in Consolidated FLO report No. 205 and, although on this occasion a closer view was obtained, there is no explanation at present of the purpose they may serve."[159]

Why was it so difficult to positively identify a Zeppelin? More curiously, why were Zeppelins operating during a time that German units on the ground knew a massive Allied bomber force was approaching the area?

This brief report is important because of the object's description: "three silver objects," "resembling zeppelins," and "moving independently of the wind." These "airship" objects were appearing with more frequency. The St. Quentin sighting report states that a "closer view" was obtained, and still there remained confusion over the object's identity. Balloons and dirigibles were apparently ruled out, indicating some form of aircraft was encountered, but if discussions continued about these phenomena, they were not conducted via normal intelligence memoranda.

Back on the ground, the Italian campaign was practically at a standstill.[160] For Air Intelligence operatives waiting to get into Rome, the Italian and European theater of operations provided plenty air prisoners of war to keep them somewhat abreast of German technical developments. The importance of air force intelligence was further emphasized and coordinated. By the order of Major General Nathan Twining, a Fifteenth Army Air Force memorandum was issued on March 15. Superseding a November 15, 1943, version, it was titled, "Capture Intelligence Interrogation Of Air Prisoners of War, Examination Of Enemy Equipment." It detailed the apparatus already set in place for such matters. The Combined Services Detailed Interrogation Center (CSDIC) was specifically set up to interrogate enemy air force prisoners and examine their documentation or anything else in their been possession. No prisoner was to be interrogated by anyone, "regardless of rank," except by the CSDIC air interrogators. Fifteenth Air Force Headquarters required all documentation sent to the A-2's attention, whether the air interrogator thought it related to enemy aircraft or something else. The memorandum required that all crashed enemy aircraft or captured air material be guarded by personnel from "the nearest Army unit" until a "representative of the Captured Intelligence Section, A-2, MAAF [Mediterranean Allied Air Force] arrived."[161]

Given the number of unconventional aircraft sightings and other aerial phenomena, the CSDIC interrogation officers were likely informed about such incidents, and instructed whom to contact. If not, perhaps at least one operative within the CSDIC was monitoring incoming unconventional aircraft intelligence.

In the meantime, the German prisoners of war had provided much corroborating information about German jet-propelled fighters captured on film. Messerschmitt and Heinkel were the two German aircraft companies that had been continually reported in connection with the He-280, Me-262, and the little known Me-163. Now the Arado Aircraft

Company was reported as producing an aircraft, designated as the Arado-234.[162] Responding to the massive amount of information regarding jet-propelled aircraft, the United States Strategic Air Force issued an article called "German Jet Propulsion–Several Years of Experimentation Lies Back of Present Developments." The article detailed the latest types of jets, indicating that a number of unique aircraft were in production. The Germans were at work on these aircraft since at least 1940, and for the last three years, intelligence had received reports indicating there were reasons for concern. If the Allied bombing campaigns had not inflicted heavy damage on the aircraft manufacturing factories, these new German jet fighters could have seen action by summer. As far as meeting them in combat, it was felt that at high speeds, they would be very efficient, but under 400 mph their effectiveness would be limited against the Allies' high-speed fighters, which had better maneuverability.[163] The Allies were not too concerned about aerial combat with jets, due to their limited ability to engage in any kind of tight maneuver. This was a very telling statement by Air Intelligence; it precludes the jets being responsible for any of the remarkable unconventional aircraft sightings.

The Normandy invasion was just a few short months away. The Allies had to control the skies; any threat to the Overlord beaches was unacceptable. Lt. General Carl Spaatz, commanding officer of the United States Strategic Air Force,[164] had to destroy the mighty German Luftwaffe.

To coordinate the bombing campaign, he assembled an excellent staff and helped create the Air Technical Intelligence (ATI) branch. This new organization represented the essential backbone for Spaatz's second most important agenda: enemy scientific and technological exploitation. From the heart of the Army Air Force, Wright Field, Ohio, men started arriving in Europe; a great task lay ahead.[165] But before intelligence gathering proceeded, Spaatz needed to ensure that his air operations were successful, aided by the most advanced technology, primarily radar. For this goal, he summoned a team of top scientists that afforded him the best information and advice. On March 4, the Advisory Specialist Group was born. David Griggs was assigned to the group, as were civilian specialists Lee A. DuBridge, Louis. N. Ridenour, Victor H. Fraenckel, and Howard P. Robertson. [166]

By early 1944, both Griggs and Robertson were connected with nearly every major military and civilian organization in Europe. They were affiliated with the Office of Scientific Research and Development's (OSRD) Scientific Advisory Committee on Radio Aids (SACRA), which focused on all aspects of radar and radio countermeasures. SACRA's importance to the success of Overlord could not be understated. Robertson now had complete knowledge of the Overlord invasion plans, and he was one of only six American scientists in this position.[167]

There is no doubt that by now, if not before, Robertson and Griggs had access to all aerial phenomena reports filtering through the Allied Air Forces. And more importantly to this story, they undoubtedly had access to key intelligence surrounding the perplexing unconventional aircraft.[168]

On April 5, Robertson met with members of the U.S. War Department's Crossbow Committee to personally discuss his first visit to the United Kingdom since being appointed to the committee in January. Robertson was questioned about the British Crossbow organizational structure, intelligence gathering, sharing of information, and interpretations of intelligence.[169] Though the German rockets could prove very successful, Robertson felt that their effectiveness as a decisive weapon was questionable. Furthermore, he felt the Allied bombings were of value and should continue to thwart the Nazi efforts.[170] Even though the bombings were in some way effective, the Germans were continuing to build rocket launch sites. Allied intelligence prepared for the worse and entertained a variety of ideas regarding Germany's use of rockets: could they be used to deliver poison gas, and could a transoceanic ballistic missile be launched from Berlin to New York?[171]

Back in London, the SHAEF command structure surrounded itself with the best scientific minds. General Eisenhower and General Spaatz saw eye to eye on this matter, and for all intents and purposes, the USSTAF would leave no stone unturned. The enemy was strong, but the sky must belong to the Allies. There could be absolutely no Luftwaffe threat to the beaches during Overlord, and that meant everything in the air had to be identified. At least that was the plan. But this was far from the case. Ordnance related objects were still encountered – and were still called phenomena. The airmen kept reporting what they saw and their Air Intelligence officers desperately tried to get the information into the right hands for identification. The SHAEF scientists were valuable in this regard. Griggs and Robertson were in the perfect position to see this material.

On April 25, 1944, another sighting occurred that surely resonated with SHAEF command. During a U.S. mission over France, an Eight Air Force B-17 crewman sighted a "probable" Me-163 jet-propelled aircraft. The witness thought it was within a couple miles when he twice saw a black teardrop shaped craft, once passing directly in front of his bomber.[172]

Reinforcing recent U.S. intelligence, British Air Ministry Intelligence (AI2(a)) had just provided its assessment of the jet situation, issuing a report entitled "German Aircraft Industry Jet Propulsion Aircraft — Production Aspect." AI2(a) felt the Germans had reached "preliminary stages" of small-scale jet-propelled aircraft production. No combat-ready jets were expected within the next six months. It was further noted that the Me-163 was rocket-propelled, and very little was known about its production. Information indicated that the Me-262 was expected to see operational use first since test results of the Me-163 had not proven very successful. Three main jet-propelled aircraft were determined to see action initially: the Me-262, He-280, Ar-234, but it was prudent to keep a watchful eye for the Me-163.[173]

British Air Intelligence was accumulating information regarding jet and rocket manufacturing facilities, airdromes, and experimental stations. The intelligence gathering effort was twofold: end the facilities' ability to help Germany's war effort and then capture them post invasion. So far, the British had learned some basic information regarding the type of research carried out at various locations: Rechlin was the chief experimental field; Peenumunde focused on rockets and jets; Aichach conducted experiments with radio controlled aircraft; Darmstadt/Greisheim conducted jet-propelled aircraft research; Oranienburg probed high altitude experimentation; Gottingen experimented with supersonic flight; and Rugen and Usedom conducted the most secret research and nothing was known about what field of study they were exploring.[174]

On the evening of April 26, 1944, RAF pilot Arthur Horton and crew with the 622 Squadron were returning from a mission over Essen, Germany. Flying at 20,000 feet, about fifty miles from their target, Horton was alerted by both his gunners that they were either being "followed or chased by 'four orange glows' at some short distance astern" that were traveling extremely fast and gaining on their aircraft.

The four objects had "short stubby wings" and were pursuing them in pairs; two from portside and two from starboard side. Mid upper gunner Bernard Dye thought the objects had a "fire-like glow" with sparks emitting from their tail, looking like "large oranges," about the size of footballs.

Horton wasted no time, immediately reacting to the objects' aggressive nature: "I, of course, had immediately 'dropped' the aircraft out of the sky, my gunner's didn't know what they were – should they fire? – by this time I was standing the aircraft on its tail and beginning a series of corkscrews and turns, with the things following everything I did, but making no move to attack us. By this time we had the throttles 'through the gate,' the gunners still asking what they should do. Apart from flying the aircraft, I had to try and answer them. But were they some form of magnetic contraption that would explode at some specific distance from us, or on contact? Did they want us to fire at them to cause an explosion?

"Out of the kaleidoscope of thought the only answer was 'If they' are leaving us alone, leave them alone. The mad gyration through the sky continued, with the aircraft shaking and vibrating with speed and stress. One of the glows faded out and disappeared. By this time, most of the crew except me and the bomb-aimer had seen the 'things.' The remaining three stayed with us, duplicating our every move, until we had crossed the coast and were heading out to sea. The episode lasted about 10 minutes. We had traveled over fifty miles, and had lost some 14,000' of height. We were at 6,000' when they disappeared. According to my gunners they just 'faded out.'"[175]

Upon returning to base, Horton and his crew were immediately interrogated by intelligence officers, who made fun of his account.[176] The intelligence officers were unable to answer any questions and there were no other crews that witnessed anything.[177] Both Horton and Dye made notes in their logbooks regarding the terrifying "rocket" encounter, personally satisfied that they had reported something real.[178]

The "things" chasing Horton and crew were very sophisticated. Their "football" size and "short stubby wings" ruled out the Hs-293, which had a sixteen-foot wingspan. American and British intelligence had concluded authoritatively that the Hs-293 glider bomb was not capable of high-speed aerial pursuits of Allied aircraft conducting extreme evasive actions, especially during night operations.

Chapter Eight

ATI and CIOS

On May 3, 1944, a British Consolidated FLO report established that pilot Horton's sighting was unique. Under a section of the report entitled "Phenomena," it referenced a sighting of projectiles resembling glider bombs observed during the night of April 11/12, 1944: "These incidents are both reported as taking place within 10 miles of each other and probably refer to one and the same phenomenon. Technical authorities have been consulted and it is believed that the objects which are now described in the following two reports may have been glider bombs.

"1. An alleged air-fired projectile was seen to follow for about a minute and to be gaining on the observer; when the corkscrew turns were made it pursued the aircraft at first, then losing height, curved away to the ground.

"2. The observer saw an object approaching from a distance of 6 miles to starboard and 2/3 miles in front; a large orange glow was emitted leaving a smoke trail. The projectile was then observed to make a turn of approximately 120° towards the aircraft, lose height and disappear into a cloud."[179]

The only aspect of the April 11 sightings that resembled pilot Horton's account was that the object seen in both cases had an "orange glow."

On May 19, Lt. General Walter Bedell Smith, U.S. Army Chief of Staff, issued a SHAEF Intelligence Directive, Number 9–Technical Intelligence. It stated that ATI personnel were "solely responsible for all matters concerned with the examination and disposal of enemy Radar, Radar and Radio navigational aids, anti-aircraft and coastal artillery gun laying and searchlight control Radar; also for all matters concerned with German Air Force equipment, including aircraft…"[180]

According to the Technical Intelligence Directive, "The term 'new equipment' as used in this directory, signifies enemy weapons, munitions, vehicles, equipments, supplies and material of war of all kinds; the existence of which is newly discovered or … [concerns topics on] which additional data are required."[181] It should be noted that "new equipment" was also an appropriate term for unconventional aircraft, either discovered in German possession or at a crash site.

Early on June 5, "S" Force moved into Rome, setting up the first U.S. command post.[182] ATI, British AI(g)2, and Office of Naval Intelligence (ONI), to name a few, were in the position to question Italian military leaders, scientists, and engineers. This was a perfect opportunity for intelligence operatives to follow-up with British SAS operative Cameron's information regarding unconventional aircraft captured on motion picture film and stored at the UNN building, most likely a high priority "target" for AI(g)2.

The struggle to obtain Rome was no easy task. Though it was a fierce struggle, it paled in comparison to the situation unfolding in the English Channel. On June 6, Operation Overlord, the invasion of Europe had commenced. Swarming the Normandy beaches were the first waves of combined Allied troops. General Eisenhower and his joint Commanders at SHAEF anxiously awaited news of a foothold on the French beaches.[183]

While the savage battles raged, the liberty ship USS George E. Badger sat just off Omaha Beach. On board, Gunner Edward Breckel scanned the horizon. Suddenly, something appeared in the sky about five miles away. It was a "dark ellipsoidal object," which was "blunted on each end like a sausage." Unable to hear any noise associated with object, Breckel noticed it was "moving in a slow, smooth, circular course at about 15 ft. above the water" with "no protruding parts like an aircraft, and was moving too low and fast for a blimp." The object remained in Breckel's view for approximately three minutes.[184]

Breckel's object was similar in appearance to one the U.S. Eighth Air Force's 401st Bomb Group reported during a mission over Augsburg, Germany on February 25; both used the word "sausage" to describe what they saw. Though the 401 Bomb Group cited a red balloon, Breckel's sighting was apparently different.

A couple weeks into the fierce Overlord campaign, the Germans themselves witnessed unconventional aircraft as they fell back from the coastal areas. It took place one evening in Couville, Normandy. Heinz Heller was with the German Army; he was the commanding officer of a truck company. They were parked in an orchard that night when one of his men encountered a strange object. It was around three in the morning. Heller and other men were spread out among the trees sleeping, when they were awoken by a gunshot. Responding quickly, Heller arose from his sleep, finding one of the sentries "in a state of great excitement." The guard had fired his weapon to alert the rest of the men.

Heller questioned the sentry. The sentry had noticed a shadow of an object. Looking up, he observed, 30 feet in the air "a round shaped thing looking like a discus of about 20 meters diameter very slightly luminescent…" Firing his weapon, the sentry felt he had stopped the object before it crossed over the orchard. It was moving at about 20 miles per hour and "then accelerated vertically at an incredible speed, shining stronger and making a swooshing noise. He did not follow it with his eyes but surmised that it might have leveled off at a very high altitude."

Commander Heller discussed whether the sighting was a balloon or missile, even entertaining the idea that the sentry had hallucinated, but those ideas proved unfounded. That morning, the orchard's owner was questioned and said his grandfather once had seen a similar "apparition" over the same field. Contemplating the sighting, Commander Heller decided to not file an official report.[185]

Within forty-eight hours of the Normandy invasion, the first Air Technical Intelligence (ATI) team had come ashore.[186] Soon more teams followed, including similar British Air Ministry teams (AI2(g)) and they began searching for rocket sites, facilities, and radar stations.[187] Issued special passes by SHAEF, ATI teams bypassed red tape, giving them "authority to commandeer any equipment" or get whatever assistance they needed to meet their goals and objectives.[188]

The intelligence gathering missions were moving through dangerous and hostile territory. Protecting them were "T" Forces (the same as Italy's "S" Force); military units were assigned the specific task of securing locations, facilities, documentation, personnel, aircraft, and anything else deemed valuable.[189]

General Eisenhower realized that numerous independent intelligence units were roaming the countryside looking for the same targets.[190] To better coordinate intelligence gathering efforts, Eisenhower established a Combined Intelligence Priorities Committee (CIPC) on June 12.[191] The Committee created of a "Black List" of high priority targets: humans, buildings, materials, and documents.

Seven "Working Parties," A through G, were formulated by category, such as radar, missiles, and aircraft. Groups of scientists and technology experts were culled from various civilian and military organizations. Depending on their expertise, they were assigned to the appropriate working parties and armed with a list of facilities, research establishments, and names of specific scientists and technology experts.[192]

In the event unconventional aircraft sighting documentation was located by CIPC "Working Parties," the categories relevant to their discovery were: Radar, including radio controlled missiles; Weapons and projectiles; and Miscellaneous air items.[193] If by now Robertson, Alvarez, and Griggs had conducted any phenomena investigation(s), certain field members attached to the CIPC working parties were likely working as liaisons with them, flagging any appropriate intelligence.[194]

I t was 4:30 a.m. on June 13, 1944, when "Diver," the V-1, made its debut against England. The German secret weapon had become a reality and the Allies were faced with a real and potentially disastrous weapon. By June 16, Prime Minister Churchill asked General Eisenhower to be as aggressive as possible in destroying the "V" weapon menace. General Eisenhower immediately instructed his deputy, Air Chief Marshall Tedder, to put forth a prioritized effort against Crossbow targets, second only to combat operations in battle.[195]

The Crossbow Committee established observational posts that quickly alerted antiaircraft batteries of incoming V-1s. The Second Tactical Air Force was responsible for countermeasures. Aircraft, radar, and human sentries scanned the skies. The countermeasures were more successful than expected, but Churchill wondered: where was the dreaded long-range V–2?

By the end of June, Howard Robertson had gone out in the field for three weeks to gather intelligence concerning captured "V" weapon launching sites. Griggs and Alavarez, who had both actually witnessed the V-1s crossing the English Channel, wrote to Edward Bowles, stating: "The flying bomb has made quite an impact on many of us over here. Ever since Louis [sic] and I first saw them crossing the South Coast, flying straight and level at two to three thousand feet immune to flak and almost to fighters, we have been captivated by the potentialities of such a weapon to complement our Air Force in bad weather and targets where our losses are high."[196]

Though the V weapons campaign had just started, the American Crossbow Committee was dissolved on July 3 and their records were transferred to the Assistant Chief of Staff, G-2. Major General Henry wrote: "The files of the Committee are being made available to the G-2 Division in order to facilitate continuity of the work. Included is all the intelligence information on CROSSBOW, together with many detailed studies, both Allied and Axis, on pertinent subjects such as rockets, refrigerant bombs, proximity fuses, electronics, bombing techniques and probabilities, fuels for rockets, turbines, athodyd propulsion units, biological warfare, German scientific institutions and personalities, balloon barrages, guided missiles, artificial deflection of earth's magnetic field, types and characteristics of explosives and war gases, concrete construction studies, trends in propaganda, German experimental programs."[197] The Crossbow intelligence files would have been an important asset to anyone monitoring unconventional aircraft.

On July 20, General James Doolittle, commanding officer of the U.S. Eighth Air Force, held a conference with the Secretary of War. During his presentation, he discussed the German jet-propelled aircraft situation, indicating that the first operational use of jet- and rocket-propelled aircraft would occur in about thirty days with an estimated thirty to forty aircraft.[198]

By July 25, Robertson, back from his intelligence-gathering mission in France, was in London with Griggs attending a very large meeting of the Interdepartmental Radiolocation Committee, chaired by Sir Robert Watson-Watt. This Crossbow affiliated committee discussed radar units and radar tracking of "Diver" (V-1), and recommended that Griggs become part of a new sub-committee to work on photographic recordings of radar tracks. The latest "Ben" (V-2) intelligence was reviewed and recommendations were also proposed.[199] Griggs was now affiliated with all aerial reconnaissance photography, giving him access to any unconventional photographs or motion picture footage.

Not long after the invasion of France, another series of massive bomb raids were conducted against German cities. As Allied troops advanced into France, Lancaster pilot George Barton was among the group of bombers hitting Stuttgart for the second time during a series of raids. Returning to his base for debriefing, he overheard another Lancaster crewman excitedly telling his account. The other crewman said that as they approached their target area, he observed "spheres" approximately "the size of a large football" following right on their tail, as though "they were caught in the aircraft's slipstream."

As with most Allied airmen, when they saw something unfamiliar they immediately assumed the objects were German secret weapons. The pilot executed evasive maneuvers to get away from the spheres, while his rear gunner tried shooting them down. Much to the crew's surprise, the "spheres" stayed right with them, and were not affected by the gunfire.[200]

The skies over Europe were about to get even more crowded. On August 1, General Spaatz sent General Arnold a detailed message describing encounters with Me-262s and Me-163s over the last several days.[201] Detailed interrogations of experienced crews indicated there was no confusion over what they had observed. An important fact was that large distances were required for maneuverability at high speeds,[202] something not relevant to strange unconventional aircraft sightings.

The Allied ground war was swiftly moving through France.[203] Prisoners of war were flooding in at an almost uncontrollable rate. With them came valuable documentation and information, some offering stunning insight into what technological advances awaited capture.

Also on August 1, Operation Tidal Wave commenced. American bombers attacked the Rumanian city of Ploesti in an attempt to destroy Hitler's oil supply.[204] Nearby, the Vega petroleum refinery was also bombed. The oil tanks were still burning when a Rumanian named Grigore Zmeuranu arrived. It was here that Zmeuranu saw a "yellow object" approaching very quickly, "several times the speed of an aircraft." At first, it was a "pinpoint size in the sky," but when it got closer, he saw "very clear outlines." The object moved as if "propelled by a vibratory movement." He heard no sound while watching the object circle the burning refinery, before flying off in the direction in which it came.[205]

Meanwhile, in the Pacific theater of operations, Japanese troops were loosing ground, falling further back towards Japan. On their heels were Allied technical intelligence teams operated by American and British personnel. The U.S. Navy's Technical Air Intelligence (TAI) branch was one of the newest intelligence gathering entities operating in the Pacific theater. The TAI field unit responsibilities were "to ensure that complete, accurate, and up-to-date technical air information" was "obtained on the Japanese Air Force…"[206]

Like their European counterparts, TAI teams were no doubt conducting aerial phenomena and unconventional aircraft investigations, based on sightings that were eluding conventional wisdom.

On the evening of August 10/11, 1944, the Twentieth Air Force's primary target was the Pladjoe refinery at Palembang, Sumatra. Assigned to the mission were Bomb Groups of the Twentieth Bomber Command. Upon reaching Palembang, the 468th Bomb Group had unlimited visibility in the altostratus layer, but below that it was limited to around six miles. They encountered a variety of enemy antiaircraft and ground defenses, including ground-to-air and air-to-air rocket fire. Enemy fighters were on the prowl, but their attacks were weak and ineffective. The mission was a success.

Arriving back at base pilot Watson, flying aircraft number 6362 immediately reported to the group's S-2 officers for debriefing.[207] They were among numerous crews whose detailed accounts were promptly sent to XX Bomber Command's air intelligence section: "Observations were reported by several crews regarding a bizarre and confusing type of new weapon, probably of the rocket type. In some cases, crews believe that the projectiles were ground released, but analysis of reports and further interrogation indicate that ground release was virtually impossible because of the unlikelihood of ground installations at many of the points where observations were made, and because of the fact that the attacks followed our aircraft continuously over great distances and in some cases out over water. Conversely, no enemy aircraft were sighted during the time of the attacks. Because of the need for clarification and identification of this weapon, crew reports are covered in detail below:

"a. One aircraft was under continuous attack for 1 hour and 10 minutes, beginning 10 minutes after leaving the target area. Reddish-orange balls about the size of baseballs suddenly appeared 'out of nowhere' on the starboard beam; a momentary flash or trail about 6 inches long preceded the red-ball effect and this was followed immediately by an explosion. The balls appeared to break up into 4 or 5 fragments that flew in all directions, and appeared in fours, threes, twos, and singly, but never more than 4 appeared at the same time. There was usually about an interval of about ten seconds between volleys. The crews estimated that they observed a total of 250-300 separate bursts during the attack. The explosions were always off the right beam, never closer than 400 yards, never farther away than 700 yards, and always accurate as to altitude. The aircraft was flying at 16,000 feet over an under-cast at 10,000 feet varying from 5/10 to 10/10. Lateral visibility was estimated as 30 miles except for occasional scattered clouds, but no enemy aircraft were sighted. There were no ground flashes observed when the ground was visible. Bursts were not observed when the aircraft flew through clouds, but reappeared when the clouds were passed.

"On one occasion, the course was altered sufficiently to allow tail guns to bear in the direction of the bursts, but 20-mm and 50-cal. fire from the B-29 had no visible effect. There was no change in the continuity or characteristics of the bursts when our aircraft reached the west coast of Sumatra and flew out over the Indian Ocean. The explosions continued until after Siberoet Island had been passed. There was no clue as to whether the projectiles were originating from below, level, or above. The B-29 was not damaged."

Two other sightings were mentioned but they were not nearly as detailed. Under the heading, "New Weapons and Tactics," the XX Bomber Command's Intelligence section was perplexed by the sightings: "In view of the reports submitted by the first crew, it appears to be virtually impossible that the projectiles could have been released from the ground, at least in that particular case. The area of attack was too great and the fire too continuous. The fact that enemy aircraft were not sighted during the attacks is unusual, particularly since visibility was good. The ability to maintain contact throughout the 1 hour and 10 minute period, to carry 250-300 projectiles, and to obtain accuracy as to altitude are other confusing aspects. Nevertheless, it is believed that the projectiles were released from one or more aircraft."

The report further stated: "It is the belief of several crews that certain enemy planes flying parallel to our aircraft and out of range relayed speed, altitude, and course information to ground batteries."[208]

In addition to sighting these "red balls," other B-29s with the 468th Bomb Group reported observing colored "lights." These were included in the Consolidated Mission Report: "(3) A/C 279 saw two Nicks over the target 4000 feet below – appeared to be camouflaged with two lights, red and green, on top of fuselage. (4) A/C 446 reported on leaving the target an airplane having amber and red lights following them for ¾ of an hour after leaving the target always approximately 10 miles back. A/C 454 saw one unidentified plane just above undercast at target area, having red and green lights on wings, moving fast at 90° heading and circling over fires."[209]

But there was another sighting that mystified the intelligence staff at XX Bomber Command's Headquarters even further. According to the 468's S-2 report, B-29 number 4494 was piloted by Alvah Reida. During debriefing, Reida said that, due to overcast, he used radar to bomb the primary target with good results. Anti-aircraft was meager. There was no fighter opposition. Under item 11 of the S-2 report concerning "Special Interest Items," pilot Reida's response: "None. 627 prepared to ditch 50 miles…" The last few words of Reida's report were illegible.[210]

Pilot Reida's key sightings during the mission were six large tanks at the refinery burning, exploding around twenty-five minutes later; seen a hundred miles away.[211]

Reida's fairly unremarkable S-2 report account is what makes his story so unusual. It is what the S-2 report does not include. This was revealed by Reida's personal account of the event after the war. The official report completely excluded any mention of his more interesting observation. Reida later had this to say about his mission against targets on the island of Sumatra: "The date was August 10, 1944. Time: shortly after midnight. There were 50 planes on the strike going in on the target and the assignment was for us to bomb then drop photo flash bombs attached to parachutes, make a few runs over the target area, photographing bomb damage from the preceding planes. The weather was broken clouds, an overcast above us. Our altitude was 14,000 feet, indicated airspeed about 210 mph.

While in the general target area we were exposed to sporadic flak fire, but immediately after leaving this area it ceased. At about 20 to 30 minutes later, the right gunner and my co-pilot reported a strange object pacing us about 500 yards off the starboard wing. At that distance, it appeared as a spherical object, probably 5 or 6 feet in diameter, of a very bright and intense red or orange in color. It seemed to have a halo effect…

"My gunner reported it coming in from about the five o'clock position at our level. It seemed to throb or vibrate constantly. Assuming it was some kind of radio controlled object sent to pace us, I went into evasive action, changing direction constantly as much as 90 degrees and altitude about 2,000 feet. It followed our every maneuver for about 8 minutes, always holding a position of about 500 yards out and about 2 o'clock in relation to the plane. When it left, it made an abrupt 90 degree turn up and accelerated rapidly, it disappeared in the overcast."

Captain Reida said that within an hour of his sighting, he was in weather that was causing St. Elmo's fire, both inside and outside of his aircraft. He said "the propellers looked like pin-wheels the way the sparks flew from them." After returning from his mission Captain Reida was debriefed, what he called a "strike evaluation and interrogation," in which he filed a detailed intelligence report regarding his mission.[212]

Though Reida states he filed the report, it is curious that neither the intelligence report written by the S-2 officers, nor the XX Bomber Command's Tactical Mission report to the Commanding General of the Twentieth Air Force made any mention of his sighting. There was no reason to exclude sightings of radio-controlled weaponry; especially since the XX Bomber Command's report went into great detail concerning rocket attacks and aerial bombings. The 468th Bomb Group's B-29 bomber crew report describing the one hour and ten minute attack from an unknown source was reported in detail, but Captain Reida's very strange, possible radio-

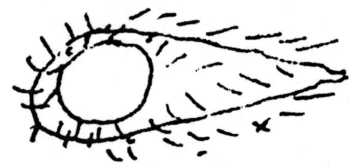

Captain Reida's drawing of object observed during mission of August 10/11.

controlled object was not. Was there a U.S. Army Air Force cover-up? Were unconventional aircraft sightings, ones thought far beyond enemy capabilities, segregated to separate air intelligence files?

Within twenty-four hours of Reida's sighting, RAF Squadron leader Brian Frow and his crew were returning from a bombing mission of oil refineries at Pelice in Southern France. Ronald Clairidge was operating the Lancaster Bomber's radar set, monitoring the screen for approaching German night fighters. Suddenly, a malfunction of some type occurred, which caused the radar unit to stop working. Clairidge quickly reported the problem to pilot Frow, who interrupted him, yelling, "What the hell was that?" Trying to see what was causing Frow so much concern, Clairidge climbed into the astrodome. Now he too saw the amazing sight. Sitting off the starboard side was a string of lights.

Clairidge stared at the spectacle: "The lights were circular, rather like portholes in a ship. The colour was a very bright yellow changing to intense white. My estimate was that they were about a thousand yards from our aeroplane. The ones nearest our Lancaster were the largest and brightest. They stretched fore and aft to what seemed infinity. After about thirty seconds I could see they were part of an enormous disc."

Stunned, the gunners held their fire, though no order was given for them to do so. The "disc" hung motionless for about three minutes, then "suddenly shot ahead and was gone." Clairidge heard "no noise of engines" and saw no signs of exhaust or vapor trail.

The sighting left the crew speechless. Nothing much was said among them during their flight home. Back at base, each crewman reported his sighting to the intelligence officers, who appeared not in the least interested or concerned about the crewmen's sighting; they listened, but asked no questions, and showed no interest in learning any further details. Yet strangely, the crew was warned not to discuss the sighting with anyone, including each other. They were told there was to be absolutely no written account of the sighting placed in their logbooks.[213]

This sighting describes an object of remarkable size, shape, and speed. An aircraft such as this in the hands of the enemy was unthinkable. It remains unknown why the intelligence officers did not interrogate Squad Leader Frow and crew. Where was the standard ridicule and sarcasm? The intelligence officer's handling of this case indicates that something had happened behind the scenes to dictate a change of policy. It seemed the unconventional aircraft sightings were escalating, but so far, they had not interfered with any military operations.

Chapter Nine

Calling Dr. Griggs

On the evening of August 13, two B-25 crews reported observing something rather mystifying. The night mission was executed to harass enemy shipping. A fighter of the 418th Night Fighter Squadron (NFS) attached to a flight of B-25s was flying out over southeast Kaoe Bay, Indonesia.

Interrogation by the 418th Night Fighter Squadron's S-2 officer revealed: "After a further interrogation of the eight crew members of the two B-25's who observed the 'very brilliant light appearing to hover for at least five minutes over the bay midway between CAPE TABOBO and CAPE JAWAL,' it has been established that the light was of magnesium flare intensity, that its position was some 200 ft. below the overcast and some 3½ miles from shore. It is therefore suggested that such a flare could have been dropped from an enemy A/C flying in the overcast, and if the flare's composition resembled that of a standard U.S. Army emergency landing flare (which opens in about 200 ft. where it is held in position by a 15 ft. parachute and gives off intense light for about five minutes), this hypothesis would be consistent in every respect with the phenomenon as reported."[214]

This report serves as a good an example where air intelligence may have mistakenly assumed the light was a flare, and placed the report under a flare ordnance category.

On September 26, B-29 bombers with the XX Bomber Command reported a variety of aerial ordnance used against them during their mission over Ashan, Manchuria. Referenced in the S-2 report as "aerial bombs," the objects used looked like a "stove pipes," "orange crates," "ball and chains," and "fire extinguishers."[215]

While U.S. bombers dodged the aerial ordnance, unconventional aircraft were reported by Japanese troops in September. An anti-aircraft battery with the Imperial Japanese Navy was on alert. They were waiting for Allied bombers when they observed a mysterious "white object," "egg-shaped," and "very brilliant," flying 8,000 feet over the island. It was the size of a B-29 bomber.[216]

A few weeks later, three Bomb Groups of the XX Bomber Command raided targets on the island of Formosa (later called Taiwan) on October 16. Encounters with fighters, aerial bombings, and rocket attacks were cited in the Operations Report to Twentieth Air Force Headquarters. Under the heading, "Possible New Weapons" the report stated: "Another crew observed a small black dot in the air at 25,000 feet above the coast of Formosa just west of Okayama. The dot seemed to hang stationary while in the crew's view. It was smaller than a flak burst, and had the appearance of an object rather than a cloud of smoke or burst from an explosion."[217]

A few days later, Eastern Air Command briefly recounted the sighting in their Intelligence Summary, but offered no comments.[218] Curiously, neither the XX Bomber Command, nor the Eastern Air Command reports suggested the "black dot" was a balloon, perhaps because it was obvious to all that it was not a balloon. Balloons were a familiar sight over the Pacific theater and were reported in all shapes and sizes.

On October 25, the XX Bomber Command sent four bomb groups on a mission against the primary target of the Omura Aircraft Assembly Plant in Omura, Japan; one of the bomb groups was the 40th Bomb Group, under the command of William H. Blanchard.[219] During the mission, three B-29 crews reported high-altitude balloons on three separate occasions.

A B-29 crew flying at 23,000 feet reported the first sighting on their approach to Omura. They were about nine minutes away, when they "observed one possible high-altitude balloon," described as "being generally round in shape." A second crew observed "a black free balloon, larger than a conventional barrage balloon, at about 15,000 feet, directly over Omura at 0116Z. The observations were made from 25,000 feet, and the balloon appeared to be rising." The third crew observed "eight to twelve large balloons" at "23,000 to 26,000 feet altitude about 10 miles south of Omura." The crew felt that the balloons were released when their "aircraft entered the target area, but the nature of release was not observed." The color of the balloons was a "silvery-gray and no cables were observed. They did not appear to be drifting and apparently remained stationary while in sight."[220] The wording of the Report of Operations suggests that the balloon conclusion for this sighting was nothing more than an educated guess.

In fact, these last few sightings suggest that some unconventional aircraft sightings were misidentified as balloons, again emphasizing the problems air intelligence had in deciphering mission report phenomena. Did U.S. air intelligence personnel categorize some unknown objects as balloons simply for a lack of any other labels to identify them?

Another suspicious sighting occurred on November 5. The entire

XX Bombardment Command was instructed to hit targets in Singapore, Malaya. Among the growing number of sightings of variously shaped high altitude balloons, one crew observed "a long purple-blue parabolic trail passed high across the nose of the aircraft at a distance of approximately 400 yards. The 'object' passed the aircraft at the height of the parabola. Further information is lacking."[221] It should be noted that the key word here is "object."

M eanwhile, in the European theater...
They were called the Polish Resettlement Corps, Polish troops who wished to fight with the Allied forces against Nazi Germany. According to witness A.W. Szachnowski: "It was the summer of 1944 in Italy, during offensive action around Loreto, Castelfidardo, and Osima. About 10:30 a.m., in an almost cloudless sky, there suddenly appeared an egg-shaped, metallically glistening, motionless object. Our anti-aircraft guns immediately opened a barrage of fire. Shells burst below the object, and after a while, our batteries stopped — when we realized the German batteries were also shelling the same object. They continued to do so for some time, but eventually stopped. The object remained motionless for another minute or so. Then it tilted about 50 degrees and suddenly moved very speedily upwards, disappearing in the blue Italian skies. At the time this was only a one-day wonder. Other emotions of the war pushed it to the back of my mind. It remained there until these discussions in the camp.

"One evening, I related the story of that sighting. Among others listening were some Polish airmen. They were very interested for they also had, on two occasions, some very strange 'escorts' in the air during bombing sorties over Germany."[222]

The Normandy hedgerows had proven a vicious battleground obstacle for Allied troops moving inland from the beaches; advances were measured by the yards. The breakout from St. Lo in early August, though costly, was a major blow to the German defenses.

Officer George Todt was with the Second Infantry Division, heading "toward Vire, near the Falaise Gap." Around 0045 hours, Todt was preparing for his round of staff work at the 38th Regimental Headquarters when he noticed something in the night sky heading west from the Omaha Beach area, towards the enemy lines. He thought he was looking at a V-1. Since Colonel Boos had wanted to see one of the German rockets, he hurried to Regimental Headquarters and summoned Colonel Boos and another officer outside to observe the rocket in flight.

While Todt, Colonel Boos, another officer, and a guard watched the passing object, Todt realized that the object was probably not a German rocket. It was heading in the wrong direction. What they were looking at was a "cherry-red light" that expanded and contracted "every few seconds, rhythmically, and without once loosing a beat."

Todt described it further: "… it was about five times as big as the largest star and perhaps a fifth the size of the moon – it seemed to be traveling silently on a straight line course towards our position at possibly 3800 feet altitude. The speed was about 120 miles per hour. Too fast for a dirigible, too slow for an airplane."

If there was any doubt the object was not a German rocket, it was put to rest when the object "arrived over the American and German lines" and "glided to a complete stop." Officer Todt timed the reddish-light sitting motionless in the sky for fourteen minutes. It then "moved away at a right angle and disappeared into the clouds."[223]

Operation Overlord involved following the troops from the beaches of France, through all their combat operations, right into the heart of Germany. By the end of August, the beaches were secure. Paris was liberated. The Nazis began falling back, taking heavy casualties as they faced the Allied onslaught. As the ferocious air and land battles unfolded, the "T" Forces were right behind the combat troops, protecting all scientific and technical "targets" for the intelligence gathering teams flooding in right behind them.

Allied command knew Hitler's Third Reich demise was on the horizon. From that point on, Operation Eclipse would take over where Overlord left off, handling the disarmament of Germany.[224] Part of Eclipse's immense disarmament plan was focused on the Luftwaffe, a phase highly anticipated by General Arnold's U.S. Army Air Force staff, especially the Air Material Command and the USSTAF ATI teams.

As of August 17, the Combined Intelligence Priorities Committee was absorbed into the much larger Combined Intelligence Objectives Sub-Committee (CIOS)[225] and the CIOS Air Intelligence gathering missions were off and running. These were in addition to General Spaatz's ATI teams, significantly increasing the number of field personnel.[226]

But still more personnel were needed to deal with this issue. On September 2, General Spaatz sent another memo to General Arnold requesting more air specialists for use in the United Kingdom. The Allied advance was accelerating so fast it was imperative that eighty new specialists be sent to augment the existing ATI teams already exploiting "captured German aviation research establishments."[227]

ATI and CIOS Air Tech teams worked in conjunction with a personal project orchestrated by General Arnold. Always the progressive thinker, Arnold wanted to start developing a U.S. Air Force for the future. He was interested in formulating "a long range blueprint" to guarantee the United States maintained complete postwar air supremacy. For this task, he chose renowned theoretical physicist Theodore von Karman to lead a specialized intelligence-gathering mission of its own: the Von Karman Mission. It was General Arnold's personal project, and its members reported directly to him.

General Arnold was motivated to jump-start his project immediately. In September, on his way to Canada for official business, he asked to meet Von Karman at LaGuardia Airport in New York. Sitting in Arnold's car near the runway, both Arnold and Von Karman discussed the genesis of their incredibly important project.[228]

Meanwhile in London, on September 6, the newly formed CIOS met for the first time. The meeting was well attended. Among the other representatives present, Howard Robertson was there, as was Commander Ian Fleming for the Admiralty and Air Commodore K.C. Buss with the Air Ministry. Representing the AAF were the Director of Intelligence, Headquarters USSTAF, General McDonald; Lt. Colonel Lewis Powell; and Chief, Air Technical Section, Colonel Howard McCoy. Their order of business: to hash out and discuss the coordination of the individual field teams and the handling of their reports. There was also a concern over what they called "pirate" bodies; separate and unknown intelligence teams encountered in the field, completely unaware of one another's existence or mission.[229]

The pirate bodies made it very difficult for a centralized coordination effort and provided a perfect cover, I might add, for a secretive unconventional aircraft investigation operating without any knowledge of their agenda by CIOS leaders.

V-1 attacks against England started diminishing as the Allies advanced through France, bombing and overrunning launch sites, severely curtailing their threat, almost crushing it entirely. The Crossbow Committee actually believed the real danger had subsided and the "Battle of London" was over. But on September 8, the Crossbow Committee was rudely disappointed. A second new aerial terror had arrived: "Ben," the code-name for the V-2. The V-2 "had changed the nature of future wars" and the Allied nations "had no rockets that could begin to compare with the V-2 in size, destructiveness, and sophistication of engineering."[230] The new weapon was out there in untold numbers. Allied command increased their bombing campaign with a vengeance; there were those wondering what other Nazi surprises lurked in the shadows.

On September 14, Air Staff at SHAEF contacted British AI2(g) in reference to very unusual sightings over the Normandy beach area during the month of July: "During the past three weeks, operators on height finding equipment located in the Normandy Beach area have observed targets flying at extremely high altitude. The general indication is that of a small plane. Rate of climb to 40,000 feet is fairly rapid, above that, to 45,000 feet, about 2,000 feet per minute, thereafter slowing down to 1,000 feet per minute at higher levels. Rate of descent observed from 47,000 to 30,000 feet on one instance was 5,000 feet per minute."

AI2(g), looking into the possibility that a "small German aircraft" had reached heights of 66,000 feet, responded: "The only German aircraft which may be capable, under certain conditions, of attaining the high altitudes mentioned, is the Me-163 rocket-propelled fighter. We have no information, however, that this aircraft has been equipped for operation at these altitudes and on the evidence of the report it cannot be concluded that the targets were in fact aircraft of this type."[231]

Despite the British air intelligence response, something was flying at high altitudes. Further corroborative intelligence was already circulating in London and Washington. The Office of Strategic Service (OSS) had reported that six stratospheric aircraft were in various stages of construction and "intended for the bombing of New York; one was actually fully operable."[232]

The OSS report represented the type of air intelligence that constantly came in from the field; approximately four to five thousand reports per month. These reports varied in reliability and this was acknowledged and taken into consideration. Nonetheless, some subjects could not be ignored: atomic energy, biological warfare, weapons, and most importantly, experimental aircraft. These reports went directly to special assistants who were responsible to the Secretary of War and his chief scientific advisor, Edward Bowles;[233] of course, Bowles's scientific advisor was David Griggs. It is among these OSS reports that unconventional aircraft sighting reports were most likely extracted and filed separately, supplying information for General Donovan's own investigation, stemming back to the Los Angeles, California sightings in early 1942. Could the OSS have been the long arm of intelligence concerning an unconventional aircraft investigation emanating out of Washington?

Another strange sighting occurred in late September when RAF Lieutenant Jeffery Wilks spotted an unusual looking object over Dover,

England. According to Lt. Wilks it happened around nine or ten o'clock at night. Spotting for the 606 Antiaircraft Battery, Wilks was very alert that evening since the anti-aircraft radar was malfunctioning. There were no clouds in the sky as he watched bombers return from a mission; one was struggling, limping home with an engine ablaze. Not long after the damaged bomber passed overhead, Wilks witnessed something that was definitely not a bomber.

The object was silent while making its approach, a red glow emitting from its rear. It was solid black in color and cylindrical-shaped. Arriving directly over the observer's position, the object changed its angle, becoming vertical, and within a matter of seconds shot straight up into the sky and disappeared. Lt. Wilks was sure he had witnessed something remarkable since he was well aware what Germany's V-1 looked and sounded like. Since the object was silent and able to change direction of its travel so abruptly, he and the hundred or so witnesses knew it was no rocket bomb. Wilks felt sure it was not one of Germany's rocket-propelled aircraft.[234]

A civilian saw another amazing unconventional aircraft that month. The witness was observing the approach of "four V-1 flying bombs, flying astern and heading in the direction of Marble Arch." According to the witness: "She noticed a bright spherical object moving at a rapid speed in the northern sky, 'like a rolling ball,' approaching the formation of V-1s. The sphere, which had the appearance of a 'soap bubble,' slowed and paced the flying bomb formation for a few seconds. When the 'bubble' approached the leading V-1, the bomb began to descend and the witness immediately took cover. After the explosion she looked again in time to see the object climbing at an incredible speed towards the NW as the other V-1's began to fall in the Pall Mall area."[235]

Antwerp, Belgium was one town that would see its fair share of destruction by the Nazi "V" weapons. During late September, the rockets were bombarding Antwerp. Lance Corporal Carson Yorke with the First Canadian Army was just outside the city when a new salvo came in that night. According to Yorke: "At about 9 p.m., I stepped out of my vehicle and on looking upward saw a glowing globe traveling from the direction of the front line toward Antwerp. It seemed to be about 3-4 ft. in diameter and looked as though it was [made] of cloudy glass with a light inside. It gave a soft white glow. Its altitude seemed to be about 40 ft., speed about 30 mph and there was no sound of any sort. I noted that the object was not simply drifting with the wind but was obviously powered and controlled. Immediately, it had gone beyond view, it was followed by another which in turn was followed by others, five in all."

Five other men joined Corporal Yorke. Most of them were not too impressed, only thinking that the Nazis had unveiled another secret weapon.[236]

Not far away in Holland, Private W.T. Smith was attached to the Lincoln and Welland Regiment. As a young child, Smith was a fan of the outdoors. Astronomy was a keen interest of his and he had spent plenty of time stargazing. On this particular evening during the fall of 1944, the sky was "very clear" and Smith could "see a lot of stars." Lying on the ground, he looked up and "saw a light" that at first he thought was a star. He knew it "wasn't a meteor because it was moving so slow compared to a meteor. It appeared to be miles and miles up. I reasoned it couldn't be an airplane, because at that time they wouldn't be flying with any lights on, also there wasn't any noise, if there was I don't think I could have heard it any ways because it seemed to be so high, directly overhead. I thought it might be a V-2, but it was going in the wrong direction. It was going in an easterly direction. I remember it so vividly because at the time it impressed me so much, I knew it wasn't a star or planet because there wouldn't be any movement to them."[237]

The witnesses had seen something far more impressive than Germany's V weapons in action, which were falling by the dozens. While the explosion was the telltale sign that the V-2 had struck, only those in the immediate vicinity heard the screaming swoosh before the bang. V-1s were another story; they moved relatively slowly and made a distinctive sound. Though they rained down upon indiscriminate targets, there was no mass hysteria; British resolve was at its finest.

In the last weeks of September, the Allies had retaken France and were moving into Germany. As the ground troops advanced, both Griggs and Alvarez collected information from top generals with the Army Air Force and Army ground forces; Griggs spent considerable time with Air Force Generals' Weyland and Quesada discussing tactical aircraft support for ground forces, the use of aircraft radar, and the specific roles of the Tactical Air Commands (TAC).[238]

With so many air operations conducted over such a huge geographic area, radar and radar counter-measures were essential in accomplishing the missions. There were many ways to deceive an enemy and such deceptions could aid in winning vital battles, ultimately affecting a campaign. Misidentifications, optical illusions, and meteorological and astronomical phenomena were all on the table.

One problem Griggs and Alvarez faced was "radar spoofs." This method of radar deception could be caused either by "electronic deception,"

"No-coherent dipoles (Chaff)," "Coherent dipoles (e.g. Ropes)," "Corner Reflectors (or physically small but high gain mechanical reflectors)," or "Other types." According to a U.S. *RCM* (Radio Counter Measures) *Digest*, single aircraft or a formation of aircraft could be simulated by such "spoofs."[239] But Griggs and Alvarez likely considered the possibility of radar spoofs before sending any unconventional aircraft sighting reports up the chain of command.

On the evening of October 20, mysterious objects were reported in the Mediterranean Theater. Over Italy, a British Beaufighter crew with the U.S. 414th Night Fighter Squadron was conducting an intruder mission over the Po Valley area. Lt. Ryan and his Navigator, Lt. Wohl, observed a "red light" that had the appearance of an aircraft light, but it disappeared and no contact was made.[240]

Within hours of each other, another Beaufighter crew, this time with the 416th NFS, was patrolling the area of Northern Florence when members saw "two orange balls diving into the hills." They were unable to get close enough to clearly identify the object.[241]

On October 23, the First Tactical Air Force (Provisional) was setting up its Headquarters in Vittel, France. Arriving with the first men was newly promoted Colonel Harold Watson. He was an excellent engineer from Wright Field in the U.S. and had personally known General Spaatz for years.[242]

An officer with the Technical Services Directorate, Colonel Watson's status grew exponentially by the day. He was issued a "blue pass" bearing the signature of General Eisenhower. The "blue pass" stated that "its bearer was authorized to examine and remove any captured aircraft or item of enemy air and air radar equipment, whether found in the field or in factories, workshops, or dumps, and was permitted to travel anywhere else required."[243]

On October 26, the War Department's Classified Message Center received a "Top-Secret–Urgent" message from General Spaatz regarding not a sighting but a strange experience that greatly troubled the higher-ups: "Four pilots of one flight 366th Squadron, 358th Fighter-Bomber Group, 19 Tactical Air Command, Ninth Air Force, had experiences on 12 October 1944 which may fall within queries put out in your WARX 35279 observations made in vicinity of Strasbourg, France while flying between the towns of Beithe and Barr between 0945 and 1015 hours.

"Pilot one reported rough engine and noise on radio while flying north south at 11,000 to 13,000 feet, pilot two complained of rough engine and excessive radio interference, also that ammeter showed fifty amps when noise and engine roughness were present, at one time when radio noise was excessive radio was turned off and ammeter returned to normal, pilot three mentioned excessive radio noise and engine roughness simultaneously, pilot four first noticed engine roughness and afterwards accompanying static on the radio.

"Radios of all here on 'C' channel at time of observations. All four pilots attempted to smooth out the engine by manipulation of propeller mixture and throttle control to no avail."[244]

The next day General Arnold sent Edward Bowles a very terse message: "See me." Penciled in on the same memo, probably at a later date was: "Conference held between ACAS/I [Assistant Chief Air Staff, Intelligence] and Dr. Bowles-Nec [necessary] action taken." Also, another hand-written message stated: "Tac & Tech note and be guided accordingly."[245]

On October 28, General Arnold contacted General Spaatz suggesting that Griggs "familiarize himself with the substance" of the incidents, and "interrogate personnel responsible for information" in the memorandum "as well as personnel involved in any subsequent experiences of this general character." Furthermore, General Arnold requested that he "be given the results of these interrogations." Attached to Arnold's memorandum was a second sheet that required necessary action be initiated within a 24-hour period.

Another hand-written note was penciled in by a Major Hearn, Jr.: "Dr. Bowles contacted regarding this cable. He in turn notified his staff who are on the alert for any information to complete this picture. He also sent cable to E.T.O. for Gen. Spaatz to advise Dr. D.T. Griggs (tech. representative) of any future cases. Dr. Griggs would interrogate the pilots and submit information to AAF Hdq."[246]

The contents of these messages offer no information as to what phenomenon was involved, but this may be the first official document to reveal that Griggs was officially requested to interrogate pilots in reference to strange airborne phenomena. It should be noted that during the postwar years right on through the present day, engine and radio interference are physical characteristics that have been associated with sightings of unconventional objects.[247]

On October 29, the Fifteenth Air Force conducted their first night mission in the Mediterranean Theater. Twelve B-17s with the 5th Wing, operating on fifteen-minute intervals, took off separately on a "Lone Wolf" operation to harass the enemy. Flying with the group was pilot William A. Schultz who taxied down the runway on the way to his target: the Marshalling Yards in Munich, Germany. Flying at 26,000 feet, they were approaching Innsbruck when tracer rounds suddenly streamed towards them. A moment later, the upper gunner yelled out that a bogie was heading their way, an apparent twin engine JU-88. In response, Schultz dropped to a lower altitude, maneuvering his plane into thick clouds, hoping they would lose the enemy fighter. He told the crew to hold their fire since their machine gun barrels had no flame suppressors on them; he did not want to give away their position and possibly draw in more fighters. His maneuver proved successful. But after getting clear of the clouds, something unusual was there to greet them.

According to Schultz: "We had broken out of the high scattered clouds when a strange phenomenon occurred. A light blue colored ball of fire approximately three feet in diameter appeared about 40 feet off our right wing tip. It actually flew along with us for about 30 seconds with streams of fire trailing down, but it was too large to be a plane."[248]

Around that same time, between 2054 and 2334 hours, Lt. Romens and Lt. Morin with the 422nd NFS were up in their P-61A Black Widow on a defensive patrol, flying between Aachen and the Rhine River. Ground Command Intercept informed them that a "fast moving target" was in the area. They went on the hunt. According to their air intercept radar, the target was about three miles away. They pursued it, but were "unable to close to visual before it went off both AI and GCI."[249]

In less than twenty-four hours yet another sighting occurred. It was the night of October 30/31. RAF Flight Engineer Maurice Juberley and his fellow crewmen of the 640 Squadron had just completed a bomb mission over Cologne, Germany. Their Halifax III was above the clouds, flying at 19,000 feet. Visibility was good with clear conditions, putting the gunners on alert; the clear weather was also a plus for the German night fighters.

The rear gunner soon reported that a "ball of fire" was following them. Juberley positioned himself in the astrodome for a better look. He could see "a circular, pale orange, clean edged light, dead astern," and approaching. Unable to determine the object's size, he thought it was a fighter without identifiable wings. It was closing in on their aircraft. The rear gunner ordered a "corkscrew to port" maneuver and the crew "lost contact with the light." Seconds later, a British plane flying nearby caught fire. The crew was unsure why but assumed it was due to an enemy fighter.[250]

For the next several nights, the 422nd NFS reported a slew of "jet" sightings during defensive patrol action, many between the Aachen and Rhine areas. On the night of November 5/6, it was no different. Between 1732 and 0005 hours, the Aachen area was still a hot zone for "jet" activity. Four separate crews in the Aachen-Bonn and Aachen-Cologne areas had reported them. The weather that night was anywhere from 7/10 to 10/10 overcast at 5,000 to 6,000 feet over the patrol areas.

One crew in particular had a particularly suspicious sighting. At 1920 hours, Lt. Siegle and Lt. Orzel were flying their P-61A on a defensive patrol in the Aachen-Bonn area, near the Vogelsand airdrome. According to their report: "...spotted jet flying 260 at Angels 14, when pilot tried to chase, jet put on power and climbed out of sight. S/L observed at same time. Pilot at first was passing jet, indicating 220. Throttled back and pulled to within ½ -1 mile and beneath when jet put on power."[251]

One way to interpret this report is that Lt. Siegle and Orzel spotted a jet, gave chase, but lost it when the jet "powered up and climbed out of sight." At the same time, they saw a single light, "S/L." Assuming the "S/L" stood for single light, it makes no sense that a night fighter would fly with any lights continuously on. Also, when the jet "powered up" to climb away, there was no mention of two lights, meaning one light for each jet engine if it were a Me-262. This suggests it was a Me-163, but there were no known rocket powered night fighter units in operation at that time.[252]

Always hungry for a new angle on pilot sighting reports, the press released a small blurb on November 7. The Associated Press out of Paris ran the story, "New Aerial Weapons Used By Germans": "The Germans are using jet and rocket propelled planes and various other 'new fangled' gadgets against Allied night fighters, Lieut. Col. B. Johnson, Natchitoches, La., commander of a P-61 Black Widow group, said today. 'In recent nights we've counted 15 to 20 jet planes,' Johnson said. They sometimes fly in formations of four, but more often they fly alone."[253]

The Associated Press did not release the night fighter unit's actual identification, due to security restrictions, but Lt. Colonel Johnson was the 422nd NFS's commanding officer. The 422nd had filed reports of jet aircraft since the first week of October. Their sightings, however, conflicted with the Allied air staff's intelligence concerning the number of operational German jet night fighter aircraft at the time.

General Spaatz's A-2 staff continually updated and disseminated the newest information among the Air Force staffs and whoever else was interested. They had recently discovered a "Top Secret" memo Hitler issued on September 4 that the Me-262 was still in an experimental stage. In his memo Hitler forbid "all references, discussions and suggestions regarding operational employment and potentialities of the Me-262, since it is still in the experimental stage and at present available only in small numbers." Hitler's warning applied to the entire staff of the German Luftwaffe.[254]

Hitler's order is pertinent, considering the widespread jet activity reported at night. There was still no confirmation of jet- and rocket-powered night fighters, but they were apparently out in number; there were five weeks of alleged jet sightings at night. Or were they something else?

Like the Air Ministry, concern and confusion at USSTAF Headquarters was mounting. Curiously, on November 13 General Spaatz sent General Arnold a message that did not mention the American 422nd NFS encounters, but instead referenced bombers of the RAF: "RAF sightings and claims of jets at night made mainly by heavy bomber crews are accepted with reserve by British Air Ministry. Possibility exists that a small numbers of jet aircraft are being employed experimentally at night, but there is no evidence that any normal night fighter units are equipped with jet aircraft."

Spaatz further stated the Air Ministry was suggesting that a "possible explanation" for many of the sightings was Germany's He-219. There were limited numbers of these aircraft, and they "may be using auxiliary jet propulsion units."

The Air Ministry was still seeking answers in the Hs-293 glider-bomb, possibly a modified version, or it was "some form of rocket flak." The Air Ministry's confusion and search for answers left Spaatz no option but to remark: "Whole position at present is uncertain."[255]

Spaatz's A-2 staff was also at a loss. They had no definitive proof other than the words of their airmen that Germans were using some type of jet-powered aircraft at night. This confusion must have caused conflict among Air Intelligence officers who knew they were dealing with a mystery. There seemed to be those who knew what was happening. Unable to say anything, they continued to openly deny the existence of strange unconventional aircraft, passing the sightings off as German jet night fighters.

Chapter Ten

Leet, Nolan, and
Intruder Schlueter

Without question, by late 1944 the Allies had witnessed an amazing array of German technological developments, and much more was still on the drawing board, months and years away from operational use.[256] Yet the sightings of unconventional objects continued.

On November 22, RAF 9 Squadron was returning from a mission against targets in Trondheim, Norway. Flying Officer Dennis Nolan and crew were somewhere over Germany, thirty to forty minutes away from their target area, at an altitude of approximately 12,000 feet. The time was around 2200 hours.

Suddenly, the rear gunner alerted the pilot to the presence of an incoming object, suggesting he take immediate evasive action with a corkscrew movement. Officer Nolan noticed what had caused his gunner's alarm. Flying at the same altitude astern of their aircraft, Nolan was able to see a clearly defined, spherical object, fluctuating in brightness, and "pyrotechnic pink" in color. The object changed from a lighter shade of pink and appeared shinier at times. Its size seemed about the same size as a "burst of heavy flak." The object was changing speeds "violently," accelerating and decelerating with "swift" and "jerking" movements, moving from side to side of their aircraft, always well astern. Watching the object closely, the rear and mid gunners thought it was possibly a German night fighter, but they did not fire on the object and it did not attack them.

Flight Officer Nolan could not recall the duration of the sighting. Worried about night fighters, all he and his crew wanted was to get the hell out of there as fast as possible. Once they arrived back at their base, the intelligence officers debriefing them showed great interest in their sighting but offered no explanations. Interestingly, Nolan underwent further interrogations by intelligence officers with the No. 5 Group Intelligence Section back at Morton Hall, Swinderby.[257]

No. 5 Group's ongoing investigation of "rocket" phenomena sightings had begun more than a year earlier. They had reached no conclusive explanation and now there were more strange cases to sort out.[258]

The next mysterious sighting occurred within forty-eight hours of Nolan's sighting, on the evening of November 24. Camped among olive trees in the southern Italian countryside, Army Air Force Captain William D. Leet prepared for a comfortable evening of food and drinks with his buddies at their camp's "Owls Club." Once inside, he was informed that one of his crewmembers was looking for him to go on a "Lone Wolf" mission over Salzburg, Germany that night. A crew was already assembled and they were looking for a pilot to fly the volunteer raid. Captain Leet had flown two Lone Wolf missions on previous occasions and both scared the hell out of him. And besides, there would be no fighter escort, just his B-17 bomber, the "Old Crow," a sitting duck for the German jet night fighters he heard that the Nazis had started using. It was a tough mission, but Leet did not want to disappoint his men, so he hesitantly agreed.

Captain Leet and his crew belonged to the 2nd Bombardment Group, 5th Wing of the Fifteenth Air Force. By 2200 hours, Old Crow taxied down the runway and up into the frigid air, committed to another nerve-racking mission. Moments later, Captain Leet got word from his waist gunner that there was a minor problem with engine number two. They

B-17 pilot Captain William D. Leet, left, 2nd Bombardment Group, 5th Wing, Fifteenth Air Force, shaking hands with his brother, Lt. Warren R. Leet. (Courtesy Richard H. Hall)

could continue, but 18,000 feet was their maximum altitude, not very high for a large bomber. Despite the problem, they decided to carry out the mission, but decided to bomb their secondary target, the marshalling yards at Klagenfurt, instead. Reaching their destination, they were pleased to find neither flak nor fighters to greet them. Finding their target, a string of freight cars below, the bay doors opened and it was bombs away. "Old Crow" had struck again, and it was time to get the bird out of there.[259]

Leet was glad the mission was going so well, but he knew something was odd: there had been no night fighters. No complaints though, he was flying over Northern Italy, near Trieste, and heading home. Seconds later, Leet noticed a blinding light and felt an "unbearable" heat. It was gone as quickly as it came.

Assuming it was a powerful searchlight crossing their path, he wondered why the Nazis had failed to notice their aircraft and blast them out of the sky. Then seconds later, a "round amber light" sitting off the left wing tip of his plane caught his attention. "None of us saw it approach or had any sight of it until it was right beside the B-17, flying along in formation with us," recalled Captain Leet. "The object's outline was a perfect circle–too perfect; its color was a luminous orange-yellow–too luminous."[260]

The upper, left waist, and ball gunners anxiously prepared to fire on the strange object, but Leet ordered them not to shoot. Not knowing what the object was, he told his men to keep it under surveillance; the object was not hostile and made no attempts to attack. Racing through his mind was a checklist of ideas.

"Not the moon, which isn't out tonight," Leet recalls thinking, "and the moon doesn't look like that, anyway. It's not exhaust from an airplane engine, which is flame and not a bit round. I can't really make out what shape it is—whether it's shaped like a sphere or if it's a disc balancing on edge—because of its unearthly light. I can't judge its size very well because I don't know how far out it is. It appears to be close to our wingtip, though, perhaps 100 yards laterally and 5 yards to the rear."

Sgt. Harris, the upper gunner, got a perfect view of the object. Captain Leet asked him to describe what he was seeing: "I don't know how to describe it," he said. "It's not an airplane or anything I have seen before. It is so perfectly round I can't believe it. I guess it's about 10 feet in diameter and 75 to 100 yards from us."

The rest of the crew concurred that the object was about 100 yards away from their B-17. Watching the entire time, the tail gunner asked Captain Leet what he thought it was. "Wish I knew," replied Leet, "but it hasn't bothered us so I don't want anyone shooting at it. I wouldn't feel right about shooting at an unknown object that seems to be from out of this world."

By now, Old Crow's nervous crew was over the Adriatic Sea, heading for the British airfield at Amendola. The object stayed right with them for about fifty minutes. Moments later, the engineer exclaimed, "It just turned off," as if a light bulb had been switched off.

The crew discussed its disappearance while Captain Leet thought about the absence of flak and the lack of enemy fighters. The apparent searchlight especially troubled him, remembering that during the mission's briefing, the intelligence officer made no mention of searchlights in the area. Leet questioned the other crewmembers about the odd searchlight. Navigator James Dehority reported that he just saw a blinding flash and felt heat. The ball gunner said he, too, saw the flash and felt the heat. Everyone concluded that it was neither ground lights nor a searchlight. And besides, searchlights did not switch on and off, finding an airplane with such incredible accuracy. Now very suspicious, Leet wondered if the strange object was some kind of advanced German technology; it would at least answer the question why flak or fighters did not attack them.

Without further incident they arrived safely back home. It was 0420 hours and they were wide-awake, full of energy, though a little shaken. Around 0500 hours Captain Leet discussed his encounter with Captain Hooton, the base intelligence officer. At first, Leet was hesitant about telling Hooton what he saw, thinking how it would sound to someone who was not there, but he told him anyway.

Captain Leet asked Captain Hooton if searchlights were being used in Klagenfurt. Hooton replied that there were no known searchlights there, probably because radar was a better method to track approaching bombers. Asking why Captain Leet was inquiring about searchlights, Leet responded by telling Hooton about the blinding light and heat. Captain Hooton said it must have been a searchlight, but Captain Leet explained that they had seen no ground lights whatsoever, and at no time was antiaircraft artillery used against them. Hooton could not believe what he was hearing. He knew there were at least forty plus artillery guns known to exist in that area.

Captain Leet, noticing Captain Hooton's incredulous look, then lowered the boom, describing in detail what he and his crew witnessed. Hooton immediately responded by stating it was a night fighter they saw, but Leet quickly interjected that they were not fired upon for fifty minutes. Hooton stood there shocked, not saying a word. Leet knew what his intelligence officer was thinking, and could not blame him, but it was the truth. Leet excused himself, knowing the rest of his crew would verify his story during their debriefing.[261]

Captain Leet's sighting is one of the most important nighttime unconventional aircraft encounters to take place late in the war. His sighting represents the first known wartime military action report that referenced heat physically felt in association with an unconventional aircraft. As expected, Captain Leet's incredible sighting mysteriously disappeared from his unit records. (The reader may recall the account in Chapter One by RAF pilot Lt. Bruce H. Thomas who actually received burns to his face and hands flying too close to a huge "light" in the sky.)

American night fighter crews had reported strange sightings since late September. Their aircraft were British Bristol Beaufighters or America's new A-20s, the P-61A "Black Widow," and they were armed to the teeth with machine guns and cannons. Roaming over the countryside, these aircraft were stealthy killers. Dealing with darkness was one thing, but many times, they were completely engulfed in cloud cover while in combat, something that proved a very dangerous combination. As usual, their "eyes" consisted of the plane's Air Intercept Radar and the Ground Control Intercept station to guide them in. The pilots were exceptional fliers and had great eyesight. They were a daring, calm, but thrill-seeking bunch of men, all of whom were specially chosen to handle the job.

One of these specialized airmen was Lt. Edward A. Schlueter. Considered one hell of a pilot, his action reports verify that claim. His buddies nicknamed him "Intruder Schlueter," citing his fearless nature, hawk-like vision, and willingness to get into the air and hunt for targets, no matter what.

On the evening of November 26 pilot Schlueter and his Radar Operator, Lt. Donald J. Meiers, were all geared up and ready to go. They were members of the 415th Night Fighter Squadron, attached to the 64th Fighter Wing, and stationed at the Longvic Air Base in Dijon, France. It was Schlueter's turn to go an intruder mission, hunting for lone aircraft, locomotives, and vehicles on the ground, or anything else of interest. That night he maneuvered his Beaufighter into position, opened up the throttle and taxied down the runway. At 1700 hours they were airborne and on the way towards their designated target area between the towns of Karlsruhe and Mannheim, Germany. The weather was fair, offering Schlueter visibility of about one and one-half miles. About an hour after reaching his patrol position, while flying at 2,000 feet, he spotted the marshalling yards at Mannheim.

Shortly after destroying a locomotive, "Intruder Schlueter" was

415th Night Fighter Squadron pilots, Lt. Edward A. Schlueter, left, and Lt. Donald J. Meiers, receiving Distinguished Flying Cross from General Glen O. Barcus in France, January 1945. (Courtesy Erik Schlueter)

leaving his kill zone when he observed something in the air that he could not readily identify. This something was "a red light flying through the area." The light "came into about 2,000 ft. of starboard then disappeared in long red streak." By 1940 hours, Schlueter had safely returned back to base. During his debriefing, he and Meiers described their combat exploits against the German troops, as well as his unusual sighting of the odd "red light."[262]

Lt. Schlueter's sighting was only the beginning of an eventful winter of strange sightings. A few days later, while still stationed at Longvic, Lt. Schlueter witnessed the odd lights again.[263] This time, however, the unit's intelligence officer, Captain Fred B. Ringwald, accompanied him and his radar operator, Lt. Donald Meiers, on the mission. Capt. Ringwald was flying along as an observer, hoping to get a glimpse of the strange aerial lights the other crews were also reporting.[264]

It was a fairly clear evening with only scattered clouds and a partial moon. Conducting a patrolling mission along the Rhine River near Strasbourg, they roamed low above the ground. Speeding through the darkness, they searched for vehicle convoys and trains, paying careful attention to avoid colliding with smokestacks, barrage balloons, and mountains, while scanning for searchlights, enemy night fighters, and flak.

While on the hunt, Capt. Ringwald noticed some lights in the distance, thinking the lights were on the hills. He asked Schlueter what he thought the lights were and Schlueter said they were probably stars. It did not take long for Ringwald to realize there were no hills in the area. There were eight to ten lights in a row, glowing orange, and moving at a terrific speed. Schlueter thought they were enemy fighters but received confirmation from GCI that no other aircraft were up there with them. Schlueter turned his aircraft into the lights, but as he maneuvered towards them, the lights blinked off. They reappeared far off in the distance and then after about five minutes they "went into a flat dive and vanished."

Lt. Schlueter continued on his mission, destroying seven freight trains, before returning to base. This time, however, Schlueter and Meiers decided not to file an official report about the lights because they did not want to be "grounded by some skeptical flight surgeon for 'combat fatigue.'"[265]

Apparently, Captain Ringwald had no problem with the crew leaving the encounter out of the report. He was with them and saw the strange lights firsthand, but for some reason, the sighting was apparently too weird for him to report as well. For now, Ringwald remained quiet. But little did he know the sightings would become quite numerous, bringing the subject to the forefront of the Allied Air Command's attention.

Ending the month of November, a spectacular unconventional aircraft sighting occurred out at sea, this time by the U.S. Navy. Fire Control Officer P. Kendall Bruce was on watch aboard the *USS Gilkiam* departing the Lingayen Gulf, Philippines. Monitoring the water and sky, Officer Bruce and a couple of other men witnessed movement behind them. Rising out of the "headlands," an object climbed to an altitude he was unable to determine. The object was a "bright green 'globe'" that sped away too slowly for it to have been a missile of any kind. He said they could think of no logical explanation for the object.[266]

Meanwhile, on December 2, the night fighter sightings began to escalate. 414th Night Fighter Squadron Pilot Lt. Baker and Radar Operator-Navigator Lt. Brown were flying their Beaufighter Mark VI on an intruder mission over the Villafranca, Ghedi Airdrome area in Italy. There was a heavy haze over the land, reaching to about 10,000 feet. During their three and one-half hour mission, they observed "a steady, seemingly hanging light." They closed their Beaufighter "…within 3 miles of light before light disappeared."[267]

During the early morning of December 5, between 0207 and 0423 hours, 422nd NFS pilot Lt. Jones and Lt. Adams conducted an intruder patrol between the front lines and the Rhine River area. They sighted an aircraft and began chasing it, closing to within a mile and a half "before it climbed out of range in nothing flat."[268]

On December 13, the *South Wales Argus* reported the Germans had "produced a 'secret weapon' in keeping with the Christmas season." The defensive weapon resembled "glass balls which adorn Christmas trees. They have been hanging in the air and are apparently transparent."[269]

According to a *Washington Post* story the next day, a dispatch issued by the United Press from Supreme Headquarters in Paris stated that crews with the Ninth Air Force were reported seeing "many silver balls floating in the air over enemy territory."[270]

By end of the first week of December, all the aircraft of the 415th NFS had arrived at their new airstrip: Toul/Ochey, France. On the night of December 14, 415th NFS pilot, Lt. Henry Giblin and his radar operator, Lt. Walter Cleary, were flying near Erstein when they observed a "light which appeared to be 4 or 5 times larger than a star going 200 mph." Poor visibility kept Giblin from getting a detailed description other than it was a "brilliant red light." Lt. Cleary was having no luck either; he was dealing with a problem: their AI had failed, creating a dangerous scenario. Despite the equipment malfunction, Giblin maintained a visual on the light as he pursued the object at around an altitude of 1,000 feet, hoping to get close enough for a better look. But his attempt failed. The red light "went out." It had simply disappeared.

Not pressing their luck, especially since their night eyes—Air Intercept—was not working, they decided to hightail it home. Upon returning to base, both men discussed the strange light at length, thinking that what they saw was the result of a bad breakfast, but nevertheless they ended up reporting it to their S-2.[271]

Then, on the early morning of December 15, sometime between 0330 and 0532, Lt. Allee and Technical Sergeant Heggie with the 422nd NFS were patrolling between Bonn and Ademan, Germany. They reported encountering and firing at a jet that they identified as a Me-163. They also saw V-1s being launched.[272]

Hours later, the *New York Times* released their morning edition. Responding to the *Washington Post* story, reporter Hanson W. Baldwin devoted a section of his December 15 feature story to the strange things aircrews were encountering on their missions. In the story's sub-section, "A Guess About The Spheres," he wrote: "The 'silver-colored spheres' that our airmen have reported encountering in the skies above Germany may be new types of floating 'windows' intended to confuse the bombing aim of our electronic 'magic eye.' During the winter months our bombers, more often than not, have been bombing 'blind' through overcasts. The target is picked up by radar and the bombs dropped by the aid of this 'magic eye.'"

Baldwin went on to accurately describe the use of "windows," the strips of tin foil dropped by the thousands, created to float slowly down, disrupting the enemy radar by camouflaging the accurate whereabouts of aircraft on the screen. Offering his own thoughts about the silver objects, Baldwin suggested: "The new 'silver spheres' might represent—but this is only an 'educated guess,' and there is no certainty that they are – the reverse of this idea. Such spheres drifting about in the sky might interfere with and confuse the radar in the attacking planes, thus making 'blind' bombing impossible, or far more inaccurate than it normally is."[273]

That same day, General Eisenhower issued a new update of the Continental Crossbow Collation and Intelligence Sections, just recently established due to the expansion of the V weapon's assault in Belgium. The Collation Section of Crossbow was: receive, coordinate, collate, and report information received from operational sources. With so many eyes trained skyward for contrails, objects, or lights indicating possible V-2 ("Ben")[274] or V-1 ("Diver") weapons in action, some were bound to be reports of unusual objects or unconventional aircraft. In any event, Crossbow was a G-2 and A-2 matter and no sighting could be ignored.[275]

By late 1944 Germany's jets and V weapons were easily recognizable objects. Their appearance had definite visual characteristics that identified them; their flight characteristics were readily recognized, and their thick, white contrails gave them an immediate signature. But darkness presented difficulties that were confusing the Allied airmen.

As the winter of 1944 spread across the European continent, airmen and squadron intelligence officers questioned whether the German Luftwaffe was responsible for the unconventional aircraft. Sighting reports received by S-2s were so numerous that the notion of so many jet-propelled aircraft being seen by so many was highly questionable.

Chapter Eleven

Smokey's Foo Fighters

As the last shades of darkness faded away, dawn's first light appeared and revealed a low-laying fog that had crept in and cloaked the forest. Moments later, the serenity was shattered by a ferocious barrage of German artillery. Operation "Autumn Mist," Germany's last big counteroffensive of the war, had commenced. It was the morning of December 16, 1944. A crippling blow was dealt all along the eighty-mile Belgium front against outnumbered American soldiers resting in the Forest of the Ardennes.[276]

Hitler had caught Allied intelligence off-guard. G-2 at SHAEF had their hands full trying to decipher exactly what was going on in that supposedly quiet sector. Alarming reports were flooding in by the dozens, but one stands out significantly in relation to the theme of this book. Among the incoming information was a "SECRET PRIORITY" memo from the headquarters of General Omar Bradley, commander of the Twelfth Army Group. The message informed G-2 about some odd occurrences that were observed just prior to the German counteroffensive. An anti-aircraft unit with the XX Corps reported that on December 13, just before midnight, two targets were picked up on radar, giving a "perfect" signal, making no noise, and traveling slow. They were engaged by anti-aircraft fire and both reacted in a "strange manner." When the anti-aircraft fire hit the first object, it disintegrated. The second object was also hit, and it dropped to the ground. The following night similar sightings occurred. Radar picked up the objects traveling at approximately 100 miles per hour and their altitude was around one thousand yards. As on the previous night, when fired upon the objects disintegrated.

In the same area three similar targets were observed, one traveling east to west. In all cases, there was no noise heard or explosion when the objects disintegrated. Responding to the downed object, a technical intelligence team was sent to the area to conduct a search.[277] Whatever had occurred prior to Germany's counteroffensive, its relevance seemed important enough for Bradley's staff to see it through.

Miles away in France, providing indirect support to the Ardennes combat front, was Major Harold Augspurger's 415th NFS. His unit sought numerous targets of opportunity essential to the German troops: supply lines, marshalling yards, and airfields, all of them vital to their counteroffensive.

The following evening, between 2205 and 2400 hours, a 415th NFS pilot conducting an intruder mission in the area of Breisach, Germany, was flying his Beaufighter at an altitude of 800 feet. Suddenly his attention was on "5 or 6 flashing red and green lights in 'T' shape." Thinking they were flak, he continued on, but about ten minutes later he "saw the same light much closer and behind" his Beaufighter. According to the 415th S-2, the pilot said he "turned port and starboard and the lights followed. They closed in to about 8 o'clock and 1,000 ft. and remained in that position for several minutes and then disappeared."[278] Once the crew returned, they filed an Operational Report that was forwarded to the A-2 with the 64th Fighter Wing.

The 415th NFS as a whole was beginning to see the strange lights almost nightly. The men were truly mystified by the sightings. Men back at base teased returning crews who reported the strange sightings, but they stopped poking fun when it was their turn and they, too, saw them. By December 18, nearly everyone in the unit had seen the strange lights and conversations around the mess tent spoke of everything from Buck Rogers to new German tracking devices. Though they had no answers, they found the strange light's antics humorous. Even as reports reached places like the 64th Fighter Wing and above, the sighting reports were greeted with skepticism and smiles.[279] But the men of the 415th NFS did not care what anyone at headquarters or above thought; they knew they were an excellent unit with top-notch airmen and had nothing to prove.

During a conversation one of the pilots suggested naming the strange lights. Nearby, pilot and operations officer Charlie Horne chimed in on the conversation and suggested calling them the "Foo Fighters"; a name gleaned from some of the men's favorite comic strip, "Smokey Stover." The cartoon followed the escapades of Smokey Stover, a madcap fire fighter who named his fire truck the "Foo" mobile. It was often stated in the comic strip, "Where there's foo, there's fire."

Officer Horne thought the name fit: "It was uh...shall we say, it was 'foo,' it was foolish... to even think about something like that, but it was kind of a phenomenon characteristic uh...thing, you know, that you just didn't expect."[280]

In the meantime, for the next two days German troops pushed through the American lines all along the Belgium front. In their wake, overwhelmed bastions of exhausted men were captured and in some places slaughtered after being taken prisoner. Though at first the weather was very poor, the sky was full of war machines. There were hundreds of Luftwaffe aircraft stalking above, engaging in fierce combat when the opportunity arose. In the city of Antwerp, V-2s had started falling, one killing close to 570 people including several hundred servicemen. The Americans were faced with the Nazis last desperate attempt to prevent them from crossing into the German motherland.

On December 19, General George Strong (Chief of U.S. Army Intelligence) sent a "Priority" memo, signed by General Eisenhower, to General Clayton Bissell (Office of the Assistant Chief of Staff for Intelligence on the War Department's General Staff) stating that "no concrete evidence as to use of new secret weapon obtained so far with the exception of report on new long range projectile." This memo may have been in reference to the new V weapon General Bradley reported. Apparently, the air technical teams sent out to the site had recovered parts of a projectile "15 to 17 centimeter caliber by 168 centimeter long" and there were three or four fins attached. It was thought the range was about fifty kilometers with rocket assistance. There were exterior markings, suggesting the "sabot construction" had rocket assistance, but all this information was only a preliminary analysis and "very scanty." It was felt that a sabot construction with fins and utilizing rocket assistance was "improbable."

In the meantime, the fragments were sent back to the U.S. for analysis. And while Strong's memo stated further information was forthcoming, he also made a point to reference the "silver-ball" phenomenon: "Information on silver colored floating balls reported in [the] press is being sought and will be cables [sic] when received."[281]

On December 20, the silver-balls story would not die. There was so much press interest regarding the objects that military command in Washington was forced to react. An Army Air Force spokesman with the Pentagon gave a brief official statement offering what they knew about the mysterious objects. His comments were reported in a "Special" to the *New York Times*, under the headline, "Berlin's Device Futile: Silver Spheres Above City Have No Effect, Capitol Says."

The story stated: "No 'detectable effects' have been noted from the mysterious 'silver balls' that, American pilots recently reported were floating over Berlin, an official Army Air Forces spokesman said today. The objects were described as silver, or silver-colored, but the AAF does not know whether they are metal, the spokesman said. He added that the descriptions had been contained in newspaper reports and that headquarters here had no reports from the theater."[282]

From the AAF spokesman's response, it is obvious that information about the spheres was suppressed. The story could have been easily diffused if the spokesman had released a statement citing previous use of simple ordnance devices, thereby ending the curiosity. But for some reason they chose to say that it was a mystery; they only had information garnered from news stories and no reports had been received from the theater of operation. One possible explanation regarding the spokesman's response: Army Counter Intelligence was handling the matter as part of some type of censorship operation; possibly, there was some kind of advantage to letting the enemy think their aerial ordnance was causing concern and confusion within the Allied command.

The silver ball reports had generated much concern and interest among the top Allied Generals. Why had the War Department's Air Intelligence staff not suggested to any of them a possible link between the silver-balls and the prior "disc" phenomena? This is very curious. The aerial phenomena observed beginning on September 6, 1943, over Stuttgart, Germany, generated a plethora of Air Intelligence memos, summaries, and reports. Some of these reports indicated that the "discs," and in some cases glass balls, were probably incendiary ordnance devices. Now over one year later, the "silver balls" were being treated as a new and mystifying item. It just seems odd and unnecessary, unless there was something else going on behind the scenes, explaining why General Eisenhower's staff had utilized precious time during the unexpected Ardennes Offensive to revisit a fairly well-known and understood phenomenon of yesteryear.

Meanwhile the crews with the 415th NFS continued to report observations of the strange and mysterious "Foo-Fighters." Five days since the last major sighting, they were back. Beginning on the evening of December 22 and well into early morning, two intruder, and six patrol missions were carried out by the 415th NFS over Germany. One crew was on a patrolling mission in the vicinity of Hagenau. It was 0600 hours and they were flying at 10,000 feet, when the crew saw two lights that "appeared to be a large orange glow" coming from the ground and heading towards their Beaufighter.

"Upon reaching the altitude of [the] plane, they leveled off and stayed on my tail for approximately 2 minutes," the pilot stated. After about two minutes, the lights would "peel off and turn away, fly along level for a few minutes and then go out. They appeared to be under perfect control at all times."[283]

Within the same time frame, another crew patrolling the Sarrebourg area also "saw lights from a plane and orange glow." They, too, thought the lights were "possible" jet-propelled aircraft.[284]

On the evening of December 23, the 415th NFS flew four more missions into Germany. Between 1730 and 2100 hours, a Beaufighter crew was sent out on an intruder mission, and not long after their mission turned into a patrolling action when the crew reported spotting a "red streak" in the sky. The crew also thought this sighting might be a jet aircraft. It was flying at 10,000 feet when they saw it at a "considerable distance."[285]

That same night, it was pilot Lt. David L. McFalls and navigator Lt. Ned Baker's turn. They were flying south of Point X, their Ground Control Intercept, when they "observed a glowing, red object shooting straight up." Suddenly, the crew was able to discern what appeared to be an aircraft "doing a wing-over and going into a dive and disappearing."[286]

Over the previous few nights, several types of jet-propelled object sightings were reported by the 415th NFS, and all were designated as foo fighter observations. As sightings came in, the 415th's intelligence officer, Captain Ringwald, listened carefully. He compared the sightings to each other, trying to find a common thread among them. One thing was a certainty: the unknown aircraft were reported frequently.

Another enigmatic encounter occurred within the first two weeks of the Ardennes offensive. Lt. Chester L. Buscio was the pilot on this particular mission. Due to the scarcity of night fighter aircraft and the large number of missions needed during the German's counteroffensive, night fighter pilots were often needed to go right back up, sometimes alternating between piloting and operating the radar. On this particular mission, pilot Lt. Samuel A. Krasney manned the AI, supporting Lt. Buscio.

Taking off one night, the Beaufighter crew headed into a thick fog, but the murkiness cleared up once over Germany. Suddenly, Buscio and Krasney were no longer flying solo. Appearing right beside them was an object the size of their aircraft. At first, Lt. Krasney was not sure what had taken place. One second they were alone, the next moment something was hanging right off their wingtip, just yards away.

The object fluctuated between grey and a reddish-glow. Lt. Krasney thought the reddish color faded due to the moon's light reflecting off tops of white clouds behind the object; against dark areas of the sky, the object's red glow was more prevalent. At times, he was able to see a wingless cigar-shape, but generally the object's shape remained amorphous within the reddish glow.

Everything was happening so quickly. Lt. Krasney was "scared shitless." He told Lt. Buscio to execute immediate evasive maneuvers. At a variety of altitudes, the object stayed right with them, sometimes close and sometimes at a distance. Whatever the object was, it had exceptional flight capabilities the Beaufighter crew was unable to duplicate. They were sure it was not an enemy prop-engine or jet-propelled aircraft. After several minutes of cat and mouse, the object "flew off and disappeared." They were unable to determine where it had gone.

Safely on the ground at Toul/Ochey, Lt. Buscio and Lt. Krasney were debriefed by Captain Ringwald; Major Augspurger was also present. When they gave their initial report, Captain Ringwald was skeptical, but eventually he said they didn't know what the objects were. He just told the guys to watch their backs up there.[287]

On December 24, the 415th NFS officers held their annual gala party. Despite the serious German counteroffensive and six crews taking turns that night conducting a variety of missions in a very active sky, they tried their best to maintain a festive mood. The next day, December 25, air battles over Belgium increased.

According to the 64th Fighter Wing's report, the 415th NFS had relatively little to report during the late evening of December 26/27, other than entanglements with a German JU-88.[288] The report for that evening also reveals no other sightings, confirming a fairly uneventful night. Oddly, this was not exactly true. According to the Captain Ringwald's [the 415th's intelligence officer] Operational Report, there was more observed that night than German JU-88 night fighters. One crew observed "red balls of fire" hanging in the air for ten seconds, and then later they saw "two yellow streaks of flame" at the same altitude off their port side. Responding to the yellow streaks, the pilot turned starboard and dropped in altitude, but the yellow streaks "disappeared from view." Contacting the crew's Ground Control Intercept, "Blunder," the pilot asked if they had enemy aircraft on their screen in that area. GCI promptly responded they did not. The crew said they could feel "what was thought to be a prop wash" which was "very distinct"; they also stated that while patrolling in another vicinity, a group of lights were observed that "made distinct lines, somewhat like arrows."

Another crew on a patrolling mission saw a row of vertical white lights, staggered evenly, appearing to be stationary at around 10,000 feet. Suddenly, they could see as many as four of the lights "swing at once," probably meaning moving as one.[289]

That evening, pilot Lt. Floyd Lott and radar operator Lt. Anderson Henshaw observed an extraordinary object. On an intruder mission, they were flying at approximately 500 feet off the ground over Worms, Germany. It was dark, but the sky was crystal clear, and at that altitude, they felt a little uneasy, considering themselves a defined target to the watchful enemy below. Lt. Henshaw was standing up, located a few feet behind Lt. Lott, in the observation bubble.

Suddenly, out of nowhere, a circular "fiery ball" appeared right on the Beaufighter's tail. It was no more than 100 feet away. "Hard right, Floyd," Henshaw yelled, wanting Lt. Lott to take evasive action, a hard starboard and dive, but Lt. Lott did not respond. "God damn it Floyd, hard right," Henshaw yelled out. This time Lt. Lott realized something dangerous was behind them and reacted.

According to Henshaw: "We made a maneuver, which was a hard right and came around to where we would've tried to come around to, and be on rear of this, whatever it was, thinking it was some kind of aircraft. But, when we made the maneuver, and came around, we were in the same position that we were originally, with the fireball still to our rear. So this situation, huh, kind of shook us up, so we got out of the vicinity."

At first both men thought they were encountering a JU-88 German Night Fighter, but they became increasingly alarmed after realizing what they were seeing made no sense. They heard no noise, saw no contrail from a jet engine, and were even more confused when they realized their radar was not picking up the object.

Since their evasive maneuver had failed, and Lt. Lott was unable to attack the object, they continued flying on a straight and level course while the triangle of lights trailed them. Lott and Henshaw anxiously watched the lighted object continue to pace their aircraft; both felt it was under intelligent control. As the minutes passed painfully slowly, Lt. Henshaw was able to get a better look at the object. It was actually three vivid, circular, reddish-blue lights, looking like flames, in a tight inverted triangle formation; he called them a "triangle of ovals." Henshaw said each of the ovals looked like the "exhaust of an aircraft radial engine," or "the size of the balls on top of a Barber's pole, the kind outside of their shop."

Lt. Floyd Lott, left, and Lt. Anderson Henshaw, France 1944-1945. (Courtesy Anderson J. Henshaw)

The triangle of lights vanished as Lt. Lott departed the area. The sighting lasted about five minutes. Once the men returned to base, they immediately reported their sighting to Lt. Anderson, an assistant intelligence officer who questioned them at length. He confirmed their sighting was similar to other crews' reports and informed them that "Corned Beef," the Ground Control Intercept, had not picked up any enemy aircraft on their radar screen. Afterwards, Lt. Anderson wrote his report and sent it to the 64th Fighter Wing.

Lt. Henshaw thought the foo fighters were something new in Germany's arsenal, designed to combat the allied night fighters. He knew that German jet-propelled aircraft were operating during the day, so it stood to reason they were operating at night.[290]

From the amount of incoming reports filed by American night fighter crews operating over Belgium and Germany, jet-propelled night fighters were operating since at least October. The problem was that there were too many variables that complicated finding an answer.

The British Bomber Command's Operational Research Section briefly addressed this issue on December 27 in their monthly report for November regarding "Losses and Interceptions." The British had struggled for months to figure out the whole rocket and jet-propelled issue. Bomber Command's Operational Research Section responded in their report entitled, "A New Phenomenon":

"A new phenomenon was first reported by crews of 6 Group after their attack on Oberhausen on the 1/2," stated the report, "and was confirmed by the experience of the other groups on the next few nights, particularly at Bochum on the 4/5.

"It was at first claimed by the crews that jet-propelled fighters had been encountered, but apart from uncertainty as to the practicability of using this type fighter at night, the apparent ease with which our gunners were able to destroy the objects made this seem improbable.

"Careful re-interrogation of the crews concerned made it quite clear, however, that some new type of weapon had been tried by the enemy and, while individual reports varied somewhat, the following general picture was provisionally deduced from them:

"The phenomenon is seen as a light, moving very fast. The general consensus of opinion is that no shape can be seen and no aircraft identified, and that the objects do not fire; when fired at by the bombers a large proportion of them burst into flames or explode. Some have been seen to explode spontaneously or dive to the ground and it is therefore assumed that they are self-destroying. No bombers have been damaged or, so far, as is known, even rocked by the explosion of these bodies.

"A tentative opinion is that they may be robot projectiles, possibly of the V-1 type, probably launched from the air into the bomber stream. On the night of 4/5, when they were seen in the greatest profusion, they appeared to have been sent into the stream, not over the target, but mainly on the return journey west of Cologne. Although bomber losses on this night were heavier than for some time previously, there is no suggestion that the new weapons played any part. There is no evidence of any aircraft destroyed or even damaged by one of them."

As far as conventional night fighter attacks were concerned, the report further commented: "The new phenomenon, already mentioned, has led to complications in compiling figures for night fighter attacks and other combats. In order to be able to use such figures as an indication of the strength of real night fighter opposition it has been necessary to ignore all reported encounters with the so-called jet-propelled bodies or with jet-propelled fighters, even if they were said to be identified, unless they fired."[291]

This meant that many of the recent foo fighter sightings reported by the U.S. 414th, 415th, 416th, and 422nd NFS were ignored. There is no doubt that some of the sightings were possible enemy aircraft and weapons. But the foo fighters were another ballgame altogether. The pilots and crews were able to distinguish the difference between foo fighters and jet fighters, even at night.

The British ORS's report had stated that yet another type of nighttime aerial object was being used against bombers and the new "robot" weapon was added to a growing list of nighttime sightings that posed more questions than answers. The whole issue was becoming increasingly more confusing and complex as the days wore on, and this confusion was borne out in the British report.

As the British report made its rounds through Air Intelligence circles, night crews with the 415th NFS were again encountering strange aerial intruders. Over the course of the evening, six missions were flown, and the first two crews up that night encountered foo fighters. But this time the sightings were a little different. A Beaufighter crew was on a patrolling mission over the Sarrebourg area, eight miles northeast of Luneville, when the pilot noticed that a number of objects were suddenly flying nearby at his altitude of 10,000 feet—and they were closing in fast. The pilot said there were "two sets of three red and white lights, one on his starboard and one on his port side at one to two thousand feet astern." Taking evasive action, he peeled off and dropped his aircraft down to eight thousand feet, and the lights "went out." Wanting to know what was happening the pilot contacted Ground Control Intercept, "Churchman," and was informed they "knew nothing of Bogies in air at that time."

Not far away, around the same time frame, a second 415th crew observed orange lights suspended in the air, "moving slowly" before disappearing. The pilot said the orange lights appeared singly and in pairs and he "observed these lights four or five times."[292]

As the sun came up on the morning of the December 28, crews with the American Third Bombardment Division prepared for a day bombing mission against targets over Neuwied and Koblenz in Germany. In the Division's Operational Intelligence Report, at 1311 hours an object was observed by one or more crews flying over Trier at 24,000 feet. "A green ball about six inches in diameter" was reported, and the object "was motionless and did not appear to have anything supporting it." Within a half an hour of sighting the "green ball," two Me-163 rocket propelled fighters were observed: one at 1331 hours, being chased by three P-51 fighters and another at 1349 hours, coming out of the clouds at 11,000 feet.[293]

By now, Major Harold Augspurger, the 415th NFS's Commanding Officer, had not personally seen the unusual objects reported by most men within his unit, though he was well aware of them, as he had listened on several occasions to their animated stories. But now it was his turn, and his time came on the night of December 28. It was a chance to use his combat experience and observational skills to help identify the culprit and diffuse the mystery that circulated wildly among his men.

The night was bitter cold, and unlike the Ardennes, the sky was crystal clear with hardly a cloud seen in any direction. There was no moon, something Major Augspurger welcomed; the illumination of a moonlit night silhouetted night fighters as they searched for prey, turning the hunter into the hunted.

Picking up speed, rolling down the steel mesh taxi strip, Major Augspurger took off in his Bristol Beaufighter named "Nightmare"; on the nose was a painting of a pure white stallion leaping into the air, symbolizing what Augspurger felt represented the nightmare difficulties in flying this type of aircraft. He was very confident that night because he had with him the unit's best radar operator, Lt. Austin Petry. They were embarking on an intruder mission leaving France behind and heading into Nazi Germany.

While over France, they flew between 8,000 and 10,000 feet, but having crossed the German border, they lowered their altitude to 500 to 1,000 feet. From here on in, Augspurger scanned the ground below, looking for targets of opportunity, searching for any signs of life and anything that had

415th Night Fighter Squadron Commanding Officer Harold F. Augspurger. (Courtesy Harold F. Augspurger)

a light. Lt. Petry sat behind him, focusing his attention on the radar screen, anticipating the sudden appearance of German night fighters. There was always the worry of flak or small arms fire, especially considering what was happening in the Ardennes forest, not far away in Belgium. Surprisingly, the sky was empty. Lt. Petry detected no enemy bogies on the AI in any direction.

Below them, nothing moved and there were no lights, just a motionless country landscape. The low–level hunt went on for about ninety minutes and proved to be an uneventful mission. It was time to turn "Nightmare" around and head back home. But moments later, while they were still over Germany, things changed. They were no longer alone in sky. Something else was flying up there with them and its lights were on.

It happened so suddenly. One second Major Augspurger was looking at his controls and the next second he looked up to find something flying parallel with them. His attention was focused upon "a white light out off to the starboard, right off the wing." Trying to think about what was flying with its light on he calmly asked Lt. Petry, "What do ya have?" Something was wrong: Petry's radar-screen remained clear. Petry looked up to verify the sighting and he saw it too.

Due to the dark sky, Major Augspurger was unable to determine how far away the light was, nor could he accurately estimate its size: it was either "a big light real far away, or a small light close in to us," he recalled. He first thought it was a flare, or maybe an aircraft but remained unsure. It gave him the impression that, whatever the light was, it was pacing them, possibly keeping them under surveillance.

Though it was unfamiliar looking, they figured the light was probably something conventional. Major Augspurger decided it was time to get a closer look. "Let's turn into it and see if we can pick it up on radar," he told Petry. Turning in towards the strange white light he opened up the throttle. "Nightmare" was bearing down on their target, heading straight towards it, and getting closer. Lt. Petry again reported nothing was showing up on their radar screen. He could not understand why because it was working just fine. But then about thirty seconds later, the target "just took off and went straight up." Climbing "straight up at a tremendous speed" for a couple thousand feet until the light vanished, simply disappearing. Major Augspurger had never witnessed anything like this before. Both men were amazed.

Their sighting had lasted about four to five minutes. After a small search of the area, they departed and headed back to base. On the way home, they discussed the encounter, feeling sure the light was not any kind of meteorological phenomenon. It was not a shooting star. Nor was it a rocket or jet. The light was solid, continuous, and there was no exhaust flame, just a round white light. They had no idea what they had witnessed, but both agreed that it acted as if it was intelligently controlled.

Once they returned to base they immediately reported their sighting to Captain Ringwald. They discussed the conventional possibilities, compared notes with the other sighting reports, including Ringwald's, but could not identify the object. All three agreed it was neither a flare, jet, or rocket, and they figured it was likely another type of German secret weapon. But while discussing the light's function and performance, they concluded that it operated in an advanced manner that was beyond conventional ordnance or aircraft capabilities. Performance wise, it flew faster than anything they had ever seen, as it streaked straight up towards the stars and then abruptly disappeared. Captain Ringwald informed them that the Ground Control Intercept radar screen had also failed to pick up any signal. Lt. Petry could not understand this. He was sure the light was within a couple of miles of them. They discussed this over and over, but it was futile. They were dealing with a real mystery.

Major Augspurger and Lt. Petry gave all the facts to Captain Ringwald who wrote an operational report and immediately fired it off to the A-2 at their command headquarters with the 64th Fighter Wing. From there, a copy was sent to the A-2 section with the XII Tactical Air Command that in turn went to the A-2 section with the First Tactical Air Force (Provisional).[294]

Their report made its way to General Spaatz's new Air Intelligence staff and most likely into the hands of his Air Technical Intelligence group.

Though foo fighter sightings had been frequently reported since October, a foo fighter sighting reported by the commanding officer of a U.S. Night Fighter Squadron had finally gained Spaatz's attention.

Chapter Twelve

Bob Wilson Gets His Scoop

On December 30, 1944, the British released a report entitled "GAF Night Fighters, A Review of Current German Tactics," written by one of Britain's best RAF interrogators, squadron leader S.D. Felkin. He compiled his data from information obtained from a German "pilot, a radar operator and a W/T operator of 3/NJG 2 shot down in Holland on the night of November 29 and from a pilot of the same Staffel[295] shot down in Belgium on the following night."[296]

The prisoners were most willing to discuss in detail a wide range of topics, including interception and homing-equipment, countermeasures, definition of reconnaissance and leader aircraft, tactics of interception, take-off, navigation, and armament. In the report's "Night Rocket Phenomena" section, the prisoners were asked about whether jet propelled fighters were used at night. Remarkably, they said that they had not heard of any jet-propelled aircraft used at night and were inclined to ridicule the suggestion. They themselves had seen rocket traces at night and had attributed them to rocket flak; they thought that rocket traces were seen, but they had to "draw their own conclusions" since there was no official statement.

The prisoners further revealed that German pilots were also observing strange and mysterious objects. According to Felkin's report: "One of the present pilots had twice encountered enormous flaming masses over Berlin some time ago; he had at first thought these to be aircraft going down in flames, but on the second occasion he was close enough to make a careful observation and could see that the rate of fall was too slow for a crashing aircraft. Again, he was told nothing officially."[297]

As operational reports passed through command channels, U.S. Air Intelligence officers diligently tried to assess everything the aircrews reported. Old and new reports describing sightings of jet-propelled aircraft circulated and kept them busy. On December 31, U.S. Air Intelligence issued an Intelligence Summary that addressed the "Pilotless 'Flying Wing.'" According to the report: "This aircraft is reported to be a small radio-controlled jet-propelled plane, somewhat resembling the Me-163, fitted with an explosive which can be detonated in the midst of a bomber formation or can be exploded by ramming another air craft.

"A US air gunner returned [sic] from the vicinity of Venlo reported that experiments were being carried out there with this novel aircraft. The attached sketch was drawn from his description; and this information, plus knowledge already gained from other sources, permits a preliminary report to be made on this new 'secret weapon.'

"This aircraft resembles a flying wing, with a span of about 20 feet. There is no horizontal stabilizer, and the vertical fin and rudder are very small in relation to the rest of the plane. The aircraft is apparently launched on a rail and for landing a skid is provided. Although there is no definite indication of radio control, the performance indicates remote control. The fact that this aircraft is filled with some sort of explosive is borne out by the reports that when one of these flying wings crashed near Venlo a terrific explosion was heard."[298]

The Venlo sighting has some relevance to the 415th NFS sighting on December 23/24, describing a glowing red light that "changed suddenly to an aircraft doing wing-over and going into a dive and disappearing." The 415th NFS sighting, however, was the only sighting similar to the one at Venlo, out of many extraordinary sightings reported by the night fighter squadrons.

Bringing in the New Year, Bob Wilson, a reporter with the Associated Press stopped by the 415th NFS base at Toul/Ochey, France. He wanted to write a story from the perspective of flying over Germany on New Year's Day, right as the clock struck twelve midnight. Assigned to take Wilson up that night were Lieutenants Lott and Henshaw. But it was not the best of evenings. Weather that night produced extremely cold temperatures, causing much icing on the Beaufighters.[299]

Sadly, that night a crew was lost, so the icy conditions gave more than enough reason to keep all flights grounded for the remainder of the night.[300] AP reporter Bob Wilson, unable to get his America over Germany story, stayed and brought in New Year's with the men.

Unexpectedly, Wilson was still able to get a story, one that was far more unusual than his original assignment. Until four o'clock that morning he mingled with the men, who were more than willing to share with him first hand accounts of their fascinating encounters. Listening and asking questions, Wilson was getting a great story.[301]

The month of December had come to a close, ending the war's pivotal year of 1944.[302] Since the war began, the RAF and AAF airmen had accumulated stories of the "Light" and the "Thing," and now the American airmen had added their own pet name to the list: the foo fighters. By the end of 1944, Air Intelligence Officers perplexed by the new foo fighter sightings were under pressure to find an answer to the phenomenon. But with each passing day, the sightings continued, and there were no answers, just theories and more questions; and in some cases, the pilots learned that encounters with the foo fighters could be downright frightening.

It was New Year's Day, 1945. While crews of the 415th NFS recounted their strange stories to reporter Bob Wilson, the Ardennes ground battle remained fierce. And then at the break of dawn, Operation "Boddenplatte" (the "Great Blow") had commenced. Close to a thousand German fighters

First Lt. Warren R. Barber, 653rd Light Weather Squadron, 25th Bomb Group, receiving the Distinguished Flying Cross. (Courtesy Mrs. Betty Barber)

began swarming the skies over Belgium, northern France, and western Holland. Their mission: attack Allied airfields and decimate their fighters on the ground.[303]

That night, the foo fighters were back again. It was a sobering experience for both pilot Lt. Jack Green and navigator Lt. Warren Barber who were conducting a Bluestocking Mission (meteorological) over Belgium, Holland, and north central Germany. The men were with the 653rd Squadron of the 25th Bomb Group (Reconnaissance). For four and one-half hours, they flew their Mosquito under radio silence orders.

They were flying at 30,000 feet over Zuder Zee on their approach to Berlin. It was 0230 hours when the strange lights first appeared.[304] According to Lt. Green, the night was "beautiful and starry." It was also very cold and at that altitude, temperatures reached 50 to 60 degrees below zero. The Battle of the Bulge was raging below them and he was able to hear communications, more than normal, between an RAF night fighter pilot and his radar control unit, who was leading him towards German Ju-88s for combat. He was concerned about the possibility of meeting up with a Me-262 night fighter, wondering how his inadequate aircraft could ever contend with such a problem.

It was not long before Green's worries started to unfold: "Suddenly, dead ahead, same altitude, were two balls of fire, orange. My God...Jets! I was looking up twin tail pipes! In that instant I froze, tense, ready to do something. But then it became apparent that they were moving in our direction and at a rate of closure that was not unusual. As they moved, they seemed to be in tandem, as if somehow connected, retaining the same apparent distance from each other. They came in a straight line towards us then moved so as to pass off our starboard wing at the same altitude. At a point about 120 degrees from our nose, they shot upwards at a rate of climb that could only be described as incredible. At a point about 70 degrees up from the horizon, the balls of fire went out.

"As we continued our flight, saying nothing, two pairs of these lights appeared suddenly off our port wing, flying level formation with us. They appeared quite close and slightly larger than those we saw first. How large were they? We couldn't tell. We had no point of reference. When sighted dead ahead they might have appeared to us as large as a radial engine might appear at a thousand yards out. They could have been very small, in fact, and close in or very large and miles away. Curiously, I don't believe Warren Barber or I said anything to each other while all this happened! Moments later these second lights went out as suddenly as they appeared."[305]

Alarmed by the sighting, Lt. Barber looked on; there were no clouds in the sky to obstruct his view. He was astonished by what he witnessed: "... heading in towards Belgium, we saw these things for the first time ahead of us, and they shot up higher than us. We were at 30,000 feet, and just got altitude, and they shot up in front of us and then zoomed towards the back and when we looked back, they were behind us, and every time they seemed to wanna just flip ahead of us and back and forward. And it wasn't like flares. We saw night flares. I've seen night flares numerous times, especially down around the submarine bases down in France... but they came up and go off like abnormal fireworks. They came up and you wouldn't see them until 25,000 feet or whatever and it wasn't anything like that."

Offering a better description, Lt. Barber described the lights as "a pair of fog lights, shooting up to 60 or 70,000 feet." The lights were bright, flying in tandem, and he could not discern any shape except they each looked like a three-foot circular light, like a ball. However, there was one especially curious aspect that puzzled him: they did not appear to be solid. As Barber continued watching, the lights ended up on Lt. Green's side. Lt. Barber said the lights "could change speed rapidly, climbing and diving, and it seemed to me that it was being used to position us." They were approaching combat on the ground where they saw small arms fire. The lights remained for about twenty minutes before they "disappeared." On the return flight, Lt. Barber thought about what he observed; the light's flight performance was beyond anything he had ever witnessed during his dozens of missions.[306]

When they arrived back at base, Lt. Green said the next day their report was given to their squadron's Air Intelligence officer who told them to keep it secret.

According to Lt. Barber: "If Jack Green will remember I wasn't going to mention the lights to anyone after we got back to the base," he explained. "Jack brought up the subject to the intelligence officer when we were making our reports the next day, then left me to do the explaining. Fortunately, two different RAF crews had already reported them. They gave a story similar to ours.

"After the intelligence Section Officer had finished with me I was walking to my room in the Officer's Club and passed the bar in the officer's mess. Jack was there. He had already mentioned our experience with the 'foo fighters' and was being razzed by a group of pilots. Clearly they were still dubious after I verified the story."[307]

Their S-2 was Captain Finis D. McClanahan, who wrote his report after debriefing both Green and Barber. Though very brief, lacking the finer details of the sighting and minus the crew's disbelief in what they had observed, McClanahan's report was sent to the Commanding Officer, 25th Bomb Group: "Crew observed pairs of bright yellowish orange lights evenly spaced which seemed to be floating around in the air, never in front, but always in rear or on either side. Lights were brilliant while on and at times faded, either in the distance, or were turned off. Aircraft was at 30,000 feet when lights were first seen. While over Zuder Zee at 0230 hours lights were seen for first time and as aircraft approached Berlin at

0310 hours two more were observed. Getting closer to Berlin, at 0330 hours, three were seen. No attacks were made on aircraft hence the crew was not certain as to identity of lights."[308]

On January 2, multiple newspapers carried Bob Wilson's story. Not mentioning who wrote the article, or which unit was interviewed, the *New York Times* was among the first major state-side newspaper to carry the story, "Balls of Fire Stalk US Fighters In Night Assaults Over Germany." It read: "American Night Fighter Base, France, Jan. 1—The Germans have thrown something new into the night skies over Germany—the weird, mysterious 'foo-fighter,' balls of fire that race alongside the wings of American Beaufighters flying intruder missions over the Reich."

"American pilots have been encountering the eerie 'foo-fighter' for more than a month in their night flights. No one apparently knows exactly what this sky weapon is.

"The balls of fire appear suddenly and accompany the planes for miles. They appear to be radio-controlled from the ground and keep up with our planes flying 300 miles an hour, official intelligence reports reveal.

"There are three kinds of these lights we call 'foo-fighters,'" Lieut. Donald Meiers of Chicago said. "One is red balls of fire which appear off our wing tips and fly along with us; the second is a vertical row of three balls of fire which fly in front of us, and the third is a group of about fifteen lights which appear off in the distance—like a Christmas tree up in the air—and flicker on and off.

"The pilots of this night-fighter squadron—in operation since September, 1943—find these fiery balls the weirdest thing that they have yet encountered. They are convinced that the 'foo-fighter' is designed to be a psychological as well as a military weapon, although it is not the nature of the fire-balls to attack planes.

"A 'foo-fighter' picked me up at 700 feet and chased me twenty miles down the Rhine Valley," Lieut. Meiers said. "I turned to starboard and two balls of fire turned with me. I turned to the port side and they turned with me. We were going 260 miles an hour and the balls were keeping right up with us.

"On another occasion when a 'foo-fighter' picked us up, I dove at 360 miles per hour. It kept right off our wing tips for a while and then zoomed up into the sky.

"When I first saw the things off my wing tips I had the horrible thought that a German on the ground was ready to press a button and explode them. But they don't explode or attack us. They just seem to follow us like will-o'-the-wisps…

"Lt. Wallace Gould, of Silver Creek, N.Y., said that the lights had followed his wing tips for a while and then, in a few seconds, zoomed 20,000 feet into the air out of sight. Lieut. Edward Schlater [sic – actually Schlueter] of Oshkosh, Wis., said that he had seen the 'foo-fighter' on two occasions and it 'looked like shooting stars.' In his first experience with them, Lieutenant Gould said, 'I thought it was some new form of jet-propulsion plane after us. But we were very close to them and none of us saw any structure on the fire balls.'"[309]

Another paper, the *St. Louis Post Dispatch* carried the same story but included Captain Fred Ringwald's account. Though listed in the news article as a staff officer, he was the 415th NFS's Intelligence Officer. The article indicates that after hearing so many crews discuss their foo fighter sightings, Captain Ringwald decided to accompany one of the crews on a mission to see for himself. Recalling the event, Ringwald said, "I saw lights off the right and told the pilot, who said, 'Oh, those are lights on a hill.'" Watching the lights for several minutes, Ringwald countered, "Well, that hill is considerably closer to us now."[310]

The most extensive treatment of Bob Wilson's report was printed in the *Tribune's* January 1 edition, under the title of "Mystery Flares Tag Along With U.S. Night Pilots." The newspaper printed basically the same story as most of the other papers, but offered more crew names of the night fighter squadron and, curiously, labeled the sightings as flares.[311]

One of the men listed who saw the so-called "flares" was flight officer and radar operator Murphy C. Painter, Jr. He was on an intruder mission

with pilot Lt. Ralph Thomas. They were flying over the area between Strasbourg and Mannheim, along the west bank of the Rhine River. At an altitude of approximately eight to nine thousand feet, Painter noticed a bright round ball out off his wing at the 3 o'clock position. Startled, by the ball's sudden appearance, he was amazed by its size: twice that of a "full moon." He said it did not appear solid, and the color was a combination of yellow, white, and red tints. The light

Lt. Murphy C. Painter, Jr., 415th Night Fighter Squadron.
(Courtesy Murphy J. Painter)

415th NFS radar operator Lt. Warren G. Rodick at observer's rear bubble. (Courtesy Warren G. Rodick)

never changed shape, but its outline was "fuzzy," and "two lengths wing span" away from his Beaufighter. There was nothing about its features that indicated it was a night fighter; Thomas had encountered a Me-262 before and he knew this was no jet since it was moving too slowly and there was no exhaust plume.

It seemed harmless in nature, but Thomas was not taking any chances. He committed his Beaufighter to an attack, executing a quick maneuver to get behind it, but as they came around, it disappeared. Lt. Painter never saw the object on his radar screen, and, in fact, he was monitoring his radar when he looked up and realized the light had vanished.[312]

Another 415th crew, involving radar operator, Lt. Warren G. Rodick and pilot Lt. Owen H. Davis, observed another alleged "flare" sighting over Germany in the area of Frankfurt and Karlsrhue. They, too, were on an intruder mission, hunting prey below. Weather conditions were challenging: a mixed evening, from clear to rain to snow. There were no enemy aircraft in the area and their radar screen was clear. But suddenly their solitude was quickly interrupted. Out of nowhere, one at a time over the next twelve minutes, three to four very bright balls flew within one hundred feet of their wing. The balls were completely illuminated. They were red, yellow, white, and blue in color and seemed to be the size of a tennis ball at arm's length. What mystified Rodick and Davis was the fact they could not discern any kind of structure within the shape of the colored lights.

For twelve minutes, Lt. Davis performed evasive action, turning, climbing to higher altitudes, trying to elude the lights, but they remained right with them; the lights were able to keep the same distance from them no matter what kind of maneuver Lt. Davis tried. Lt. Rodick remembers being inquisitive while he watched the spectacle. Since the lights appeared over enemy territory, he felt they were some kind of markers to track their Beaufighter's height and speed. But no antiaircraft fire or enemy night fighter attacks came. The chase finally ended when the lights simply disappeared.[313]

Night fighter pilot Lt. George Shrock and radar operator Lt. Garland Moore were among those also named in the *Tribune's* "flare" sightings article. They were flying an intruder mission over eastern France and western Germany when one second the sky was clear and they were alone, and then the next second, they had company. Flying about two to three hundred yards off their wing were a string of lights, twelve to fifteen in number, orange to yellow in color, and twice the length of their aircraft. Lt. Shrock did not overreact but maintained his speed and course, watching the odd display of lights that seemed to be pacing them.

Checking and rechecking his AI, Lt. Moore saw nothing on the radar screen. He, too, was not alarmed by their presence, just curious about what they were. Watching closely, he felt the lights were not displaying any type of hostile maneuvers, and it was his impression they were monitoring his aircraft's movement. For about the next four or five minutes the lights followed them over enemy territory before disappearing as quickly as they appeared.[314]

A very small but interesting article that appeared that day in the *Palestine Post*, "Strange Goings On In West" by William Steen, a special correspondent for Reuters, indicated there were more strange things besides foo fighters being observed in the skies over Europe, according to SHAEF. "Strange things are happening at the front this New Year's Eve," he wrote. "American pilots reported seeing green Thunderbolt fighters shadowing them over Germany and ground troops swore they saw a large, oval cylindrical-object believed to be an observation balloon, floating over the German lines. Both puzzles remain unsolved."[315]

By January 3, the foo fighter story continued to make headlines. "Nazi Balls of Fire Race Along with US Night Raiders," proclaimed another U.S. paper. The article's foo fighter account was brief, but another section, under the heading of "Interference Attempt," was particularly noteworthy. It was the first scientific effort to explain the foo fighters and the silver spheres as German devices.

"Floating and plane-following balls in fire-like color, added to the silver globes encountered over German lines by American airmen, might not be as mysterious as would seem in cabled dispatches," C.E. Butterfield, AP [Associated Press] radio editor says.

"This is just a guess, but on the little information available the colored and glowing globes might well be added elements in attempts to interfere with radio signals and radar detection.

"While dispatches hint that they are radio controlled, the fact that they travel along with a plane or stay a certain distance ahead would tend toward the belief that they instead are magnetic," Butterfield commented. "Thus, the metal of a plane would attract them, at the same time holding them at a distance. Radio control from the ground or another plane would not permit such apparent accuracy in control."

Regarding the illuminating features of the objects, he figured "the glow, coupled with the possible magnetic action, might come from the gas they contain to aid in their electrical qualities and to add to their buoyancy."[316]

Butterfield had interjected a new and disturbing theory, one that was speculative but still plausible. General Spaatz's Air Technical Section probably took note of Butterfield's theory, forwarding a message to ATI field teams exploiting German territory, and to Air Prisoner of War Interrogators.

In the same paper, another article entitled "Great Balls of Fire!" added further details about the mystery: "Effie Mac of the comic strip Muggs and Skeeter has an expression 'Great Balls of Fire!' which she uses in moments of stress. Evidently our night fliers over Germany can well afford to use the term, too, when they encounter the latest German 'secret weapon' (if that is what it is) which they are calling 'foo fighter' balls of fire. No one seems to know what the strange contrivances are, or what they are supposed to accomplish."

The newspaper gave an account of the types of objects seen, based on Bob Wilson's breaking story: "An American plane flies over Germany at night and suddenly, alongside one wing, a large red ball of fire appears. It maintains its position off the wing no matter what the speed, never coming closer and never fading away apparently until many miles have been covered. Or the 'foo fighter' ball of fire may appear as a vertical row of three lights ahead of the plane. No matter how fast the plane may travel it never quite catches up with those weird lights. Eventually, they disappear as suddenly as they arrive. The third phenomenon is described as a cluster of perhaps 15 lights at some distance from the plane which flicker on and off 'like a Christmas tree.' They, too, keep pace with the racing plane.

"There are all kind of speculation as to what these devices are and what they are supposed to accomplish. One is that the effect is supposed to be largely psychological which frankly sounds pretty far-fetched since it has yet to be shown that any of these things can harm the plane. A more likely explanation was offered by an AP radio and science expert [probably C.E. Butterfield]: he suggested that perhaps the devices are intended to interfere with radio transmission from the plane or to help the Germans operate some direction device such as radar."

Another theory the article suggested was "that these devices whatever they may be are intended to act as location finders for anti-aircraft batteries. If a certain type of 'foo-fighter' ball attaches itself to the flight path of a plane at night, anti-aircraft batteries might be able to plot the course of the plane much more accurately, making due allowance for the distance between the satellite and the plane than would be possible through the use of searchlights."

According to the article, the "soundest theory" was that the foo fighters "perhaps contain some kind of gas activated by the presence of the metal in the plane and that and that a magnetic attraction keeps them at a prearranged distance from the plane, but never letting the plane outrun them until the force in the contrivance is expended." It was felt that this explanation accounted for one flier's account when he could not escape the foo fighter at 260 mph, and once during a chase at 360 mph over the course of twenty minutes.[317] However unlikely these explanations, they reveal a real confusion and a serious grasping for answers.

In the meantime, military sources in Washington and London were closed mouth about the matter. Butterfield's article had gained critical attention, and as a result was not very popular with the night fighter pilots who had personally witnessed the foo fighters perform incredible flight maneuverability and reach outrageous speeds.

While newspaper accounts presented the public with a variety of theories, some were quick to point out that there were no definitive explanations. By January 1945, sighting reports indicated that a German secret weapons program of astounding capabilities seemed to exist. But behind the scenes, McDonald's staff could not explain away the astounding unconventional sighting reports; there was no captured material, no documentation, or POW interrogations that accounted for anything remotely resembling the foo fighters or balls of fire.[318]

Chapter Thirteen

Foo or Phoo?

Increased press coverage of the foo fighters was starting to turn heads back in Washington. On January 4, 1945, the War Department sent a message to Air Intelligence at SHAEF: "Press reports red balls of fire accompanying planes in flight termed 'Foo-Fighters' by air personnel; Desire explanation if available."

Alleged photograph of foo fighter. Source unknown.
(Courtesy Janet Bord and the Fortean Picture Library)

SHAEF A-2 took immediate action. A handwritten note on this War Department message noted that the commanding officer of the Second Tactical Air Force was spoken with and he assured A-2 that "they will make further inquiries."[319]

But this message is rather odd. The War Department was requesting old information; the "red balls of fire" was a phenomenon already seen for months. Curiously, it seems AP reporter Bob Wilson's article had touched a nerve. Why the War Department issued the message is unclear. Was it completely ignorant of sightings prior to the breaking story? It is unlikely. Were the foo fighter sighting accounts a compartmentalized subject matter?

SHAEF's Air Intelligence officer, RAF Air Commodore Colin Grierson responded in a "SECRET" message to the War Department's request on January 5: "...Careful investigation shows that on one occasion only has a red ball of fire accompanying an aircraft been reported (.) This in November by IX Tactical Air Command when formation reported ME.109 joined formation in number five position and was seen to emit what appeared to be a red ball of fire which followed the aircraft for some 2-3 seconds. ME.109 then broke away. FOOFIGHTER not known here."[320]

Grierson's response suggests that he, too, was unaware of sightings now called the foo fighters. His reply in reference to the Me-109 story had absolutely no connection to the "Foo Fighters"; they were observed longer than one or two seconds and there were no enemy aircraft ever reported in the area during a sighting. Could Grierson have had no knowledge of the RAF's prior "Light" and "Thing" sightings and the RAF's No. 5 Group's investigation?

It should be noted that when Air Commodore Grierson queried about the foo fighters in January 1945, he had been in intelligence for less than a year. Starting in May of 1944, Grierson became Chief Intelligence Officer, Allied Expeditionary Air Force, to relieve Claude Pelly who needed to concentrate on "Operation Crossbow" efforts.[321]

Meanwhile, civilian newspapers were alive with theories. On January 5, one stateside paper, *The Hartford Courant*, was quick to notice the way Washington was handling the foo fighter mystery, citing that Army spokesmen continued to keep a "discreet silence" from the subject. Physicists suggested that ball lightning or a "new variation of St. Elmo's fire" was the culprit.

According to the article, St. Elmo's Fire is an age-old phenomenon. Throughout nautical history, numerous stories were written about "the mysterious fire" that on occasion illuminated the masthead of ships at sea. Modern day physicists continued to explain the glow as "the result of discharged atmospheric electricity usually appearing as a tip of light at the point of such objects as church steeples." There were also reports of "sounds" associated with the appearance of the lights, making a "crackling or fizzing noise."

The article stated that another possibility for the foo fighters was "ball lightning," which displayed "some of the characteristics described by aviators who have been pursued by the 'foo-fighters.'" While most of the explanations offered some answers, they were partial at best. One troubling characteristic, one that most airmen did agree upon, was that the foo fighters' illuminated presence brought unwanted attention from both the enemy on the ground and in the air, sort of like "a dog with a tin can tied to its tail."[322]

While news focused on the foo fighter phenomenon in Europe, they were observed over the Pacific Ocean as well. On the night of January 10 eight B-24s of the 42nd Bomb Group, and two with the 11th Bomb Group, were on a "snooper mission." Their target: Iwo Jima. Some ten miles south of the island, several crewmen "observed an amber light pass parallel and at the same altitude off the right wing and disappear into the clouds."[323]

In *Science News Letter*, released on January 13, opinions were leaning more towards enemy weaponry. It was reported that although the mysterious "Foo-Fire" had scientists "guessing" about their nature or purpose, they generally agreed the objects were not radio-controlled. They were convinced there was no known possible way a ground-operated unit could control the objects in tight turns, maintain close proximity to the aircraft, etc. Physicists felt that if the objects were able to conduct such close formation with the aircraft, there must be some kind of magnetic or other force involved.

It was felt the foo fighters were neither incendiary nor explosive ordnance, but instead were conventional ordnance "intended to dazzle the eyes of the pilots, breaking down their carefully built-up night vision." Another idea was that the foo fighters were a type of target indicator, serving as guide for aiding flak gunners in finding the "elusive dark shape of the plane itself." Or, they were brilliant flak bursts, designed to produce "spots before the eyes," known as after-images. It was suggested that "an after-image seen out of the corner of one's eye might easily produce the impression of a ball of fire hovering near the wing-tip."[324]

On January 15, both *Time* and *Newsweek* picked up the story. "If it was not a hoax or an optical illusion, it was certainly the most puzzling secret weapon that Allied fighters have yet encountered," *Time* reported. The article, only a few paragraphs in length, rehashed the same sighting information other news agencies had recounted for days, and reiterated that scientists were "baffled" by the strange lights. *Time* noted that "front-line correspondents and armchair experts" were having a "Buck Rogers field day." Aside from radio-control, electrical, or magnetic possibilities, other explanations involved something "to dazzle pilots," visual tracking devices for antiaircraft gunners, and disrupting the plane's radar. But *Time* included the newest theory, one that the Office of Strategic Service and

British MI6 had for some time been receiving classified reports about: cutting "a plane's ignition, thus stop its engine in midair."[325]

Newsweek's article kept closer to the tone of Bob Wilson's original AP story. It was based primarily on the descriptions of foo fighters reported by Lt. Donald Meier and Lt. Schlueter of the 415th NFS. *Newsweek*, however, introduced another possible explanation not revealed in other press accounts. Information about a radio-controlled, rocket-propelled flying wing, similar in appearance to the Me-163, and "designed to crash into Allied planes" was presented, but this theory was discounted by one pilot's account; he made a careful observation of a foo fighter following him and "detected nothing but spheres."[326]

Apparently *Newsweek* had good inside sources, since Mediterranean Allied Air Force Headquarters had just released its Secret Air Intelligence Summary on January 14, the day before *Newsweek* came out with their story. "'Flying Flak' – An Experimental Pilot-less Aircraft" was a reissue of the United States Strategic Air Force-Europe update, keeping the Venlo, Netherlands Flying Wing sighting an important topic.[327]

The foo fighter stories had struck a nerve. Battle lines were drawn. Crews who witnessed them first hand were developing a serious animosity towards the scientific community whose explanations just did not fit the bill. But the scientists continued trying to explain away the sighting accounts, insulting the pilots with a multitude of absurd reasons, ignoring their observational skills, combat experience, and their intelligence.

The foo fighters were always illuminated, most of the time brilliantly. They could remain motionless in the sky and fly at speeds that far surpassed six hundred miles per hour. In almost one hundred percent of the sightings, no flak or enemy night fighters were observed, including jet-propelled aircraft. According to most crews, jets were distinctive and easy to recognize, due to their flight characteristics. Most witnesses felt the foo fighters were pacing and observing their night fighters, were under intelligent control, but were not hostile.

While civilian scientists continued debating the foo fighter phenomenon, Army Air Force officials were quietly reacting behind the scenes. The foo fighter mystery had garnered serious attention within SHAEF; it was a real threat that needed to be addressed. With the major Allied invasion of France less than six months away, no one wanted any unexpected surprises. If the foo fighters represented an experimental Nazi secret weapon that would soon become an operational combat device, SHAEF had to counter it immediately.

On January 16, an official inquiry into the foo fighters was initiated.

Lt. Colonel Leavitt Corning, Jr., A/C of S, A-2, Headquarters, XII Tactical Air Command, sent a "Secret" memo to the Commanding General, First Tactical Air Force (Provisional), specifically for the Assistant Chief of Staff, (A/C of S) A-2. Under the subject of "Night Phenomenon," the memo stated:

"1. The following is quoted from training and tactical information supplied by the 415th Night Fighter Squadron for the month of December 1944:

"'We have encountered a phenomenon which we cannot explain; crews have been followed by lights that blink on and off changing colors, etc. The lights come very close and fly formation with our planes. They are agitating and keep the crews on edge when they encounter them, mainly because they cannot explain them. It is requested further information be furnished on this subject, such as similar experience of other night units'.

"2. Further information is requested."[328]

Four days later on January 20, the First Tactical Air Force's Executive Officer, Major S. V. Boykin, responded to Lt. Colonel Corning's request, for the Assistant Chief of Staff, A-2: "There have been no instances reported. Before an investigation can be made it will be necessary to have more complete information, such as colors of the lights, their intensity, size, duration, and at what altitudes seen; also if the lights are observed at any specific hours. Do subject lights cross Allied lines and in what direction are they seen to travel? Also, has it been noted: on what part of the aircraft are they carried, i.e. wing, tail, prop; and how close do they approach our aircraft?"[329]

XII Tactical Air Command needed better information for a response to the First Tactical Air Force. Apparently, when the 64th Fighter Wing received the 415th NFS Operational Reports, all the 64th A-2 sent XII Tactical Air Force were condensed versions of the 415th NFS mission reports. To clarify exactly what was being sighted, John E. Wooley, signing for Lt. Colonel Leavitt Corning, Jr., A/C of S, A-2, contacted the 415th NFS S-2, Captain Ringwald, requesting information about the foo fighter sightings.[330]

While the First Tactical Air Force's A-2 staff waited for further information, one of the most important developments in relation to this story occurred at SHAEF headquarters. The Scientific Intelligence Advisory Section (SIAS) was established under the guidance of Dr. Victor H. Fraenckel. The section was composed of U.S. and British staff members, who were advisors "regarding the acquisition and exploitation of intelligence and information concerning scientific, technological, and kindred developments, processes, and concepts which the Germans have produced." Other functions of SIAS included: advising CIOS, handling "requests for scientific intelligence," and "to coordinate the subject matter of all intelligence investigations in the scientific and technological field conducted in Germany" during SHAEF's leadership.[331]

SIAS was a needed organization within SHAEF, providing essential aid to General Eisenhower's command in assessing many aspects of the enemy's situation. The creation of SIAS was perfectly timed since SHAEF's Air Staff now wanted the American foo fighter sightings investigated.

Meanwhile, as days passed, the Germans were getting closer to capitulation, and Hitler's secret technology was ravenously sought. One source providing the most current information was *The Commander's Intelligence Digest*, a report "designed as a convenient reference covering all aspects of the war for the Air Commander-In-Chief." Culled from a large source of intelligence officers, their expertise represented many aspects of the war situation, including political, industry, psychological warfare, and economic.

On January 19, General Arnold received his latest digest. The section, "An Evaluation of German Capabilities," provided him with an "estimate of German capabilities" for 1945. It included sections such as "Radio and Radar," "The German Air Force In 1945," "Flak," "Passive Defense," "U-Boats," "Counter-Intelligence," and most relevant to this story, "Other Weapons."[332]

Under the report's Flak section, aerial ordnance, either dropped by aircraft or released by exploding shells, referenced the variety of objects that were reported as early as mid-1943. Staring in mid-December the press began carrying stories of "silver spheres."

While ordnance like the silver spheres seemed explainable, General Arnold's newest digest still listed them as "unexplained phenomena," stating the objects "might conceivably result in some new development in the future." The report went on to reemphasize that "large numbers of silver spheres, alternately described as glass balls, balls of cotton wool, etc., have been reported during the past year at various altitudes; latterly at lower levels (up to 10,000 ft.). It has been suggested that they may be intended as some form of check on radar information or that they may be filled with some type of gas or other material designed to interfere with the functioning of aircraft weapons. Similar suggestions were made with respect to what was known as the 'Swarm of Bees' phenomenon. As far as is known, no damage has yet been definitely ascribed to the presence of these phenomena."

The importance of General Arnold's Digest report revolves around sightings like the summer 1944 raid against Stuttgart, Germany during which an RAF crew reported "spheres" the "size of a large football." Here again, is another example of terminology mixing two different types of sightings. Could this be the reason why flak ordnance remained so confusing for unit air intelligence personnel trying to accurately assess eyewitness observations?

The "Other Weapons" section of General Arnold's digest dealt with "actual or potential weapons, which the Germans may use against USSTAF operations." These items were addressed in order of operational pertinence. The first item was information concerning the V-1 and V-2 missiles, which were definitely operational. Surprisingly, the next items mentioned were "untried weapons such as the 'PHOO' bombs, Magnetic Waves, and gases applicable to aircraft"– these items were thought "to offer no new threat of really serious proportions."

Interestingly, the name "Phoo" and "foo" are obviously identical in sound and pronunciation, however, the intelligence officers reporting the "Phoo" bombs were apparently citing information that related to "Flying Wing" sightings. "Occasionally reports by pilots and the testimony of prisoners of war and escapees describe this weapon as a radio-controlled, jet-propelled, still-nosed short-range, high performance ramming weapon, for use against bombing formations," stated the report. So far, the weapon had proven unsuccessful, but they had "passed over formations and performed various antics in the vicinity of formations." To be effective against bomber formations, it was determined that a couple hundred of these weapons were needed. It was believed the quantity was far too great for Germany to produce, so there was no "real menace expected in 1945."[333]

By the end of January, foo fighters reminiscent of those seen by Lieutenants Green and Barber on January 1 over the Ardennes area were again reported on January 29/30. On this occasion, another one of Major Augspurger's 415th NFS Beaufighter crews was conducting an intruder mission over Germany. Nearing the end of their mission, at 0010 hours the crew observed two amber colored "lights in the air at 2000 feet between Wissembourg and Landau." When first noticed "one light was 20 to 50 feet above the other," and they were "about a foot in diameter." The amber lights followed their Beaufighter, closing in to about one thousand feet away "off to the starboard and rear," and when the pilot turned into them, they "disappeared." The encounter lasted only about thirty seconds.[334]

On January 30, Captain Ringwald, the intelligence officer for the 415 NFS and a foo fighter witness, responded to the XII Tactical Air

Captain Fred B. Ringwald,
Intelligence Officer, 415th
Night Fighter Squadron.
(Courtesy Fred C. Ringwald)

Command's request for more information. The following is his complete report:

"In compliance with paragraph 2 of 1 Ind., the following extracts from the Sortie Reports of various pilots who have encountered the Night Phenomenon are submitted for your information.

"Night of 14-15 December 1944 —'In vicinity of Erstein (V-9381) flying at 1000 ft. observed large red light at 2000 ft. going East at 18:40 hrs., traveling at approximately 200 MPH.'

"Night of 16-17 December 1944 — '20 miles north of Breisach (W-0173) at 800 ft. observed 5 or 6 flashing red and green lights in 'T' shape. Thought they were flak. About 10 minutes later saw the same lights much closer and behind me. We turned port and Starboard and the lights followed. They closed in to about 8 O'clock and 1000 ft. and remained in that position for several minutes, and disappeared.'

"Night of 22-23 December 1944 — 'Patrolling at Angels 10, from Sarrebourg to Strasbourg, North, and South of highway. At 0600 hrs., saw two lights coming towards a/c from the ground. Upon reaching altitude of plane, they leveled off and stayed on my tail for approximately 2 minutes. Lights appeared to be a large orange glow. After staying with a/c for approximately 2 minutes, they would peel off and turn away, fly along level for a few minutes and then go out. They appeared to be under perfect control at all times. Lights were seen somewhere in the vicinity of Hagenau.'

"Night of 23-24 December 1944 —'Observed reddish colored flames at considerable distance and at approximately 10,000 ft.'

"Night of 23-24 December 1944 — 'Approximately 10 miles south of point X (Q6745) noticed to NE approximately 5 miles a glowing red object shooting straight up; changed suddenly to a plane view of A/C doing a wing over and going into dive and disappearing.'

"Night of 26-27 December 1944 — 'At 0145 hrs., saw two yellow streaks of flame flying at same level at approximately 3000 ft. off port side. We also saw red balls of fire that stayed up for 10 seconds approximately 45 miles away. After seeing yellow streaks, made starboard vector lost altitude and streaks disappeared form view. Called GCI Blunder and asked if any E/A were in vicinity. They answered No. Instructed to return to Angels 10. We felt was thought to be prop wash; very distinct. Noticed several groups of lights off port while patrolling in vicinity of Q-9050 and R-1556. Lights made distinct lines somewhat like arrows.'

"Night of 26-27 December 1944 — 'While on vector 090 near V-7050 during patrol we observed airborne white lights. They staggered evenly, vertically, and we could see from 1 to 4 swing at once. They appeared stationary at 10,000 ft.'

"Night of 26-27 December 1944 — 'Observed light at same altitude while in vicinity of Worms. Observer saw lights come within 100 ft. Peeled off and took evasive action but light continued to follow for 5 minutes. Light then pulled up rapidly and went out of sight.'

"Night of 27-28 December 1944 — 'While on North heading in patrol area noticed in vicinity of Q-1378 lights suspended in air moving slowly and would then disappear. Were orange in color. Lights appeared singly and in pairs. Observed these lights four or five times during period.'

"Night of 27-28 December 1944 — 'Eight miles NE of Luneville at 1910 hrs., saw three sets of three lights (red and white) one on starboard and one on port from 1000 ft. to 2000 ft. to rear and closing in at Angels 10. Pulled up to Angels 8 and lights went out. Called Churchman to see if there was anything in the area; received a negative reply.'

"Night of 30-31 December 1944- 'Saw a group of lights flying through the air 30 or 40 miles east of base while flying at Angels 9-10.'

"Night of 1-2 January 1945 – 'Saw* Foofighters North of Strasbourg and North of Severne.'

"Night of 14-15 January 1945 – 'Observed a large orange glow in sky approx. 5 ft. in diameter in vicinity of Ingweiller at 6000 ft. at 2000 hrs.'

"Night of 29-30 January 1945 – 'At about 0010 hrs. sighted a Foo fighter about half way between Weissembourg and Landau. Foo fighter was off to the starboard and rear at Angels 2. Lights were amber and one was 20 – 50 ft. above the other and about 30 seconds duration. Foo fighter was 1000 ft. away and following. The lights were about a foot in diameter. Lights disappeared when Travel 34 turned into them.'

"2. In every case where pilot called GCI Control and asked if there was a Bogey A/C in the area he received a negative answer.

"*Foofighters is the name given these phenomenon by combat crews of this Squadron."[335]

By the middle of January 1945, balloons became a serious military issue. The Japanese were launching them into the jet streams that carried them towards the United States and Canada. These particular balloons carried high explosive shells designed to explode on impact. There was concern whether they contained biological agents.

The public was not informed about the balloon threat, and in fact, a press blackout was strictly enforced. Coastal defense units in the U.S. and Canada were kept busy chasing down observation reports, but not all sighting reports were clearly identifiable as balloons.

On January 18, the Western Air Command RCAF (Royal Canadian Air Force) reported a baffling sighting. According to Captain Parker BCMR (British-Canadian Military Reserves), he was at Oyster River, near Vancouver Island and the Campbell River, when he spotted a "large silvery cylinder or balloon." It was flying at around fifteen to twenty thousand feet. He watched as it floated past Mt. Alexander and "appeared to discharge another balloon or object which dropped for about a minute and then enlarged itself. The first balloon or object continued south while the second balloon or object moved west and could still be seen at 2359Z time in the area of Butte Lake."[336]

The description of the object indicates the witness was not sure about what he actually observed; this is further borne out by continued use of the phrase "balloon or object" throughout the message. And the fact that something was either discharged or released from it is odd, especially since the falling object expanded and then moved in an entirely different direction. The expansion of the object suggests a balloon by nature, but its ability to travel in another direction, once released, is questionable.

The month of January 1945 was unprecedented by most accounts. Foo fighters continued to display highly sophisticated technological capabilities. The most worrisome aspect is that some of the objects could not be tracked on radar, either the aircraft's radar units or those on the ground. This kind of technology represented a real problem that needed immediate attention, specifically the attention of U.S. radar experts Luis Alvarez and David Griggs. Allied Command had no choice: an investigation of the foo fighters was needed more than ever.

Chapter Fourteen

Scientists Say "Pooh"

The month of February 1945 started off with more weirdness. On the night of February 2, a 415th NFS Beaufighter crew was traveling over the Colmar area when at 1845 hours a "green" light appeared in the sky. Passing by their starboard side, it was "moving rapidly," traveling at three to four thousand feet altitude in an East to West direction about four miles ahead of the crew.[337] A green light was not a normal light for aircraft at night.

Two days later, John Wooley, XII Tactical Air Command, sent a copy of Captain Ringwald's January 30 foo fighter report to the attention of the Assistant Chief of Staff, A-2, First Tactical Air Force (Provisional).[338] By the next day, Colonel C.A. Young, First Tactical Air Force, sent the report right to the chief intelligence officer at SHAEF. His message is as follows:

"1. Forwarded for your information 2. This headquarters has no further information or explanation in connection with these phenomena. 3. It is believed that further investigation is warranted. Since appropriate technical personnel are not available within First Tactical Air Force, this matter is forwarded for such investigation as may be advisable."[339]

On February 8, a 415th NFS Beaufighter crew was returning from an intruder mission between Breisach and Strasbourg, when the crew reported that for approximately one minute they observed a "yellow light at 9,000 feet" that was "ten miles northwest of Strasbourg."[340]

On the evening of February 9/10, a 415th NFS crew flying near Riegel, Germany, reported a "very bright light moving slowly through the air at 6,000 feet, which lasted for 20 seconds," but the crew was unable to determine its point of origin.[341]

SHAEF Air Staff finally responded to the foo fighter phenomenon, having no other choice but to utilize key scientific personnel at the highest level. On February 11, Air Commodore Colin Grierson, A.C. of S., A-2, Air Staff, SHAEF, wrote to the First Tactical Air Force: "1. Reference to your 3rd Endorsement on the subject of night phenomenon originated by the 415th Night Fighter Squadron, there is no information at this Headquarters which might explain the nature and cause of the lights and other phenomena described by the pilots of this Squadron. 2. This matter is, therefore, being referred to the Air Ministry in order to find out whether any further information can be obtained from that source. It is also hoped to make arrangements for an Air Technical Intelligence Officer from USSTAF to visit the Unit concerned."[342]

That same day, Air Commodore Grierson sent off another "Night Phenomena" memorandum to Colonel Bradley, chief technical intelligence officer at USSTAF headquarters: "1. Attached are copies of papers received from the First Tac. Air Force (Prov). From the number of reports quoted in the 2nd W/Ind from the 415th Night Fighter Squadron, it would seem that there must be something more than mere imagination behind the matter and in view of the fact that pilots and crews are becoming slightly worried by them, it is considered that everything possible should be done to get to the root of the matter. 2. Copies of the reports have been sent to the Air Ministry for their consideration, and the Scientific Investigation Division of this Headquarters (Mr. Robertson) has also been asked to consider the problem. 3. In the meantime, it is suggested that it might be as well for an Air Technical Intelligence Officer to visit the Unit concerned and obtain reports and impressions at first hand from aircrew personnel."[343]

Howard Robertson was manning yet another key position that gave him complete access to all material surrounding the foo fighter and unconventional aircraft phenomenon, including photographs and motion pictures. He had access to some of the best engineering and scientific minds; their expertise covered a wide variety of scientific backgrounds. Robertson was also able to call upon colleagues such as Alvarez and Griggs. At his disposal was any intelligence agency or scientific field team he chose to access, as well as captured enemy military personnel, scientists, and technology experts. And, due to his ties with the London Mission, he was able to obtain information on the phenomenon gathered by the British Air Ministry over the years.

The first officially acknowledged foo fighter investigation was underway. Robertson was at the ship's helm and the ship was SIAS. Air Commodore Grierson's memorandum had officially acknowledged that two investigations of the foo fighters were now initiated: one by an Air Technical Intelligence Officer who would proceed to the 415th NFS camp in Toul/Ochey, France, and conduct first-hand interviews with the crews, and a second investigation headed by SHAEF's Robertson.

But there was yet another group of men looking into the phenomenon; they arrived at the 415th NFS base, not from France, but from Washington. According to the 415th NFS's commanding officer, Major Augspurger, the visitors showed up and bypassed him, immediately contacting Captain Ringwald. The foo fighters were technically Ringwald's concern, since he was the unit's intelligence officer and interrogated the crews.

Major Augspurger knew the Washington men were "definitely there to investigate the Foo Fighters," and that "secrecy surrounded the whole issue." But they never spoke with him in person while they were there. He did not give it much thought since he was so busy with other matters. Even Augspurger's commanding officer, General Barkus of the 64th Fighter Wing, made no mention of the Washington men's visit; in fact, Barkus never spoke with Augspurger at any time about the foo fighter sightings.[344]

Major Augspurger recalled that "the men went up on a flight or two with one of the pilots" but was not sure if they saw any foo fighters during their flight(s). He also assumed they wrote a report, but did not see one and received no information thereafter.[345]

On the other hand, operations officer Captain Charlie Horne, who had come up with the name foo fighter, had considerable contact with the visitors. The men from Washington were "skeptical people." They did not believe what the crews were reporting and thought the men were "going nuts" and "needed a vacation" or should "perhaps go home."[346]

Captain Ringwald asked Captain Horne if he wanted to take one of the Washington men up on a flight. Horne agreed; he told Ringwald if the Washington man was up to the task, so was he. So up they went. Captain Horne piloted, Captain Ringwald manned the radar and radio, and one of the Washington men stood behind, looking over Horne's shoulder.

"That little boy from Washington who went with me, he was scared to death," recalled Horne, who told the Washington man: "Don't worry son, I haven't been shot down yet. Maybe this will be the first time." They were lucky that night. There was no action, but there were no foo fighters either.

With no firsthand sightings to report, the next day the men departed Toul and headed back to the U.S.[347] Whether the Washington men stopped at SHAEF Headquarters to talk with General Spaatz or Howard Robertson, or for that matter any of Eisenhower's Air Staff, is unknown; in all likelihood they spoke with someone. It is unknown who the men from Washington were, but they may have represented a War Department investigation, emanating from Edward Bowles's office, and one of them may have been David Griggs. Why the Washington men stayed only a day is puzzling since sightings were occurring almost nightly.

As the foo fighter investigation took shape, the 415th NFS reported another incredible sighting on February 13/14. While conducting an intruder mission, a Beaufighter crew flying between Rastatt and Bishwiller suddenly encountered two sets of lights while at 3,000 feet. Immediately the night fighter attacked. Turning into them, one set of lights "went out and the other went straight up 2-3,000 ft., then went out." Bringing his plane around, the pilot was surprised to see the "lights in their original position again."[348] Within twenty-four hours, another 415th NFS Beaufighter crew was flying between Landau and Freiberg on an intruder mission, when the crew's attention was drawn to a "string of lights north of Freiberg, (1 red one in center, 4 white ones on each side) blinking off and on."[349]

On the night of 15/16, it was the 414th NFS's turn to report odd lights again over Italy. For two and one-half hours, pilot Lt. Shaffer and radar operator Lt. Ayres conducted a patrolling mission in their P-61-B Black Widow over Leghorn and Pontdera. It all started around 0130 hours while they were at 15,000 feet, close to the Pisa Air Base, when they spotted and circled a "flare."

About ten minutes later, another "flare" appeared between Pisa and Pontdera, and ten minutes after that, they observed a third "flare" that "seemed to spiral" in the vicinity of Pisa. "The flares were observed to burn at 6,000 feet then disappear below overcast." Then again, within minutes, the crew "saw a spurt of flame, which went out immediately just west of Viareggio." They observed the flame between an altitude of ten and thirteen thousand feet. Lt. Shaffer immediately took his Black Widow night fighter in for the kill. "During the chase two more spurts of flame were observed with the last spurt of flame continuing until it was lost in clouds below 6,000 feet," he commented. Their Black Widow was hitting an air speed of 290 mph, and reaching 400 mph on the dive. Throughout the chase, Lt. Ayres was "unable to obtain an AI contact." The crew felt they were chasing a jet-propelled aircraft for fifty miles on a straight course right out over the sea, before losing it in the clouds. They had to call it quits because of a shortage of fuel and headed back home.[350]

On the night of February 16, 416th NFS crewmen Lt. Kangas and Lt. Herron were airborne at 2250 hours. They were on a ground control intercept and patrolling mission along the coast. The crew noticed something flying at around 11,000 feet near La Spezia. Lt. Kangas turned towards the aircraft to investigate. It looked to him that "white flares were dropped by what looked like a jet-propelled aircraft." The chase was on. For the next six minutes, the Black Widow crew bore down on the alleged jet, closing in to about one mile, but it "disappeared in a hole of the overcast." Lt. Kangas indicated they were moving at a 380 mph ground speed and the GCI said that they had "clocked him at 458 mph." The odd thing surrounding the chase was there was "no radar contact what-so-ever, airborne, or otherwise."[351]

Sightings of alleged jet-propelled night fighter aircraft were reported repeatedly on February 15 and 16. With these reports in mind, it should be noted that another issue compounded the problem for the foo fighter investigation. Not every night fighter squadron called the objects foo fighters. Over the course of my investigation, on several occasions I heard that commanding officers with some night fighter units forbade their intelligence officers to use the term foo fighter in their operational reports because the term sounded too silly; they were not going to allow such nonsense forwarded up the chain of command. To ensure this new mandate was followed, the S-2s were instructed to inform the crews that they were observing "jets" or "flares," not some kind of mystery object. This policy, if enforced, was not only a suppression of facts, but served to muddy the waters of an already murky subject.

Back over Massa and the Central Po Valley area of Italy, on the night of February 17, a Beaufighter crew with the 416th NFS was airborne at 1755 hours. The crew was flying west of Massa when they "saw what appeared to be a red ball of fire traveling a curving course," heading West. The crew said "it climbed then dove out of sight in the valley South of Massa," and it "did not emit spurts of flame" and "did not appear to be Jet A/C."[352]

Also conducting an intruder mission in the Central Po Valley was a 414th NFS crew. At 2120 hours pilot Lt. Schaeffer and radar operator Lt. Ayres were cruising at eight to ten thousand feet, a couple thousand feet above the fog. Twenty minutes had passed and all was quiet: no flak and no enemy aircraft. Suddenly, out of nowhere, Lt. Schaeffer "observed 2 very bright lights which appeared directly in front of him." Immediately he reacted, firing on the lights and "strafed the area beneath them." The crew said that the lights "appeared in pairs" at "about 8-10,000 feet, and stayed on for approximately 2 minutes."[353]

In response to recent activity over Italy, the 416th NFS commented as follows in their operations records: "Our crews are beginning to report mysterious orange-red lights in the sky near La Spezia and also inland. These 'foo fighters' have been pursued, but no one has been able to make contact. GCI and Intelligence profess to be mystified by these ghostly manifestations. The hypothesis that the foo-fighters are a post cognac manifestation has been disproved. Even the teetotalers have observed the strange and mysterious foo-fighters which have also been observed in France and Belgium."[354]

Though press coverage on the foo fighters had nearly died, on February 18 a new article found its way into print, keeping the story alive. "Fireballs? Science Says 'Pooh!' Beaufighter Crews Insist 'Foo!'" reported Ed Clark, a staff correspondent with the First Tactical Air Force (Provisional). The article struck a nerve with the night fighter crews, rekindling their infuriation over the attack on their credibility by skeptical scientists. Clark's article reemphasized negative and disbelieving attitudes that were gathering momentum back in the U.S. "Discussion of the 'foo-fighters,' weird thingamajigs spotted by US night fighters over enemy territory reached a new peak here today," the small article began, "indicating that the 'foo-fighters' were figments of the imagination and strictly from the realm of make-believe."

The article mentioned *Time* magazine's January 15 comment on the subject. It also included a response from a couple of airmen. Incensed by *Time's* article, Lt. Owen H. Davis and his navigator, Warren G. Roderick [actually Rodick], both with the 415th NFS, but not cited as such, were so irritated they now went on record saying, "If we're starting to see things now, we'd better quit and go home."

Clark's article ended with these words: "They [Beaufighter crews] described them as balls of colored light which rise from the ground in Krautland, and move in on the US night fighters, shortly after they near, or cross the battle lines. Sometimes they are in sets as multiples of ten. Their color has ranged from red to orange, yellow, white, and even blue. Playing it safe, no Beaufighter crew has yet allowed the 'foo-fighter' to close in."[355]

Clark's news story raises an important question regarding German defensive weapons that requires clarification. He stated that the objects rose "from the ground" once the airmen were "near or crossing enemy lines." At odds with this statement was the fact that very few night fighter operational reports described the foo fighters as rising from the ground. Most sightings were unexpectedly observed in the air, appearing out of nowhere, and disappearing in the same fashion. To give some credence to Clark's statement, it is possible that some crews simply did not see where the objects came from until the lights were closing in on their aircraft. But for most others who saw them, it was an absurd comment coming from people who did not know the facts and had no idea what was observed during the encounters.

While the 415th NFS crews vented their anger over Ed Clark's story, new sightings came in that night from in Italy. A crew with the 416th NFS was conducting a ground control intercept patrol over Leghorn and

La Spezia again, when within thirty minutes the crew observed a "blinking light" about twenty miles away near La Spezia, lasting for about forty-five seconds. Due to the distance, the pilot was unable to make an accurate observation. About forty-five minutes later, the light appeared much closer. This time it was a "reddish white light going off and on in spurts about 6 or 8 miles away, near La Spezia at 10,000 ft. going NE." Turning into the light, the pilot gave chase for about ninety seconds, but the light flew an "erratic course" and "faded out" before the Mosquito could attack.

About ten minutes later, the pilot saw the same type of light flying at 9,000 feet, traveling around ten miles south of La Spezia. Again he pursued the light as it turned and headed North, and then moments later, turned East, before fading out. The pilot stopped pursuing the light when he was within five miles of La Spezia because he felt there might be an "Ack Ack [anti-aircraft] trap." But within fifteen minutes, the light was back, approximately ten miles South of La Spezia.

This time the pilot decided to ignore his reservations about a possible anti-aircraft trap and he chased the light anywhere it went. Below, the town was still. Piercing the night's silence was the whining Mosquito's engine as it reached 300 mph, racing across La Spezia in hot pursuit. Much to his surprise, his aircraft drew no enemy gunfire. Unfortunately, his efforts were fruitless. As he pushed his aircraft harder, the light "faded," disappearing in the darkness.

The Mosquito crew was just about to call it a night when approximately an hour later it "saw the same light" around ten miles away. Another game of cat and mouse ensued, as the pilot immediately started the chase. While at 10,000 feet, for over two minutes the pilot tried to catch up to the strange "light," which he described as a "glow that alternates between weak and bright." The pilot's efforts failed again. The strange light had eluded his every attempt to engage it in combat. Making the entire evening's event even more mysterious was the fact that the enemy had made no attempt to jam their GCI radar, and the aircraft's radar operator never made contact on his Air Intercept.[356]

The next couple of nights were rife with sightings of conventional lights, ones that were stationary and displaying flare-like characteristics. A crew with the 414th NFS was one of four P-61 B crews up on the evening of February 21. Pilot Lt. Rausch and radar operator Lt. Lindlof reported heavy fog covered the Po Valley area during their two-and-one-half hour plus patrol.

They first reported seeing a stationary "cluster of 11 or more orange colored flares" that burned for four minutes. Moments later, while flying over the Masa area, they saw a "cluster of 15 orange balls of fire" at about 5,000 feet, "appearing every time their fighter approached area." They appeared five different times and burned for about four minutes.[357] That same night over Piacenza, another Mosquito crew with the 416th NFS was on an intruder mission when they reported seeing "two large red balls of fire" hovering between 4,000 or 5,000 feet for about ten minutes.[358]

On February 22, David Griggs was busy writing two separate letters to his boss, Edward Bowles. In the first letter, he wrote: "John Trump and I recently made a week's tour of the front. Following your suggestion, we saw something of the ground commanders and had very satisfactory interviews with Bradley, Hodges and Patton. We also saw first Spaatz, then Vandenberg, Quesada and Weyland." Griggs went on to discuss radar and bombing tactical issues.[359] In his second letter, he wrote about the results of having just spent a day and a half at "Pinetree," the Eighth Air Force Headquarters. There he spoke with General Doolittle's operations officer, General Orville Anderson, and the topic of their discussion was radar. The radars employed by the Army Air Forces made Griggs optimistic about the war's end, "barring any developments wholly outside our present intelligence." In closing, Griggs asked Bowles to give Luis Alvarez his best, and, interestingly, he thanked Bowles for his February 14 letter "and the enclosed memoranda" which were "of the greatest interest."[360]

Griggs was in the right place at the right time. His presence in the European theater coincided with the numerous sightings and Howard Robertson's foo fighter investigation. Griggs weeklong visit to the front put him in contact with the big guns, especially General Spaatz. Did Griggs and Spaatz discuss the foo fighter investigation? It was General Spaatz's intelligence man who was asked to visit the 415th NFS headquarters in February regarding the foo fighters. Was Griggs one of the men from Washington who visited the 415th NFS at Toul/Ochey, France?

Chapter Fifteen

Air Ministry at a Loss

On February 22, 1945, as David Griggs was writing his letters to Edward Bowles, a 416th NFS Mosquito crew was over the Central Po Valley at 2230 hours, conducting a GCI intruder sweep and a patrol of the La Spezia area. Hanging over the water, about twenty miles West of Leghorn, they noticed three lights, red-orange in color that "burned about a minute." Strangely, the lights "did not appear to be flares."[361]

Alleged foo fighters in flight. Source unknown.
(Courtesy Janet Bord and the Fortean Picture Library)

The sighting that took place five days later indicated that something other than flares was hovering over Italy's countryside. During another GCI patrol over the area north and south of Bologna, the crew vectored onto a "bandit" that was up at 20,000 feet, but when they got to its altitude, "no contact was made." That fast, it was gone. Communication with their GCI, Rhubarb, had revealed that "there was nothing there." Then, at 2000 hours, the crew observed "three lights" at 10,000 feet in the "shape of a triangle." Now in pursuit, the radar operator was unable to make AI contact on his screen. Nevertheless, the pilot continued closing in on the lights. Zeroing in for a kill, his Mosquito was around 2,000 feet away, when suddenly the "lights disappeared."[362]

Meanwhile on the west coast of the U.S., February marked the end of a three-month spree of "unusual blips" picked up by the Naval Air Station in Pasco, Washington. The "blips appeared out of nowhere and proceeded from Northwest of the Air Station to the Southwest and consequently off the radar screens." Responding to the "blips" on at least two occasions was a F6F Hellcat fighter, which was "given orders to shoot down anything that appeared to be hostile." During each pursuit, no aircraft were located, so the Hellcat returned to base.

On another occasion Naval officer R.W. Hendershott, flying a SNJ aircraft, was contacted by ground radar "to make contact with one" of the blips, flying at a "very high" altitude. According to the radar operators, two blips were traveling about the same speed as a single-engine Piper cub aircraft. Though Officer Hendershott saw nothing, he was convinced the radar "blips" were real.[363]

Further south, another mid-winter sighting occurred in New Mexico. Sergeant James L. Lease, who was stationed at Fort Sumner Air Force Base, and E.E. Dickey were driving south on the Santa Rosa Highway, heading back from a little rabbit-hunting excursion in the countryside when, at around three in the afternoon, they saw the "glint" of a "flying object" coming across the mountaintop to their right. Lease commented that the object looked like fast flying P-38s. According to Dickey, the object hung in the air near a small gas station/grill, about twelve to fourteen feet off the ground. It remained motionless.

"The air seemed to vibrate with electricity—like one feels or hears walking under a high-line," Dickey commented. "Then it suddenly *swept away*—like a dragonfly over water—no turning—looked like an upside-down canoe shape—not over 3 to 4 ft. in highest spot—*no protrusions*—it was all so fast—color of weathered aluminum—grayish. I tried to think, [had] I seen small sight holes, but not sure. All *too fast*—out of sight in seconds —but we knew we was seeing something *not of our own making*."

Both men sat in their car stunned, "not breathing." Soon the object was gone. Sgt. Lease could not believe what he had seen and asked if Dickey had seen the same thing. He advised Dickey to say nothing because "they in the military had been told this over other sightings," possibly over sightings in Italy. Arriving at the Ft. Sumner drug store, they continued discussing the sighting and Sgt. Lease emphasized that if their sighting were reported, the military authorities "would say they were drunk."[364]

On March 3, 1945, the 41st Combat Bombardment Wing was part of a task force striking targets in Misburg, Germany. One crew with the 379th Bomb Group witnessed the flight of a V-2 over the North Sea and four over the Zuider Zee. According to the 379th Bomb Group's Antiaircraft Report, two "balloon-like silver balls" were observed. Unfortunately, the report supplied no other details.[365]

It is unknown why the intelligence officer debriefing the crew stated "balloon-like silver balls." Surely, someone in the task force had a pair of binoculars to get a closer look for an accurate description. In any case, the balloons over Germany were becoming a concern, as were the Japanese trans-Pacific balloons.[366]

How many unconventional aircraft resembled balloons, floated, or remained motionless in the sky, and were designated as balloons by various units observing them?

An Air Intelligence Summary for the Mediterranean Allied Air Forces (MAAF) indicates that Air Intelligence was struggling to positively identify all aerial sightings. Confidence among the MAAF air staff, however, reflected a strong belief that the sightings were German experiments: "Reports of German ground-fired antiaircraft rockets have been received ever since the air offensive against the Reich began. However, since the possibility existed that the so-called 'rockets' could easily be confused with air-to-air rocket fire, these reports were at first viewed with skepticism. Large numbers of strange phenomena have been reported, from both day and night operations. Aside from those which have only been reported once, and which may be attributed to abnormal conditions of observation or other 'freak' circumstances, the unusual manifestations which have been reported by air crews returning from operations from over German territory appear to resolve themselves into [several] categories..."

The categories listed were: "Scarecrow Flares," German high-altitude "Rockets," German low-altitude flak rockets, and an assortment of specific caliber rockets and other low-level rocket types.

The report's conclusion further strengthened the case for German weaponry: "With regard to high-altitude rockets, since the early part of 1944 the belief has been growing that a large portion of the observations of rockets is in fact due to other phenomena. For example, in daylight, the trails left by smoke bombs dropped by U.S. aircraft might, after a lapse of time, be reported as rocket traces. At night, it is thought that the light flak tracer, and, occasionally, emanations from experimental aircraft have led to similar reports.

"In spite of this, however, and in spite of continued lack of evidence from photographic or other sources or as a result of captured German equipment in liberated territory, the opinions of many observers is [sic] that some sort of high-altitude flak rocket is being employed, though on a much smaller scale than was at first indicated. This opinion, which is based upon observations difficult to discount by any of the alternatives described in this article, is divided as to the exact nature or purpose of such a projectile. Bearing in mind the 'rocket consciousness' of Germans, it is probable that rocket projectiles of several types are under trial or in limited use."

The conclusion further noted that recent evidence revealed that the Germans were experimenting with guided antiaircraft missiles. Air Intelligence was instructed to watch for any new signs of this development.[367]

MAAF's air staff felt quite certain they had enough evidence to support the view that the sightings were ordnance related. Their stance followed the same line of thinking proposed by the RAF nearly a year previously. But the foo fighters were different, as the following makes clear.

The MAAF report mentioned that the Germans were experimenting with guided antiaircraft missiles, a subject that was taken very seriously. The OSRD's London Mission was running its own Guided Antiaircraft Project (GAP), including representatives of the U.S. Navy and NACA (National Advisory Committee of Aeronautics). In a letter from H. Guyford Stever, scientific liaison officer with the London Mission, to M.A. Tuve, at the U.S. embassy in London, the GAP was discussed.[368] Regarding Germany's progress, Stever stated that the RAF and USAAF were "rife" with reports of a German "sub-sonic guided chaser plane" resembling the Me-163 but without a cockpit. This new "chaser-plane" was called the Me-328. It had an estimated speed of 525 mph and had flight duration of several minutes.

Stever thought the Me-328 was remote controlled but since most sightings occurred during partial overcasts, ground control of the aircraft was unlikely. Consideration of an enemy aircraft controlling it by radio link, via visual guidance, was entertained, but no antennas were ever seen to warrant this belief. Crew interrogations revealed the remote control missile/plane dived through their bomber formation, climbed rapidly back up above, and then repeated the aerobatics. Confusion existed regarding the craft's purpose, and it was not understood if the missile/plane was designed to explode on proximity or ram the Allied bombers; no reliable reports were available to assess the situation further.

"With the considerable guff about foo-fighters and other secret weapons that is now being passed around verbally and by the newspapers, every flyer interprets what he sees in a pretty exciting way," Stever continued. "We have established as many contacts as possible with Service Intelligence organizations, so that we get up-to-the-minute reliable news. Bob Robertson [Some people called Howard P. Robertson, Bob.] of this office is now working for G-2 SHAEF on Scientific Intelligence and has been briefed on our problems, so we have a good contact with headquarters."[369]

Stever's letter conveys the importance of Robertson as their primary conduit with SHAEF. He was also admitting the foo fighter was in a category by itself. The bottom line was that OSRD needed answers.

On the night of March 5, 1945, 653rd Reconnaissance Squadron of the 25th Bomb Group assigned one of its aircraft to conduct a Bluestocking mission to determine the weather conditions over Holland and northern Germany. At 2247 hours, Mosquito pilot Lt. Smith and his radar operator, Lt. Kuehn, observed "a large orange ball" in the sky at approximately 5,000 feet below their aircraft, around twenty miles away. The ball hung "in the air for a period of about five seconds." Lt. Smith dropped his Mosquito down to around 15,000 feet, and minutes later he observed a "similar ball" that was "moving horizontally at the same altitude" as his aircraft; and this time, he observed the ball, also around twenty miles away, for close to fifteen seconds before it disappeared. Major Finis D. McClanahan, the group's S-2, stated in his report the "phenomena" was unknown.[370]

March 7, 1945, marked the first step towards piercing Hitler's Third Reich.[371] The crossing of the Bridge at Remagen opened a new chapter for Allied Air Intelligence. British and American Air Technical Intelligence teams were more than ready, anxiously waiting their chance to complete their mission. They had high hopes of finding Germany's advanced aeronautical secrets. There was surely contemplation over whether the foo fighter mystery was a powerful platform for new and exotic weaponry.

On the evening of March 9, the 25th Bombardment Group conducted another meteorological mission. Major Bozarth was pilot and Lt. Anglum was his navigator. They crossed the English coast, over the North Sea, tracking the weather in an area designated as a bombing run route to follow hours later. They were flying at 10,000 feet, just above the overcast. Down below were the North Friesian Islands, hidden from view in the fog.

Suddenly, three lights appeared; one was low and two were at about 15,000 feet above the Mosquito. They "had the appearance of white flares dropped in air" and they looked similar to parachute flares, even fading out like flares. Their operations report was sent to the 25th Bombardment Group Headquarters, stating that the crew had observed "3 Foo fighters."[372] The crew's report indicated they were observing flares, so either other units used the term foo fighter as sort of a novelty name, or there was something different about the objects. Perhaps they had a strong resemblance to flares. Did the white lights fade-out, as flares normally do, or did they blink out like so many foo fighters were reported to do?

Another phenomenon affecting Robertson's foo fighter investigation was St. Elmo's Fire, which confused the issue, and was cited as an answer to the sightings by skeptical scientists. But the following report clearly of St. Elmo's Fire differs sharply from reports of foo fighters.

In the Pacific, Captain William Gifford was a B-29 Commander with the 73rd Bombardment Wing. On March 9, he and his crew were flying a mission at an altitude of 4,800 feet and cruising at 201 mph. Their plane was escorted by storms and lightning as they traveled towards their destination. Over the course of thirty minutes, his crew was unnerved by the light show, but he insisted it was harmless and not to worry.

But moments later, there was cause for concern. The B-29's wingtips, propellers, aerials, and protruding surfaces were engulfed with "sheets of fluid looking fire"; the two props on his left were a "mass of whirling flames." A couple of minutes later, there was a loud explosion. The right gunner reported the number three engine was "covered in flames." Captain Gifford then saw a sheet of flames racing along the left wing towards his cockpit window. As the flames grew near, their color changed from white to a pinkish hue, ending up as a "pinkish ball of fire around the nose" of the B-29.

"An instant later, a tremendous explosion occurred, both audible and felt." It filled the entire cockpit with brilliant light. For around half a minute, Captain Gifford was stunned by the explosion's force, and by the intensity of light it expelled. Regaining his composure, he smelled burning metal and noticed smoke was filling the cockpit. "My first conscious thought was that the bombs in the bay had exploded," Gifford explained. Crawling towards him, his co-pilot put his light on the instrument panel. Everything was fine. The instruments were operating as normal, and he noticed the B-29, after dropping steeply to the right, was recovering its normal position. Captain Gifford and crew made it back home with no further incident.[373]

This account of St. Elmo Fire does not fit any of the characteristics associated with foo fighter sightings. It should also be noted that most foo fighter sightings took place during clear weather.

On March 13, the Air Ministry finally responded to Air Commodore Grierson's February 11 request about its knowledge of the phenomenon, now commonly referred to as foo fighters. "Balls of Fire-Red" was printed in large bold letters on the very short memorandum: "Bomber Command crews have for some time been reporting similar phenomena. A few of the alleged aircraft may have been Me-262 and for the rest, flak rockets are suggested as the most likely explanation. The whole affair is still something of a mystery and the evidence is very sketchy and varied so that no definite explanation can yet be given."[374]

That night four P-61-B crews with the 414th NFS were patrolling the front line south of Bologna, Italy. At 1940 hours, pilot Lt. Schaeffer and his navigator, Lt. Ayers, were at 3,000 feet when they saw "100 balls of orange fire" illuminating the whole area around them. A couple of hours later, the last patrolling mission flown by pilot Lt. Price and his radar operator, flight officer Wilkinson, observed two "balls of foo fire" flying 15 miles south and west of Bologna.[375] "Foo fire" was the newest name associated with the phenomenon.

Five days later, on March 18, Air Commodore Grierson reported back to the First Tactical Air Force (Provisional), relaying Air Ministry's response concerning the 415th NFS's sightings: "1. With reference to requests forwarded from XII Tactical Air Command, through your Headquarters on the subject of night phenomena (foo fighter)... dated 11 February, a reply has now been received from the Air Ministry who say that Bomber Command crews have for some time been reporting similar phenomena. 2. The Air Ministry's view is that a few of the alleged aircraft may have been Me-262's and for the rest, flak rockets are suggested as the most likely explanation. 3. It is regretted that no further, or more definite, information can be given."[376]

Air Ministry's very brief memorandum offered little information, just reconfirming that the sighting remained a mystery. British intelligence officers were sticking to their belief that the sightings were new versions of known types of ordnance and weaponry. But flak rockets, though more advanced, did not exhibit the performance of the foo fighters.

SHAEF Air Staff was back to square one: continue collecting sighting reports. Growing in complexity, the Air Intelligence gathering missions were making great progress. If the foo fighter was an enemy weapon, a good chance existed that answers were among the mass of enemy documentation exploited by the Air Intelligence teams.

On the ground, CIOS created its newest intelligence tool: advanced eyes, designed to aid the advancing 6th, 12th, and 21st Allied Army Groups.

These were teams composed of six specialist/experts: a physicist, armaments expert, metallurgist/chemist, Naval Technical Rep., Air Technical Rep., and an engineer (tanks, vehicles, etc.).[377] Approved by SHAEF, they were officially called the Consolidated Advanced Forward Teams (CAFT).[378] Placed among or right behind advancing combat troops, CAFT teams made initial determinations of who was needed to examine each "Target" as it was found or located.

Another special Air Intelligence unit was created in addition to the Air Technical Intelligence teams already in the field. This new specialized unit was focused more on the operational aspect of intelligence gathering: aircraft, radar, airfields, and facilities. Two of the primary functions of this unit were "to obtain technical information from captured enemy aircraft and equipment on subjects of tactical importance against which counter-measures can be initiated (Radar and GCI frequencies, new armament, etc.)."[379]

The creation of this new ATI team suggests compartmentalization existed among the already existing Army Air Force ATI teams. For example, if two ATI teams had a list of "targets," only one team might have full knowledge of the foo fighter investigation, providing a direct and expeditious link to Robertson's foo fighter investigation.

On the night March 18, a 416th NFS crew was flying their Mosquito 25 miles northwest of Florence, Italy. The prowling Mosquito experienced no antiaircraft flak, nor encountered any enemy aircraft. But suddenly, they were no longer alone. Something else was flying with them. A "light" is all that was visible. The radar operator checked his Air Intercept screen, but it was blank, offering no indication of anything in the light's position. When the operator checked to see if his radar unit was operating properly, GCI asserted that it, too, had "no contact" on its screen.

The mystery light was moving at about 13,000 feet. Changing from patrol mode to intruder mode, the pilot turned his Mosquito in its direction for the kill, bearing down on the lone glow. The chase was on. For the next thirty minutes, the pilot kept right on the light's tail, racing along at 260 mph and climbing up to 16,000 feet. Throughout the chase, the crew clearly saw the light. Then suddenly, "the light disappeared" and the pilot was chasing darkness.[380]

While over the town of Speyer, Germany, members of the 415th NFS "saw 2 'Foo' Fighters – 1 orange ball and 1 green one" during a mission on 19/20 March. The crew said that the foo fighters "seemed to be closing in from portside," but the pilot was quick to evade them.[381]

Over those same nights, the skies over Italy and Germany were also alive with alleged jet-propelled night fighters,[382] some of which seemed to be aggressive. "It is suspected that the increased use of upward-firing armament by enemy night fighters may have commenced, but there is no reliable evidence to suggest that jet-propelled fighters have so far been employed," stated the British Operation Research Section on March 22. For nearly two months, a flood of reports described combat encounters with alleged jet-propelled night fighter aircraft: Me-262s and Me-163s. The RAF had accumulated a number of accounts that identified the Me-163 as firing on the British bombers, technically making this aircraft the first rocket-propelled fighter. But no British bombers were reported shot down by any jet-propelled fighter, and it was noted that many of these jet-propelled fighters were shot down, which was considered highly suspicious.

A couple of examples took place two weeks prior in February. A crew with the 78 Squadron was returning from its mission against targets in Chemnitz. There were no clouds and the visibility was good. The pilot and his mid-upper gunner noticed two marker beacons on the ground. They noticed a red light "superimposed on the normal white signal." Suddenly, the "reflection of the jet glow on the runway" was spotted as the jet-propelled aircraft, one that they could not identify, "climbed at great speed" towards their Halifax bomber; one witness could see wings and a fuselage as it tore down the runway. Within thirty seconds, the jet was upon them, closing in at 500 yards. The rear gunner opened up with his machine gun. It was a direct hit; the jet exploded into two burning pieces.

A second sighting occurred that same night of an alleged Me-163. The Lancaster crew said the jet attacked them, firing within four hundred yards of their bomber. But it missed them. Giving it no more chances, they responded, blowing it clean out of the sky. And there was another account describing a missile or jet as a "flying wing, giving off a yellowish-red intermittent glow" as it followed the bomber well within machine gun range, but it did not open fire. The British bomber obliged, sending it down in a sea of flames.

ORS followed up: "While the details quoted above are not necessarily accurate in view of the difficulties of observation at night, it seems likely that the enemy is introducing a new method of defense." [383]

That "method of defense" was contributing to the confusion that steadily mounted among the Allied air intelligence staff. More and more cases poured in presenting observations of guided missiles or aircraft that looked like the Me-163s were in operation. But among these sightings, the sophistication of some of the objects observed kept the Allied Air staff puzzled. By March 1945, there was still no verifiable proof that the Germans had accomplished success with jet-propelled guided missiles. All the while, Allied ATI and various other intelligence teams pushed closer towards Germany in hopes of finding answers.

The following sighting is another example that reflects the variety of observations designated as foo fighters, although their appearance, flight characteristics, and actions, clearly denotes ground-fired ordnance. On the night of March 23, 414th Night fighter crew, Lt. Gravel and Flight Officer Moore were conducting an Air Drome intruder mission over the Bergamo, Ghedi area. It was 2015 hours. The P-61B was at an altitude of 1,500 feet when both crewmen spotted "two spurts of gun fire on the ground." Seconds later, they witnessed "2 balls of foo fire" that "appeared about 600 yds. Dead ahead." The balls burned for approximately three to four minutes. At 2100 hours, "two more appeared in their path and this time they also observed two solitary gun flashes prior to their appearance. This time, however, after approximately one minute of glowing, one of the two burst like a projectile. The other continued to glow."[384]

A couple hours later, a 415th NFS crew was on an intruder patrol over Germersheim, Germany. They were vectored in on a target by GCI, who reported that they were picking up a "stationary airborne object." The crew went for a look, but when they arrived, there was nothing there.[385]

Chapter Sixteen

The Pacific Balls of Fire

New Guinea was an early prize for the Japanese army during the early war years, but by July 1944, after brutal to-the-last-man fighting, U.S. Marines recaptured it.[386] By mid-March 1945, New Guinea was under Allied control and considered fairly safe. Close by, after suffering from its intense battle at Iwo Jima, the *USS New York* was returning to combat duty. Escorted by two destroyers, it set sail to join up with the Seventh Fleet.

The weather that day was sunny and clear. Around 1300 hours general quarters sounded, electrifying the calming nature of the warm sea air. Alert, Corporal Donald Pratt and his crewmembers prepared for an attack by Japanese forces, possibly suicide aircraft. Pratt was a 40mm gunner. He was ready, waiting for the order to fire. Nerves tense, he watched, but the sky was clear. No Japanese planes appeared.

On the *New York*'s radar, things were different. The radar screen was picking up a single blip. It had appeared out of thin air. Just seconds later, the blip was in view. Cpl. Pratt watched as the object hovered motionless, almost directly over the battleship. Captain K.C. Christian was watching through his binoculars, as were approximately 2,000 other navy crewmen, some with their own binoculars.

The object was "silver in color," "very shiny" and "did not change colors," Pratt said. "It was much larger than the brightest star would be, but smaller than a full moon." Quietly, it continued hovering above them, just matching the *New York*'s speed and course.

For thirty minutes, the *New York* and her two escorts anxiously braced themselves for something to happen. The strange object did nothing, but its presence was too much for the naval vessels to stand by and do nothing. Was this a Japanese secret weapon waiting for the right time to strike? Or was it waiting for more of them to show up and attack in number? Captain Christian did not wait to find out. There was no need to receive damage first and then respond, so he ordered a first strike.

Two of the *New York*'s three-inch antiaircraft guns cut loose on the object, sending a hail of lead arching high into the air. But the object did not move or appear affected by the gunfire. Since it was useless and a waste of ammo, Captain Christian ordered his guns silent. Within seconds of their cease-fire, the object "climbed up at a fantastic rate of speed until it was out of sight, and off the radar scope." Corporal Pratt said "everyone aboard the ship was stunned by this; they had never seen anything like it."

The general quarters sounded, and the ships were again alone at sea. The men discussed the incident for days, trying to make sense of what they saw. "Anyhow, we knew, after watching it for a few minutes that it was not any type of plane because our ship was only traveling at around twelve knots," Pratt explained. "A plane could not travel that slowly without stalling the engine and dropping into the ocean. It was too sunny and bright that day to be a star, and it was not a balloon...not in the middle of the Pacific. We didn't know what it was."[387]

Airmen in the Pacific were seeing an increase in aerial pyrotechnic activity. The Japanese were "throwing the book" at them, revealing that they were becoming proficient with such ordnance as rocket-assisted air-to-air weapons. Documentation found on the islands revealed valuable information regarding new ordnance; however, a clear picture of the weapon's identity or operational use was not established.

On March 24, a memorandum from the Headquarters Allied Air Force, South West Pacific Area (SWPA), circulated among air intelligence, describing Japanese rocket encounters. "Round-The-Clock Rocket Attacks: Japan and Sumatra" was the title of the article. Mirroring the March 22 ORS report's remark that the Germans were possibly introducing new air defenses, the article began: "Persistent but inconclusive B-29 reports of the use of rockets by interceptors over Japan and Sumatra may herald new Japanese defensive tactics." Excerpts from the XX Bomber Command's February 6 and the August 10/11, 1944 missions were included. SWPA's commented: "Projectiles described seem to be much smaller than 'foo-fighter' balls encountered in Europe. Also, the Japanese projectiles have a horizontal trajectory indicating an air release. The 'foo-fighter' reportedly seems to have been more or less suspended, with limited movement. Since at no time was a point of origin discovered by the 29's this may really be a 'Buck Rogers' special."[388]

Apparently, the SWPA Intelligence officers had limited access to foo fighter reports. Their comment that foo fighters were "more or less suspended, with limited movement" was way off mark.[389]

That evening the SWPA received more observations for their database. The XXI Bomber Command commenced with operations against mainland Japan, sending their B-29s on a raid to destroy the Mitsubishi Aircraft

Engine Works in Nagoya, Japan.

B-29 crews observed a variety of pyrotechnic activity: a "yellow ball of fire about 6 inches in diameter"; "orange and red flashes"; "six white balls of fire"; apparent rocket bursts resembling gas explosions, appearing reddish-orange in color, "far brighter than A/A fire"; "a grayish ball of fire about the size of a soccer ball"; and a "red ball of fire" coming up from below.[390]

Back in Europe, the very next day, U.S. Army ground troops in Germany witnessed something bizarre. On the night of March 25, 1945, overcast hid the moon from view, and there was no fog present. Company A, U.S. 44th Armored Infantry Battalion, 6th Armored Division, was busy settling in for the evening, bivouacked on a wooded hill along the Autobahn between Mannheim and Darmstadt, Germany.

It was an overcast night but not foggy. Infantryman John Norris was busy digging his foxhole. Looking up, he noticed a few strangers were slowly passing by his camp. Watching in amazement, he used his pair of 7x35 field glasses view them.

The following is his account: "Between 10 and 11 o'clock in the evening, I observed 6 or 7 objects obliquely approaching our position through the air. The objects were circular in my view of them and could well have been spherical. They glowed steadily with a bright yellow-orange color and were about as bright as a full harvest moon. Several other men in the area were awake, and saw these objects and wakened their buddies who also saw them. The light from these objects was sufficient to cast distinct shadows behind the trees and to show the whereabouts of two men some thirty feet away who were not in their foxhole at the time.

"The objects moved along roughly parallel course which brought them across the Autobahn from the west at an altitude of about 150 feet. As a group, they lost altitude as they moved, so that they were at treetop level or a little below as they passed our position.

"At first, we assumed these objects to be some sort of unfamiliar flare but soon realized that they were not flares because: 1) Though the light they gave off was visible and annoying to us, it was hardly bright enough to have been useful to an airborne or distant observer; 2) They did not drift down to the ground as a parachute-supported flare does, but followed a transverse course without the aid of any wind or breeze; 3) Although the group followed a fairly well defined path, the individual objects were not fixed with relationship to each other or with relationship to the general path, but moved upward, downward, back along the flight path, and forward as if individually controlled.

"Their deliberate hither-and-yon behavior suggested intelligent probing and gave one the sensation of being peered at. The men, who were by now all watching these objects, crouched lower in their foxholes; those who had got out of their foxholes moved cautiously keeping in the shadows (which were themselves moving, of course) of trees.

"The path of these objects carried them into full visibility from time to time and then into partial or complete obscurity behind tree tops. Within 5 or 6 minutes of our first seeing the objects, they were totally hidden from view by the forest – somewhat denser in the direction of their flight than in the area where we were dug in.

"The following morning, by sighting in the same directions and from the same position, I was able to determine that the objects must have passed behind certain trees and in front of certain others and thus make a close estimate of their actual distance and hence of their true size and speed. They were 3 or 4 feet in diameter and moved soundlessly at speeds of from one to perhaps ten miles per hour. About 30 men saw them clearly and agreed on what they had seen when, following their disappearance, the men discussed this phenomenon."[391]

Infantryman John Norris is the only known U.S. Army ground trooper to report foo fighter type objects. Mannheim and Darmstadt were in an area where foo fighters were observed on numerous occasions, and the date of his sighting matches other foo fighter activity precisely. These strange lights are curiously similar to those floating through the Ardennes forest a couple days before the German counter-offensive.

In the meantime, U.S. bombers were hitting German jet-production facilities hard; they attacked airdromes, airfields, and research facilities, anything that suggested German jet-propelled aircraft activity. In the Italian theater, due to the Germany's diminishing war capabilities, it was considered "unlikely" that German jet fighters stationed in northern Italy would pose a threat to American bombers.[392]

So far, the Luftwaffe had put into operation two jet-propelled and one rocket-propelled aircraft: the Me-262, Me-163, and Ar-234. But the numerous jet-propelled encounter reports were not adding up; intelligence supported the opinion there were not many Me-262 night fighters in existence and there was no proof of a Me-163 night fighter at all. The British agreed with American assessments that jet and rocket night fighters were unlikely; however, the British suspected, despite a lack of information, that something jet-propelled was roaming the night sky.

On March 26, the Air Ministry's chief interrogator, Group Captain S.D. Felkin, learned that the Germans were building a new triangle shaped tailless aircraft called Delta, an invention of Alexander Lippisch, the designer of the Me-163 and a glider expert.[393] Lippisch's Delta Tailless aircraft, if flown as predicted, was similar to a bat-winged jet propelled aircraft seen in December 1944 by U.S. airmen. Even if the Delta series became operational, however, American foo fighters and British balls of fire sightings represented something far more exotic.

By the end of March, the last of Hitler's V-2s had been fired. The skies over Europe were much friendlier since Allied aircraft flew virtually unchallenged. Field Marshall Goering's mighty Luftwaffe was nearly decimated. His jet aircraft had come into operation far too late to be effective. And now, as the Allies advanced into the Ruhr Valley industrial area, the last of the major airfields that supported the Luftwaffe were being overrun.[394]

With each passing day, General Spaatz's First Tactical Air Force (Provisional) continued preparing for its new phase of existence, changing from combat operations to exploitation status. As the Allied advance brought a close to hostilities, the knowledge supporting Germany's real Flash Gordon and Buck Rogers technology was falling into Allied hands, including the Russians. Germany was a technological wonderland. General Arnold and his staff anxiously awaited news that Nazi Germany's scientific and technological achievements were being located.

B
ut the war was far from over. The skies of the Pacific were still extremely dangerous. All U.S. forces approaching mainland Japan expected to encounter a fiercely aggressive enemy.

On March 29, 1945, the XXI Bomber Command Air Intelligence staff released a report, which stated: "Japs Have A Bagful of Tricks, *But They Don't Work*! In the European Theater of Operations, the Germans have

From XXI Bomber Command Air Intelligence Report, March 29, 1945. (Courtesy NARA)

experimented with a great variety of 'secret weapons' and special antiaircraft devices," began the report. "None of these has proved effective against our bombers. It seems that the Japs—-with their usual flare for imitation—have likewise tried a number of weird weapons against B-29's of the XXI Bomber Command."

Under the name "Nightmare Devices," XX Bomber Command briefly cited some sighting descriptions, including: "Two orange-red bursts with tails," "Balls of fire traveling at very high speed," "Three green balls that appeared to float down," and "Two large balls of red fire apparently attached together, floating down."

Like the airmen in the European theater who used the word "flare" to describe what they saw, the Pacific crews did the same. One crew described "three flares" approaching them as if "radar-controlled" due to the fact that the objects followed and turned with their aircraft. Another crew reported a "White flare coming up slowly and bursting with a starfish-like flash."

The XXI Bomber Command Air Intelligence officers further advised the S-2s: "Such reports have a definite intelligence value. We want them. Keep them coming. But don't let them scare you. Up to date not a single plane has been reported lost or damaged by these 'secret weapons'—except in the Japanese newspapers. The only effective weapons against our bombers are still the fighter plane and the antiaircraft gun."[395]

Over the next couple days, on March 30 and April 1, 1945, the skies over the Pacific came alive. The target: Mitsubishi Aircraft Engine Works in Tokyo. Conducting the raid was the XXI Bomber Command. That night B-29 crews experienced a large variety of aerial encounters. The tactical mission report included a variety of enemy categories.

Listed in the report as "Flying Objects," one B-29 crew "observed a dark object coming towards them." Oddly, the object "disintegrated" before reaching the bomber, falling to the ground, and exploding. Under the heading of "Possible Remote Control Flying Bomb," the same crew reported that "something was following" their B-29 as they approached land's end. As the object gained on the bomber, the pilot increased the B-29's speed and executed "gentle turns," but the object kept coming. Two "long streams of flame" were observed coming from the object, and it was not long before it exploded. Under the heading "Possible Rocket Bombs," a B-29 crew observed something taking off from the ground. A "long red steak of flame" was all the crew saw, but then the "object pulled up into a steep climb and made a turn to the right, coming around in front and well ahead" of their plane. Circling them, the object approached the rear of their aircraft and then it, too, exploded.[396]

During the evening of April 3 and the early morning of April 4, the skies over Honshu rumbled again with the sound of heavy bombers. The XXI Bomber Command's tactical report had only one enemy air opposition heading: "Balls of Fire." Though several bombardment wings participated in the raid and reported sightings, crews with the 73rd Bombardment Wing headquarters provided the best reports, and they considered the following reports among "the most complete observations made."

According to Lt. Althoff, they had just completed bombing the secondary target and were approaching land's end. Their altitude was 9,000 feet at the time when he first saw the "ball of fire" coming in on his B-29 at about the five o'clock. It was about 300 yards behind his B-29 and the "ball of fire was about size of basketball." Immediately, evasive action was taken, but the ball of fire cut to the inside of the plane and continued to follow. Lt. Althoff said that it appeared that the ball of fire could not keep up with the B-29's evasive maneuvers, the weaving turns, but when the bomber was flying straight, the ball of fire caught up to them. One of the other crewmen said he saw a "streamer of light behind the ball of fire, which was faint and not steady." The light faded as it turned with the B-29, but increased in intensity on the straightaway.

Playing cat and mouse, the B-29 and its pursuer were over the Pacific Ocean. Diving to 6,000 feet, the B-29 was able to obtain additional air speed, and the ball of fire fell behind, eventually turned around, and gave up its pursuit, heading back to the coast. Watching the object retreat, Lt. Althoff noticed a "streamer of light," but then the light "faded abruptly." The blister gunner thought he had seen a "wing in connection with ball of fire; and it had a navigation light burning on left wing tip." But now the chase was over. It had followed them for approximately six minutes.

Lt. Schmidt was in another B-29. His plane had departed the target area, which they bombed from at 6,100 feet. Gaining another 900 feet, he noticed a ball of fire, emitting a "steady phosphorescent glow," following him. Immediately the B-29 took evasive action, "gaining and losing 500 ft. and also changing course as much as 35 degrees and varying airspeed from 205 to 250." Flying into the clouds, they thought the maneuver had worked, but as they emerged, the ball of fire was right on the B-29's tail. Twice more the pilot steered his bomber into the clouds and twice more when he came out, the ball of fire was right there behind his plane. Then, over Tokyo Bay, the ball of fire "disappeared" not too far behind the fleeing B-29.

Capt. Bricker's B-29 was at 8,000 feet, leaving his secondary target behind. The waist gunner was looking towards the ground below when he saw an "amber colored" searchlight. But he was wrong. The light was not on the ground, but airborne and moving, climbing in altitude, and gaining on them. There was no time to waste. The B-29 ascended, reaching an altitude of 12,000 feet. The ball of fire tagged right along, so the pilot dropped his B-29 down another 2,000 feet, but the "ball of fire" still followed.

In the meantime, the radar operator reported that another aircraft was picked up off their tail, about a mile out. The tail gunner "then observed stream of fire emanating from object following them, and coming out in bursts; one burst about twenty-four inches long, and then about a 6 inch break, followed by another burst of flame about 24 inches long." This kept up for about eight minutes, before the flame extinguished. He said the ball of fire was about twelve inches in diameter, and no explosions were observed.

During the whole experience, the pilot varied the B-29's altitude from 800 to 1200 feet, but the "ball of fire" mimicked his plane's every move, falling behind occasionally. The tail gunner further noticed that the flame "appeared to gain and diminish in intensity," but was not sure if this related to its varying distances. The ball of fire was last seen about 30 miles out over the ocean. The crew saw no explosions.[397]

General Curtis LeMay, commander of the XXI Bomber Command, headquartered in Guam, immediately sent the April 3/4 intelligence report to the commanding general of the Twentieth Air Force, in Washington D.C., via teletype.[398]

While crews were interrogated about the Honshu Island raid, a massive formation of B-17 Flying Fortresses was heading over the North Sea towards targets near Berlin, Germany. During the mid-morning hours of April 7, navigator Captain Louis Sewell's aircraft came under attack by a German fighter. The aircraft dove in and leveled off, then rolled into a dive, positioning itself under the B-17. Oddly, the aircraft did not attack, however this was understandable since it was not a German fighter. It looked more like a V-2 and was executing skilled maneuvers without wings.

Once under Captain Sewell's aircraft, the wingless aircraft came to a complete stop. At this time, Captain Sewell's B-17 was positioned overtop the "object" and the ocean below. The rest of his crew and many other crewmen flying in formation witnessed the spectacle. Suddenly, the unconventional aircraft accelerated to "about two thousand miles per hour" as it raced out of sight.

Once Captain Sewell returned to base, his and other B-17 crews reported the sighting to intelligence officers. This time Sewell's radio operator had taken several pictures of the object. The film was rushed away for developing. Captain Sewell heard nothing more about the strange aircraft, but he said that was standard operating procedure.[399]

As usual, nothing about the missile-like unconventional aircraft seen by Captain Sewell and numerous crews that day was mentioned in any memoranda; this sighting was apparently far too hot for communication via normal intelligence channels.

Meanwhile, on Okinawa, the technical intelligence unit of the Tenth Army made a very significant discovery. During their advance, ground troops had captured a cache of Japan's newest fully functional piloted rocket-propelled flying bombs and a number of others that were unassembled. Tenth Army headquarters determined that the piloted rocket bombs were probably being produced in large quantities for use in the near future, but there was no evidence they had been used operationally thus far.[400]

It's worth noting here that the intelligence report produced on the April 3, 1945, Honshu Island incidents stated quite clearly that the observed balls of fire were, to some extent, definitely controlled.

On April 7, the Director of Intelligence, Air Intelligence Branch, Army Air Forces, Pacific Ocean Areas, issued the staff's take on things, as the report's cover sheet states: "This is an attempt to describe the phenomenon and to define it with an eye toward the most recent Japanese fields of interest and developments."

The intelligence report, addressed the three types of sightings designated as the balls of fire phenomenon. This new assessment report shows the level of thought and effort by technical intelligence officers to determine what the objects were, based on a few verbal accounts.

The report indicated that after careful review of the crewmen's observations, and after "certain factors" were "substantiated," three new weapons may account for the balls of fire sightings. The first theory was that the ball of fire exhibited performance capabilities indicating it was a jet-propelled aircraft.

"A jet powered unit would throw off intermittent spurts of flame as it propelled itself forward," the report stated. "This exhaust pattern of a jet unit may have been the amber colored searchlight observed by the waist gunner. He noted that the light was closing in on his plane both as to altitude and distance. The blister gunner on another crew claimed that he saw a wing in connection with the 'ball of fire'; the wing had a navigational light on its left tip. This plus the fact that the 'ball of fire' turned back after it had chased the bombers for a certain distance, lends evidence that either the 'ball of fire' is controlled manually or by a control plane."

Their second theory was that the ball of fire was a "sonic controlled flying bomb propelled by a jet powered unit," which they explained this way: "This bomb could be easily launched from the aircraft that have been reported on all recent missions over the mainland of Japan. The fact that the B-29 was followed through layers of clouds as well as evasive action, points toward some control of a sonic device." To further support this theory, it was suggested that the B-29 was able to outdistance the ball of fire during maneuvers because the sonic control was not sophisticated enough to keep up with the B-29 except on straight-aways; this accounts for the lost ground during the evasive maneuver.

The third possibility noted by the intelligence report was that the ball of fire was a "radio controlled aircraft consisting of a warhead and a jet powered unit." Though no observations of control-planes were reported, Air Technical Intelligence felt this was due to the crewman's attention on the light, not the surrounding sky. And if it was a control-plane in the limited visibility, evasive maneuvers by the B-29 accounts for the ball of fire falling behind, as reported.

The Pacific Air Intelligence had given their best shot in trying to identify the sightings, but it was impossible to be more definitive with only "fragmentary evidence of an initial experience with this weapon."[401]

Message activity among the Pacific commands covered the balls of fire story in detail, and offered post crew interrogation sighting details whenever possible.[402] It was quite apparent to the Twentieth Air Force that the Japanese interest in Germany's advances with guided missiles was the underlying issue, a key factor in developing the three most logical possibilities explaining the balls of fire. Newly discovered documentation in Germany was helping to shed light on the German and Japanese sharing of technology. Nazi Germany was near collapse, but it continued to surprise the Allies with an influx of updated weaponry.

The British offered their opinion on "controlled" bombs and missiles: "It is clear that even at this late stage of the war, the Germans are still trying to put into operation effective controlled missiles as a defense against night bombers. Although it is not possible to draw a definitive conclusion from the Schmidding documents as to whether any of the above missiles have yet been used operationally, reports from night bomber aircrews, over the past months, have frequently referred to supposed winged missiles which could well have been the Hs-298, X-4, or Hs-117. Some of these reports have noted especially the tendency of the missiles to follow the bombers during evasive action, strongly suggesting the use of remote control and/or homing devices. It seems reasonable to conclude therefore that these controlled missiles have to some extent been put into operation and that an increasing use will be made of them in the near future."[403]

In the XX Bomber Command's *Weekly Air Intelligence Digest*, the balls of fire were regarded as possible Japanese versions of the German V-1. Even more intriguing was the suggestion of a connection between the balls of fire and the "round black objects" following F-5 pilots over China.[404]

On the night of April 7, a XXI Bomber Command raid was conducted against targets in Nagoya, Japan. Crews reported seeing a "ball of fire" changing colors from "orange to red" and moving parallel to their aircraft as they headed over the water in the direction of landfall with the main Japanese Islands. It was 500 feet below them and changed course with their aircraft.[405]

When General Arnold read about the balls of fire sightings in his "Incoming Message Log" on April 8, he immediately wanted to know exactly what these objects were. Penciled in his briefing messages was the following note: "Intelligence to obtain Dr. Von Karman, Dr. Bush and any other worthwhile view." If anyone knew what the balls of fire were, it was Von Karman and the men he had hand chosen for his mission in Germany. Penciled in beside the extract about the suicide rocket-propelled projectiles on Okinawa, Arnold wrote: "Intelligence — does this connect with 'balls of fire'?" [406]

Arnold wanted answers. Those few simple handwritten sentences suggest his questions were quickly acted upon by his staff, including Air Materiel Command and Edward Bowles.

From the descriptions supplied by Twentieth Air Force B-29 crews, the Pacific balls of fire were apperaing in far greater numbers than those seen by British and Americans in the European and Mediterranean theaters of operations.

Chapter Seventeen

"Circles of Light"

On April 11, 1945, a flak intelligence memorandum was released describing the various anti-aircraft weaponry and defenses the Japanese had at their disposal. Under the heading of "AA Rockets," the report stated: "The indicated experimental use of ground-to-air rockets by the Japanese is still unconfirmed by photographs, captured equipment, documents, or known damage to our aircraft. Manifestations of Jap rocket research appear in recent B-29 reports of 'Balls of Fire' over Tokyo, which followed the planes for as long as six minutes, and are described as similar to the 'balls of fire' or 'Foo Fighters' encountered over Germany last summer."[407]

Curiously, the intelligence memorandum stated the foo fighters were encountered over Germany "last summer," not the fact that the real activity under the name of foo fighter flourished from December 1944 throughout 1945.

For almost a month, the balls of fire were the focus of attention throughout the Pacific theater of operations. On April 26, General Curtis LeMay's XXI Bomber Command's Air Intelligence staff produced a five-page report representing the most up-to-date information and theories on the balls of fire. Under the report's "Japanese Air Defense – Balls of Fire" section, U.S. Air Intelligence knew that the Japanese were experimenting with their air defenses since their conventional fighters and antiaircraft were not proving successful. U.S. Air Intelligence was expecting an "ever increasing number of inventions similar to V-1, V-2, jet propelled fighters, rocket-propelled fighters, flying wings, radio controlled bombs, and all the other appurtenances of the flying circus."

"Are These Fireballs?" was boldly printed in the next section of the report. In reference to piloted flying bombs, the report asked: "Has this development any relationship to our combat report of 'balls of fire'? While it becomes readily apparent that all of these reports have stemmed from the same causative source, it does not appear beyond the realm of possibility that some of the so-called 'balls of fire' may have been generated by the rocket motor of the 'Viper'. In one form or another as many as 302 sightings by 140 crews which may be classified under the heading 'balls of fire' have been reported. While a large percentage of these sightings have continued for at most two-three minutes, some have persisted for as long as 15 minutes."

A sampling of the various sightings were included, twelve in all, and due to a wide range of characteristics, it was suggested that half were probably under human control, all within the capabilities of the captured Viper (also known as the Baka). While the report did not dismiss radio-controlled missiles, the difficulty surrounding their use at night was insurmountable.

LeMay's Air Intelligence staff was confused by the absence of daylight sightings, explaining: "In like manner, it is difficult to explain this phenomenon in terms of normal jet or rocket-propelled fighters such as have been used by the Germans in the European Theater of Operations," stated the report. "Perhaps the simplest explanation is that these balls of fire are generated in some unknown fashion by a conventional Japanese night fighter. The problem is yet unresolved."[408]

On April 30, Hitler was dead and all hopes of a great Germany and thousand-year Reich was no more. The Allies were now able to focus all of their attention on the Japanese Empire. The Pacific balls of fire were the latest aerial ordnance related puzzle, but a newer phenomenon emerged in the South Pacific near a place called Truk.

It was the evening of May 2. Nine B-24s with the 11th Bombardment Group's 431st Squadron were heading out on a "night harassing bombing mission" against Japanese air installations. According to the VII Bomber Command's intelligence report: "The crew of plane #616 over FALA ISLAND, TRUK ATOLL, at 021802Z observed 2 airborne objects at their 11,000 foot altitude, changing from a cherry red to an orange, and to a white light which would die out and become cherry red again. These objects were out on either wing and not within range of caliber .50 machine guns. Both followed the B-24 thru all types of evasive action. A B-24 took a course for Guam and one of the pursuers dropped off at 021900Z after accompanying the B-24 for an hour. The other continued to follow never approaching closer than 1000 yards and speeding up when the B-24 went through the clouds to emerge on the other side ahead of the B-24. In daylight it was seen to be bright silver in color."[409] The report went on to cite various observations by other B-24 crews on the raids, but none mentioned seeing anything like plane #616's crew.

The sighting could not have been of the BAKA, Japan's piloted, rocket-propelled, suicide aircraft bomb, which was not capable of such lengthy flights, or the balls of fire, which performed in flight much differently. The changing of colors from cherry red to an orange, to white, and back to cherry red again was odd, as compared to reports from previous missions by B-29 crews.

On May 4, the Deputy Commander of the Twentieth Air Force on Guam sent a "Confidential" message to the War Department in Washington and to the Commanding General Army Air Forces, Pacific Ocean Area, describing the "phenomenon" observed by the B-24 crew.

Their report described the object as "two red circles of light" that "grew bright yellow or white like electric light or phosphorous glow" as they traveled. The B24's evasive action indicated that the object had no trouble matching the pilot's maneuvers and maintained the same position and distance from the plane. Throughout the night, the object remained only a light, due to lack of moonlight masked by high clouds.

At daybreak, the object appeared as a "steady white glow." The crew thought they could see a "wing shape and silver color," but the object was too far away and the sun's glare obstructed a clear view. The report further stated that the entire crew was carefully interrogated and a check with Guam ground-based radar units revealed that their screens showed nothing at the time. This puzzling event caused the Twentieth Air Force's deputy commander to ask, "Can you suggest possible explanations?"[410]

The War Department's classified memo revealed further details not mentioned in the original VII Bomber Command Mission report. Visually, the light was described as orange, not cherry red, changing to a bright yellow resembling an electric light, or a phosphorous glow. The possibility that the object was a jet-propelled aircraft was unlikely since at no time was there any sign of exhaust. And no known jet aircraft could maintain such lengthy flights.

The most curious detail was the crew's observation of a possible "wing shape." Whatever the object was, it appeared under intelligent control and was capable of mimicking evasive maneuvers by the B-24, maintaining the same relative distance at all times. Complicating matters, as compared with the European foo fighter sightings, the objects were not picked up by ground radar in the area.

The first official attempt to explain the sighting came on May 8, when the Office of the Director of Intelligence, Headquarters Army Air Forces, Pacific Ocean Area, issued an Air Intelligence Memorandum entitled "PLANES or STAR??" This important memo reveals the same sort of confusion over the sighting as those expressed by XII Tactical Air Force and SHAEF regarding the foo fighters.

The Pacific Air Intelligence Branch felt the B-24's sighting over Truk was an encounter "as baffling phenomena as the Balls of Fire seen by the B-29s while over the Japanese mainland." The details of the original report were discussed, with nothing new added. Regarding radar returns, the crew felt "the light was never close enough to the bomber to give a single blip on the radar..." Air intelligence felt that "the report from Guam radar units plus the fact that the light was always seen on the right side of the B-24, and that even when the bomber turned into the light no rate of closure was noted tends to make the possibility of a jet powered or even a conventional type aircraft a doubtful one."

Air intelligence felt the "light" that turned back after pacing the B-24 for over an hour "may or may have not been an aircraft." The other light, which continued to stay with the B-24, was "not" an aircraft, and it was "very possible" that it was astronomical in nature; explaining that since the light "never closed" to the B-24, changing "from an orange color to a white phosphorescent glow," it "was nothing but a star or planet." To clarify further they said that when celestial objects start their early morning hour ascent in the sky, they burn "brightly with a myriad of colors" during their travel; this type of phenomena was previously witnessed by crews "in latitudes near the equator," while conducted operations against targets in the Gilbert and Marshall Islands.

The assistant chief of Air Staff Intelligence offered another possible explanation from his preliminary evaluation of the sighting: "It is believed the lights observed were those of an unknown type mounted on Japanese aircraft with the capabilities of an IRVING [a Japanese night fighter] on an experimental or observation mission. While certain jet exhaust flame characteristics are apparent, the range and length of light greatly exceed the known capabilities of friendly or enemy jet aircraft. While observations vary considerably from characteristics of 'Balls of fire' recently seen over Japanese homeland, there is great need for intelligence on all air phenomena. In the future, when such sightings are within range of interceptors, it is recommended that radio silence be broken and a scramble ordered with pilots briefed especially for intelligence requirements of the mission."[411]

On May 8, 1945, the world had reason to celebrate: Germany had surrendered. While celebration erupted around the world, the brutality of war continued in the Pacific. Two days later, General LeMay, commander of the XXI Bomber Command, supplied Washington with further updated details regarding the balls of fire encountered on the April 13/14 bombing mission. The report offered nothing revelatory. Overall, the most interesting detail of LeMay's message was that the balls of fire were "circular" or "spherical" in shape. [412]

On May 12, the U.S. Seventh Air Force's intelligence staff issued a five-page report. Contained in the report's "Tactics" section was a lengthy piece entitled "Fire-Balls, By Screw-Balls." The Seventh Air Force Air was certainly in agreement with General LeMay's intelligence staff. Included were extracts from an April 11 Air Intelligence Memorandum, Army Air Forces Pacific Ocean Areas, and LeMay's April 26 report. Other than keeping the balls of fire sightings in the news, the Seventh Air Force contributed no other information about the phenomenon other than a comment: "At the present time no definite information has become available which would identify either the source or components of this unexplained 'weapon.'"[413]

On May 14, the XXI Bomber Command conducted a daytime incendiary mission against urban industrial sites in northern Nagoya. They reported a sighting similar to the 415th Night Fighter Squadron's observations of foo fighters. According to the 58th Bombardment Wing's Tactical Mission report: "A/C 4861 was followed by an unidentified plane described as a ball of fire. The object was first sighted directly after bombs away at 1848Z. This red or 'flame colored' light stayed at the five o'clock position until the B-29 began to take evasive action. The object fell behind, and then caught up again. An attempt was made to pull away and speed was increased. The object stayed in the same relative position apparently with no effort. Power was then reduced, and the object also slowed down. As far as could be judged, the object stayed approximately 300 yards behind the B-29. Its light appeared to be about the same size as a B-29 landing light."[414]

Each time General LeMay's Air Intelligence staff thought they had figured out the latest aerial phenomena, they would receive another report that didn't quite fit their explanations. It can be safely surmised that General LeMay had probably determined that the oddball phenomena represented something very simple: the sightings were nothing more than the enemy's futile attempt to harass his mighty Air Force.

In the meantime, with hostilities over in the European and Mediterranean theaters, there were plans for General Doolittle's Eighth Air Force to pack up and move to the Pacific. General Spaatz was also handing over Griggs and the Scientific Advisory Group within weeks. General Spaatz had already discussed with Bowles that he felt an Advisory Specialist Group attached to the Far East Forces was needed to support

General George C. Kenney's effort in the Pacific.[415]

Bowles agreed with Spaatz's idea and notified General Kenney, informing him that Griggs was the perfect choice. Bowles explained that Griggs "has been concerned with H2X, Shoran, and other types of bombing aids, including AI, and has been active in effecting the utilization of SCR-584 and MEW radars for control of fighter bombers. He represents a unique combination of technical ability with operational experience, is open-minded, imaginative, and dynamic, and is a pilot." Bowles pointed out that having Griggs as "principal advisor on radar" and maintaining "direct contact" with Bowles' office "on certain matters" afforded Kenney access to "many resources of personnel and facilities." Attached to the headquarters of the Southwest Pacific Area, Griggs was "to act as Advisory Specialist" on Kenney's staff.[416] General Kenney agreed.

Griggs finished up his work in Europe and was off to the Pacific theater. While there is no evidence to suggest that Griggs was to remain in contact with Bowles on "certain matters," it does, however, suggest the possibility that those "certain matters" were related to unconventional aircraft; Griggs' knowledge of the European foo fighter sightings was a valuable asset for any investigation being conducted by the Twentieth Air Force.

On the evening of May 14, 1945, a very important German mission was taking place beneath the waters of the Atlantic. Heading for Japan was one of ten German U-boats loaded with a large cache of war technology. The German submarine U-Boat 234 (U-234) was on its way through very hostile waters, hunted by a very aggressive and determined opponent. The Allied Naval Command had recently issued a warning that if all U-boats did not immediately surrender, they faced destruction at first sight.

At 2141 hours, the *USS Sutton*, an antisubmarine warfare (ASW) ship, received confirmation that U-234, under the command of Lt. Commander Johann Heinrich Fehler, was surrendering in the North Atlantic. The *USS Sutton* had captured a great trophy and it was escorting U-234 towards guarded waters along the east coast of the U.S. where the Coast Guard continued escorting it to the final destination of Portsmouth, New Hampshire on May 19.[417]

Preliminary examination of U-234's manifest revealed a gold mine. It was full of aviation-related items of prime importance to the AAF. On board were three completely disassembled aircraft: a Me-262, Me-163, and a Me-309 single-engine fighter. There was a "high-altitude pressure cabin for the proposed Henschel 130 stratospheric aircraft," an assortment of jet engines, and complete sets of blueprints and documents associated with all the above.[418]

U.S. personnel poured in for a chance to interrogate the U-234's unique and very valuable passengers.[419] There were nine Germans on board. At the top of the list was Air Force General Ulrich Kessler. The Japanese were waiting for him to "supervise" the incorporation of the German aircraft and anti-aircraft weapons into their own defenses. He was particularly well versed with fire control devices, anti-aircraft guided missiles, and remote control missiles.[420]

Kessler informed his interrogators that Japan was very interested in German jet-propelled fighters, but they had not received prior information about the Me-262. The Japanese had received plans for the Me-163 and by December 1943, they were conducting test flights with "production aircraft rather than a prototype glider." This shocked the ONI interrogators. If the Japanese were successful and had built a large Me-163 force, the B-29s were in for a rough time, and there would be little "hope of a quick ending to the war." Kessler's revelation destroyed the Allied assessment that Japan had failed in producing operable turbo-jet aircraft.[421]

Another passenger on the U-boat was Oberleutnant der Luftwaffe Erich Menzel, an air communications "specialist," who provided Tokyo's Military attaché technical aide.[422] Menzel had become an expert in many fields and contributed to "the development of new radar systems, bomb-sights, radar reconnaissance methods, and radio-controlled weapons."[423]

Then there were the men from Messerschmitt: August Bringewald and Franz Ruf. Bringewald was Willi Messerschmitt's "right hand man" and the Messerschmitt factory's top engineer. An "expert" on "airframes for jet and rocket propulsion," he was sent to get the Me-262 into mass production, and get the Me-163 program up and running. To compliment Bringewld's plans, Ruf, a "procurement specialist," was prepared to supervise the building of jet and rocket factories; and get tools and machinery in place for Japanese production.

But the passenger most important to Allied air intelligence was Luftwaffe Colonel Fritz von Sandrart. Formerly in charge the city of Bremen's anti-aircraft defenses, he was involved with the latest experimental anti-aircraft weaponry.[424] His background afforded him possible knowledge pertaining to the foo fighter mystery.[425]

On May 21, RAF Wing Commander H. Priestley sent the ONI a list of thirty questions for their interrogation team to ask the prisoners of war. Number twenty on the list addressed the balls of fire. Interrogating officer, Captain Halle asked Colonel Sandrart: "Allied air crew operating over

Germany late last year reported encountering colored balls of fire. What is the explanation of those balls of fire? Where they due to use of some secret German weapon? If so, what was that weapon and how successful was its use?"

According to Captain Halle's report: "P/W [Prisoner of War]asserts that the colored balls of fire encountered by air crews operating over Germany were only experimental weapons and later shelved as impractical in operation. It was a weapon used by the air force and not by the Anti-Aircraft units. Planes would climb far above the ceiling of enemy bombers and release a bomb with a time-fuse, which theoretically would detonate on the level of the attacking formation. The successes however placed the idea back into experimentation phase. The P/W is at loss to give any further information and suggests that technical people in the Luftwaffe and especially those familiar with experiments be approached."[426]

Though Colonel Sandrart's answer was helpful, it did not provide anything useful. He was describing another device, one not nearly as sophisticated as the foo fighters. Again, there was a problem with terminology. "Balls of Fire" was a term also used to describe flares, rockets, jet and rocket flames, meteors, stars, and a host of other ordnance devices. Colonel Sandrart was describing a weapon, not a phenomenal object that defied the latest aeronautical developments.

The Messerschmitt men, Bringewald and Ruf, were asked the same question. According to interrogators Lt. Abels and Lt. Youkstetter: "One of the informants saw the 'balls of fire' over Munich once and assumed that they were a new type of AA defense operating on an acoustical principal. No definite explanation of the phenomenon could be offered."[427]

The RAF's interrogation of U-234's passengers had revealed nothing further about the balls of fire, other than it was a mystery even to the Germans. It is unknown what questions U.S. Air Intelligence asked about the phenomenon as the days progressed.

Chapter Eighteen

The Secrets Flood In

Hitler was dead. The Nazis were no more. Germany belonged to the superpowers. For a brief moment, the Allied armies were comrades and friends, but the chill of a cold war quickly divided the people of the east and west. Before zones of occupation were enforced, the mad rush to exploit Germany continued with increased fervor. The hunt for Nazi weapons, scientists, technicians, facilities and documentation intensified day by day. The Allies understood it was a combination of time, expediency, and a little luck that stood between them and untold bounty.

Thanks to the plethora of Allied agendas, operations, and missions, answers for many questions were soon forthcoming. But Robertson's foo fighter investigation seemed a different story: answers for unconventional aircraft remained elusive. Finding a German solution to the problem certainly appeared doable, as Robertson had access to the wealth of Germany's aeronautical information.

Germany's advanced aircraft designs, secret weapons, facilities, and the men attached to them were extremely important to General Arnold's postwar air force. Since the summer of 1944, the Combined Intelligence Objectives Committee (CIOS) and the USSTAF's Air Technical Intelligence teams had captured much German technology to compliment Arnold's vision. One prize the United States had in custody was the architect of Germany's Luftwaffe: Reichmarschall Hermann Goering, who was very willing to talk.

For two hours on May 10, Goering sat before a group of his Allied peers. Anxious to question him at length, General Spaatz; General Vandenberg, Commanding General of the Ninth Air Force; Brigadier General Paul Barcus; Major Alexander de Serversky, a Special Consultant to Secretary of War; and Bruce Hopper, a historian for the USSTAF, were all ears. It should be noted that at least one member of this panel was associated with the foo fighter phenomenon: General Spaatz, whose USSATAF ATI intelligence men were sent to investigate foo fighter sightings reported by Major Harold Augspurger's 415th Night Fighter Squadron. Given the significance of foo fighter sightings over recent months, Goering was a prime source to ask about them.

General Spaatz asked Goering many questions that day, but one question was of particular significance to the foo fighter sightings. Spaatz asked Goering if he had the chance to go back in time and redesign the Luftwaffe, "what would be the first airplane" that he would develop? Goering replied: jet fighters and bombers, especially the Me-264, the bomber that was designed to fly to America and back. Goering further stated, "I might add that according to my view the future airplane is one without fuselage (flying wing) equipped with turbine in combination with the jet and propeller."[428]

Flying wing reports started coming to General Arnold's attention during the summer of 1944. When General Arnold asked Von Karman to come on board to help with his futuristic American Air Force project, Arnold wanted to know if pilot-less, remote-controlled rockets, using television or radar as a guidance system was possible.[429] Robertson probably suspected these types of aircraft accounted for many foo fighter sightings, but they certainly did not account for sightings like those of Sergeant Cockcroft, Lt. Sabinski, or Captain Leet.

The capture of Lippisch and his Delta designs were very important. Also eagerly sought were two other Germans associated with wingless aircraft designs: Walter and Reimar Horten.

On April 7, the Horten Brothers were arrested by U.S. troops near Gottingen, Germany. They were among the Luftwaffe's best aviation experts.[430] On May 19, General Spaatz received word that General Arnold wanted "immediate shipment" of "complete specifications, data photographs, and blue prints on Horten flying wing and equipment" sent to the Assistant Chief of Air Staff Intelligence.[431]

Another shining moment came on April 22. An ATI team, led by Colonel Donald Putt,[432] stood at the edge of a small forest called Volkenrode, just on the outskirts of Braunschweig.[433] Hidden among the trees were dozens of buildings spread around the landscape, masterfully camouflaged. Putt was amazed. He realized there was something very important about the place: it was home to seven wind tunnels of various sizes.[434]

Colonel Putt knew the facility required General Arnold's main investigative team's attention. Putt contacted Von Karman, who upon arrival "was impressed." In fact, in a letter to General Arnold, Von Karman wrote: "...probably 75 to 90 percent of the technical aeronautical information in Germany was available at this establishment and that information on research and development, which had not been previously investigated in the United States, would require approximately two years to accomplish in the United States with the facilities found there. This also included jet engine research that was determined ahead of the US program by 'six to nine months.'"[435]

General Spaatz's special project was now up and running. The new ATI teams that had been organized in recent months worked under the codename of Operation LUSTY (Luftwaffe Science and Technology, also referred to as Luftwaffe Secret Technology), which was commanded by Colonel Harold Watson. LUSTY's first priority was determining how much intelligence Germany had shared with the Japanese.[436] The second priority was the collection of enemy equipment and documentation. For the second stage, Colonel Watson handpicked a team to quickly locate and fly the Me-262 and other aircraft into U.S. hands.[437] His band of pilots, engineers, and field crew were called "Watson's Whizzers," an appropriate name for those "whizzing" around the sky.[438]

By May, the British AI2(g) and headquarters of AAF Intelligence in Washington released brief information about the capture of the Horten Brothers and their "flying wing" aircraft. The British report specifically referenced HO-9, offering technical information about its design and alleged ability to reach 550 mph at 20,000 to 25,000 feet.[439]

The Allies recovered tons of German documents; if there was any documentation remotely associated with the foo fighters, it should have appeared in these recovered documents. CIOS was responsible for locating some of the most important caches of Germany aeronautical research and development. They had recovered the German Luftwaffe Archives. Immense in scope, they offered a tremendous amount of material relevant to operations but also included "copious details on designs and production of aircraft weapons."

Near Gotha, "a cache of approximately five tons of Top Secret Documents, covering the entire field of German arms development and industrial mobilization for war" were located in a salt mine. Fortunately, they were recovered from Nazi SS soldiers in the process of destroying them. Another incredible discovery of documentation was found in an abandoned mineshaft where the 250,000 volumes of the German Patent Office were hidden.

The Herman Goering Institute at Braunschweig "provided access to a great concentration of research and development on advanced German jet propulsion, aero-dynamics and long-range guided missiles." CIOS considered the Goering Institute to be Germany's equivalent of America's Wright Field or Britain's Royal Aircraft Establishment (RAE) facilities. Many more months were required to fully exploit the institute. The

American and British scientists were hard at work conducting their on-site investigation; they had no doubt "new information concerning advanced aviation, rocket and jet fuels" was at their fingertips.

CIOS's single most important "target" was the former minister of German Armaments and War Production, Albert Speer. A second personality of great value was Professor Werner Osenberg, head of the Reich Research Council's Planning Board. The capture of Osenberg and staff was most fortunate for the Allies, as they were able to provide a complete scientific and technological picture of war-time Germany. Documents found in their possession afforded CIOS "a list of 15,000 of the leading German technicians, together with information concerning armament developments in which they were engaged." The "list" was priceless in its value to assist interrogators during their investigations of Germany's armament and weapon advances. The recovered documents also covered Germany's entire guided missiles program.[440]

Osenberg was also leader of the Defense Research Council under Goering's command. When a new weapon went from the research phase to the first prototype phase, it was then transferred administratively to Albert Speer's office.[441]

The unexpected discovery of Mittelwerke, an immense underground facility located at Ilfeld, north of Nordhausen and south of the Harz Mountains, was made by the lead elements of the U.S. Third Armored Division during their push into Germany. They soon realized they were standing in Germany's V weapons factory.[442] Mittelwerke was the "final assembly" facility for the V-1 and V-2. Other production taking place included other rocket weapons and jet engines for the Me-262. The Americans were now mainly concerned with locating the Mittelwerke documentation because the facility also controlled and directed all aspects of Germany rocketry.[443]

As Mittelwerke was scoured by scores of Allied scientists and intelligence personnel, active interrogations of Germany's leading scientists and technical experts took place. They included Wernher Von Braun and his rocket team, who had surrendered and were now at Camp Dustbin. Arriving at Nordhausen was another important prisoner, Walther Riedel, who was "Chief of the rocket motor and structural design section" at Peenumunde. Interestingly, as his interrogation unfolded, interrogators learned more about what truly interested many of Germany's rocket scientists. Riedel said that the scientists wanted to build "passenger-carrying rockets, trips to space stations revolving about the earth as satellites, space mirrors which could be used for good and possibly evil, short trips around the moon, and daring explorations of space."

Flying in on May 18, SIAS men Fraenckel and Robertson arrived at Nordhausen to pick up Riedel and other scientists and take them back to Camp Dustbin for interrogation. Major Staver, who was conducting his own interrogations, said that it was a poor idea to interrupt an investigation already in progress. Robertson agreed. Aside from picking up the prisoners, Robertson was also interested in the whereabouts of the Peenumunde documentation. He checked his notebook and offered Major Staver a lead.[444] According to an interrogation of prisoner of war Major V. Ploetz, General Dornberger had provided information as to the whereabouts of the V weapon production documents; they were "walled into a mine shaft in Maliwark at Bleicherode."[445]

The Peenumunde documents were found, but only some were located in Bleicherode. The main lot of the documentation was hidden in the town of Dornten. Dynamite blasts had sealed them behind stone rubble, securing them from easy discovery. Around the clock, the Americans dug out the debris to retrieve the most important documents in Germany, all fourteen tons of them.[446]

By May 25, Director Georg Rickhey and the cases of documentation were on a C-47 heading to General Spaatz's Headquarters. Waiting for their arrival, General Spaatz and the Assistant Secretary of War for Air, Robert A. Lovett, were in a conference discussing the nature of the Mittelwerke discovery. According to Colonel Beasley, Rickhey held more secrets about the cave. There was no time on the first visit to search them fully, but the Americans knew they were missing the microfilm containing all of Mittelwerke's documents. Further interrogation of Rickhey was needed.[447]

Other CIOS discovered documentation relevant to the foo fighter investigation surrounds radar and electronics. Specifically known as the "Schornsteinferger" Project, the documentation contained "radar camouflage and the development of materials absorbing electromagnetic and supersonic waves" and revealed Germany's progress regarding "complete anti-radar coverage of submarines and other equipment."[448] The Schornsteinferger Project documentation possibly contained information accounting for why the American night fighter units had such difficulty picking foo fighters up on ground control or air intercept radar, if indeed foo fighters were of German origin.

The discovery of anything anti-radar was undoubtedly revealed to Bowles, Griggs, Alvarez, Jones, and Robertson. Again, if Germany was indeed operationally utilizing such technology, some aspects of the foo fighters, such as their design, flight capabilities, and propulsion system, were still unexplainable.

The American Air Intelligence teams' investigation of Nordhausen, Dornten, Bleicherode, Volkenrode, and Kochel were goldmines of information that held answers to the question: Was Germany responsible for the unconventional aircraft? Unless operational unconventional aircraft were actually located, the documentation would hold the answer. But there is an even more relevant question: Has all this recovered documentation been disseminated to the public?

By the end of May, Robertson had become chief of the Field Intelligence Agency, Technical (FIAT). Established at SHAEF headquarters, FIAT's purpose was to "Coordinate, integrate, and direct the activities of the various missions and agencies interested in examining, appraising, and exploiting all information pertaining to German economy other than direct military intelligence."

FIAT provided "centralized information services and facilities covering this technical intelligence field," and established and governed "the collection of technical, especially scientific, and industrial information." The agency oversaw and controlled the "disposition of personnel, documents, equipment, and installations of primary value."[449]

Robertson had complete authority over where he sent his personnel, as long as the area was within General Eisenhower's jurisdiction.[450] His chances of finding answers to the foo fighter mystery increased exponentially. But so far, enemy technology had revealed nothing to account for the astounding sightings. So far, no evidence had surfaced to confirm that the foo fighters were German technology. The foo fighters and other unconventional objects remained a mystery.

Chapter Nineteen

Multiple Choice

On May 21, 1945, the U.S. Ninth Air Force reprinted the XXI Bomber Command's "Air Intelligence Report" regarding the Twentieth Air Force's encounters with balls of fire over the Pacific. Concern among U.S. air intelligence was spreading fast. Airmen braced themselves for the unexpected. Danger lurked in the night sky. There was no doubt that Japan had faith in their "rosy dream of secret weapons." Despite the multitude of ordnance and weaponry thrown at the U.S. bombers, they remained relentless and the bombing missions intensified.[451]

General LeMay's bombers were busy unleashing a terrible firestorm against targets in the heart of Japan: Tokyo. Throwing a one-two punch, the B-29s roared overhead and released their incendiaries on two separate nights. The first mission (181) struck on May 24, and the second, mission (183) hit its mark on May 26.[452]

On both nights, as expected, enemy resistance was fierce. Within days, the Twentieth Air Force's commander had received a report detailing the balls of fire and Bakas seen during the missions. Strangely enough, comments by LeMay's Air Intelligence revealed they were still confused by the variety of sightings: "Some Balls of Fire, (Flares?), hang in the air, stationary over the target area for several minutes. Others appear to move about; some have been seen to crash and explode on the ground: others, (Rockets?), seem to follow the B-29's."

The XXI Bomber Command Air Intelligence staff divided the balls of fire and Baka sightings into three tentative categories: (1) "Illuminating Flares," a ground-launched device that hung and floated in the air, and used to illuminate the sky and the aircraft;(2) "Rocket Projectiles," a ground or air-launched weapon that was "probably electrically controlled" and designed to shoot B-29s out of the sky; and (3) "Midget Aircraft. Jet-propelled. Ground launched or launched from a mother aircraft. Piloted controlled (Baka) or electronically or sonically controlled War Head; possibly self-destroying mechanism."[453]

The XXI Bomber Command's messages to Washington represented a solid attempt by their Air Intelligence staff to identify the aerial encounters. The "classification" system allowed Air Intelligence to handle the constant influx of varied reports.

With the war in Europe over, much needed supplies, equipment, and personnel were heading to the Pacific Theater of Operations. AAF Captain Sewell, who had had an unconventional aircraft sighting on April 7, was about to encounter another. On May 25, Sewell was part of a Transport Squadron that was using B-17s for ferrying troops from the European theater to the Pacific. He was in flight from Port Lyautey, Morocco to Dakar, Senegal during the early morning. From the cockpit, Captain Sewell and several others first noticed an object between five and ten miles away, flying, and sometimes hovering. Opposite the sun, its finish, "shiny 'like aluminum,'" bounced the sun's rays, revealing its "elliptical or disc" shape. Over the course of eight hours, "they saw it 6 or 7 times through the clouds."[454]

By the end of May, observations of jet-propelled aircraft were reported all over the Pacific. Intensifying the problem was the discovery of a German and Japan exchange program regarding jet aircraft. The B-29s were vulnerable. There was no way to avoid it. Washington was worried.

On June 8, General Kenney authorized the release of a memorandum to all commanders and units, including group levels, of the Far East Air Force: "Effective at once there will be attached to the FEAF Headquarters Dr. David T. Griggs, Dr. Thomas A. Murrell, and Dr. E.G. Schneider, civilian specialists on radar and related electronic equipment and techniques." Kenney's memo further stated that "the services of these men have been placed at the disposal of the Far East Air Forces through the cooperation of Dr. Edward Bowles, Expert Consultant to the Secretary of War and Special Consultant to the Commanding General, Army Air Forces." General Kenney expected all units to assist in educating the Advisory Specialist Group by providing them with firsthand knowledge of problems.[455]

As the top advisory specialist to the FEAF's General Kenney, Griggs was most likely briefed on the variety of aerial sightings, including the balls of fire and the "circle of light." His familiarity with the European foo fighter sightings enabled him to draw information from many reports, helping in determining if the Pacific and European balls of fire sightings were the same type of object.

"Combat crews should make every effort to obtain detailed data on any unusual sightings and report them accurately to their S-2s," stated Air Intelligence of the XXI Bomber Command in their June 9 Air Intelligence

Report. "The value of such information cannot be stressed too highly, for all knowledge of the enemy gradually fits into the big picture." In light of all the new aircraft the Japanese were introducing into combat, it was important to stress upon the bomber and fighter crews that no detail was too little, especially since another "one-way" plane was apparently on the scene.

Newly acquired information indicated the Baka had a big brother: Suzuka 24. Based on a reliable prisoner of war interrogation, Suzuka 24 was ground launched and resembled a Baka, but had a larger wingspan. Air Intelligence officers suggested a propulsion system similar to the German Me-163; possibly explaining some of the "so-called balls of fire" sightings. Allegedly, the Suzuka was capable of forty-to-sixty minute flights, explaining why the Baka, primarily an anti-shipping weapon with short range and lack of maneuverability, was not responsible for following B-29s for such extended amounts of time.

Meanwhile, General LeMay's Air Intelligence staff offered their best opinion regarding the "circles of light" sightings over Truk Island. "'Light' Follows B-24s From Truk" headlined the article, which included details from the May 8 Pacific Ocean Areas memo, "Planes or Stars??" But this new article provided details of their conjecture. In Washington, the office of the Assistant Chief of the Air Staff, Intelligence (A-2) had looked into the sighting. Washington Air Staff had reason to believe that stars were not the answer.

Their evaluation stated: "Few of the characteristics of this air phenomenon as reported relate to those other 'Balls of Fire' sightings recently reported over the Japanese homeland. This observation is similar in degree only to but two of more than 50 such sightings.

"It is probable the lights observed are those of an unknown type carried on a Japanese aircraft possessing flight capabilities of the Irving, engaged on an experimental, diversionary, or observation mission.

"It is possible, but highly improbable the lights were from a jet type aircraft because the duration of flight greatly exceeds the known capabilities of any enemy or friendly jet aircraft."

According to their analysis: "The action of the lights indicate [sic] that there was intelligence within the object. Therefore, it was a type of aircraft that could carry a man. Because visual contact was not possible throughout the flight, some form of airborne radar was used, permitting tactics as reported."

The report suggested that the object was a Japanese aircraft, possessing similar flight characteristics to the Irving, which has a 1300-mile flight range, and that it was possibly conducting an experimental, diversionary, or observational flight. Truk Island was known to have underground hangers and facilities, and was well established as a Japanese base for some time. Air Intelligence knew the Irving aircraft was formerly stationed on Truk Island in the past. The overall lack of aircraft available to the Japanese Air Force was considered the reason why the "Circles of Light" did not approach the B-24s.

They proposed that due to the scarcity of enemy aircraft the enemy was conducting an experiment, possibly "for unknown uses of the light phenomenon or for airborne radar," and "the approach to the Guam base without attack might be a diversionary tactic to be followed by a closing movement in a similar operation in the future. Such maneuvers were employed by the Germans."

Evidence also suggests that the Japanese were using airborne radar, permitting their aircraft to track the B-24 as indicated in the crew's mission report. Another possible Japanese tactic mentioned the use of aerial searchlights. "The light phenomenon could have been this or lights of other types mounted on the aircraft. The changes in color could have been aided by atmospheric conditions."

Though the "size and appearance of the light phenomenon" suggested that the aircraft used jet propulsion, this was ruled out. "Inasmuch as the known capabilities of both enemy and friendly jet type aircraft do not exceed a flight time of approximately three hours it is regarded as highly improbable that this was a jet type plane. Assuming the plane was to return to base the elapsed time of flight would be approximately six hours."

LeMay's A-2 staff thought it "was possible, but not probable" that the lack of radar return may have been associated with recent information regarding Germany's "Schnorkel" [sic] submarine program, which had to do with using paint as a radar deterrent.[456]

Here again, LeMay's A-2 staff provided logical and conventional explanations, but it was still little more than educated guesswork. The "Circle of Lights" sighting was observed over a fairly long period of time. In defense of the B-24 radar operator, and the ground radar operators on Guam, it seems doubtful that both operators failed to detect the alleged Japanese aircraft, especially over such a long period of time; these men were able to focus their attention on the sighting without the stress of combat engagement.

It is hard to believe, as the report suggests, that the B-24 radar operator was an "un-alerted" observer, especially as the lights represented a possible threat. Furthermore, it was a clear day over Guam. It seems reasonable to suggest that the same kind of atmospheric/celestial misidentification had occurred on prior occasions and reported, however, this was not the case. The fact that Guam was a key U.S. base suggests the island was well protected. So, it is likely the radar operators were alert; there was no excuse for the base defenses to suffer a sneak attack by Japanese Kamikazes.

On June 18, 1945, the XXI Bomber Command conducted a night raid against urban targets on the main Japanese islands of Kyushu and Honshu. Many enemy encounters kept the bomber crews busy; they were becoming seasoned observers able to distinguish various Japanese ordnance and weaponry easily. But some things were difficult to identify. One crew reported that a ball of fire paced their B-29, flying parallel for about one minute, before it aborted its pursuit and "disappeared."

It was reminiscent of the Truk Island "circles of light" phenomenon: "One crew observed a fluctuating light, round in shape that changed alternately from bright red to dim orange. The light was first observed near land's end and it trailed the aircraft for a considerable distance (the crew was unable to estimate the distance, but apparently it was over a mile). The object trailed for approximately 42 minutes out to sea, or roughly 125 miles. The crew was of the opinion that the object gained a half-mile during this period. At no time was a wing or fuselage observed in connection with the light. The object finally faded out. Two other crews from the same group made similar observations on leaving the target but, after some time, concluded that the object was a star. The crew making the first report felt very strongly that what they had seen was not a star."[457]

Within twenty-four hours, the XXI Bomber Command's B-29s were back in action. The bombers were heading for three targets: the urban areas of Toyohashi, Fukuoka, and Shizuoka. During the mission, B-29 crews reported a variety of aerial phenomena: "One B-29 was followed by a strong white light after bombs away. This light never closed, nor fell back, even when the B-29 increased its speed. The enemy plane was finally lost in a cloud. The crew reporting they believed the plane was a night fighter."

Flying over Fukuoka, a B-29 crew observed "one bright 'ball of fire'" approaching at a very high speed. The B-29's pilot immediately took evasive action while the machine gunners fired away. The gunners missed, or they hit it with no apparent results. The ball of fire was right on top of them, just fifty yards away, passing right under the bomber. The crew saw no fuselage or any wings as it passed under the B-29 and disappeared.[458]

By the middle of June, unit S-2s interrogating returning crews were still faced with the somewhat overwhelming problem of accurate identification.

Aerial sightings were difficult to translate into reports for higher command levels to ascertain exactly what was encountered. The sighting reports included too many words describing the objects: lights, aircraft, enemy fighters, objects, Balls of Fire, Bakas, Vipers, rockets, flares, and "glows." These different descriptions kept the exact nature of each sighting open to debate.

Further complicating matters was the use by the crews and S-2s of uncertain phrases regarding sightings: "believed to be," "it was possible," "was of the opinion," "was probable," and "may possibly be." Despite the confusion, the U.S. Pacific Air Forces kept Air Staff in Washington busy with a constant flow of updated reports. All the A-2 staff was capable of doing was collect, collate, and file reports, while their analysis and evaluations filled in the gaps until verifiable proof was available.

Chapter Twenty

The Skies Stay Busy

The Navy's Technical Air Intelligence Center (TAIC) was concerned by the threat posed by the Japanese use of German technology. On July 1, they released a report, "Possible Japanese Jet and Rocket Development," that covered six items: Piloted V-1s; Version of Me-163; Ground Launched Anti-Aircraft Rocket; Air or Ground Launched Guided missiles, specific to the German X-4, Hs-117, Hs-293, Hs-294, and Hs-298 series of weapons; Rocket Firing Aircraft; and the "BAKA." It is important to note that TAIC's report listed all of these separate items under the single heading of "Balls of Fire."

According to the report: "Data on this phenomenon is still conflicting and descriptive details are at such variance, that it is not possible to single out any specific missile or aircraft to fit all cases. A wealth of German experimental and production information has been given to the Japanese in minute detail and there is strong evidence that versions of the Me-163, piloted V-1, and some ground launched projectiles may be in limited production."

Under the "Ground Launched Anti Aircraft Rockets" section of the briefing, TAIC stated: "Colored balls of fire were reported by the Allied air crews over Germany in 1944; no satisfactory explanation has yet been received from German sources except that they may have been either antiaircraft rockets designed to operate automatically when approaching a bomber formation, or possibly air launched Hs-293s. A further possibility for some of the 'slow and hovering' balls of fire is a ground rocket that may contain an illuminating and/or an incendiary agent that drifts downward on a parachute."[459]

TAIC's statement about Allied aircrews observing balls of fire over Germany in late 1944 mirrors question number 20 from the list of questions the RAF had ONI interrogators ask of the German U-234's passengers. Again, TAIC's report was another example of the use of "balls of fire" as nothing more than a label, or heading, a catch-all for the various types of objects sighted.

As the TAIC report made its rounds, LeMay's bombers roared in for another concentrated attack against four urban areas on the islands of Honshu and Kyushu in the early morning hours of July 2. The XXI Bomber Command's four Combat Wings were delivering another hellish incendiary firestorm.

After bombing their target, one bomber crew about twenty minutes from the coastline and flying at 15,000 feet reported that they noticed "two balls of fire" that were "below and on either side of the aircraft." They "were much larger than supercharger glow, but of somewhat the same color," and "did considerable maneuvering, fading away to a bare glow for almost a minute and then coming on brightly for 30 to 40 seconds." The B-29 crew held their fire, and upon reaching the coast, the balls of fire "disappeared" from view.[460]

No statements in the Tactical Mission Report indicated whether the unknown "aircraft" were single or twin engine craft, if they were picked up on radar, or if the B-29 crew assumed they were Japanese aircraft.

Meanwhile Naval Intelligence was dealing with the phenomenon of strange radar returns being reported by U.S. ships in the Pacific. Prepared for the worst, time and time again, the ships stood ready for action. Many were unnerved, thinking they were under attack by an on-coming group of enemy aircraft. After the tense moments were called off, they would realize there was no enemy.

On July 6, the U.S. Navy released an Air Operations Memorandum. A very small mention made under the heading of "Radar Decoy" noted that on May 22 the *USS Twining* "recovered a radar decoy balloon about eight feet in diameter from which was suspended a light wooden frame covered with tinfoil-coated paper." The U.S. Navy's Air Technical Intelligence Group felt that some of the "false echo" phenomena of recent operations were caused by decoys launched from the Nansei Shoto islands.[461] This was the latest in a series of articles written by the Navy about the mysterious pips, spooks, echoes, phantoms, and ghosts that radar operators on U.S. ships were witnessing for several months near Nansei Shoto and other areas.

According to the command of the *USS Independence*, strange radar returns were generally encountered at night; they "usually moved on a very definite course (very often northwesterly) at speeds running 25 to 60 knots," but usually between 40 and 45 knots. Aircraft and destroyers sent on patrol to find the culprits were never able to find anything, even though the "ghosts" would on occasion "merge with ships." The radar "ghosts" were usually detected about twenty-five to thirty miles away. Sometimes they faded out, only to reappear as "suddenly" as they had vanished. Sometimes it was possible to track the pip or ghost "into the sea return and out again on the other side."

According to the *Independence*'s report: "These echoes were seldom picked up on the SG, and never on the SK, and elevating the SM antennae to a point where the pip from a surface vessel would disappear had no effect on the phantom echo. The altitude of such contacts usually read 1500 feet (as in the case of legitimate surface contact), but occasionally as high as 3500. The appearance of the pip in the "R" scope was perfectly conventional at long ranges, and it was only when the 'ghost' had closed to ten or fifteen miles that the operator could tell the difference. Even then, it took an experienced operator to recognize the slight difference in the pip from one caused by a ship. The main recognition of these 'ghost' tracks has been their speed."[462]

Both the *USS Audubon* and the *USS Lewis Hancock* had encounters with the "Galloping Ghost of Nansei Shoto." It was April 24 when the *Audubon* was shaken from its calm at sea. Radar operators had picked up "unidentified aeroplanes" heading their way. A general alarm was sounded. All hands reported to their stations. The ship's radar showed a pip "some eight miles away moving down the starboard side" at twenty knots. It was "fuzzy" then "strong." The lookouts saw nothing on the horizon coming their way. On the screen, it was getting closer at a range of five miles. The radar operator determined that no aeroplane was heading their way. In his opinion, if it was anything, it was a flock of birds, possibly pelicans.

Though no one actually saw the birds, the radar operator's gut instinct was right on target. Previously, on April 22, when the *USS Hancock* was northeast of Okinawa, the SG radar picked up an unidentified target at six miles, confirming a "low flying air target" was heading their way. The target was moving between 60 and 100 knots, and it gave "a pip like a battleship." The target's movements were "erratic" and resembled those of similar events during the previous months. Two miles out and approaching, the target was observed: "a tight formation of more than fifty birds, of unknown species." According to the Navy's Combat Information Center (CIC): "No such groups of birds had previously been observed in this area, but so similar to the Nansei Shoto Ghost were the radar indications produced that it is believed many previously reported phantoms may be of the same feather. On three occasions since then, this vessel has undergone the same experience."[463]

Whether Navy Intelligence determined the strange radar returns were fish, fowl, weather, or radar decoys, the ghosts of Nansei Shoto were something more than wildlife to one combat information officer aboard a U.S. aircraft carrier; the witness chose not to disclose the name of his ship.

It happened during the summer of 1945. Combat Information Center officer James Dawson was responsible for directing fighter aircraft on task force defense and tactical missions and was the main source of information to the ship's commander.

Dawson's ship was part of a task force streaming along the string of islands known as the Nansei Shoto Archipelago. It was their mission to guard the American troops on Okinawa as they dodged Kamikazes and floating mines. The weather was great that day. Visibility was fifty miles. At that moment, the other intercept officer asked Dawson if he knew what the very large plot was that the radar operator just reported. According to the radar operator, it looked like "200-300" unidentified aircraft. The men were staring at a possible massive Japanese force. Dawson was worried and called for a fighter to get a look at the oncoming mass.

Things got worse when he realized the impossible was happening. The mass was traveling nearly 700 mph at 12,000 feet. Two U.S. fighters approached. The general alarm was sounded. The ship's crew ran to their battle stations and the pilots ran to their planes. Dawson was sure an enemy attack was imminent. Dawson waited to hear what the lone fighters had to report. The radar showed the mass at 65 miles and beginning to break up into "tentacles," heading right and left. Dawson recognized it as an old Japanese tactic; to him, this meant a Japanese aircraft carrier was in the area supporting dive-bombers, high altitude bombers, and torpedoes that were heading towards his ship

Dawson was confused. According to intelligence, there were no reported Japanese aircraft carriers in operation. It did not matter; this was a Japanese attack reminiscent of the battle of Midway. The two U.S. fighters got closer to the target and then merged into one big blob. Dawson and the others held their breath. They waited for a word from the pilots, but nothing came. The radarscope showed the tentacles of the massive blob starting to pass around the ship.

Then the loudspeaker broke the tension. Word came from the fighters that they had "nothing in sight." Everyone in the control room was dumbfounded. The radar screen showed the tentacles completely encircling the ship in a ring. On deck, there was nothing in sight. "What the hell's going on down there?" shouted the Captain through the speaker. He thought Dawson was "crazy." But too many people saw the event on the radar screen to do anything but ask questions. The nerve-racking experience was over.

In its aftermath, Dawson said that the technical officers who witnessed the radar ghost offered "vague speculations," claiming it was due to "faults in the radar gear, emanations from other ships, and enemy countermeasures." Dawson said there were "mutterings about a Doppler effect which even we knew was nonsense. We looked at them coldly, and they dropped their eyes. They had no name for this enemy."[464]

Dawson's account was far more eventful than those reported by the *USS Audubon* or *Hancock*. The speed of the approaching mass and its mimicking of known Japanese tactics is suspect. If this event was a countermeasure, it was very sophisticated and effective. His superior officers refused to entertain that idea for one minute, blaming the radar instead. Dawson's experience that day, and how it affected those around him, left an indelible mark upon his memory. He was convinced that what he and the crew witnessed was not a radar malfunction, but something else.

The U.S. Office of Naval Intelligence offered no explanations for the radar ghosts, only educated guesses and conjecture. The "Ghosts of Nansei Shoto" remained unknown.

On July 7/8, there were no radar ghosts seen during a bombing mission against targets in the Japanese city of Sasebo. [465] Eighteen B-29 bombers were part of raids conducted against Nagasaki, Omura, and Yawata. One lone B-29 crew encountered an object reminiscent of Lt. Roman Sabinski's June 1942 encounter.

"We were flying at approx. 9000 feet," said the B-29's flight engineer, "when the 'Foo' appeared to join us and 'fly formation' abeam our left horizontal stabilizer. Our rear gunners reported it first. It followed us for many miles. Our airplane Commander (AC) ordered a burst of gunfire after we were sure it was not another B-29. (This was a single sortie bomber stream type of mission.) The tracers were seen to appear to hit the blob of light but nothing happened. Sometime later, the Foo broke formation, swooped under the B-29, and vanished in the distance at approx. the 2 o'clock position which is where I was able to observe it from my position on the right side of the nose section…

"It was impossible to accurately estimate the distance separating the Foo and our airplane as there was nothing to compare [it to] within the dark night sky. It was a big ball of fuzzy orange-red light and nothing more." Later that morning he and his crew were debriefed and their report was taken by the unit's intelligence officer. Interestingly, soon thereafter, the flight engineer and the rest of his crew were assigned to a "rest camp at Hickam Field, Oahu, Hawaii." The flight engineer always wondered if their rest camp excursion was "coincidence or war nerves."[466]

On the night of July 12/13, the XXI Bomber Command instructed five combat wings to conduct a precision radar attack against urban area targets in four cities on the island of Honshu. Enemy fighter opposition was negligible. No Bakas or balls of fire observed, but near the city of Kawasaki, one B-29 crew encountered a "light Phenomenon." According to the report, the B-29 crew said they saw a single "enemy aircraft" flying at 16,000 feet, and it "appeared to have a large orange light traveling" with it "at the same speed." The crew was unable to determine "whether the orange light was on the aircraft or was parallel to it."[467]

This report may be the first official documentation of a Foo fighter observed pacing an enemy aircraft. Unfortunately, the report offered no further details. The "large orange light" was very similar to those often described as amber colored lights seen in the European theater.

There was one person working in the Pacific theater who must have recognized the similarities between the Truk Island "circle of lights," the RAF's "balls of fire," and AAF's foo fighters, and that was David Griggs. Since June 8, Griggs was the head of General Kenney's Advisory Specialist Group and was aware of all the aerial phenomena encountered over the Pacific. The Truk Atoll "circles of light" sighting must have interested him as it was a radar related sighting. The lack of radar with these objects was an operational issue of the utmost importance, affecting the safety of General Kenney's Air Forces. Reports displaying negative radar results from ground and air units needed immediate attention.

Everywhere Griggs visited, he heard about the balls of fire encounters. He wanted to see one first hand, so he tagged along on a mission specifically for that purpose. At one point during his investigation (exact date unknown), Griggs decided to accompany a crew during a raid. He conducted a pre-mission inquiry with the B-29 crew for a considerable amount of time. The crew had seen many balls of fire and they were eager to have Griggs aboard. The crew told Griggs about one instance where they shot at one. He listened but was unable to give the crew a solid answer. He knew they were describing something real.

Once Griggs and the crew were airborne, they watched the sky carefully as the B-29 approached the Japanese coastline. They were coming in west of Tokyo, flying at 15,000 feet, preparing for their incendiary raid. Climbing up to the top astrodome canopy, Griggs manned the navigator's spot, giving him a clear and unobstructed 360-degree view. Suddenly, Griggs heard the waist gunner yell through his headset, "Fireball coming in!" Sure enough, there was something there. Griggs saw the object. Unfortunately, it was not coming towards them. The men were so anxious to prove what they had seen in the past that they had misidentified the moon rising in the night sky. Griggs knew that all the sightings were not the moon or some other kind of false alarm. He understood the crew's eagerness to show him just how strange the balls of fire really were.[468]

While Griggs was accumulating sighting information about the Pacific balls of fire, back on the U.S. mainland a far more incredible sighting occurred during the middle of July. Navy pilot Roland D. Powell and five other pilots observed something that surely would have astounded Griggs.

Stationed at the Naval Air Station, Pasco, Washington, pilot Powell was part of a new air group formed to prepare for future aircraft carrier operations in the Pacific. Flying F6F "Hellcats," the new group was stationed only sixty miles away from the Hanford Atomic Reactor plant. Unknown to the pilots were Hanford's activities regarding the Top Secret atomic bomb project. All they knew is that this was a location they were to guard at all costs against possible enemy attack.

That day, shortly after the alarm sounded, Powell and five other "Hellcat" pilots were airborne. They were briefed that "radar had detected a fast-moving object," now sitting motionless over the Hanford facility. Arriving in the area around noon under a beautiful clear sky, the pilots had no visual on the object until they climbed to a much higher altitude. Then they saw the unidentifiable object. It was "very bright and had a "saucer-like appearance." One pilot yelled over the radio, "What the hell is that?"

None of the pilots had ever seen anything like it. The object, according to Roland, was "the size of three aircraft carriers side by side, oval shaped, very streamlined like a stretched-out egg and pinkish in color." He further stated "that some kind of vapor was being emitted around the outside edges from the portholes or vents," and "the vapor was being discharged to form a cloud for disguise."

They placed a radio call to base for further instructions since they were already getting close to the peak performance altitude of their aircraft, 37,000 feet. Ordered to keep pursuing the object at the expense of the aircraft's engines, they pushed their "Hellcats" to 42,000 feet. It did not matter because the object was hovering at an estimated altitude of 65,000 feet. The object remained for another twenty minutes, "hovering in a fixed position," and then went "straight-up" and "disappeared." The "Hellcats" returned to base. The unconventional aircraft was apparently unconcerned with their presence. But unconcerned is one word the Pasco Naval Air Station did not have in its vocabulary.[469]

Another summer of 1945 sighting occurred over the Pacific near the Aleutian Island of Adak. On the way back to Seattle, Washington, the U.S. Army Transport *Delarof* was most likely returning from dropping munitions and supplies off at Adak. The trip home was quite a remarkable experience and not because of a Japanese submarine. Around sunset, fourteen men were going about their duties. Suddenly, crewman Robert S. Crawford "heard shouts from some of the crew." Several men had observed something about one mile away rise out of the water. Turning to look, Crawford "saw a large round object which had just emerged from the sea."

The object, about 150 to 250 feet in diameter, "climbed almost straight up for a few moments, then it arced into level flight, and began to circle the ship. All observers were convinced it was large object." Silently, it "circled the ship two to three times." The gunners watched it cautiously, holding their fire since the object showed no hostility towards the ship. After a couple minutes, it departed towards the south and disappeared. Looking in that direction, the crew "saw three flashes of light from the area where it had vanished."

For the remainder of their journey home, *Delarof*'s captain ensured that security precautions were taken, posting extra watch in case other objects were encountered. Upon arriving back at Seattle, fourteen witnesses signed a written summary of the account.[470]

The month of August 1945 began with another unusual sighting. At the time, the Japanese islands were a scene of constant air and sea bombardments. On Okinawa, Captain William A. Mandel commanded a small military outpost. Captain Mandel's training was mainly in antiaircraft. He was well versed in aircraft recognition, both Japanese and American. The weather was clear that day. Standing on a cliff, high above the beach, Mandel caught a glimpse of an aircraft as it approached along the island's coast. At first, he thought it was a "Navy Corsair returning to Kadena Airfield before sundown, as was custom." The aircraft was only a "few hundred feet higher" than his position. But as he continued watching, thoughts of a Japanese Zero crossed his mind.

According to Captain Mandel, the object "was cigar-shaped, metallic and without markings or visible openings of any kind except at the after end." He estimated its length was about thirty-five to fifty feet as it passed him no more than a couple hundred feet away. Mandel realized it was not a U.S. Corsair or Japanese Zero. He noticed its speed remained constant, barely breaking one hundred miles per hour. There was no noticeable change in its altitude or direction. After the cigar-shaped object passed him, it traveled along the coastline and "followed the coastline, eventually disappearing in the direction opposite to its appearance."

The sighting had so mesmerized Captain Mandel that it never crossed his mind to retrieve a pair of field glasses or camera; he just stood there and stared at the object for a good five minutes. When he thought of leaving to find someone else, the object was long gone. Thinking it was a Japanese secret weapon, he wondered if more were coming. But none came.

That night, while lying in his sleeping bag, Captain Mandel hoped that whatever it was, it belonged to the Americans. He thought to himself that the nation possessing such a "new weapon" would certainly win the war.

The sighting had so shocked Captain Mandel that he decided to not tell anyone about the sighting. Worried about ridicule, he casually asked around if any officers or enlisted men had witnessed anything out of the ordinary that day. Since their replies were all "negative," he said nothing else about the incident because he didn't want his CO to question his sanity.[471]

But Mandel was probably not alone. Okinawa was full of activity and the sighting took place during the day. There was also plenty of opportunity for an U.S. naval vessel and Navy and Army Air Force aircraft to spot such a slow moving object. There is no reason to believe Mandel was the only witness.

In any case, Captain Mandel did not have to worry about Japanese secret weapons too much longer. During the early morning of August 6, a B-29 bomber, Enola Gay, was over the Japanese city of Hiroshima. The B-29's bomb doors opened. The defining moment had come. Silently falling through the sun filled sky, "Fat Boy" spiraled earthward. The world's first atomic bomb was released upon humanity. A few seconds later, an incredible blinding flash marked the beginning of a new, terrifying age.

On August 15, the Second World War was over.[472] Japan had surrendered. The Allied invasion was cancelled. In the meantime, the Fifth Air Force began securing all the areas of occupation. Until one hundred percent of the Japanese aerial threat was eradicated, no one was landing anywhere. E. L. Moreland, who headed the U.S. scientific mission into Japan, and his team were poised and ready. Griggs' balls of fire investigation continued. The Pacific Air Intelligence staff had provided him with nothing of significance, other than numerous sighting reports. Contact with the crews had proven very interesting, but they, too, provided no answers, just colorful stories and more questions. Griggs' personal attendance on at least one operational flight had proved disappointing. But with access to captured Japanese documentation, scientists, and airmen, an answer to the aerial phenomena possibly awaited him in Tokyo.

The U.S. Fifth Air Force was designated as the "occupational air force" and its intelligence responsibilities included disarming the Japanese military in the area, using counter-intelligence to secure their area, and photographing the areas. The initial troops moving into Tokyo consisted of three echelons: the first, a very small group of intelligence men; the second, arriving a couple days later for preliminary investigation; and the third was composed of primary personnel for exploitation.[473]

General Douglas MacArthur sent in a task force of 150 men to prepare the way for his main body of troops. On August 28, they landed at Atsugi airfield, near the city of Yokohama, under the command of Colonel Charles Tench, who was the first American officer to set foot on Japanese soil.[474] For the first wave of men flying into Atsugi, it was a historical moment, shared in spirit by all the American forces. But as the task force approached, something occurred that was not on the agenda.

In broad daylight, Colonel Tench's men were flying towards Japan. As a member of the first troops into Japan, Sergeant Leonard Stringfield was packed in a C-46, number 304. On board was "special equipment" that he and nine others with the Fifth Air Force intelligence team were bringing with them. Their flight plan was depart Ie Shima, make a short stop at Iwo Jima, and then fly on to the Atsugi Air Field on the island of Honshu, Japan.

They were flying at 10,000 feet, between the Japanese islands of Ie Shima and Iwo Jima, when their "C-46 suddenly developed trouble in the left engine." Suddenly, "the plane dipped," and the engine struggled to keep working. It "sputtered oil" and the C-46 began to lose altitude, dropping approximately 25-50 feet. It was at this moment that Stringfield saw something that completely caught him by surprise. Looking out his "starboard-side" window, he was "shocked to see three teardrop-shaped objects." Looking carefully, he determined that the "three unidentifiable blobs" were "about the size of a dime held at arm's length." They were "brilliant white, like burning magnesium."

Flying in a "tight formation," the objects "were traveling in a straight line through drifts of clouds, seemingly parallel to the C-46 and equal to its speed." Stringfield became alarmed; they "seemed to be intelligently controlled." He was convinced they were not U.S. aircraft reflecting the sun. In fact, they were like no aircraft he had ever seen. They were extremely advanced; Stringfield saw no wings or fuselage, and there was no outline of a solid object behind the mass of luminescence. Being familiar with the latest intelligence reports and summaries describing the shape and characteristics of Germany's jets and the Japanese Bakas, he was quite sure they were not enemy jets.

Sergeant Stringfield's postwar painting of objects observed over Pacific. (Courtesy Mrs. Dell Stringfield)

Suddenly, Sergeant Stringfield's attention was roused by a commotion coming from the cockpit. Seconds later, the alarmed co-pilot made his way back to where Stringfield and the rest of the men were sitting. Looking at everyone, he said, "We're in trouble," and then handed Harry Berning a pair of binoculars to help him find a place to land. Berning was "plenty scared." The plane was going off course and they were flying through heavy clouds. Stringfield was on the plane's left side and Berning was on its right, so Berning was unaware of the objects.

Sergeant Stringfield continued to watch. Whatever they were, he was sure they were "responsible" for the plane's behavior. The entire event lasted about thirty seconds before the three objects "disappeared into a cloud bank." When they pulled away, the C-46's engine "revved up" and returned to normal again. The plane immediately began to gain altitude. Whether coincidentally or not, the C-46 fully recovered from its engine problem and was able to safely arrive at Iwo Jima without further incident.

During the trip's final leg, Sergeant Stringfield watched the clouds closely, waiting to catch another glimpse of the objects, should they return. They did not. Getting off the plane, Stringfield wanted to report the sighting, but Iwo Jima was a bustling staging area and "there was no real place to report anything" of that nature.

The flight crew was off somewhere getting briefed, so Stringfield was unable to question the pilots. With no time to waste, he and the rest of his team immediately conducted a major check-up of their C-46. This was when he noticed that "oil had splashed all over the side of the craft from the left engine." Other than that mess, there were no other apparent problems with their plane, and they were soon on their way.

A couple hours later, Stringfield and the rest of the first echelon Air Intelligence members arrived at the Atsugi Air Drome. Again, there was no time to waste. Preparation for the arrival of the second and third echelons of the intelligence mission was a priority. Unfortunately, by the time Stringfield had a few minutes rest, it was too late. The pilots were long gone, whisked away to debriefing, so he was unable to corroborate anything he had witnessed. Stringfield learned he was the only person in the rear of the plane who saw the strange objects, but he believed the pilot saw them as well. They were both on the same side of the aircraft. He felt the pilot must have seen something, especially when the engine started experiencing trouble.

Sergeant Stringfield thought that after the pilots were debriefed, the S-2s would interrogate him and the other team members about the objects, but that never happened. So, he never filed an official report. Though he was unable to catch up with the pilots, he was sure they had reported the objects. Much later, another source told him that the "magnetic-navigation instrument needles" in the cockpit "went wild."

Stringfield's foo fighter sighting is remarkable in many ways. First of all, the Fifth Air Force had established complete air superiority in the area. There was no way that the Far East Air Forces were going to allow a formation of advanced Japanese aircraft to operate near this intelligence mission. If the three objects were Japanese aircraft, were somehow lucky enough to get off the ground, and then managed to fly over the lone stretch of open water between Ie Shima and Iwo Jima, their mission had proven futile. If it was a last ditch effort to strike a U.S. warplane, the Japanese pilots had passed on a golden opportunity to attack Stringfield's defenseless C-46.[475]

Chapter Twenty-One

Dr. Griggs in Japan

On September 6, 1945, David Griggs and E. G. Schneider (also a specialist on radar and related electronic equipment and techniques), representing General Kenney's Advisory Specialist Group with FEAF, arrived at the Atsugi Air Drome with four other military officers and four men from E.L. Moreland's Pacific Branch, OSRD. Calling themselves a Scientific Intelligence Mission, they were formally set up under Moreland's guidance. Moreland was advisor to General MacArthur and headed the new Scientific and Technical Advisory Section of the Pacific Armed Forces General Headquarters.

The primary objective of their mission was to "discover the organization of Japanese Scientific War Research, together with personalities, programs and laboratories," and to "establish a target list" of "Japanese scientific personnel" as per G-2 (Army Intelligence).[476] In addition to the Moreland/Compton mission, a Japanese ALSOS Mission composed of eight members, including Griggs, was established under the leadership of Luis Alvarez.[477]

Griggs arrived at the Atsugi Air Drome prepared to conduct his scientific mission, part of which involved the balls of fire investigation. He did not have to go far. His presence at Atsugi occurred on the exact same day as Sergeant Stringfield's sighting. If the C-46 pilots saw the same objects as Sgt. Stringfield and filed a report, in all likelihood Griggs would have been briefed on the sighting.

Griggs knew that "about three" regions generated a "high frequency" of foo fighter sightings over South Tokyo.[478] Armed with an excellent interpreter, he was able to draw information from a huge list of important Japanese scientists at his disposal.[479] In Tokyo, Griggs conducted interrogations and gained the confidence of one Japanese officer attached to Japanese headquarters. During questioning, Griggs relayed the Balls of fire information to the Japanese officer, who in turn found the sightings just as interesting as the United States Army Air Force had found them. The circumstances in Japan were repeating those in Germany; the enemy seemed as surprised by the unusual sightings as the U.S. was.

Griggs believed the Japanese were cooperative with the interrogators of the Compton Mission and were not withholding any information regarding the balls of fire. The information in the records he was amassing indicated there was no record of aerial observations of the balls of fire by Japanese ground personnel or by Japanese pilots. Griggs said he felt he'd "really looked and found zero."[480]

Meanwhile, the South Pacific sky was still host to strange lights. One was seen between September 25 and 27, while the *USS Beaver* (AS-5/ARG-19),[481] a submarine tender with Submarine Squadron 45, was anchored in Buckner Bay, Okinawa. Machinist-Mate First Class George M. Reynolds had completed his four-hour watch in the engine room. Tired and very hot, he grabbed a shower, put on some clean clothes, and "went up on the main deck" to "cool off and lay down." It was about 0100 hours. Reynolds was in a good mood. He was very happy the war was over. Joining the Navy in 1941, he had "made it" through the entire conflict, having escaped several harrowing experiences.

"It was beautiful and clear that night, as I laid there looking up at

Machinist-Mate First Class George M. Reynolds. (Courtesy George M. Reynolds)

the stars," recalled Reynolds. "Not realizing there's a fourteen hour difference between me and my girlfriend back in Maryland, I wondered if she was looking at the same stars, and all this stuff. Catching my eye, I noticed a star directly above me. It was a bluish, a bluish white, and it stood out like it was close; standing out stronger than all of the other ones. Wondering if it was an airplane, I doubted it because I could see no running lights on; no red lights, green lights, nothing like that. As I continued to watch, it started to move. And it moved down towards the south, made a right hand turn, then went over to the west, and stopped. It stood still. Then it started moving again, returning back into the general area that it had originally started from."

The "bluish light was about the size of a dime at arm's-length" and it moved in a slow fashion. Reynolds was puzzled by the light's behavior, but since it posed no threat, he fell asleep. The next day, he told his buddy Harry Owens about his odd sighting. Owens suggested maybe it was a helicopter or something. Reynolds felt it was no helicopter because he "did not hear any sound and it stood perfectly still in the sky, too still for a helicopter." Though he knew the "bluish light" was odd, he chose not to file a report.[482]

On September 28, Lt. Colonel A.R. Sullivan, Jr., with the U.S. Signal Corps, sent General McDonald, USSTAF, a message regarding two important subjects, the first involving "Remote Interference with Aircraft." Sullivan informed McDonald that "investigations have been completed on the subject and it is considered that there is no means presently known which was in development or use by the German Air Force which could interfere with engines of aircraft in flight. All information available through interrogations, equipment, and documents has been thoroughly investigated and the subject may be closed with negative result."

Interference with aircraft had been reported since well before the 1940s. By January 19, 1945, General Arnold was informed in his *Commander's Digest* that there were two reported cases, and many rumors of electrical interference of some kind affecting aircraft engines. Colonel Sullivan's message had come exactly one month after Sergeant Stringfield observed the three luminous objects while his C-46 malfunctioned and suggests the military was aware of the sighting. It is unknown, however, whether Colonel Sullivan's memo involved a discussion of known research efforts designed for combat use, or effects caused by the proximity of mysterious unconventional aircraft.

The second part of Sullivan's memo dealt with the balls of fire. It read: "As far as can be determined from extensive interrogations, investigation of documents, and field trips there is no basis of fact in the reports made by aircrews concerning balls of fire, other than that phenomena similar to balls of fire may have been produced by jet aircraft or missiles. This subject may be considered closed with negative results."[483]

Again, Sullivan ended the memo with the words: "this subject may be considered closed with the negative results." The balls of fire investigation was not complete, however. Griggs was still in the Pacific. Colonel Sullivan was telling General McDonald that certain balls of fire sightings were not based on fact, and they were only "similar" to the reports of balls of fire that seemed to be "produced by jet aircraft or missiles." This means

Sullivan was definitely discussing two types of balls of fire sightings: (1) conventional ordnance, rockets, and aircraft related sightings, and (2) aircraft that defied conventional explanation. Either Colonel Sullivan was in the know regarding unconventional aircraft sightings, or he simply reported information accumulated outside the investigations by Robertson and Griggs.

On September 28, the same day that Colonel Sullivan wrote his memo, Griggs was still in Tokyo. During his time with the Moreland/Compton mission, he was unable to reach any definitive conclusion about the balls of fire sightings. He thought many of the sightings were the result of combat stress but was puzzled over those sightings reported by experienced pilots. He felt the "European type was much rarer," which was probably a reference to the foo fighter sightings.

The Griggs visit to Japan was a brief one, only a few weeks. He was convinced that some balls of fire sightings were not Japanese secret weapons. His findings, though not conclusive, were included in his report.[484] Once complete, the report probably ended up on the desk of his new boss General Kenney. But since the Griggs investigation was ongoing, he may have bypassed General Kenney altogether. Copies of the report surely ended up with General Arnold and General Spaatz, and most certainly on the desk of his direct boss, Edward Bowles. Unfortunately, his foo fighter reports have not been located.

As the Griggs balls of fire report circulated quietly behind the scenes at Allied command, another report was released. On December 15, Theodore Von Karman handed General Arnold the cumulative efforts of his Scientific Advisory Group's work entitled, *Toward New Horizons*. Von Karman wrote the introductory volume, "Science, the Key to Air Supremacy," accompanied by thirty-two other volumes written by his team on research programs in a variety of fields. Throughout the work, Von Karman emphasized the need for scientists and Air Force leadership to respect one another and establish a cohesive working relationship; this had to be executed with complete compliance by both parties in order to achieve optimal success.[485]

The month of December also saw the release of a story penned by Jo Chamberlain for the *American Legion Magazine*. In his article, "The Foo Fighter Mystery," Chamberlain cited accounts by the 415th Night Fighter Squadron over Europe, the Truk Lagoon "circles of light" sighting, and the Pacific balls of fire reports. There were no new facts in his story, no new sighting reports, and no new comments by Air Intelligence officers. Chamberlain, like many in military intelligence, believed the strange observations were German technology.

Bringing his story to a close, he wrote: "The foo-fighters simply disappeared when Allied ground forces captured the area east of the Rhine. This was known to be the location of many German experimental stations. Since V-E Day, our Intelligence officers have put many such installations under guard. From them we hope to get valuable research information—including the solution to the foo-fighter mystery, but it has not appeared yet. It may be successfully hidden for years to come, possibly forever.

"The members of the 415th hope that Army Intelligence will find the answer. If it turns out that the Germans *never* had anything airborne in the area, they say, 'We'll be all set for Section Eight psychiatric discharges.'

"Meanwhile, the foo-fighter mystery continues unsolved. The lights, or balls of fire, appeared and disappeared on the other side of the world, over Japan—and your guess as to what they were is just as good as mine, for nobody really knows."[486]

Chamberlain's foo fighter article was the last in-depth article to cover one of the war's biggest mysteries. It was the end of 1945. But there was one thing Chamberlain did not know: the foo fighters never went away.

Chapter Twenty-Two

And So...

From 1933 through 1945, unconventional aircraft were observed around the world. These flying objects were given a variety of names: "mystery planes," "ghost aviators," and "phantom fliers," "freaks," "meteors," "comets," "balls of fire," the "light," the "thing," and the "foo fighters." Nearly a decade later the CIA's 1953 Robertson panel report would state that, "If the term 'flying saucers' had been popular in 1943-1945, these objects would have been so labeled."

As of December 1945, Allied Air Intelligence had provided no answers regarding the unconventional aircraft phenomenon. Efforts to explain the sightings resulted in a quagmire of contradiction, speculation, and educated guesses. The ground based Air Intelligence gathering missions had failed to find answers. Interrogation of prisoners of war, including high-ranking officers, engineers, and scientists provided no answers. No enemy documentation was uncovered validating secret projects to account for the sightings. And there was no indication that any unconventional aircraft were shot down or captured during the conflict.

There is no denying that many of the Allied Air Force sightings were explainable by conventional means, simply as a misidentification of German or Japanese ordnance and weaponry. Accurate identification of the sightings proved increasingly difficult, however. There were antiaircraft flares and rockets, both short and long-range. There were jet and rocket-propelled aircraft. And there were jet-propelled experimental devices, including remote control versions. In all, the enemy had introduced an impressive array of technology.

Nonetheless, some sightings defied conventional explanation. The most fantastic sighting accounts described aircraft that were saucer-, cigar-, or circular-shaped; possessed remarkable flight capabilities and extraordinary speeds; and evaded radar. Unfortunately, many of these sighting reports have not been located. They are either still buried in various publicly accessible archives awaiting discovery, or they are hidden away among military and government libraries inaccessible to the public.

Year after year, as the war went on, Allied air intelligence remained confused about the sightings, as they tried explaining them away as conventional ordnance and weaponry, misidentifications, and natural phenomena. Despite their efforts to identify and categorize the various phenomena, highly advanced unconventional aircraft sighting reports remained unexplainable, prompting air intelligence personnel to ridicule the eyewitness observations.

In light of Germany's operational weaponry, the Allies could not ignore any sightings of technological merit, no matter how remarkable In the United States, most branches of service were using a decimal system to file information regarding every imaginable topic: food, weather, clothing, armaments, medicine; the list is quite extensive. Most branches of service followed the same decimal file, but there were variations. The U.S. Army Air Force used the decimal 000.9 for files on "natural and unnatural phenomena."

For example, on March 9, 1944, an AAF crew reported "three silver objects about 30 ft. long" that resembled "Zeppelins and although moving in unison independently of the wind, were apparently not interconnected." The report further said that "although on this occasion a closer view was obtained there is no explanation at present of the purpose they may serve."

The March 9 sighting report is important because of the way it was filed by the U.S. War Department. The War Department General Staff/ Special Staff (WDGS/SS) placed aerial phenomena reports in a "Special Binder" under the file number 9815, which included flak, flares, rockets, etc. These items were assigned their own decimal number, and the March 9 case was placed under decimal file number 6535, "Phenomena."

The U.S. War Department's "Special Binder" reveals that time was taken to compile records of the most challenging observations. And the very existence of such a "Special Binder" suggests that there may also have been a secret unconventional aircraft monitoring committee.

The foo fighter sightings were not representative of the entire unconventional aircraft – or UFO – phenomenon, but only played a significant role for several months. Why then did the foo fighters receive specific mention in the 1953 Robertson panel report? Was the foo fighter investigation part of a larger unconventional aircraft effort conducted by the War Department? We know that when the foo fighter press coverage reached a peak during the winter of 1945, men from Washington arrived at the 415th NFS headquarters to investigate.

The SHAEF-sanctioned American foo fighter investigation is the only officially acknowledged UFO-related investigation conducted by the United States during the war. But rumors have persisted over the last several decades that there were more.

The first rumor appeared in 1950 in retired Marine Corps Major Donald Keyhoe's first UFO book, *The Flying Saucers Are Real*. Keyhoe had established many contacts within the Pentagon; the military men Keyhoe knew were veterans and well informed. Many felt the UFO phenomenon was more than imagination and posed a real cause for concern. Some supported the extraterrestrial hypothesis, while others felt the Russians had achieved aerial superiority from captured German scientists and technology.

In 1949, Keyhoe was at the Pentagon searching for a copy of the newly released Project Saucer report. He discussed the matter with two men he had worked with, Al Scholin and Orville Splitt, in the Pentagon's magazine section of Public Relations. But they told him there was no way he was going to see that documentation: Project Saucer was "still classified secret."

Later that morning, Keyhoe received a strange telephone call at home from a guy named "Steele" (Keyhoe chose to protect the man's real identity) who claimed he was a "former Air Force Intelligence officer" in the European theater during the war. Steele was curious, too, about the foo fighters observed over Europe during the end of the war. Steele questioned Keyhoe about what he knew about the subject. Keyhoe said he had just begun checking into the story, and although very familiar with UFOs, he was not familiar with the term foo fighter, asking, "Wasn't that some kind of missile fired from the ground?"

"No," Steele responded. "Intelligence never did get any real answer, so far as I know. They were some kind of circular gadgets, and they actually chased our planes a number of times. We thought they were something the Nazis had invented – and I still think so." Steel further suggested that Keyhoe get a hold of an Eighth Air Force intelligence report.

After a little digging around about Steele, Keyhoe telephoned Splitt at the Pentagon. He wanted to know if Splitt had heard about the foo fighters. Splitt said yes. Keyhoe then asked if the Eighth Air Force had conducted a foo fighter investigation, and Splitt said yes again. Wanting to know if he could have a look at the report, Splitt put him on hold and went to check. When he returned he said, "Sorry, it's classified." Keyhoe had received the first official verbal confirmation that a foo fighter investigation had been conducted by the U.S. Eighth Air Force.[487]

Verification of just such a U.S. Army Air Force report regarding a foo fighter investigation came in 1952. On April 23, a staff member signing for Lt. W.W. Ottinger, Executive, Evaluation Division, Directorate of Intelligence, responded to a Mr. [name blacked out] in California. According to the letter, Colonel Ottinger said that "careful consideration" was given to questions asked by this person. And one answer he provided was very revealing. "An evaluation of the World War II 'Foo Fighter' reports was made at the end of the war," stated Ottinger. "Because of the lack of adequate data, this evaluation was necessarily very general in nature. Essentially, it was concluded that these reports were the result of misidentification of conventional objects and did not represent any unusual phenomena."

Whether this Air Force staff member was talking about the Eighth Air Force report that Keyhoe had heard about is not known. If not, his response suggests that there may have been more than one. Was he perhaps referencing the Griggs report?[488]

The Keyhoe-Steele story adds further credence to an alleged 1943 British UFO investigation referenced by American journalist Frank Edwards in his 1967 book, *Flying Saucers: Here and Now!* According to Edwards, a British Lieutenant General Massey was involved with a War Office investigation of foo fighters "as early as 1943," ending sometime in 1944.[489] The "Massey Project" was probably a reference to RAF No. 5 Group's investigation of "rocket phenomena," and General Massey was a pseudonym to protect the officer's identity.

So far, however, little information has surfaced regarding British officials who were in the know about foo fighter investigations conducted by the British military. In 1935, Sir Victor Goddard was the Air Ministry's first Deputy Director of Intelligence. Responding specifically to a 1978 letter asking whether the British Air Staff had initiated a foo fighter investigation, Goddard stated: "To the best of my knowledge there has never been any official study of the foo-fighters. This implies Treasury sanction; it suggests that in the middle of the war against Germany when we had our hands full and it was far from certain that we could survive, the Air Ministry was concerned that a UFO menace existed; it most certainly was not."[490]

Sir Goddard's truthful assessment reflects a possible confusion over terminology. Case in point: the Air Ministry never used the term foo fighter, instead calling their sightings "balls of fire." British Bomber Command definitely sanctioned investigations of so-called "rocket phenomena." Technically speaking, rockets were UFOs and they were a "menace." The mystery is whether or not the Air Ministry considered all "rocket" sightings enemy ordnance and weaponry.

One scientist having knowledge of the Air Ministry's air staff activities during the war was Reginald V. Jones, the Air Ministry's Chief Scientific Intelligence Advisor. When questioned in 1996 about his knowledge of the foo fighters, Jones stated: "In answer to your letter there was no Committee on 'foo-fighters' during my time with the Air Ministry during the war or with the Ministry of Defense afterwards. If there had been any such inquiry, it would have been primarily an Air Force matter. . ."[491] Granted the RAF Bomber Command would carry out such investigation(s), but any generated reports would certainly have reached the Air Ministry.

During the height of the foo fighter sightings, Jones was in contact with a colleague of his: Howard Robertson. During that time, Robertson was in charge of SHAEF's foo fighter investigation. Though there is no documentation supporting an Air Ministry foo fighter investigation, there is reason to believe an investigation existed under another name: Balls of fire. Again, it is important to emphasize that from late 1944 until war's end, foo fighter was a name primarily used among AAF crews.

It was not until the 1990s that we learned that the Office of Strategic Services (OSS) had conducted an investigation of the foo fighters. According to CIA historian Gerald K. Haines: "During World War II, US pilots reported 'foo fighters' (bright lights trailing US aircraft). Fearing they might be Japanese or of German secret weapons, OSS investigated but could find no concrete evidence of enemy weapons and often filed such reports in the 'crackpot' category. The OSS also investigated possible sightings of German V-1 and V-2 rockets before their operational use during the war."[492]

Carrying out the foo fighter investigation was most likely handled by the OSS's Secret Intelligence, Technical Section. Two primary functions of this branch were: one, cooperating with military and government agencies for detailed investigations in the field; and two: "Assisting in obtaining information on particularly active technical matters, and carrying on investigations in the US and foreign countries regarding special alleged inventions and developments."[493]

The strong CIA link to the foo fighter investigation is cemented in the 1953 Robertson panel report. Three of the panel's most prominent members, including the person whose name titles the report, were civilian scientists who collaborated with U.S. military forces and were involved with official foo fighter investigations during the war: Alvarez, Griggs, and Robertson. As this book makes abundantly clear, these scientists all had connections to the highest levels of military commands and government agencies in the U.S. and Britain.

Robertson was one of those scientists. During the war, he was attached to the OSRD's London Mission, U.S. and British CROSSBOW Committees, Scientific advisor to General Doolittle's U.S. Eighth Air Force and General Spaatz's USSTAF, Chief of SHAEF's Scientific Intelligence Advisory Section; and Chief of the Field Intelligence Agency, Technical (FIAT).

Luis Alvarez, of the MIT Radiation Laboratory, was affiliated with most radar related issues in conjunction with the Allied Air and Ground Forces. He was also the inventor of Ground Control Approach (GCA) radar and Microwave Early Warning System (MEW)[494] and was part of the United States Atomic bomb project, putting him in contact with the ALSOS Mission, as well as being a member of the Moreland/Compton mission.

Griggs was Chief Scientific Advisor to Edward Bowles of the War Department; Chief Scientific Advisor to General Arnold, Commanding General of the entire Army Air Forces; Chief Scientific Advisor to General Spaatz, Commanding General of the United States Strategic and Tactical Air Forces; and expert consultant to the War Department's Edward Bowles, who was the chief scientific advisor to the Secretary of War; a member of the Advisory Specialist Group attached to General Kenney and General Spaatz; and a member of the Compton mission.

The 1953 Robertson Panel report clearly references Griggs as the most knowledgeable person on the subject of foo fighters. Since Griggs and Alvarez were both radar experts, radar evasion was probably the aspect of these unconventional aircraft sightings that most concerned the Allies. And there is no denying that Germany was experimenting with paints, jamming devices, and aerial debris designed to foil radar detection.

Unfortunately, there is very little known about what Robertson and Alvarez learned during the foo fighter investigation. There is, however, a small amount known about Griggs' role. In 1969, atmospheric physicist James McDonald, then a professor at the Institute of Geophysics, University of California, contacted Griggs.[495] McDonald spoke twice with Griggs on the telephone, asking about his personal involvement with the foo fighter investigations, his conclusions, and the whereabouts of his reports.

All that's left of McDonald's interview with Griggs is a couple pages of handwritten notes. Interestingly, McDonald noted that Griggs "did volunteer quite a bit of comment," but that he was "non-committal all throughout," guarding his answers during their conversation. From what McDonald could ascertain from his brief telephone interviews, his impression "was that no real conclusion was ever reached" about the foo fighters or balls of fire.[496] To this day, the Griggs investigative reports regarding the foo fighters and balls of fire have not been located.

By the end of 1945, there was absolutely no evidence to indicate that all the unconventional aircraft sightings were enemy related. The balls of fire and foo fighters during the war became the "Ghost Rockets" of 1946. This new term was introduced primarily due to flights of flying objects over Sweden, Finland, Norway, and Denmark; eventually extending throughout Europe including Portugal, France, Tangier, Italy, Greece, and India.[497] By the summer of 1947, the term "flying saucer" had arrived and spread globally. Then by 1956, the U.S. Air Force was calling them "Unidentified Flying Objects" (UFOs).

Epilogue

Postwar Thoughts

Over the years, as the war grew distant in the minds of veterans, some scars and memories remained vivid. For some, memories of strange aerial sightings and encounters haunted them, causing confusion as they reflected back upon their experience. In many instances, as the UFO phenomenon continued expanding with frequency and in complexity far past the end of World War II, veterans realized they had seen the same sorts of objects during the war. They, too, were witness to something unknown.

Lt. Roman Sabinski's 1942 sighting remains the most riveting account of its kind. Years after the war, Sabinski reflected upon his amazing encounter: "I don't say that this was – we didn't have any names 'flying saucers' or 'foo-fighters' because I never had any before that date – occurrences of that sort. So any conclusion that could be made out, that had to be made by someone else. I still don't know what it was."[498]

Another interesting account was Captain William Mandel's sighting of a cigar-shaped object in late August 1945 over Okinawa. He felt sure it was a Japanese secret weapon, possibly based on some magnetic method of propulsion. After realizing he was the only one who had reported it, he kept the sighting to himself. It was not until years later, that Mandel's sighting was finally vindicated in his own mind. He was startled upon opening an issue of *Life* magazine. There before him was a picture of a cigar-shaped object exactly like the one he had seen during the war.

The *Life* article indicated that the objects were possibly extraterrestrial craft; that idea had never occurred to Mandel. Now he was finally able to break his self-imposed silence and tell his wife and friends that he, too, had seen the same thing. In 1967 Mandel wrote a letter to astronomer J. Allen Hynek, a long time UFO investigator for the United States Air Force. In his letter, Mandel said that he was not seeking publicity, since in his experience anyone claiming to see a UFO was regarded as "some kind of nut." For twenty years, he remained frustrated because he was unable to verify his sighting.

In his letter to Hynek, he wrote: "The most interesting point to be considered, I think, is that not until several years later did I first hear of the terms 'flying saucer' and 'UFO,' nor was I aware that others before me had recorded similar sightings. It certainly did not occur to me at the time that I might be witnessing the passage of an interplanetary vehicle."[499]

In 1966, one of the only known foo fighter articles appearing in the press was "Joe Thompson and the Foo-Fighters." Major Joe Thompson commanded the 109th Tactical Reconnaissance Squadron. During the war, he and his men flew P-51 Mustangs "equipped with powerful aerial cameras and four 50-caliber machine guns." While over the Rhine Valley, Major Thompson observed "four or five objects that looked like silvery footballs" stationary in the sky.

Major Thompson assumed they were German and continued with his mission. He returned and reported the account to his S-2. Only later did he learn that "captured intelligence reports said the Germans had seen the objects, too—and thought they were put up there by the Americans!"

When the flying saucer wave of 1947 erupted across the country, Major Thompson became interested in the UFO phenomenon. He maintained a balanced viewpoint, aware of the problems surrounding accurate information, and kept an open-mind. Thompson offered a final thought in the magazine: "We have been flying on this planet for only 63 years and we are now planning to send astronaut to the moon. This is a long way to go in 63 years, but we still don't know all the answers."[500]

Major Augspurger was the Commanding Officer of the American 415th Night Fighter Squadron during the winter of 1944/1945. His unit was responsible for naming the foo fighters. During those months, even Major Augspurger saw one himself. He, like Major Thompson, decided they were Nazi secret weapons. After the war, he realized the foo fighters were not airplanes, jets, rockets, nor were they secret weapons. They were not flares or barrage balloons, and they certainly were not the moon or stars.

In 2003, I asked Augspurger what he thought the foo fighters were. He replied: "Well, I think it was extraterrestrial objects of some kind. I, at that particular time, I didn't think much anything like that, but as time goes on, I think that it was something from outer space. I just believe in those things. But what we saw, . . . I think it is extraterrestrial, something from outer space. Now I think they. . . probably came down to Earth to see what the heck was going on there."[501]

When asked about whether he discussed the sightings with his chief intelligence officer, Captain Ringwald, Augspurger replied: "We didn't talk a whole lot about what it was or anything...we just reported what we saw. The other fellows did, too. But I didn't know. There had to be a record kept of it in intelligence."

On January 1, 1945, pilot Lt. Jack Green and radar operator Lt. Warren Barber encountered their foo fighters. After the war, Barber attended a lecture where an ex-intelligence officer was speaking about the war. The speaker talked about intelligence matters regarding stories of soldiers in the service who had escaped German and Japanese captivity.

After the presentation, Barber spoke with the intelligence man, and recalls: "I, after World War II, went to a meeting up to Bell Aircraft in Niagara Falls and was invited by another fellow who was in P-61s as a navigator and gunner in the Pacific. And they talked about everything, practically, and afterwards I asked, 'There's one thing you haven't mentioned, the foo fighters that we saw. And he said, 'Are you one of those pilots and navigators who saw it?' And I said, 'Yeah.' He said, 'You know that's one of the big things about World War II that's never been quite really solved.' He said that the German pilots that were up that night reported identically the same thing as the British and us."

I spoke to Barber in 2003 and recorded the following interview.

Keith Chester (KC): How did the ex-intelligence officer know that? [How were they aware of the German sightings?]

Warren Barber (WB): They got the report. This was an intelligence officer after World War II and he'd been at a debriefing of German pilots, too, and he said they came up with the same identical story, and they could never figure out what it really was.

KC: I see. So this intelligence officer, do you remember his name?

WB: I don't remember his name. But... as I said, he came in to visit an aircraft group up at the falls.

KC: Let me clarify one point. Now he was telling you that the German pilots had been reporting it that same night?

WB: The same night.

KC: How was he able to get the same information on the same night? That's what I'm curious about.

WB: That's what I didn't ask him. He said it was the same night. He said the British had reported it and we reported it, and my first thought, of course, it was something that the Germans had tried.[502]

When Barber originally reported his January 1 sighting to his S-2 debriefing officer, he was told about the British night fighter crews' observation. It certainly suggests Barber's sighting was very significant, since the ex-intelligence man lecturing at the Bell Aero Club meeting remembered the event so clearly.

Lt. Jack Green had this to say about their foo fighter sightings when I interviewed him in 1966: "I recalled reading about them in about two or three articles before this flight of ours. They had been explained away as being nothing more than St. Elmo's fire, which the English couldn't seem to recognize, or as possible hallucinations. By now, I had had a lot of experience with St. Elmo's fire in a variety of forms. What we saw, Warren and I, was yet quite another type of display for which no possible accounting could be given then or, for that matter, has been given to date."

According to Barber, after the war he and Jack Green decided that what they had witnessed was a flying saucer. Barber is unsure of what he witnessed and still feels the foo fighters they encountered that night were something the Germans were flying. Despite their difference of opinions, Barber emphasized he had the utmost respect for Jack Green, who he felt was honest, intelligent, and whole-heartedly steadfast.[503]

As I mentioned in the introduction, this book came about following my 1991 interview with Leonard Stringfield. Stringfield diligently scrutinized his own account and wrote about it in two books. Up until his untimely death in 1993, he could only come to one conclusion: UFOs were extraterrestrial.

During the war, Stringfield had no access to air intelligence matters regarding foo fighters, other than what was disseminated through normal channels. His duties at the time were primarily clerical and he was publisher of his unit's newspaper.[504] Here now is a portion of my interview with Stringfield:

Keith Chester (KC): Did the craft appear to be intelligently controlled?

Leonard Stringfield (LS): Well, they seemed to have been because the fact is that they retreated when they got close to the aircraft. There was a definite retreat back into the cloudbank and they disappeared. Now the opinion was, at that time, before I got on the plane and had learned about these things, was that they possibly could have been enemy devices, manufactured by the Germans, who were highly technical people, to cause psychological affects on the pilots. Also, they could have been used to throw off radar as interference.

KC: What are your feelings about this idea?

L.S.: Well, that was the opinion back in 1944 and 1945. No one had any expertise at that time about anything beyond what we owned, you know, what we had here on Earth. And, we were in wartime. So, the thought was that we were connected with enemy psychological weapons or something to throw our radar off. Now the strange thing is that years later our intelligence briefing of what was left of the Luftwaffe, the German air force, discovered that the German pilots were encountering the same thing and they thought they were ours. So it didn't belong to either one of us. And my opinion, in later years, it was not German, American, or British or Japanese. And that they were forerunners, the precursors, of the UFO of today. You know it goes back to World War II.

KC: Have you since then come into contact with individuals, or pilots, who have seen the foo fighters?

LS: Oh, yes. See, at that time, when I was in the Philippines, months earlier, there were reports. I remember receiving intelligence reports about these… well they called them foo fighters. They weren't UFOs then. They were unidentified objects that had the ability to out maneuver our aircraft. They were seen in both the ETO—European Theater—and ATO—Asian Theater, and there was no explanation. So when I got back and settled down again and got into the UFO business, why I realized that what I had seen was one and the same thing that they were seeing in 1947, you know Ken Arnold right up to the present day, the precursors.

KC: Do you feel that these objects were secret research developments within the government?

LS: No. That's my opinion. As I said, the Germans were seeing the same thing as our pilots.

KC: In 1945, most of the key German scientists had been taken out of Germany and moved to the U.S. and Britain.

LS: Yeah, they were working on the V-2 rocket. They had nothing to do with…these things were free flying. What I observed was over the Pacific Ocean. It was so many hundreds of miles outside Iowa Jima. And there was nothing left of the Japanese air force at that time. And, why would the German's take their secret weapon clear over Japan? [Laughs.] You know, it doesn't add up.

KC: Exactly, especially so close to the war's end.

LS: Well, why they…you know, the Germans had surrendered in May of that year. The Japanese surrendered on September 4. The Germans were out of it. So I see no connection whatsoever. And looking back through the years, there is no connection with the Russians manufacturing [those things], or the Americans.

KC: When the war ended, and after you progressed with your own research, did you ever contact Air Force officials and present your questions to them?

LS: Oh yes, I even called the Pentagon back in the '50s, talked to their spokesman, and to their PIO, Public Information Officer, about that sort of thing, that phenomenon during World War II. They claim they had no explanation.

KC: Mr. Stringfield, since you were in the intelligence community, did you have any inside contacts?

LS: No, the only thing I had was memoranda, as I remember, back in the Philippines, which was back in 1944-45, that indicated that our airmen were seeing these things in the skies over the European theater and the Asian-Pacific theater, and had no explanation for it.

KC: Do you think there were investigations conducted?

LS: Well, the only thing they had at that time was briefings. When a plane comes in that was on a combat mission, the same as today, their briefed and debriefed. Everything that they know or observed is reported. Not that they can come to any conclusions, but they can take the information.

KC: Since the 1940s, in light of all your research, have you come to any conclusions: Do you feel the UFOs are of an extraterrestrial nature?

LS: That's my opinion, where I lean, yes. I think the evidence that we have highly suggests that we're dealing with extraterrestrial craft.

Until there is evidence to verify that the unconventional aircraft of World War II were enemy aircraft or weaponry, it is the testimonies of veterans like Lieutenant Roman Sabinski, Captain William Leet, Sergeant Cockcroft, Lieutenant Jack Green, Major Harold Augspurger, and Sergeant Leonard Stringfield that bear witness to an extraordinary phenomenon seen during World War II, which, very likely, were not of this Earth.

Appendix

Dr. Goudsmit and ALSOS

The Robertson Panel report was a pivotal document regarding the foo fighters and provided an important starting point for my research. We know that the CIA cited Alvarez, Griggs, and Robertson as the three important scientists who during the war were affiliated with the foo fighter investigations. But there is one other member of the Robertson Panel that was not mentioned in this regard, and I feel that he was just as involved as the others. His name is Samuel A. Goudsmit.

Given his affiliation with Alvarez, Griggs, and Robertson, I suspect that, at the very least, he was peripherally involved with the foo fighter investigation. Here's why.

The year was 1939. Many scientists, having already fled Europe to escape the rising Nazi regime, came to the United States armed with knowledge of a new scientific breakthrough: there existed the possibility of creating a bomb so powerful it was capable of generating incomprehensible mass destruction. The scientists clearly understood there was no time to spare; President Roosevelt had to be informed and convinced of its danger. On October 11, in an effort to emphasize the dire circumstances, a handwritten letter from renowned scientist Albert Einstein was delivered to Roosevelt. Einstein's letter was a plea from a group of renowned immigrant scientists, urgently requesting that the President understand that atomic energy in the hands of a madman such as Hitler could have devastating consequences. Understanding the gravity of the situation, Roosevelt authorized the building of the atomic bomb.[505]

By 1943, the U.S. Army's "Manhattan Project," the codename for America's atomic bomb effort, was making exceptional progress in the desert of Los Alamos, New Mexico. Understanding the project's importance to the war's outcome, President Roosevelt was well aware that the Germans, Italians, and Japanese also had the same scientific knowledge at their disposal. Roosevelt's critical concern was how far the enemy had progressed with a program of its own. Winston Churchill was absolutely overcome with anxiety over this dilemma. He knew that Britain was the first place Hitler's bomb would be used.

General Leslie Groves, commanding officer of the Manhattan

Project, discussed the severity of the situation with Vannevar Bush, his chief scientific advisor and head of the Office of Scientific Research and Development (OSRD), and Army Intelligence Chief Major General George Strong. Until Allied forces were able to get into Germany, U.S. Army Intelligence had determined that prominent scientists in Italy were the best sources in revealing just how far Germany had progressed with the bomb. Plans were made to capture and interrogate several prominent Italian scientists, plus recover all pertinent documentation.

To achieve this goal, an Army operation codenamed ALSOS was established and placed under the command of Colonel Boris T. Pash, who would provide the safety for a team of scientists headed by James Fisk, an exceptional physicist with the OSRD. A few days later, while in Washington Colonel Pash accompanied General Strong to a meeting with the Secretary of War, Henry Stimson. Colonel Pash was given a letter to personally deliver it to either General Eisenhower or his Chief of Staff, General W. Bedell Smith, detailing the specific needs of the operation and emphasizing the "extreme urgency and overriding priority." Without further delay, the ALSOS Mission was a go.[506]

What does the history of the atomic bomb have to do with unconventional aircraft you wonder? There is reason to believe that air intelligence members attached to the ALSOS mission were also engaged in fact-finding on unconventional aircraft. ALSOS needed to know whether a zeppelin, hot-air balloon, plane, jet, or rocket would be the delivery system for the most advanced weapon of the war.

In early 1944, the Allied Armies advanced through Italy, but several months remained before they reached Rome. When ALSOS entered Naples, they were accompanied by the following intelligence units: G-2 (Army Intelligence) Advanced Allied Forces Headquarters; G-2 Fifth Army, Naval Intelligence Unit (ONI); Combined Services District Interrogation Center (CSDIC); Joint Intelligence Collection Agency (JICA); Office of Strategic Services; British Naval Intelligence; and the I Informazioni Militari (they apparently provided assistance). Regardless of its primary task, the ALSOS mission aimed to determine the extent of the Italian and German war efforts with "new weapons and materials of war."

The ALSOS scientists met with the Italian Minister of Communications, the Chief of Naval Ordnance, Lt. General Matteini, and staff of the Italian Naval Academy. Select professors with the University of Naples and officers of the Italian Navy and Air Force were also interrogated. The most promising interrogations unfolded between January 19 and 22, 1944. The assistant chief of production for the Air

Ministry, Major Mario Gasperi, had been captured. A former Italian Air Attaché to Berlin for six years, Gasperi was considered an "outstanding man." He was the only person available who was capable of offering a complete picture of the German Luftwaffe. He was questioned about missiles, rockets, homing devices, jet and high altitude bombers, but apparently had no groundbreaking information to reveal;[507] most likely he had been questioned about unconventional aircraft sightings.

Meanwhile, back in Washington, arguably the most important U.S. intelligence-gathering operation of the war was approved on May 11. Due to the success of the Italian ALSOS Mission, Colonel Pash was placed in charge of its European counterpart.[508] He was given a letter to personally hand deliver to General Eisenhower from Secretary of War Simpson: "Lt. Colonel Boris T. Pash who will deliver this letter, has been designated Chief of the Scientific Intelligence Mission organized by G-2 of the War Department to procure intelligence of the enemies' scientific developments. The Director of the Office of Scientific Research and Development is assisting G-2 in the conduct of this mission, and I consider it to be of the highest importance to the war effort."

A couple weeks later, Colonel Pash attended a meeting in Washington at the Office of Scientific Research and Development. Vannevar Bush introduced Pash and his ALSOS staff to their new scientific chief, Samuel A. Goudsmit.[509] As scientific chief, Goudsmit was afforded special latitude with ALSOS that can be viewed as significant to the discovery of unconventional aircraft intelligence or actual specimens. In the advent of "unforeseen situations," if Goudsmit deemed them important, he had the authorization to alter the atomic bomb intelligence-gathering plan and obtain "special agents" and "investigators" as needed.[510]

Early on the morning of June 5, 1944, "S" Force moved in and set up the first U.S. command post in Rome.[511] Air Intelligence flooded into Rome. The first caches of German information lay waiting. If SAS operative Cameron's information proved correct, the UNN building was a definite high priority "target."

By late August, Paris was in Allied hands. Goudsmit and his ALSOS team were also there.[512] Proof that Goudsmit was monitoring air intelligence matters in addition to his atomic bomb agenda is seen in two reports he personally penned on September 9, 1944: "German Air Ministry –Foreign Liaison" and "Rockets, Ionosphere and Stratosphere Research."[513] These two reports certainly provided SHAEF with more confirmation that Germany had exceeded aeronautical advancements made by the U.S. and also supported the OSS report of one operational stratospheric aircraft.

While wrapping up loose ends in Paris, Colonel Pash received a memorandum, "ALSOS Organization for Operations in Germany," from Goudsmit: "The primary aim of ALSOS is to obtain intelligence on enemy scientific research applied to warfare. Scientific developments in which we believe the enemy to be ahead of our own achievements have first interest; those secret war researches which might be stopped or continued underground and used in a following war have priority. The bulk of the intelligence will have to come through personal investigation of German scientists in military, governmental, and industrial research institutes. The finished apparatus itself is of only secondary importance to ALSOS."

He further wrote: "Intelligence leading to precise location of enemy research centers and key research workers must also be gathered by ALSOS personnel. The interests of ALSOS Navy personnel go beyond these narrow aims, and include intelligence of a more technical nature— captured equipment of new types, new manufacturing processes, etc."[514] ALSOS provided agencies requiring assistance in other areas whenever possible. Intelligence agencies that were in "more frequent contact with ALSOS" were Navy Technical Mission Europe; Army Service Forces; Air Forces, under the General direction of USSTAF; CIOS; Technical Industrial Intelligence Committee; and Scientific Intelligence Advisory Section, G-2, SHAEF.[515] Both General Spaatz's USSTAF and SHAEF's SIAS are very important since they were about to become key player in the foo fighter investigations.

In late 1944, Goudsmit's connection to the War Department put him in contact with Bowles's expert consultant, Griggs, as well as General Spaatz and Howard Robertson, a member of CIOS and the future chief of SHAEF's Scientific Advisory Section. These men were well connected to another circle of men, all whom either knew each other, or were familiar with each other's work: General McDonald, Colonel McCoy, and Colonel Watson, all of the USSTAF; Luis Alvarez; and R.V. Jones, liaison between the USSTAF and Air Ministry. (All of these men were in some way connected to the UFO phenomenon in the postwar years.)

By the end of March 1945, ALSOS was across the Rhine, right behind the advancing front line troops in very dangerous territory, as everywhere there were pockets of resistance. But the ALSOS team was not deterred. For Goudsmit's combat scientists, Thuringia, Germany was of the greatest importance. General Dever's 6th Army Group had made astounding progress and ALSOS were very close to their two most critical targets: the town of Stadtilm in Thuringia and the Hechigen-Besingen complex in Wurttemberg. The American scientists were so excited about the prospect of getting into these two places that just mentioning them put them in a state of "frenzy." They did not have to wait long.

Around April 10, Colonel Pash was informed to get his troops ready and prepare for some important news. He got word to wait there, combat ready, because "a friend of Sam's by the name of Dave" was on his way and had important news. Piloting a light plane, David Griggs arrived from Paris. Griggs said the word was they were immediately going to Stadtilm, and their sights were on a laboratory. Then Griggs lowered the boom: ALSOS "would be looking for an actual Nazi atomic pile." Colonel Pash's impression of Griggs was that he "was a man whose scientific stature was second to none." Pash had no problem fitting Griggs into his battle-ready combat unit.

Things got rolling. Griggs information was so motivating it lit a fire under an already blazing effort by Pash's soldiers and Goudsmit's scientists. It was happening so fast, Colonel Pash had to put the operation together on the move. Colonel Pash, Griggs, and ALSOS were heading right for Stadtilm. Within twenty-four hours, the men were there and Griggs was one of the first to secure the laboratory. They were looking at real proof: Germany was intending to construct an atomic bomb.[516]

Hearing the news, Goudsmit knew his presence was needed immediately. Using the telephone lines was too dangerous for his top-secret mission, but he had an ace up his sleeve. Griggs had promised Goudsmit help "whenever an emergency arose," and this was one such emergency.[517]

Griggs was rushed to Heidelberg by air, and from there he got in his own plane and flew back to Paris, where Goudsmit was waiting. They wasted no time; they were quickly airborne and heading right to Stadtilm. Griggs landed his small plane in a field, and before turning the prop off, Goudsmit had jumped out and was running towards a jeep waiting for his arrival. This was his shining moment. His scientists had hit a home run and by April 12, ALSOS's "Operation Big" was in progress.[518]

While the ALSOS scientists conducted their exhaustive investigation, Griggs probably communicated his concern over unconventional aircraft that had been reported. Major sightings had plagued the Allied Air Forces for at least five months, and if they were man-made, and an advanced aircraft of this type was employed as a vehicle to carry atomic devices, there was a chance some answers existed among the documentation found at the facilities.

Since May of 1944, AAF personnel had been attached to the ALSOS Mission progressing through Europe. On March 23, 1945, General Clayton Bissell, assistant chief of staff with the War Department's Military

Intelligence Division, sent a "Secret" memorandum for the AAF's assistant chief of staff for intelligence. Two scientists with the National Advisory Committee for Aeronautics (NACA), Henry J. Reid, and Russell G. Robinson, were actively involved. According to the memorandum: "In particular, the Mission is investigating details of enemy scientific progress in aerodynamics (compressibility phenomena), airplane stability and control, automatic devices and instrumentation, servo mechanisms, fuels and lubricants, bearings, pitons and rings, ignition, and the theory of airplane structure."

General Bissell further stated: "A maximum of five representatives, either from Army Air Forces Technical Teams now operating in the European Theater, or from Army Air Force Headquarters in Washington, can be accommodated as Mission members at present. It is believed their attachment would prove of mutual benefit to the War Department intelligence and intelligence of interest to Army Air Forces. The Division will continue to keep you informed of all ALSOS Mission targets pertaining to enemy aeronautical scientific research and development. ALSOS Mission reports on those subjects are distributed to the AAF through established channels."[519]

Goudsmit's ALSOS Mission had succeeded in gaining the Pentagon's confidence that Germany had not completed their atomic bomb program, and it appeared that Japan was out of the running as well. His mission was now able to focus upon more aeronautical concerns, much to the delight of the Army Air Force.

Goudsmit certainly came across important foo fighter documents given the wide range of Air Intelligence items he came across. In addition to his two September 9, 1944, reports, he wrote fifty-five reports, including "Research Department, German Air Force," "Information Concerning Forschungsfuhrung (Research Dept.) of GAF," "Report on V-Weapons," "Peenemunde Project," "A German Report on Aeronautical Research Establishment at Braunschweig (LFA 'Herman Goering')," and "Research of Remote Control Devices in Germany."[520]

Goudsmit's ALSOS Mission certainly helped Robertson's foo fighter investigation. Considering Goudsmit's friendship with Griggs, and his affiliation with the Army Air Forces and SHAEF, I believe that there is much the Robertson Panel report failed to point out regarding the mysterious foo fighters, or more appropriately, UFOs.

Acknowledgements

I would like to express my sincerest gratitude to the following people: Patrick Huyghe and Anomalist Books for bringing this book to life; Jerome Clark for his valuable assistance and extending me the courtesy of writing the Foreword; Jan Aldrich, Wendy Connors, Carl Feindt, Barry Greenwood, Richard Hall, Norman Malayney, Murphy J. Painter, Nick Pope, Nick Redfern, Fred C. Ringwald, Erik Schlueter, Dell Stringfield, John P. Timmerman, and Janet Bord with the Fortean Picture Library, for generously supplying documentation and photographs from their personal collections; the staff of the Military Reference Branch of the National Archives at College Park, Maryland, especially Military Reference Archivist David Giordano and Archive Specialists Edward Barnes and Doris Jackson.

I would like to especially thank the following veterans for sharing their extraordinary experiences: Harold F. Augspurger, Warren R. Barber, Donald F. Flaherty, Anderson J. Henshaw, Samuel A. Krasney, Willis D. Locke, Garland H. Moore Jr., Murphy C. Painter, George M. Reynolds, Warren G. Rodick, Louis A. Rogers, Frederick O. Sargent, and Leonard H. Stringfield.

To my family and close friends, but most of all to my wife Nancy for her love and long standing support of all my endeavors over the last twenty-five years.

Please note that these people do not necessarily share the viewpoints or opinions expressed within.

Glossary

A-2- Air Intelligence
AA - Anti-aircraft
AAF- Army Air Force
AAI(c)- British Air Force Intelligence
ADI(k)- Air Intelligence (prisoner interrogation)
AFC- Air Force Committee
AGL- Airborne Gun Laying
AI- Air Intercept (Radar)
AOC- Air Officer in Charge
ASV- Aircraft-to-Surface vessel
ATI- Air Technical Intelligence
CA - Coastal Command
CBS- Columbia Broadcasting System
CIOS- Combined Intelligence Objectives Subcommittee
CIPC- Combined Intelligence Priorities Committee
COI- Coordinator of Intelligence
CSDIC- Combined Services Detailed Interrogation Center
DDI- Deputy Director of Intelligence
FLO- Flak Liaison Officer
G-2- Army Intelligence
GAP- Guided Aircraft Project
GCA- Ground Control Approach
HB- Heavy Bomber
HE- High Explosives
JICA- Joint Intelligence Collection Agency
MEW- Microwave Early Warning System
MI6- Military Intelligence (Secret)
MI14(E)- Military Intelligence (anti-aircraft: Flak)
MI5- Military Intelligence (Security)
MIT- Massachusetts Institute of Technology
NFS- Night Fighter Squadron
NACA- National Advisory Committee on Aeronautics
NARA- National Archives and Records Administration
NASA- National Aeronautics and Space Administration

NRDC- National Defense Research Council
ONI- Office of Naval Intelligence
ORS- Operational Research Section
OSS- Off ice of Secret Services
POW- Prisoner Of War
PWB- Psychological Warfare Board
RAE- Royal Aircraft Establishment
RAF- Royal Air Force
RCAF- Royal Canadian Air Force
S-2 - Squadron Intelligence
SACRA- Scientific Advisory Committee on Radio Aids
SHAEF- Supreme Headquarters Allied Expeditionary Force
SIS - Secret Intelligence Service
SIAS- Scientific Intelligence Advisory Section
SWPA- South West Pacific Areas
TAC- Tactical Air Command
TAI- Technical Air Intelligence
UFO- Unidentified Flying Object
UNN- United Nations News
USSTAF- United States Strategic Air Forces - Europe
WDGS- War Department General Staff

Notes

Introduction

[1] Beverly Springfax, a high school teacher in Maryland, had relayed her account to several of her English classes in the early 1980s. According to her story, Springfax revealed that during summer months of 1969, through the Civilian Employment Training Agency (CETA), she was hired to work at the Pentagon with the Office of Civil Defense. Her position was personal secretary to a Colonel Sullivan, who was with the United States Army. It was a very small staff, just Colonel Sullivan and herself. One day, while working at her desk, she overheard a conversation between Colonel Sullivan and other Army officers in his office. They discussed "...what they should do with the remains of a crashed flying saucer." Twenty years later, she felt it was okay to reveal this information, since UFO stories were so publicized.

[2] I later discovered that his encounter had scared him immensely. In fact, years later, while visiting with UFO author/researcher Richard Hall, he told Hall that the foo fighter sighting had left such an impact on him that upon his retirement from the Army Air Force, he decided to never fly again in an aircraft; instead he would take a train. I heard this account from Richard Hall in 2003.

[3] Released by the Central Intelligence Agency (CIA) in the 1970s, via the Freedom of Information Act (FOIA).

Chapter 1: Among the War Clouds

[4] "Mystery Aeroplanes Of The 1930s, Part II," by John A. Keel, *Flying Saucer Review*, Vol. 16, No. 4, July/August 1970, pp. 10-11.

[5] Charles Fort, *The Fortean Society & Unidentified Flying Objects*, by Loren Gross, privately published, 1976, p. 45.

[6] Unfortunately, no further details are known about the RAF encounter, other than newspaper articles and the 3 Fighter Squadron's historical records. To my knowledge, their account is the first to officially acknowledge UFO sighting by a unit of the British RAF. It is also the first military pre-war report referencing a "'huge' circular light" causing mechanical malfunction to aircraft and physiological effects on humans. "Aircraft UFO /Encounters Prior To 1942," by Jan Aldrich. http://www.project1947.com/jan42.htm.

[7] Charles Fort, *The Fortean Society & Unidentified Flying Objects*, by Loren Gross, privately published, 1976, pp. 46-48; *Above Top Secret: The Worldwide UFO Cover-Up*, by Timothy Good, William Morrow And Company, 1988, p. 13.

[8] "Mystery Plane Is Hunted By Swedish Army Fliers," *New York Times*, January 1, 1934, pg. 21. Article supplied by Carl Feint.

[9] *Above Top Secret: The Worldwide UFO Cover-Up*, by Timothy Good, William Morrow and Company, 1988, p. 13.

[10] Explaining the sighting requires a real stretch of the imagination. According to phenomena researcher and author John A. Keel who has extensively researched the Scandinavian sightings:

"Arc lights had come into use in the Nineteenth Century but these required heavy, powerful energy sources. Any flying craft using an arc light would have necessarily been overloaded with batteries or a large generator" and "these would not have been bright enough to provide a satisfactory explanation for the brilliant UFO lights."

Mr. Keel further suggests that arc lights, a relatively new invention, were the most powerful lights available in the 1930s. Without them, aircraft used normal landing lights that were no more powerful than lamps attached to automobiles. "The Mystery Aeroplanes Of The 1930s, Part 1," by John A. Keel, *Flying Saucer Review*, Vol. 16, No. 3, May/June 1970, p. 11.

[11] *Above Top Secret: The Worldwide UFO Cover-Up*, by Timothy Good, William Morrow and Company, 1988, p. 13; "Mystery Plane Is Hunted By Swedish Army Fliers," *New York Times*, January 1, 1934, pg. 21. Article supplied by Carl Feint.

[12] "Mystery Plane Reported": *New York Times*, January 10, 1934, p. 11. Article supplied by Carl Feindt.

[13] "Mystery Aeroplanes Of The 1930s, Part II," by John A. Keel, *Flying Saucer Review*, Vol. 16, No. 4, July/August 1970:p. 12. Mr. Keel has keenly suggested: "It is amusing to find that these 1934 newspaper articles indulge in all the wearisome debates of witness reliability and alternate theories which would be repeated over a decade later in the 'ghostrocket' flap of 1946 and the 'flying saucer scare' of 1947."

[14] "Finnish Alarm Grows Over 'Ghost' Planes," *New York Times*, February 4, 1934; supplied by Carl Feindt.

[15] "Mystery Aeroplanes Of The 1930s, Part III," by John A. Keel, *Flying Saucer Review*, Vol. 17, No. 4, July/August 1971, p. 19.

[16] "Mystery Aeroplanes Of The 1930s, Part II," by John A. Keel, *Flying Saucer Review*, Vol. 16, No. 4, July/August 1970, p. 14.

[17] "The Mystery Aeroplanes Of The 1930s, Part I," by John A. Keel, *Flying Saucer Review*, Vol. 16, No. 3, May/June 1970, p. 13.

[18] "Mystery Aeroplanes Of The 1930s, Part II," by John A. Keel, *Flying Saucer Review*, Vol. 16, No. 4, July/August 1970, p. 11.

[19] "Mysterious Planes Soviet's, Oslo Hears," *New York Times*, January 14, 1935, p. 2. Article supplied by Carl Feindt.

[20] "Mystery Aeroplanes Of The 1930s, Part II," by John A. Keel, *Flying Saucer Review*, Vol. 16, No. 4, July/August 1970, p. 11.

[21] *Charles Fort, The Fortean Society & Unidentified Flying Objects*, by Loren Gross, privately published, 1976, p. 48.

[22] *Strange Skies: Pilot Encounters with UFOs*, by Jerome Clark, Citadel Press Books, 2003, p. 6.

[23] "Mystery Aeroplanes Of The 1930s, Part IV," by John A. Keel, *Flying Saucer Review*, Volume 17, No. 5, September/October 1931, p. 22.

[24] *Charles Fort, The Fortean Society & Unidentified Flying Objects*, by Loren Gross, privately published, 1976, pp. 48-49.

[25] *Mysteries of The Skies: UFOs In Perspective*, by Gordon Lore, Jr., and Harold H. Denault, Jr., Prentice-Hall, Inc., 1968, pp. 136-137.

Chapter 2: From War of the Worlds, To a World at War

[26] *New York Times*, Monday, October 31, 1938; Script of *The War of the Worlds*, by H.G. Wells, as performed by Orson Welles and the Mercury Theater on the Air, and broadcast on the Columbia Broadcast System on Sunday, October 30, 1938, from 8:00 to 9:00 p.m., http://members.aol.com/jeff1070/script.html.

[27] Transcription from live broadcast: July 27, 1939; courtesy of Wendy Connor's Faded Disc Archives, 2004.

[28] The first flight of the Douglas DC-3 took place on December 17, 1935. http://en.wikipedia.org/wiki/Douglas_DC-3

[29] *Mysteries of the Skies: UFOs in Perspective*, by Gordon I.R. Lore, Jr., and Harold H. Deneault, Jr., Prentice-Hall, Inc., 1968, p. 138.

[30] *The Second World War: A Complete History*, Revised Edition, by Martin Gilbert, An Owl Book, Henry Holt and Company, 1989, pp. 3-4.

[31] *Most Secret War: British Scientific Intelligence, 1939-1945*, by DR. R.V. Jones, Book Club Associates, Great Britain, 1978, pp. 57-66.

[32] *Strange Secrets: Real Government Files on the Unknown*, by Nick Redfern and Andy Roberts, Paraview Pocket Books, 2003, pp. 54-55.

[33] Whether or not Jones studied the 1930s "mystery plane" reports, by 1940 he certainly had access to reports of strange aerial phenomena.

[34] "Administrative Report of OSRD Activities in The European Theater," Part Two of Report of OSRD Activities in the European Theater During the Period March 1941 through July 1945. NARA (National Archives and Records Administration). By the summer of 1941, the NDRC became the Office of Scientific Research and Development (OSRD)

[35] The mission included members: "Sir Henry Tizard (Mission Leader, Brigadier F.C. Wallace (Army), Captain H.W. Faulkner (Navy), Group Captain F.L.Pearce (RAF), Professor John Cockcroft (Army Research),Dr. E.G. Bowen (Radar), and A.E. Woodward Nutt (Secretary). "The Tizard Mission to the USA and Canada," by Dr.

E.G. Bowen, pp. 1-2, http://www.radarworld.org/tizard.html.

[36] "Administrative Report of OSRD Activities In The European Theater," Part Two of Report of OSRD Activities in the European Theater During the Period March 1941 through July 1945. By the summer of 1941, the NDRC became the Office of Scientific Research and Development (OSRD)

[37] *The Office of Strategic Services: America's First Intelligence Agency*, A publication of the Central Intelligence Agency, 2000, p. 2.

[38] *Mysteries of the Skies: UFOs in Perspective*, by Gordon I.R. Lore, Jr. and Harold H. Deneault, Jr. Prentice-Hall, Inc., 1968, p. 130-131.

[39] *The Second World War: A Complete History, Revised Edition*, by Martin Gilbert, An Owl Book, Henry Holt and Company, 1989, pp. 272-278.

[40] *Mysteries of the Skies: UFOs in Perspective*, by Gordon I.R. Lore, Jr. and Harold H. Deneault, Jr. Prentice-Hall, Inc., 1968, p. 140.

[41] *Mysteries of the Skies: UFOs in Perspective*, by Gordon I.R. Lore, Jr. and Harold H. Deneault, Jr. Prentice-Hall, Inc., 1968, pp. 140-141.

Chapter 3: Over Coasts and Valleys

[42] *Mysteries of the Skies: UFOs in Perspective*, by Gordon Lore, Jr., and Harold H. Denault, Jr., Prentice-Hall, Inc., 1968, p.76.

[43] Naval Intelligence had been informed by reliable sources that "an attack could be expected within the next ten hours." "The History of the Fourth AA Command, Western Defense Command," Jan 9, 1942 to July 1, 1945 (extract), The Computer UFO Network (CUFON):http://www.cufon.org/.

[44] *"Mysteries of the Skies: UFOs in Perspective,"* by Gordon Lore, Jr. and Harold H. Denault, Jr., Prentice-Hall, Inc., 1968, p.76; "The History of the Fourth AA Command, Western Defense Command," Jan 9, 1942 to July 1, 1945 (extract), The Computer UFO Network (CUFON): http://www.cufon.org/.

[45] "The History of the Fourth AA Command, Western Defense Command," Jan 9, 1942 to July 1, 1945 (extract), The Computer UFO Network (CUFON): http://www.cufon.org/.

[46] *The Army Air Forces In World War II: Volume I, The Plans and Early Operations*, January 1939 To August 1942, Edited by W.F. Craven and J.L. Crate, University of Chicago Press, 1948, p. 283.

[47] *Mysteries of the Skies, UFOs in Perspective*, by Gordon Lore, Jr. and Harold H. Denault, Jr., Prentice-Hall, Inc., 1968, pp. 76-83.

[48] *Above Top Secret: The Worldwide UFO Cover-Up*, by Timothy Good, William Morrow and Company, 1988, pp. 15-17.

[49] "1942 'Battle of Los Angeles' Biggest Mass Sighting In History New Photo Analysis," by Jeff Rense, no date, http://www.rense.com/ufo/battleofla.htm.

[50] *Above Top Secret: The Worldwide UFO Cover-Up*, by Timothy Good, William Morrow and Company, 1988, pp. 15-17.

[51] Testimonies given after the event at the 37th Brigade Headquarters in Washington reflects a very unusual degree of confusion and conflicting details.

[52] It was later learned that a meteorological balloon was sent aloft that night.

[53] *Mysteries of the Skies: UFOs in Perspective*, by Gordon Lore, Jr., and Harold H. Denault, Jr., Prentice-Hall, Inc., 1968, pp. 76-84.

[54] *The Army Air Forces In World War II: Volume I, The Plans and Early Operations*, January 1939 To August 1942, Edited by W.F. Craven and J.L. Crate, University of Chicago Press, 1948, p. 283.

[55] *Journal-Every Evening*, Wilmington Delaware, Thursday, February 26, 1942: 1, 4. Article supplied by Carl Feindt.

[56] The *Army Air Forces In World War II: Volume I, The Plans and Early Operations*, January 1939 To August 1942, Edited by W.F. Craven and J.L. Crate, University of Chicago Press, 1948, p. 284.

[57] *Journal-Every Evening*, Wilmington, Delaware, Thursday, February 26, 1942: 1, 4. Article supplied by Carl Feindt.

[58] Memorandum for the President, signed George C. Marshal, Chief of Staff, February 26, 1942. Document provided by Fund for UFO Research.

[59] The so-called Battle of Los Angeles represents the first major wartime press coverage, and possibly the first attempted deception by the United States government, of UFOs.

[60] *UFOs and the National Security State: Chronology of a Cover-up 1941-1973*, by Richard M. Dolan. Hampton Roads Publishing Company, 2002, pp. 5-6.

[61] *Mysteries of the Skies: UFOs in Perspective*, by Gordon Lore, Jr. and Harold H. Denault, Jr., Prentice-Hall, Inc., 1968, pp. 141-142; Letter: Rev. Robert H. Moore to Ed J. Sullivan, Civilian Saucer Investigations April 7, 1942. Document provided by Jan Aldrich.

[62] *The Office of Strategic Services: America's First Intelligence Agency*, A publication of the Central Intelligence Agency, 2000. Donovan went about recruiting some of the best minds in the country, seeking them out in college and universities and well-respected business establishments.

[63] Other important developments also occurred on June 13, 1942. Nazi scientists had tested A-4, the world's first ballistic missile, launched from Usedom, a small island sitting just off north Germany's Coast in the Baltic Sea. The A-4 was hidden at Germany's

top-secret joint Army/Luftwaffe research center: Peenumunde. *The Rocket and the Reich-Peenumunde And The Coming Of The Ballistic Missile Era*, by Michael J. Neufeld, Smithsonian Institution, Free Press, Division of Simon And Schuster, 1995, p. 161.

[64] Transcript of Ray Sabinski interview, provided by Wendy Connors; "UFO Sighting From an Aircraft" – Report Form, provided by Barry Greenwood, *MUFON Journal*, Number 290, provided by Jan Aldrich.

[65] That summer, as Lt. Sabinski and crew were getting the hell scared out of them, the first planes of the new U.S. Eighth Air Force arrived in Britain. *The Mighty Eighth, A History Of The Units, Men and Machines Of The US Eighth Air Force*, by Roger A. Freeman Cassell & Co., 2000, pp. 4-7.

[66] "Administrative Report of OSRD Activities in The European Theater, Part Two of Report of OSRD Activities in the European Theater During the Period March 1941 through July 1945." NARA. By summer of 1941, the NDRC became the Office of Scientific Research and Development (OSRD). A visiting member with the London mission during the fall of 1941, Robertson became a full resident member soon thereafter.

Chapter 4: What Phenomenon Is It?

[67] *The Second World War: A Complete History, Revised Edition*, by Martin Gilbert, An Owl Book, Henry Holt and Company, 1989, p. 350.

[68] "U.S. Navy 1942 Sighting," Mutual UFO Network, 103 Oldtowne Road, Sequin Texas, *MUFON Journal* 1983; MUFON UFO Sighting Report Form by Robert Neville (field investigator). The witness to this sighting chose to remain anonymous. It should be noted that on 11-13-74 the witness stated in a "MUFON UFO Sighting Report Form" that his sighting had occurred sometime between October 8-10. But further questioning by investigator Neville revealed the sighting occurred two days prior to the Guadacanal invasion. This author believes the witness wrote the wrong date, and the actual date was August, which would match official military history and documented UFO sightings also occurring in early August of 1942.

[69] A letter, likely the late 1950s, sent to the editor of *Fantastic Universe*, who forwarded it to Civilian Saucer Investigations (CSI). Copy provided by Jan Aldrich; *Above Top Secret The Worldwide UFO Cover-Up*, by Timothy Good, William Morrow And Company, Inc. New York, 1988, p. 18.

[70] *Flying Saucers Uncensored* by Harold T. Wilkens, p. 224. The witness requested that his real name not be used in any report.

These three Pacific sightings must have caused great concern at the U.S. War Department and Britain's Department of War, and may have started an Office of Naval Intelligence (ONI) investigation. Regarding Major Brennan's encounter, his sighting is the first known wartime case to mention an actual symbol on the craft. But more astounding is the fact that the aircraft flew into and out of water. Again, there is no known documentation available to corroborate these stories.

[71] *The Second World War: A Complete History, Revised Edition*, by Martin Gilbert, Holt and Co., 1989, P. 339.

[72] Headquarters, Coastal Command, Intelligence Command, Intelligence Summary, No. 166, 30 august to 6 September, 1942. NARA.

[73] Telephone conversation with aviation expert Don Berliner, July 11, 2004.

[74] "1942 Sighting On The Russian Front," by J. Burns BSc., supplied to author by researcher Jan Aldrich. The witness (name withheld) relayed his story to his son-in-law. Unfortunately, the witness could not recall the exact date. The author of the magazine article noted that the object's size was more than twice the size of the Hindenburg airship.

[75] Letter to Dr. David T. Griggs, from Dr. Edward L. Bowles, Expert Consultant to the Secretary of War, 18 August 1942. NARA.

[76] Operational Research Section, Bomber Command, Report 53, "A Note On Recent Enemy Pyrotechnic Activity Over Germany," September 25, 1942. Public Records Office File: AIR 14/2076. Crown copyright exists. Document provided by Nick Pope.

Chapter 5: Neither a Dream, Nor a Buck Rogers Invention
[77] On October 12, Headquarters, Bomber Command, sent a memo titled "Enemy Defenses-Phenomenon" to eight Bomb Groups. Attached was the September 25 ORS "Pyrotechnic" Report. (Memorandum, Enemy Defenses-Phenomenon, from Air Vice-Marshal, Senior Air Staff Officer, Headquarters, Bomber Command, to Headquarters, Numbers One through Five, Ninety-one through Ninety-Three Groups, 12 October, 1942, Public Records Office File: AIR 14/2076. Crown copyright exists. Document provided by Nick Pope.

[78] Headquarters, Eighth Fighter Command, ETOUSA, *Weekly Intelligence Summary*, 12 October thru 18 October 1942. NARA.

[79] RAF Station Syerston to Headquarters, No. 5 Group (Attention Major Mullock, M.C., FLO), 2 December, 1942, Public Records Office File: AIR 14/2076. Crown copyright exists. Document provided by Nick Pope.

[80] Memorandum, Enemy Defenses-Phenomenon, from Headquarters, No. 5 Group, to Headquarters Bomber Command, 3 December, 1942, Public Records Office File: AIR 14/2076. Crown copyright exists. Document provided by Nick Pope.

[81] Military Intelligence Division, WDGS, Subject: Consolidated Flak Liaison Officer Report, 14 December, No. 133, for period 28 November through December 14, 1942. NARA.

[82] The witness requested complete anonymity.

[83] C.J.J. and his crew were interrogated, but so far no information concerning their mission report has been recovered. Civilian Research, *Interplanetary Flying Objects Newsletter* (CRIFO), Jan. 7, 1955. Edited by Leonard Stringfield.

[84] There was an extensive amount of film shot, in the millions of feet, during the war, both

black and white and in color. So there is a good chance that good deal of wartime UFO footage exists.

[85] Newspaper article: "Wartime Experience," by Mr. B.C. Lumsden. Date unknown. Document provided by Jan Aldrich.

[86] MI14(E) Periodical, AA Intelligence Summary, No.7, MI14(E), War Office, 18, Dec. 1942. NARA.

[87] On December 26, the U.S. Eighth Air Force devoted three full pages to the subject of Flak Phenomena, reprinting the December 18, MI14(e) summary in their *Weekly Air Intelligence Digest*. Air Intelligence staff with the Eighth Air Force offered no new information or further comments. Eighth US Air Force *Weekly Air Intelligence Digest*, week ending Dec. 26, 1942. NARA.

[88] Command Information Intelligence- Series No. 43-1, "Notes on Recent German Pyrotechnic Activity," January 13, 1943. Document provided by Barry Greenwood.

[89] Gunner's Briefing Notes, January 11, 1943. NARA.

[90] Interrogation Form 384th Bombardment Group, January 11, 1943. NARA.

[91] Military Intelligence Division, WDGS, Military Attaché, Germany, Subject: Consolidated Flak Liaison Officer Report, No. 139, 25 January, 1943, for period 9-17 January, 1943. NARA.

[92] Antiaircraft Section European Theater of Operations United States Army, Antiaircraft Notes No. 16, March 2, 1943. NARA.

[93] U.S. Army Air Forces in the Middle East, Periodic Intelligence Summary, March 20 – March 27, issued on March 27. NARA.

[94] Military Intelligence Division, WDGS, Military Attaché Report, Germany, Subject: Consolidated Flak Liaison Officer Report, No. 159, 27 May, 1943. NARA.

[95] Military Intelligence Division WDGS, Military Attaché Report, Subject: Consolidated Flak Liaison Officer Report, No. 161, 30 May, 1943. NARA.

[96] "Foo-Fighters the RAF Experience" by David Clarke and Andy Roberts, *UFO Magazine*, page 9; BUFORA - UFO Sighting From An Aircraft - Report Form. Provided by Jan Aldrich

[97] Though there was mention that two crews reported the "scarecrow" flares, this was the only phenomenon sighted. Military Intelligence Division WDGS, Military Attaché Report, Germany, Subject: Consolidated FLO Report, 25 to 28 May 43, No. 162, MI14(E), War Office, 2 June 1943. NARA.

[98] "RAF Officer's UFO Experiences, Subject: A Report of UFO Sightings," by Gordon W. Cammell Royal Air Force, retired; *Strange Secrets: Real Government Files on the Unknown*,

Nick Redfern and Andy Roberts, Paraview Pocket Books, 2003.

[99] Letter: David T. Griggs to General H.H. Arnold, June 11, 1943, NARA.

[100] The British War Office's MI14(E) had assigned a flak liaison officer with the U.S. First Bombardment Wing to report high altitude B-17 Flying Fortress daytime missions, including "the experiences with anti-aircraft over selected targets, enemy methods of fire control, counter-measures, and evasive action recommended, for the period of August 1942 to June 1943." The VIII Bomber Command report Anti-Aircraft Memorandum No. 5: Report of Flak Liaison Officer, First Bombardment Wing on 'German Anti-Aircraft Defense against Daylight High Altitude Bombing Formations'." The report was discussing the use of what would be later called "window," aluminum strips of various size and shapes, used as a deterrent to foul-up accurate radar readings. It was sent to the Chief of Military Intelligence in the War Department, Washington, D.C. and was considered of interest for the entire Army Air Force and Anti- Aircraft Commands. Anti-Aircraft Memorandum No. 5, Headquarters VIII Bomber Command, July 22, 1943. NARA.

[101] British AA Command Intelligence Review, No. 149, reprinted in Antiaircraft Notes No. 44, Antiaircraft Section, European Theater of Operations United States Army, September 22, 1943. NARA.

[102] *Weekly Air Intelligence Digest*, Eighth U.S. Air Force, September 5, 1943. NARA.

Chapter 6: Silvery-Discs, Pie-Plates, and the Light
[103] Secret 384th BG memo to A-2 Duty Desk, Section 'A'; Report of Operations 6 September 1943, Headquarters VIII Bomber Command to Commanding General, Headquarters Eighth Air Force, October 18, 1943; AA Gun Fire Report – Stuttgart, prepared by Second Lt. S.F. Araus for Major W.E. Dolan, station S-2 Officer, September 6, 1943. NARA.

[104] 384th BG, Stuttgart Briefing Notes, September 6, 1943. NARA.

[105] Report to Commanding Officer, Headquarters AAF Station No. 106, Office of the Intelligence Officer, Subject: Group Leader's Narrative of Mission flown 6 September 1943. NARA.

[106] AA Gun Fire Report – Stuttgart, prepared by Second Lt. S.F. Araus for Major W.E. Dolan, station S-2 Officer, September 6, 1943; Secret 384th BG memorandum, ATTN: A-2 Duty Desk, Section 'A'; received by Signals Office, 7 September. NARA.

[107] 384 BG memorandum, ATTN: A-2 Duty Desk Section 'A'; received by Signals Office, 7 September. NARA.

[108] Confidential Memo, Attention: A-2 Duty Desk, First BW, Subject: Additional Information On The Observation Of Silvery Colored Discs On Mission To Stuttgart, 6 Sept., 1943. NARA. Note the different terminology used in the description of the objects. They are described initially as "discs," but then "balls" within the same paragraph.

[109] Antiaircraft Weekly Intelligence Bulletin No 15, Allied Force Headquarters Antiaircraft & Coast Defense Section, September 11, 1943. NARA.

[110] Message from General Eaker to General Arnold, September 12, 1943. NARA.

[111] Memorandum to Lt. Colonel Harry W. Besse from Major W.W. Spencer, Chief, Tactical Section; Subject: Possible Explanation of Silvery-Colored Discs Used on Stuttgart Mission, 6 September, 1943, dated 16 September, 1943, NARA. The Eight Air Force's A-2 section addressed the issue on September 19: "'Silver' Air Incendiaries on Two Fronts," US Eighth Air Force *Weekly Air Intelligence Digest*, Sunday, 19 September, 1943. NARA.

[112] Memorandum from W.M. Burgess, Colonel, G.S.C., Chief, Information Division, Office of Assistant Chief of Air Staff, Intelligence, to Commanding General, Eighth Air Force; Attention: Colonel Lucius Ordway, A-2, Subject: Phenomena Observed on Stuttgart Mission, 6 September 1943, dated September 22, 1943. NARA.

[113] *AA Intelligence Review* No. 153, 17 September to 24 September, 1943. NARA.

[114] *Weekly Air Intelligence Digest*, Eighth Air Force, Sunday, 26 September 1943. NARA.

[115] Headquarters VIII Bomber Command, Narrative of Operations, Operation 115, October 14, 1943. NARA
    In his 1960 book, *Black Thursday*, author Martin Caidin presented the first reference to an aerial phenomenon seen over the city of Schweinfurt, Germany by American bomber crews during the famous raid on October 24, 1943. Citing information from official military memoranda, then unavailable to the general public, Caiden reported the bomber crew's observations of "disc"-shaped objects during their raid. Students of UFOlogy have come to know this particular document as the "Schweinfurt Memo." Over the last five decades, the Schweinfurt sighting has been referenced in UFO literature, becoming a pivotal case promoting a belief that the "discs" were extraterrestrial spacecraft. It was not until the late 1990s that Caiden's claim was corroborated with the discovery of documentation found in an ocean of records at both the Unites States National Archives and England's Public Records Office. Researchers were now able to confirm the Schweinfurt "discs" and put them into perspective. "WWII Document Research (in search of 'Foo-Fighters')," by Andy Roberts, (originally published in: *UFO Brigantia*, No. 66, July 1990; "Schweinfurt-A Mystery Solved?" by Andy Roberts, 2000, http://www.project1947.com/articles/arwwr.htm.
    Though the Schweinfurt "discs" have proven conventional in nature, they remain important to this book; Air Intelligence had added one more item to their phenomena category that inadvertently masked some sightings of real disc-shaped UFOs.

[116] Loading Lists for 546 Bombardment Squadron (H), AAF Station No. 106, 14 October 1943. NARA.

[117] Memorandum from RAF, Oakley, to USAAF 384th Bombardment Group, October 14, 1943. NARA.

[118] "Defense Against the Fortress," Headquarters Eighth Air Force, Office of the Assistant

Chief of Staff A-2, Special Report No. 83, 28 August 1943. NARA.

[119] Eighth US Air *Weekly Air Intelligence Digest*, Vol. III, No. 14, Force, Sunday, 3 October, 1944. NARA.

[120] Message from General Devers for General Strong, October 8, 1943. NARA.

[121] *Crossbow and Overcast*, James McGovern, William Morrow and Company, 1964, pp. 38-39.

[122] Memorandum For The Director, New Developments Division: Subject: Organization and Functions, New Developments Division, War Department, October 13, 1943, from Henry L. Stimson, Secretary of War. NARA.

[123] Air Force General Information Bulletin 17, November, 1943, Assistant Chief of Air Staff, Intelligence. NARA.

[124] One of the more extraordinary accounts describing a sighting of unconventional aircraft surfaced in Italy during the 1990s. Though compelling, it is included here, but must be viewed with skepticism until further validating information surfaces. This information was supplied by an operative (demanding complete anonymity) who worked "together with Morpugno, Pontecorvo, and Mario Soldati, as well as with the famous Colonel Stevens of the BBC."

[125] In 1998, Italian researcher Fabio di Rado conducted an interview with a man (requesting complete anonymity) who provided this account. In addition to his testimony, he provided copies of still photographs of the films he viewed. The pictures were downloaded onto a CD, along with other documents by researcher Fabio di Rado. "Foo Fighters and the SAS," *UFO Magazine*, Jan./Feb. 2002.

[126] Churchill had appointed Under-Secretary at the Ministry of Supply Duncan Sandy to study the state of German secret weapons. Sandy's investigation led him to the conclusion that Peenumunde was very significant. He was informed that neither the British or Americans, nor Russians had achieved any measurable success, other than "small rockets with limited range." *Crossbow and Overcast*, by James McGovern, William Morrow and Co., 1964, pp. 11.

[127] *Crossbow and Overcast*, James McGovern, William Morrow and Company, 1964, pp 38-39.

[128] This case was extracted from Project 1947, UFO Reports – 1943, http://www.project1947.com/fig/1943a.htm. According to Jan Aldrich, this case was from a letter to Project Bluebook written in 1952 by the witness who was a Civil Aeronautics Administration safety agent in Seattle.

[129] Consolidated Flak Report (5-17 Dec 43) No. 192, MI 15, War Office, December 22, 1943, NARA.

[130] Wells made reference in his flight log (of which he kept a copy): "Screaming Dog-

fight with the 'light'." Wells was unable to remember if he had reported his December 14 "light" sighting to the 255's Intelligence Officer after arriving back at base; he assumed he did, but generally, the aircrews in his unit were not debriefed unless they had encountered an enemy fighter. Wells further recollected that typically the intelligence officers showed little interest in the light sightings.

Wells was assigned to the 73 Hurricane Night Fighters, flying May through July 1943 in the Tunisia area. "Many" crews had seen the light and he remained skeptical until personally witnessing the light. Later that year, he transferred to the 255 Beaufighter Night Fighters, and the December 14, 1943 sighting became his second encounter with the light; and they were reported with regularity. Personal Correspondence: Wells and researcher Andy Roberts, August 16, 1987. Supplied by Jan Aldrich, Project 1947.

[131] The article also referenced crews observing red and silver discs. 115 Squadron Newsletter article: "Bang On," Issue 1, December 31, 1943; supplied by Nick Cook. Crown Copyright exists.

Chapter 7: Rockets, Airships, and Balloons
[132] *The United States Army In World War II: The European Theater of Operations, Cross-Channel Attack* by Gordon A. Harrison, Konecky & Konecky, 1950, pp. 46-51.

[133] SHAEF included the Supreme Commander, General Eisenhower; his Deputy Supreme Commander, Air Chief Marshal, Sir Arthur W. Tedder; Chief of Staff Lt. General Walter Bedell Smith; Army Intelligence, G-2, Major General K.W.D. Strong and Brigadier General Thomas J. Betts; and Air Defense Division Chief, Major General A.M. Cameron. *The D-Day Companion: Leading Historians Explore History's Greatest Amphibious Assault*, Editor Jane Penrose, The National D-Day Museum, New Orleans, 2003, p. 76; "Administrative Report of OSRD Activities in The European War, Part 2 of Report of OSRD Activities in the European Theater During the Period March 1941 through July 1945," NARA.

[134] Extract From Raid Report M/463 Squadron Night 2/3 January 1944. Crown Copyright exists. Document Supplied by Nick Pope.

[135] Memo from Headquarters, No 53 Base, to Headquarters, No. 5 Group, January 30, 1944. Crown Copyright exists. Document Supplied by Nick Pope.

[136] Headquarters, First Bombardment Division, Report of Operations, Kiel, Germany, Tours, France, January 5, 1944 to Commanding General, Eighth Air Force. NARA.

[137] Major Jesse M. Barrett, Group S-2, 303rd Bombardment Group, Narrative of Mission, 5 January 1944, to Commanding Officer, 303rd Headquarters AAF Station 107, 5 January, 1944. NARA.

[138] Operational Report, 306th Bomb Group to Commanding General First Bombardment Division and Commanding General Fortieth Combat Wing, Attention A-2. NARA.

[139] Headquarters 2nd Bombardment Command, Tactical Report of Mission, 5 January 1944, to Commanding General, Eighth Air Force, AAF Station 101. NARA.

[140] Captain Edward R. Burkardt, Group S-2 Officer, Mission Report to Headquarters 17th Bombardment Group (M) [Medium Bombers], 6 January, 1944. NARA.

[141] As of March, British Intelligence "was still unable to provide Prime Minister Churchill or the *Crossbow* Committee with any specific details about the German long-range rocket," spelling disaster for the allied soldiers. The Crossbow Committee told Eisenhower that, to the best of their knowledge, there were no missiles, but they were not entirely sure. General Leslie Groves, the commanding officer overseeing America's atomic program, was also concerned that the Germans were able to launch a concentrated barrage of missiles carrying radioactive warheads along the French coast. Eisenhower's advisors were correct. General Eisenhower would have to make hundreds of decisions, "two of them unknown to the men of the invasion forces and to any but his closest advisors": German atomic capabilities and long range rockets. Eisenhower was worried about the possibility of long range strikes hitting the staging areas in England. *Crossbow and Overcast* by James McGovern, William Morrow and Company, Inc., 1964, pp. 51-60.

[142] Under the umbrella of Major General S.G. Henry's New Developments Division, the Committee on Countermeasures against German Secret Weapons held their first meeting. In attendance, as well as members of G-2 (Army Intelligence) and the AAF, three scientists were present: A.L. Loomis, Roger Adams, and H.P. Robertson. General Henry reemphasized the importance of resolving the German long-range projectiles. General Henry turned over the meeting to its new chairman, Colonel C.P. Nicholas. Colonel Nicholas stated that although the committee was an American organization, if they rejected any conclusions or information by their British counterparts, they had to inform them. The committee focused on countermeasures, not intelligence matters. Plans were laid to send an officer and scientist to the theater immediately to exchange ideas with the British. "Minutes of First Meeting of Committee on Counter-measures against German Secret Weapon," 6, January, 1944. NARA.

[143] Memorandum for the Chairman n Counter-measures against German Secret Weapons, January 7, 1944. NARA.

[144] Report from Headquarters, MACAF to Headquarters, MAAF (REAR), Headquarters MAAF (ADV.), and CSDIC, AFHQ 28 January, 1944. NARA.

[145] Memo, Subject: Rocket Phenomena, from Group Captain, Headquarters, No. 52 Base, to Headquarters, No. 5 Group, 29 January, 1944. Crown Copyright exists. Document Supplied by Nick Pope.

[146] RAF document, February 2, 1944 (partially typed and hand-written). Crown Copyright exists. Document Supplied by Nick Pope.

[147] Memorandum signed by [name illegible], February 6, 1944. Crown Copyright exists. Document Supplied by Nick Pope.

[148] Report from Headquarters, No. 5 Group, Subject: Rocket Phenomena. Sent to No. 51 Base, RAF Stations; Swinderby, Winthrop, Wigsley, Syerston; No. 52 Base, RAF Stations, Scampton, Dunholme, Fiskerton; No. 53 Base, RAF Stations, Waddington, Bardney, Skellingthorpe; No. 54 Base, RAF Stations, Coningsby, Metheringham,

Woodhall; and RAF Stations, East Kirkby, Spilsby, dated 9 February, 1944. Crown Copyright exists. Document supplied by Nick Pope.

[149] Minutes of Special Meeting of the Crossbow Committee with E. L. Bowles, January 31, 1944; Interview with E.L. Bowles, Office of the Secretary of War, on 31 January 1944. NARA.

[150] Interview: E.L. Bowles, Office of the Secretary of War, 31 January 1944. NARA.

[151] 384th Bomb Group, Briefing Notes, February 8, 1944. NARA.

[152] Confidential Operational Report, 303rd Bomb Group, no date, NARA.

[153] 92nd Bomb Group, Confidential report to: A-2, First Bombardment Division and 41st Combat Wing Command, 4 February 1944. NARA.

[154] Confidential 482nd Bomb Group, Operational Narrative Report, Mission of 4 February 1944. NARA.

[155] 384th Bomb Group Interrogation Form, February 8, 1944, NARA.

[156] Major W.E. Dolan, Station S-2, 384th Bomb Group, Group Leader's Narrative of Mission Flown on 8 February, 1944, to Commanding Officer, Headquarters 384th Bombardment Group, AAF Station No. 106, Office of the Intelligence Officer, 8 February, 1944, NARA.

[157] Whether they were balloons or not, the Frankfurt sightings were indicative of what was to come in the postwar years. For decades, balloons have been the official explanation by the military and government, becoming a scapegoat explanation for many UFO sightings. Those readers interested in a classic UFO/balloon controversy should research the infamous 1947 case surrounding an incident near the small town of Roswell, New Mexico.

[158] Military Intelligence Division WDGS, Military Attaché Report, Germany, Subject: Consolidated Flak Liaison Officer Report, 7 March, 1944 (19-24 Feb 44), No. 205, MI15, War Office, 27 February 1944; NARA.

[159] Brief note marked "Secret," Germany, 6535 (R) Phenomena, Source: Military Attaché London-66474-9 March 1944 – filed Special Binder; Military Intelligence Division WDGS Military Attaché Report, Germany, Subject: Consolidated Flak Liaison Officer Report. NARA.

[160] On March 15, the battle for Monte Cassino, a famous Monastery and key German stronghold, kept the allies from advancing, and was again the site of an intense battle. First, there was a massive aerial strike, followed by a concentrated and brutal artillery barrage. It was soon followed by an aggressive infantry attack. After the smoke had cleared, amazingly Monte Cassino was still in German hands. *The Second World War*, Revised edition, by Martin Gilbert, Henry Holt and Company, 1989, An Owl Book Henry Holt and Company, 1989, p. 509.

[161] Confidential Memorandum Number 45-7, Capture Intelligence Interrogation Of Air Prisoners Of War Examination Of Enemy Equipment, by command of Major General Nathing Twining, March 15, 1944. NARA.

[162] "United States Strategic Air Forces In Europe Air Intelligence Summary," No. 18, For Week Ending 12 March, 1944. NARA.

[163] "United States Strategic Air Forces In Europe Air Intelligence Summary," No. 19, For Week Ending 19 March, 1944. NARA.

[164] USSTAF was composed of the Eighth and Fifteenth Air Forces, and Spaatz had administrative control over the Ninth Air Force, which was specifically designated to support the Cross Channel invasion.

[165] General Spaatz assigned the job to his Deputy Commanding General for Administration, Major General Hugh Kneer. It was General Kneer's responsibility to make things happen. Wright field personnel reported to Colonel H.G. Bunker, commander of the Directorate of Technical Services and its new subdivision, the Air Technical Intelligence Section (ATI). General George McDonald, known for his ability to "fix things," was his Chief of Intelligence. General McDonald was not directly in charge of the ATI. McDonald felt all intelligence matters should be under his control, something he was determined to accomplish; until then, Wright Field ran the show. *American Raiders: The Race To Capture The Luftwaffe's Secrets*, by Wolfgang W. E. Samuel, University Press of Mississippi, 2004, pp. 65-66.

[166] Bowles informed Griggs on March 4 that in addition to his other responsibilities, he was assigned to General Spaatz's office to "assist in the introduction and application of the H2X radar blind bombing equipment." Bowles further informed Griggs that he was free at all times to discuss any technical matter. Letter to Griggs from Edward L. Bowles, Expert Consultant to the Secretary of War, and Communications Consultant to the Commanding General, Army Air Forces, March 4, 1944; Letter, Subject: Advisory Specialist Group, from Lt. General Spaatz to Commanding General, Eighth Air Force, 4 March, 1944. NARA.

[167] "Administrative Report of OSRD Activities In The European War, Part 2" of Report of OSRD Activities in the European Theater During the Period March 1941 through July 1945. NARA.

[168] Robertson was also a consultant to Operational Research Section, Eighth Air Force; member of OSRD's London Mission; and member of the War Department's Secret Weapons Committee, New Developments Division.

[169] He was able to answer the committee without certainty and wanted his audience to realize his discussion was impromptu and not an official report. There was too much that needed clarifying. Basically, the British were receiving a huge amount of intelligence from a variety of sources. The Air Ministry seemed to be operations center, and Air Marshal Bottomley was overseeing the whole of Crossbow. The British were sharing complete information with the United States. The consensus was that the German rockets were a real potential menace, but their numbers, ability to destroy London and

other large cities, and threat to the outcome of Overlord, could not be determined with reliability. Even at this late date, only educated assessments could be offered. Report Of Meeting Of Crossbow Committee, New Developments Division, War Department Special Staff.

[170] Report Of Meeting Of Crossbow Committee, New Developments Division, War Department Special Staff, Room 3C-960, Pentagon Building, On 5 April 1944, 2 P.M.-3:50 P.M.

[171] *Crossbow and Overcast*, by James McGovern, William Morrow and Company, New York, 1964, p. 40.

[172] Air Intelligence had not yet realized the Me-163B was rocket propelled. United States Strategic Air Forces In Europe Air Intelligence Summary, No. 26, For Week Ending 7 May 1944, NARA.

[173] AI2(a) Report No. 114/44: German Aircraft Industry Jet Propelled Aircraft-Production Aspect, April 17, 1944. NARA.

[174] Colonel H.G. Bunker, Director of Technical Services, home of the new Air Technical Section had requested a list of the German experimental stations on March 28. The list was supplied by British AI2(g), but it was several months old. Thus far, the aircraft firms that were known numbered about seven in all: Arado, Blohm &Voss, Donier, Fieseler, Focke-Wulf, Gotha, and Heinkel. Each of the firms had several affiliated test or experimental stations, but nothing was known about the Gotha firm. In-house letter, subject: German Experimental establishments, to Colonel H.G. Bunker, Director of Technical Services, from Captain Robert L. Abbey, Headquarters, European Theater of Operations, United States Army, Air Technical Section, Technical Intelligence, ASC –USSTAF, 19 April, 1944. NARA.

[175] Personal correspondence: Arthur Horton to researcher Andy Roberts, May 19, 1987. Document provided by Jan Aldrich.

[176] Horton, interviewed years later, said "…there was great hilarity at having been 'chased by rockets,' but I can assure you it wasn't very funny at the time." Personal correspondence from Arthur Horton to researcher Andy Roberts, May 19, 1987, and personal correspondence from Bernard Dye to researcher Andy Roberts, May 26, 1987. Document Provided by Jan Aldrich.

[177] According to Dye: "This incident happened on my second operation, our next 28 operations which we were in combat with three German night-fighters, but thank goodness no more 'orange' objects which were very frightening, I for one thought they would hit us and then explode." Personal correspondence: Bernard Dye to researcher Andy Roberts, May 26, 1987. Document provided by Jan Aldrich.

[178] Personal correspondence: Arthur Horton to researcher Andy Roberts, May 19, 1987. Provided by Jan Aldrich; Personal correspondence: Bernard Dye to researcher Andy Roberts, May 26, 1987. Documents provided by Jan Aldrich.

Chapter 8: ATI and CIOS

[179] Consolidated FLO Report MI15. War Office, May 4, 1944. NARA.

[180] Also included were "airfields and airfield construction, air installations, stores, parks and dumps, but excepting flak weapons, weapons and equipment of airborne troops and equipment or supplies common to ground and Air Forces. The excepted are Ground Force responsibilities.

[181] In case "new equipment" was discovered, an agreement between the War Office and War Department established that the first specimen would be sent to authorities in England and the second piece would go to the appropriate U.S. authorities. Army groups on the ground would send reports without delay to the appropriate headquarters; enemy radar and Luftwaffe equipment to the Allied Expeditionary Air Force and "all new equipment" directly to SHAEF. Intelligence Directive No. 9, Technical Intelligence, SHAEF, May 19, 1944. NARA.

[182] Final Report of "S" Force Operations, Headquarters "S" Force, C/O HQ. Fifth Army, US Army, to Commanding General, Rome Area, 17 June, 1944. NARA.

[183] According to author James McGovern, who was a post-war "intelligence agent in Germany for five years," none of the soldiers fighting out from the beaches and cliffs toward Carentan, Isigny, St. Lo, and Caen could know this. Nor could they know that Chemical Warfare troops had followed them ashore with Geiger counters but had found no traces of radioactivity. And they could not know that the failure of the secret weapons to attack them had greatly relieved the few Allied leaders who knew of the threat. After two weeks, the beaches were secure. No rockets armed with radioactive material greeted the assaulting forces. The secret weapons had failed to make an appearance and "reply to the invasion." However, it would not be long before the V-1s began launching against England, not the Normandy beaches. *Crossbow and Overcast* by James McGovern, William Morrow and Company, Inc., 1964, pp. 51-60.

[184] *CRIFO Newsletter*, January 7, 1955, Vol. 1, No. 10, Leonard Stringfield, editor and publisher.

[185] Official Organ of the Inter-Continental Aerial Research Foundation, "Flying Saucer Digest" Vol. 1, No. 1, August 1958. Document provided by Jan Aldrich.

[186] *American Raiders: The Race to Capture The Luftwaffe's Secrets*, by Wolfgang W.E. Samuel, University Press of Mississippi, 2004.
    "Wright Field had graduated 'crash teams,' two or three men with jeep and trailer, fully equipped for independent, field function." The initial ATI members attached themselves to a "Ninth Air Force unit building airstrips at the beachhead." "ATI and Operation LUSTY," Part 1, by Norman Malayney, 1995, p.17.

[187] ATI teams were under the command of Major John Gette, who reported to Colonel E.T. Bradley, who in turn was reporting to senior staff officer of the entire program was Colonel Howard McCoy. AI2(g) Section, under the Wing Commander Wheeler was the organization that the American Air Technical Intelligence teams, units, sections, branches, etc. modeled themselves after.

From beginning of the war, AI2(g) was responsible for exploiting enemy air equipment; the Air Ministry's Scientific Intelligence, ADI (Science), under the leadership of Dr. R.V. Jones, OSRD's London Mission, with whom Robertson was affiliated, and the prisoner of war interrogation branch, ADI (K), were all connected to AI2(g). They were operating all over Europe and Germany. Memorandum to Members of USAAF Technical Teams in Europe, date unknown. NARA.

This organization was most likely instrumental in aiding British Bomber Command's attempt to find an answer to the very perplexing UFO sightings since the war began. Memorandum to Members of USAAF Technical Teams in Europe, date unknown. NARA.

[188] Everything was shipped back to Wright Field for further evaluation; they would follow up with reports of their findings. "ATI and Operation LUSTY," Part 1, by Norman Malayney, 1995, p.17.

[189] On July 27, Intelligence Directive Number 17 -"T"- Force was established by the command of General Eisenhower, and signed by U.S. Army Chief of Staff, Brigadier General W.B. Smith. The "T" Force the directive stated: "It is hoped that the capture of large towns both in enemy occupied and enemy territory may mean that much valuable and special information including documents, equipment and persons, both enemy and others, may become available to the Allied Forces." Supreme Headquarters Allied Expeditionary Force, Office of Assistant Chief of Staff, G-2, Intelligence Directive Number 17, "T" Force, by Command of General Eisenhower, signed by W.B. Smith, Lt. General, US Army, Chief of Staff, 27 July, 1944. NARA.

[190] Combined Intelligence Priorities Committee was "under a British or American chairman and composed of 1 or more representatives, of each nationality, of Navy, Army Air Force and economic warfare, (including American representative of OSRD)." War Department Incoming Message from CG, SHAEF, London, England to War Department, June 12, 1944. NARA.

[191] The CIPC met for the first time on 17 June. Its members began their major task of coordinating the Intelligence gathering. Minutes of Combined Intelligence Priorities Committee, First Meeting held in Conference Room 'B', Great George Street, S.W. 1, on 17 June, 1944, at 2:30 P.M., NARA.

[192] On June 22, a second meeting of CIPC was held, and this time, the European's ALSOS mission chief scientist, Goudsmit, was present (See Appendix Two). In attendance was Commander Ian L. Fleming, whose experience in this field was of greatest value. Britain's most advanced Intelligence operation was the Admiralty's No. 30 Assault Unit, later called 30 AU RN (Assault Unit Royal Navy). This British Royal Commando unit was headed by Commander Fleming. This was the same Ian Fleming whose exploits with this commando group had become well known; their tales would become an inspiration for Fleming's postwar spy novels about agent 007, James Bond. Minutes of Combined Intelligence Priorities Committee, First Meeting held in Conference Room 'B', Great George Street, S.W. 1, on 17 June, 1944, at 2:30 P.M. NARA.

[193] Though unconventional aircraft were not mentioned, categories for "working parties" were listed in: Minutes of Combined Intelligence Priorities Committee, First Meeting

held in Conference Room 'B', Great George Street, S.W. 1, on 17 June, 1944, at 2:30 P.M. NARA.

[194] By July 25, 1944, Robertson, back from an intelligence gathering mission in France, was in London with Griggs attending an important meeting of the Interdepartmental Radiolocation Committee, chaired by Sir Robert Watson-Watt. It was a Crossbow affiliated committee, and they discussed radar units and radar tracking of "Diver" (V-1), recommending that Griggs become part of a new sub-committee to work on photographic recordings of radar tracks. The latest "Ben" (V-2) intelligence was reviewed and recommendations were also proposed.

[195] *Crossbow and Overcast*, by James McGovern, William Morrow and Company, 1964, pp. 59-62.

[196] This sighting inspired him so much he pressed to have a Chinese copy of the weapon be made in mass production for use against the Germans. Curiously enough, many people in England did not consider the V–1 to be of great military importance, but fortunately Air Chief, Marshal Tedder and the U.S. Air Secretary, Mr. Lovett, agreed with his idea. Letter from Dr. Griggs, Headquarters United States Strategic Air Forces In Europe Advisory Specialist Group to Dr. E.L. Bowles, Expert Consultant, Office of the Secretary of War, Washington, D.C., June 27, 1944. NARA.

[197] Memorandum from S.G. Henry, Major General, U.S. Army, Director, New Weapons Division for the Secretary, Attention: Colonel Edwin Cox, Joint New Weapons Committee, July 3, 1944. NARA.

[198] Notes On Conference with General Doolittle, July 20, 1944.

[199] Inter-Departmental Radiolocation Committee Meeting, CROSSBOW, Minutes of the Sixth Meeting on Tuesday, 25, July, 1944. NARA.

[200] *Strange Secrets: Real Government Files on the Unknown*, Nick Redfern and Andy Roberts, Paraview Pocket Books, 2003, pp. 53-53.

[201] Me-262 was expected to see action soon in the United Kingdom as armed reconnaissance, and then for attacks against troops on the ground. Me-163 was considered an interceptor for defending industrial targets, primarily in the Hamburg, Bremen, Berlin areas. Very long runways were needed for the Me-163 and they were seen in Denmark, Norway, and Munich. Message from General Spaatz, Commanding General USSTAF, Strategic Air Forces In Europe, London, England, to General Arnold, Commanding General AAF, War Department, Incoming Classified Message, 1 August 1944. NARA.

[202] United States Strategic Air Forces In Europe Air Intelligence Summary No. 38, For Week Ending 30 July, 1944. NARA.

[203] *The Second World War: A Complete History, Revised Edition*, by Martin Gilbert, an Owl Book, Henry Holt and Company, 1989, p. 568.

[204] Ibid; pp. 448-449.

[205] *Flying Saucer Review*, Vol. 15, No. 1, Jan-Feb., 1969, p.3. Article Supplied by Jan Aldrich. It should be noted that the exact date of this sighting is unknown. The only information provided was that it was the summer of 1944. But the sighting does, however, correspond with the Ploiesti bombing campaign that began in August and continued for another year, totaling twenty-two missions.

[206] Technical Air Intelligence Center, Summary #1, Technical Air Intelligence Organization and Functions, Issued by the Division of Naval Intelligence, By Combined Personnel of United States and British Services for the Use of Allied Forces, Technical Air Intelligence Center, Naval Air Station, Anacostia, D.C., 1 August 1944, NARA.

[207] Consolidated Mission Report, Section: Narrative Summary, Group 468, Filed Order Number 5, Mission Number 5, 10 August 1944, prepared by Heckinger and Steinmetz, 14 August 1944. NARA.

[208] Tactical Mission Report, Field Order No. 5, Mission No. 5, 10-11 August 1944, Targets On Island of Sumatra, NEI, Pladjoe Refinery, Palembang, Moesi River, Prepared by Intelligence Section, XX Bomber Command. NARA.

[209] Consolidated Mission Report, Section "Enemy Tactics," Group 468, Field Order Number 5, Mission Number 5, 10 August 1944, prepared by Heckinger and Steinmetz. NARA.

[210] S-2 Flash Report, Aircraft Number 4494, Pilot Reida. NARA.

[211] Consolidated Mission Report, Section: Bombing Data, Group 468, Field Order Number 5, Mission Number 5, 10 August 1944, prepared by Heckinger and Steinmetz. NARA.

[212] Personal correspondence: Mr. Reida to Richard Williams, April 18 [day unclear], 1953. Document provided by Jan Aldrich.

[213] "Bomber's Moon," by David Clarke and Andy Roberts, *UFO Magazine*, Volume 23, No. 7, July 2003.

Chapter 9: Calling Dr. Griggs

[214] Memorandum from S-2, For Final Mission Report #226-DX-11, 13 August 1944, 418th Night Fighter Squadron, APO 565, to Commanding Officer, 418th NFS, Attention A-2. NARA.

[215] Analysis of Fighter Opposition: XX Command Mission #9, 26 September, 1944. NARA.

[216] "Wartime UFO Seen by Japanese Navy," *Space*, January 1959, p.5. Provided by Jan Aldrich.

[217] Report of Operations, 16 and 17 October 1944, from Headquarters XX Bomber Command, APO 493, to Commanding General, Twentieth Air Force, Washington, D.C., 28 October 1944. NARA.

[218] Eastern Air Command, *Weekly Intelligence Summary*, November 10, 1944. NARA.

[219] For those who are not familiar with the alleged UFO crash and retrieval operation in Roswell, New Mexico, in July of 1947, it was Colonel "Butch" Blanchard who was the Commanding Officer of the 509 Bomb Group. The 509 was stationed at the Roswell Air Base and it was the only unit capable of carrying the atomic bomb. It was during the first week of July that UFO history was made; the event became known as the Roswell incident.

[220] Headquarters, XX Bomber Command, APO #493, Report of Operations, 25 October 1944, to Commanding General, Twentieth Air Force, Washington 25, D.C., 4 November 1944. NARA.

[221] Headquarters, XX Bomber Command, APO #493, Report of Operations, 5 November 1944, to Commanding General, Twentieth Air Force, Washington 25, D.C., 4 November 1944. NARA.

[222] "The Anglo-Polish U.F.U. Research Club," A.W. Szachnowsi, date unknown. Article supplied by Jan Aldrich.

[223] "A View of the News: George Todt's Opinion." Date and periodical unknown; there is a good chance this article was written for the *Herald-Examiner* daily newspaper.

[224] *American Raiders: The Race To Capture The Luftwaffe's Secrets*, by Wolfgang W.E. Samuel, University Press of Mississippi, 2004, pp. 86-87.

[225] Combined Intelligence Priorities Committee, Minutes of the sixth meeting of the Committee held in Conference Room "d," Offices of the War Cabinet, Great George Street, S.W.1., on 16 August 1944, at 10:30 a.m., CIPC (44), Sixth Meeting, August 17, 1944. NARA.

[226] General Spaatz's ATI teams were definitely on the look out for superior aviation technology, possibly more advanced than the jet or rocket-propelled aircraft. Within two weeks, he contacted General Arnold at the War Department requesting more Air specialists to the United Kingdom. The allied advance was accelerating so fast it was imperative that close to eighty new specialists were added to augment the existing ATI teams to further "exploit captured German aviation research establishments." In all, there were thirty-eight technical categories, covering every aspect of aviation. Wright Field would determine who would go on the fact finding missions, selecting personnel from Material Command, NACA, CAA, OSRD, technical universities, and contractors. Incoming Classified Message from CG, Strategic Air Forces In Europe, London, England to War Department, September 2, 1944. NARA.

[227] Their expertise included jet-propelled aircraft, aircraft performance, and designs for rocket, pressure cabins, and wind tunnels. In all, there were thirty-eight categories, covering every aspect of aviation. Wright Field determined who would go on the fact finding missions, selecting personnel from Material Command, NACA, CAA, OSRD, technical universities, and contractors. At least half of the men were to be equipped with 35mm cameras for documentation purposes. Incoming Classified Message from CG,

Strategic Air Forces In Europe, London, England to War Department, September 2, 1944. NARA.

228 By December 1, 1944, General Arnold's group was officially known as the Army Air Force Scientific Advisory Group (USAAFSAG) *The United States Air Force Special Studies: The USAF Scientific Advisory Board – Its First Twenty Years, 1944-1964,* Thomas A. Sturm, pp. 2-5.

229 CIOS Minutes of First Meeting, September 6, 1944. NARA.

230 *Crossbow and Overcast,* by James McGovern, William Morrow and Company, New York, 1964, pp. 82-86.

231 Memo from AI2(g), to DG of S; CIO, HQ, AEAF; and CIO, HQ, ADGB 14 September, 1944. NARA.

232 Report generated by a Free French operation. An Air Force engineer had supplied the information after he had collected it while traveling through Germany. He had learned it "despite the measures taken by the Germans to preserve secrecy." FF-19 Report, September 26, 1944; released on October 13, 1944. NARA.

233 Technical Section, SI-History, February 9, 1945. NARA.

234 Personal Correspondence from Ted Peters, Ph.D. to Walt Andrus, MUFON, September 30, 1986. Document provided by Jan Aldrich. Unfortunately, there is no known official military documentation that can help substantiate Lt. Wilk's story. With over 100 witnesses, there must have been some kind of paperwork generated.

235 *BUFORA* [British UFO Research Association] *Journal,* Vol. 5, No.5, Jan./Feb. 1977, p.20. Document supplied by Jan Aldrich.

236 *Flying Saucer,* 1958, Number 31; provided by Barry Greenwood.

237 Letter to Donald Keyhoe from W.T. Smith, May 15, 1964; provided by Jan Aldrich.

238 Letter to Dr. Bowles, Expert Consultant to the Secretary of War, from Dr. Griggs, United States Strategic Air Forces In Europe, Advisory Specialist Group, October 17, 1944. NARA.

239 RCM (Radio Countermeasures) Digest No. 9, October 1, 1944. NARA.

240 Daily Operations Report; 414th NFS, October 20, 1944. NARA.

241 Daily Operations Report; 416th NFS, October 20, 1944. NARA.

242 In September, anxious to personally get involved with the ATI field teams, he was greatly pleased about receiving orders for overseas duty. Arriving in London at Bushy Park, he was stationed at the USSTAF Headquarters (Rear). Here he spent countless hours with British intelligence learning "everything they knew about German science

and technology, where they were headed and what new things might appear on the scene." Not long after, he was off across the English Channel, landing at Villacoublay airfield, just outside of Paris, where he reported to the main USSTAF Headquarters in St. Germain, France. American Raiders, *The Race To Capture The Luftwaffe's Secrets*, Wolfgang W.E. Samuel, University Press of Mississippi, 2004, pp. 72-85.

[243] Watson began immediately familiarizing himself with the "A" List, composed of information sought after by many of his friends, back at Wright Field. Colonel Watson's agenda was firmly established during the first week of October. He was invited to an informal lunch with General Spaatz. The core of the USSTAF officers surrounded the table: Brigadier General McDonald, Director of Intelligence; Major General Kneer, Spaatz's Deputy of Administration, and Watson's boss; and Major General Anderson, Operations. General Spaatz discussed the "V-weapons, the ME-262s, Arado-234, ME-163, and other advanced aircraft that potentially could give the Air Corps problems." Colonel Watson clearly understood what General Spaatz specifically desired; get those aircraft into the hands of engineers' back at Wright Field as soon as possible.

[244] War Department Classified Message Center, Incoming Classified Message: From Commanding General, US Strategic Air Forces in Europe, London, England, to War Department (Top Secret- Vandenberg to Arnold from Spaatz, signed Eisenhower), 26 October, 1944. NARA.

[245] Within twenty-four hours, the message was down graded from Top Secret to Secret. Top Secret Memorandum: to Dr. Bowles from General Arnold. NARA.

[246] War Department Classified Message Center, Secret War Department Outgoing Message, TOP SECRET, General Arnold to General Spaatz, Commanding General, US Strategic Air Forces In Europe, London, England, 28 October, 1944. NARA.

[247] It should be noted that during the post war years, right on through today, engine and radio interference have been physical characteristics associated with UFO sightings.

[248] *The Raven*, newsletter of the 301st BG, August 1994. It appears at http://www.project1947.com/acu2.htm.

[249] Air Intercept (AI) was a radar unit within the aircraft, and Ground Control Intercept (GCI), was a ground based station that guided aircraft. Operational Flash Report, No. 6, from 422nd NFS, to Commanding General, IX Tactical Air Command, 29/30 October, 1944. NARA.

[250] In a postwar interview, Flight Engineer Juberley said no allied aircraft were lost on the Cologne raid, and that he had heard other accounts of crewmen belonging to the 640 Squadron who had reported similar observations at their Intelligence debriefings. He also learned that according to men with Air Intelligence, Germany was using jet-propelled aircraft for the first time. Personal correspondence: Maurice M. Juberley (possibly misspelled) to researcher Andy Roberts, June 21, 1987. Document provided by Jan Aldrich.

[251] According to the "Contact Report": section of their report it read: "1 Chase, 1 AI contact

which faded." Operational Flash Report, No. 1, from 422nd NFS to Commanding General, IX Tactical Air Command, 5/6 Nov. 1944. NARA.

[252] Operational Flash Report, No. 2, from 422nd NFS to Commanding General, IX Tactical Air Command, 5/6 Nov. 1944. NARA.

[253] *New London Evening Day* (Connecticut), November 7, 1944, p.1; Article provided by Richard Hall.

[254] United States Strategic Air Forces in Europe; Air Intelligence Summary, No. 52, For Week Ending 5 November, 1944, p. 5. NARA.

[255] SECRET in Log Message, General Spaatz to General Arnold, November 13, 1944. NARA. The last line of the message actually said, "Whole position as present is uncertain."

Chapter 10: Lett, Nolan, and Intruder Schlueter
[256] The United States and Britain were rushing to introduce their own jet fighters and ballistic missiles, but at the time they were unable to get anything into operation that could immediately challenge the German military war machine. In the U.S., General Arnold's Air Technical Service Command's (ATSC) Wright Field scientists and engineers were deeply involved with far-reaching and progressive projects. In addition to the Wright Field group was General Henry's New Development Division, the National Defense Research Committee, and the National Advisory Committee for Aeronautics. Projects included: radar and radio controlled weaponry, tracking and control systems, television, radar homing devices, heat seeking missiles, tailless and supersonic pilotless aircraft. "TOP SECRET" War Department Classified Incoming Classified Message, from Director Air Technical Service Command, to War Department, 16 November 1944. NARA.

[257] "World War II Foo-fighter Phenomena Report" Form. Document provided by Jan Aldrich.

[258] Results of No. 3 Group's investigation have not been located.

[259] *To Rule The Sky*, by Lou Jagues, Jr. and William D. Leet, B-L Enterprises, Publishers, 1979, pp. 144-154.

[260] "The Flying Fortress and The Foo-Fighter," by William D. Leet, *The MUFON UFO Journal*, 1979. Document supplied by Richard Hall.

[261] *To Rule The Sky*, by Lou Jagues, Jr. and William D. Leet, B-L Enterprises, Publishers, Copyright 1979, pp. 144-154.

[262] Mission Report: 415th Night Fighter Squadron, November 26/27, 1944; "The Foo Fighter Mystery," Jo Chamberlain, *American Legion Magazine*, December, 1945. Article provided by Anderson Henshaw NARA.

[263] During the last week of November, the 415th Night Fighter Squadron started moving

the first elements of their unit from their air base station at Longvic, near the town of Dijon, to Ochey, near Nancy, France. They set up camp and waited for planes to arrive on December 6.

[264] "The Foo Fighter Mystery," Jo Chamberlain, *American Legion Magazine,* December 1945. Article provided by Anderson Henshaw.

[265] "The Foo Fighter Mystery," Jo Chamberlain, *American Legion Magazine,* December 1945. Article provided by Anderson Henshaw.

[266] Personal correspondence: P. Kendall Bruce to NICAP (National Investigations Committee of Aerial Phenomena), Washington, D.C., Jan. 20, 1965. Document provided by Jan Aldrich.

[267] 414th Night Fighter Squadron, Daily Operations Report, Mission 108, 2 December, 1944, by First Lt. Wallace H. Geisz, S-2. NARA.

[268] 422nd Operational Flash Report No. 10, to Commanding General IX Tactical Air Command, 4/5 December, 1944. NARA.

[269] *Strange Secrets: Real Government Files on the Unknown,* Nick Redfern and Andy Roberts, Paraview Pocket Books, 2003, pg. 49.

[270] "SECRET" Out Log Message from St. Germain, France to General Spaatz, 18 December 1944. NARA.

[271] 64th Fighter Wing Mission Report of 415th NFS, December 14/15, 1944, NARA; Excerpt from Operations Report as cited in War Diary 415th Night Fighter Squadron, December 15, 1944, NARA; Report from Captain F.B. Ringwald, Intelligence Officer, 415th Night Fighter Squadron, to AC of S, A-2, XII Tactical Air Command, APO 374, US Army, 30 January, 1945. (The actual date of this sighting was the evening of December 14, though there are references to December 15. The exact date is confused only because the Mission report is dated as Dec. 14/15. This is a minor detail. The crew of this mission was mentioned by name in Jo Chamberlain's *American Legion* article in December 1945, and their account matches the official 415th NFS Operational Report. It was this sighting that Captain Ringwald cited as the first Foo Fighter sighting he sent extracts to the XII Tactical Air Command on January 30, 1945.

[272] Operational Flash Report to Commanding General, IX Tactical Air Command, from 422nd NFS, December 14/15, 1944. NARA. By the end of the first week of December, all the aircraft of the 415th NFS arrived at the Toul Ochey airstrip.

[273] *New York Times,* December 15, 1944.

[274] On September 8, 1944 "Ben," Crossbow Committee's code-name for the V-2 had arrived. The V-2 "had changed the nature of future wars" and the allied nations "had no rockets that could begin to compare with the V-2 in size, destructiveness, and sophistication of engineering." *Crossbow and Overcast,* by James McGovern, William Morrow and Company, New York, 1964, pp. 82-86.

[275] Supreme Headquarters Allied Expeditionary Force memorandum, Subject: Functions of Continental Crossbow Collation and Intelligence Sections at Supreme Headquarters, Allied Expeditionary Force, by command of General Eisenhower, issued by T.J. Davis, Brigadier General, USA, Adjutant General, 15 December, 1944.

Chapter 11: Smokey's Foo Fighters

[276] In the first weeks of December 1944, while the sky was busy with action overhead, Hitler's final large-scale attempt at breaking the allied advance moved into place quietly under the cloak of night. Allied Intelligence failed to put together a clear picture of the German counterattack preparation; concentrations of troops, aircraft, tanks and equipment were being amassed on the Western Front, but assessments indicated the German's were only preparing for the American attacks and they were not capable of launching an effective offensive. *The Second World War: A Complete History, Revised Edition*, by Martin Gilbert, An Owl Book, Henry Holt and Company, 1989, pp.616-617.

[277] Secret Incoming SHAEF Message from 12th Army Group TAC to SHAEF Main for G-2, December 16, 1944. NARA.

[278] Report by Captain F.B. Ringwald, Intelligence Officer, 415th Night Fighter Squadron, APO 374, US Army, to AC of S, A-2, XII Tactical Air Command, APO 374, US Army, 30 January, 1945, NARA; 64th Fighter Wing Mission Report of the 415th Night Fighter Squadron, December 17/18; Excerpt from Operations Report as cited in War Diary 415th Night Fighter Squadron, December 18, 1944. NARA. There are minor date discrepancies: the 64th Fighter Wing lists the sighting as 2205-2400, December 17; the 415th War Diary, quoting from Operations report, lists date as December 18; and Captain Ringwald report lists sighting as night of December 16/17.

[279] "The Foo Fighter Mystery," by Jo Chamberlain, *American Legion Magazine*, December 1945. Article provided by 415th NFS pilot, Anderson Henshaw; War Diary 415th Night Fighter Squadron, Ochey Air Base, France, December 1944. NARA.

[280] Personal Interview with Charlie Horne, "Supernatural Belief Traditions: The Traditions of Belief and Disbelief and the Role of the Memorate as an Illustrative Dialogue," Jeffery A. Lindell, date unknown, http:/www.project1947.com/articles/londfoo.html; Personal correspondence with Harold Augspurger, November 23, 2003, and personal correspondence with Anderson Henshaw, November 7, 2003, and http://en.wikipedia.org/wiki/Foo_fighter.

There is a little confusion over who named them first. Charlie Horne claimed he was the one who named them, and he may have been the one, but others of the unit, including Major Augspurger, recalls it was Lt. Donald Meier who named them the Foo Fighters.

[281] Army Air Force "SECRET" In Log, 21 December, referencing memo for Bissell from Strong, signed Eisenhower. NARA.

[282] *New York Times, December 21, 1944. Article provided by Richard Hall.*

[283] Report by Captain F.B. Ringwald, Intelligence Officer, 415th Night Fighter Squadron,

APO 374, US Army, to AC of S, A-2, XII Tactical Air Command, APO 374, US Army, 30 January, 1945. NARA.

284 64th Fighter Wing, Mission Report: Mission Report of 415th Night Fighter Squadron, December 22/23, 1944. NARA.

285 64th Fighter Wing, Mission Report: Mission Report of 415th Night Fighter Squadron, December 23/24, 1944; Report by Captain F.B. Ringwald, Intelligence Officer, 415th Night Fighter Squadron, APO 374, US Army, to AC of S, A-2, XII Tactical Air Command, APO 374, US Army, 30 January, 1945; 64th Fighter Wing, Mission Report of 415th Night Fighter Squadron, December 23/24, 1944. NARA.

286 Excerpt from Operations Report as cited in War Diary 415th Night Fighter Squadron, December 24, 1944. NARA; Sixty-Four Fighter Wing Mission Report of 415th Night Fighter Squadron, NARA; "The Foo Fighter Mystery," by Jo Chamberlain, *American Legion Magazine*, December 1945. Article provided by 415th NFS pilot, Anderson Henshaw.

287 Lt. Krasney had several Foo Fighter sightings over the course of several months. Each sighting remained a mystery. The foo fighters were altogether different than jets. Samuel A. Krasney: Foo Fighter Questionnaire, 11/10/2006; Interviewed on 11/7/04, 11/10/06, 11/13/06, 11/14/06.

288 64th Fighter Wing, Mission Report: Mission Report of 415th Night Fighter Squadron, December 26/27, 1944. NARA.

289 Report by Captain F.B. Ringwald, Intelligence Officer, 415th Night Fighter Squadron, APO 374, US Army, to AC of S, A-2, XII Tactical Air Command, APO 374, US Army, 30 January, 1945. NARA.

290 Report by Captain F.B. Ringwald, Intelligence Officer, 415th Night Fighter Squadron, APO 374, US Army, to AC of S, A-2, XII Tactical Air Command, APO 374, US Army, 30 January, 1945, NARA; Personal telephone Interview with Mr. Anderson Henshaw, November 24, 2003; Personal correspondence: Foo Fighter Questionnaire, completed by Mr. Henshaw, November 7, 2003.

291 Operational Research Section, Bomber Command, Report No 116, December 27, 1944. NARA.

292 64th Fighter Wing, Mission Report: 415th NFS, December 27/28, 1944, NARA; Report by Captain F.B. Ringwald, Intelligence Officer, 415th Night Fighter Squadron, APO 374, US Army, to AC of S, A-2, XII Tactical Air Command, APO 374, US Army, 30 January, 1945. NARA.

293 Third Bombardment Division Operational Intelligence Report-Tactical Targets, A-2, Third Bombardment Division, 28 December 1944. NARA.

294 Personal Correspondence, November 23, 2003. Telephone Interviews with Harold

Augspurger: November 29, 2003, January 1, 2004, May 2004, and October 1, 2004.

Chapter 12: Bob Wilson Gets His Scoop

[295] A Staffel is the Luftwaffe's equivalent to a RAF's squadron. www.fishponds.freeuk.com/nluftbri4.htm

[296] ADI(K), the British organization was a part of the Air Ministry, specifically dealing with Air Intelligence matters, obtained through Air Prisoners of War. When reports were generated utilizing this kind of information, a bold lettered statement was made at the top of each report, citing where the contents of the report had been acquired. The statement informed the reader that the document in hand still awaited verification, and no mention of it was to be made in Intelligence Summaries of Commands or anywhere else.

[297] ADI(K) Report No. 700/1944, GAF Night Fighters, A Review Of Current German Tactics, S.D. Felkin for Wing Commander, Air Interrogation, 30 December 1944. NARA.

[298] United States Strategic Air Forces In Europe Air Intelligence Summary No. 60, For Week Ending 31 December, 1944. NARA.

[299] "The Foo Fighter Mystery," by Jo Chamberlain, *American Legion Magazine*, December 1945. Article provided by 415th NFS pilot, Anderson Henshaw; Telephone interview with Anderson Henshaw, May 12, 2004.

[300] Captain Owen Jones and his radar operator, Lt. Susman, were tackling an intruder mission. It was not long before they encountered a German night fighter and engaged in a brawl. Unfortunately, their luck was not with them that night. They were struck first, receiving a deadly volley of lead from the attacking fighter. Lt. Susman was severely injured and their aircraft's rudder and controls were shot out. Limping along, Captain Jones knew that his aircraft and Lt. Susman were in horrible shape. He had to make a decision: either bale out or try to bring the aircraft in and save his friend. Deciding to stay with his Beaufighter and save the life of his friend, he struggled to keep the aircraft airborne. Getting to within thirty miles of the air base, he tried his best but it was not enough. One engine had already failed and the other was conking out, finally sending the plane spirally down, crashing, and killing both men. Telephone interview: Anderson Henshaw, May 12, 2004.

[301] "The Foo Fighter Mystery," by Jo Chamberlain, *American Legion Magazine*, December 1945. Article provided by 415th NFS pilot, Anderson Henshaw.

[302] Over the last several months, the Germans had introduced the V-1 and V-2, the Me-262 jet-propelled aircraft and the Me-163 rocket-propelled aircraft. There were scattered reports of many jet-propelled variants including remote or radio-controlled versions.

[303] By day's end, the Luftwaffe had achieved complete surprise, inflicting a heavy toll on allied aircraft, but their overall objective had failed. The disappointment of Operation "Boddenplatte" was due to a variety of reasons and their effort to destroy the Allied fighter force caused only a minor setback; it would only take two weeks before the

destroyed aircraft would be replaced. But overall, the Ardennes Offensive and Operation Boddenplatte was a psychological blow to Allied Intelligence. There was a definite need to reassess Germany's Luftwaffe potential and threat. *To Win the Winter Sky: The Air War Over the Ardennes, 1944-1945*, by Danny S. Parker, Combined Books, INC., 1994, pp. 373-374.

[304] Report from Group S-2, Captain Finis D. McClanahan, Headquarters 25th Bombardment Group (Reconnaissance), APO 634, Subject: S-2 Mission Report, Bluestocking 1/ 2, 653 Sq., Mosquito 626, Pilot-Green, to Commanding Officer, 25th Bomb Group., Rcn., APO 634, US Army, ATTN: Group S-3, January 1, 1945; provided by Norman Malayney.

[305] *Aerial Intelligence of the Eighth Air Force*, by George Sesler. Taylor Publishing Co., Dallas, Texas, 1996, pp. 150-152.

[306] Personal correspondence with Warren Barber: Foo Fighter Questionnaire, December 2, 2003; and Telephone Conversation November 16, 2003.

[307] *Aerial Intelligence of The Eighth Air Force*, by George Sesler.; Taylor Publishing Co., Dallas, Texas, 1996. Pgs. 150-152. Lt. Jack Green had this to say about their foo fighter sightings: "I recalled reading about them in about two or three articles before this flight of ours. They had been explained away as being nothing more than St. Elmo's fire, which the English couldn't seem to recognize, or as possible hallucinations. By now, I had had a lot of experience with St. Elmo's fire in a variety of forms. What we saw, Warren and I, was yet quite another type of display for which no possible accounting could be given then or, for that matter, has been given to date."

[308] Report from Group S-2, Captain Finis D. McClanahan, Headquarters 25th Bombardment Group (Reconnaissance), APO 634, Subject: S-2 Mission Report, Bluestocking 1/2, 653 Sq., Mosquito 626, Pilot-Green, to Commanding Officer, 25th Bomb Group., Rcn., APO 634, US Army, ATTN: Group S-3, January 1, 1945. Document provided by Norman Malayney.

[309] *New York Times*, p. 1, January 2, 1945. Article provided by Carl Feindt.

[310] *St. Louis Post Dispatch*, January 2, 1945. Article provided by Jan Aldrich.

[311] "Mystery Flares Tag Along With U.S. Night Pilots," (reprinted from previous day's late *Tribune*) January 2, 1945. Article provided by Anderson Henshaw.

[312] Personal correspondence with Murphy C. Painter, Jr.: Foo Fighter Questionnaire, January 1, 2004; Telephone conversation on January 24, 2004.

[313] Between December and January, Lt. Rodick had no less than nine sightings. Personal correspondence with Warren Rodick: Foo Fighter Questionnaire, January 10, 2004.

[314] Personal correspondence with Garland Moore: Foo Fighter Questionnaire, November 22, 2003.

[315] *The Palestine Post*, January 2, 1945; provided by Jan Aldrich.

[316] Unknown newspaper article: from the archives of Richard Hall. Possibly: *The New London Day*, (hand-dated January 3, 1945, p. 10). Article provided by Richard Hall.

[317] New London, Connecticut newspaper, *The Day*, January 3, 1945. Article provided by Richard Hall.

[318] Back at the USSTAF Headquarters, Chief of Intelligence, General McDonald had accumulated information determining there were at least one hundred to one hundred and twenty-five Me-262s in operation. Close to four Me-262s hundred by April, and possibly up to two hundred and fifty built each month through June. This was very disturbing news and General McDonald felt this information represented "a serious threat." The German's were throwing a tremendous effort into their jet-propelled aircraft program and this could not be ignored. If these figures proved accurate, by the summer of 1945, Germany's jet-propelled interceptors could change the whole course of the war. General Spaatz had no other choice. He had to react swiftly, initiating a stepped-up aggressiveness completely focused upon destroying the German danger. *Piercing The Fog: Intelligence and the Army Air Forces Operations in World War II*, John F. Kreis, General Editor, Air Force History and Museums Programs, 1995, p. 245

Chapter 13 Foo or Phoo?

[319] SHAEF INCOMING MESSAGE, from AGWAR from Bissell, signed Ulio, to SHAEF Main A-2, January 3, 1945. NARA.

[320] Message from Air Commodore Grierson, Air Staff SHAEF, to AGWAR, January 5, 1945. NARA.

[321] *Most Secret War*, by Dr. R.V. Jones, Book Club Associates, 1978, p. 115 Bombing V weapon launch sites was not proving successful. Prime Minister Winston Churchill immediately set up the Crossbow Committee within the British War Cabinet to review up-to-the-minute reports, implement a fresh start, and make changes of staff members and scientists throughout the program. According to Jones, "He (Pelly) was succeeded in the middle of May by Air Commodore Colin Grierson who, once again, was completely new to Intelligence." Jones further commented: "The strain was beginning to tell on Colin Grierson, for whom I was profoundly sorry. He had been thrust into a very difficult post only a week or two before the flying bomb campaign opened, and he found himself working in a field in which he had no previous experience." p.425.

[322] *Hartford Courant*, January 5, 1945. Provided by Jan Aldrich.

[323] Mission Report No. 11-140, from First Lt. Kinsey Jones, Assistant A-2, VII Bomber Command , to Headquarters VII Bomber Command, 17 January 1945. NARA.

[324] *Science News-Letter* for January 13, 1945. Article provided by researcher Jan Aldrich.

[325] *Time*, January 15, 1945. From Project 1947 website: www.project1947.com/fig/1945a. htm.

[326] *Newsweek*, January 15, 1945. From Project 1947 website: www.project1947.com/fig/1945a.htm.

[327] Air Intelligence Weekly Summary, No. 113, Headquarters, Mediterranean Allied Air Forces Intelligence Section, 14 January 1945. NARA. Interestingly, that same day the OSS also received another field report from Switzerland describing the flying wings as "Fledermaus planes" that were going to be brought into service by May. "Fledermaus planes are the shape of a kite (or bat), are without armament, are rocket propelled, have reinforced noses, and are designed to ram invading bombers," the report stated. Report, "Germany – Air/Technical, from Switzerland to OSS London, 14 January, 1945. NARA.

[328] Memo from Leavitt Corning, Jr., Lt. Colonel, G.S.C., A/C of S, A-2, Headquarters XII Tactical Air Command (ADV), to Commanding General, First Tactical Air Force (Provisional), US Army. ATTN: AC/ of S, A-2, January 16, 1945. NARA.

[329] This very important memo represents the first official document that confirms that an American investigation of the foo fighters was initiated. Memo from S. V. Boykin, Major AC, Executive Officer, Headquarters, First Tactical Air Force (Provisional), to A/C of S. A-2, XII Tactical Air Command, January 20, 1945. NARA.

[330] Memo from John E. Wooley, for Lt. Colonel Leavitt Corning, Jr., A/C of S., A-2, to S-2, 415th Night Fighter Squadron, January 23, 1945. NARA.

[331] Supreme Headquarters Allied Expeditionary Force (REAR), G-2 Division, Staff Memorandum No. 135, dated 16 January 1945, Subject: Establishment of Scientific Intelligence Advisory Section in G-2 Division, to all members of CIOS, 22 January 1945. NARA.

[332] *The Commander's Intelligence Digest*, "An Evaluation Of German Capabilities In 1945," Headquarters, United States Strategic Air Forces In Europe, Office of the Director of Intelligence, 19 January 1945. Document provided by Jan Aldrich.

[333] *The Commander's Intelligence Digest*, "An Evaluation Of German Capabilities In 1945," Headquarters, United States Strategic Air Forces In Europe, Office of the Director of Intelligence, 19 January 1945. Document provided by Jan Aldrich.

[334] 64th Fighter Wing, Mission Report: report of 415th NFS, January 29/30, 1945. NARA; War Diary of the 415th Night Fighter Squadron, January, 1945. Provided by Barry Greenwood; Report from Captain F.B. Ringwald, Intelligence Officer, 415th Night Fighter Squadron, to A/C of S, A-2, XII Tactical Air Command, January 30, 1945. NARA.

[335] Report from Captain F.B. Ringwald, Intelligence Officer, 415th Night Fighter Squadron, to A/C of S, A-2, XII Tactical Air Command, January 30, 1945. NARA.

[336] Report from Military Attache, Ottawa, to Incoming Briefs for General Arnold, US Army Air Force, 21 January 1945, NARA.

[337] 64th Fighter Wing Mission Report: 415th NFS, February 2/3, 1945. NARA.

[338] Memo from Headquarters XII Tactical Air Command (ADV), APO 374, US Army, to the Commanding General, First Tactical Air Force (PROV), APO 374, US Army; Attn: A/C of S., A-2, 4 February, 1945. NARA.

[339] Memorandum from Colonel Leavitt Corning, Jr., A/C of S., A-2, Headquarters XII Tactical Air Command to Commanding General, First Tactical Air Force (PROV), ATT: A/C of S., A-2, 5 February 1945. NARA.

[340] 64th Fighter Wing Mission Report: 415th NFS, February 7/8, 1945. NARA.

[341] 64th Fighter Wing Mission, Report: 415th NFS, February 9/10, 1945. NARA.

[342] Memorandum from C.M. Grierson, Air Commodore, A.C. of S., A-2, Air Staff, SHAEF to First Tactical Air Force (Provisional), February 11, 1945. NARA.

[343] Memorandum from C. M. Grierson, Air Commodore, A.C. of S., A-2, Air Staff, SHAEF to Headquarters, USSTAF, for the attention of Chief Technical Intelligence Officer, Colonel Bradley, February 11, 1945. NARA.

[344] Based on interviews with Major Augspurger, 415th NFS Commanding Officer, and Captain Horne, 415th NFS Operations Officers, they felt the visitors were from Washington. Thinking about it today, Augspurger feels the Washington visitor's affair was a bit odd. Back then, he was too busy with other matters to give it much thought. In hindsight, Major Augspurger feels that as the commanding officer, the visitors should have introduced themselves to him out of respect and protocol.

[345] Author's personal telephone Interview with Harold Augspurger, 11/29/03, and Foo Fighter Questionnaire, 11/23/03.

[346] From "Supernatural Belief Traditions: The Traditions of Belief and Disbelief and the Role of the Memorate as an Illustrative Dialogue," by Jeffery A. Lindell in a personal interview conducted with Charlie Horne, Operations Officer 415th NFS, November 1993; http://www.project1947.com/articles/lindfoo.html.

[347] Author's personal telephone Interview with Harold Augspurger, 11/29/03, and Foo Fighter Questionnaire, 11/23/03; Supernatural Belief Traditions: The Traditions of Belief and Disbelief and the Role of the Memorate as an Illustrative Dialogue, by Jeffery A. Lindell in a personal interview conducted with Charlie Horne, Operations Officer 415th NFS, November 1993, http://www.project1947.com/articles/lindfoo.html.

[348] 64th Fighter Wing, Mission Report: 415th Night Fighter Squadron, 13/14 February 1945. NARA.

[349] 64th Fighter Wing, Mission Report: 415th Night Fighter Squadron, 14/15 February, 1945. NARA.

350 414th Night Fighter Squadron Daily Operations Report, 15/16 February, 1945. NARA.

351 416th Night Fighter Squadron Daily Operations Report, 16/17 February 1945. NARA.

352 416th Night Fighter Squadron, Daily Operations Report, 17 Feb. 1945. NARA.

353 414th Night Fighter Squadron Daily Operations Report, 17/18 February, 1945. NARA.

354 416th Night Fighter Squadron, Daily Operations Report, 17 February 1945, as cited in "Supernatural Belief Traditions: The Traditions of Belief and Disbelief and the Role of the Memorate as an Illustrative Dialogue," by Jeffery A. Lindell, for Dr. J. Johnson, http://www.project1947.com/articles/lindfoo.html.

355 "Fireballs? Science Says 'Pooh!' Beaufighter Crews Insist 'Foo!'" Article states February 18, most likely released on the 19, unknown newspaper, clipping provided by 415th NFS veteran Anderson Henshaw, November 2003.

356 416th NFS Daily Operations Report, February 18, 1945. NARA.

357 414th NFS Daily Operations Report, February 21, 1945. NARA.

358 416th NFS Daily Operations Report, February 21, 1945. NARA.

359 Griggs had also visited the frontlines as a sounding board, listening to what the Generals had to say in relation to the use of radar with the Air Tactical Support units. Memorandum to Lt. General Spaatz form Dr. David T. Griggs, Expert Consultant, Office Secretary of War, February 17, 1945. NARA.

360 Letter to Dr. Edward Bowles, Expert Consultant to the Secretary of War, from Dr. David T. Griggs, Advisory Specialist Group, Headquarters, United States Strategic Air Forces IN Europe, February 22, 1945.

Chapter 15: Air Ministry at a Loss
361 416th NFS Daily Operations Report, February 22, 1945. NARA.

362 416th NFS Daily Operations Report, February 27, 1945. NARA.

363 "Hand written report" by Commander R.W. Hendershott, USNR, Seattle Washington, "of a sighting given to Aerial Phenomena Research Association, Seattle, Washington (Board members of APRA are also acting as NICAP Subcommittee, Washington Unit #1) - signed June Larson, NICAP Subcommittee, Washington Unit #1, February 10, 1961. Document provided by Jan Aldrich.

364 Letter from E.E. Dickey, February 28, 1993; provided by Jan Aldrich.

365 Report of AA Fire, Headquarters, 379th Bomb Group, March 3, 1945. NARA.

[366] Along the west coast of the U.S., during January 19 through the 22, coastal defense units reported sightings of balloons "not identified as of domestic origin," although an air search of the areas "failed to confirm the observations." Weekly Intelligence Summary, No. 64, Headquarters 14 Antiaircraft Command, issued March 3, 1945. NARA.

[367] Air Intelligence Weekly Summary No. 120, Headquarters Mediterranean Allied Air Forces Intelligence Section, March 4, 1945. NARA.

[368] He explained that the dispersal of technical reports was forwarded to various groups studying the subject elsewhere and said there was talk of a new group being organized to conduct research on the whole field of guided missiles and jet propulsion.

[369] Letter to Dr. M.A. Tuve, Embassy of the United States, from H. Guyford Stever, Scientific Liaison with the OSRD London Mission, Subject: GAP News Letter, March 5, 1945. NARA.

[370] Operations Narrative of the 653rd Bombardment Squadron (Weather Reconnaissance) Mission, to Headquarters, 25th Bombardment Group (Reconnaissance), AAF Station 376, APO 634, 5 March 1945; S-2 Mission Report, Bluestocking 3/27, 653 Squadron, 25th Bombardment Group, to Headquarters, 25th Bombardment Group (Reconnaissance), 7 March 1945; supplied by Norman Malayney.

[371] *The Second World War: A Complete History*, Revised Edition, by Martin Gilbert, An Owl Book, Henry Holt and Company, 1989, pp. 647-648.

[372] Headquarters 25th Bombardment Group (Reconnaissance), Subject: S-2 Mission Report, Bluestocking 2/43, 653rd Sq., to Commanding Officer, 25th Bomb Group, (Rcn.), 10 March 1945. Document provided by Norman Malayney.

[373] "I have seen St. Elmo's Fire on many occasions," he told his S-2. "I have never known or heard of St. Elmo's Fire being dangerous to an aircraft. On two previous occasions, when the A/C in which I was flying was hit by lightning, there was no indication except that a streak of lightning had whipped past near the fuselage, with only minor damage to radio equipment. The envelope of an A/C in sheets of fire and subsequent explosions is the first knowledge I have ever had that an A/C in flight may be severely damaged or destroyed by lightning. It is possible that if we had had bomb-bay tanks aboard, the A/C would have been completely destroyed by the flash explosion." Letter from Headquarters XXI Bomber Command to National Advisory Committee of Aeronautics, Washington, D.C., March 25, 1945, referencing Letter of Transmittal from Headquarters: 73rd Bombardment Wing to Commanding General, Air Technical Service Command, Wright Field, Ohio, thru XXI Bomber Command. NARA.

[374] After careful discussion with "various Departments concerned," Group Captain E.D.M. Hopkins, responded for the Air Ministry's Deputy Director of Intelligence. SECRET Memorandum, "Balls of Fire-Red," from the Air Ministry, DDI 2, signed E.D.M Hopkins, Group Captain, to Air Commodore Grierson, AC of S, A-2, Air Staff SHAEF, 13 March 1945. NARA.

[375] 414th NFS Daily Operations Report, 13 March 1945. NARA.

[376] Memo from Air Commodore Grierson, SHAEF, to First Tactical Air Force (Provisional), March 18, 1945. NARA.

[377] By March, new adjustments were proposed within the organizational structure of CIOS. Its staff was always busy adjusting and restructuring their intelligence operations. Their goal was producing a more effective organization, not repeat work already conducted by other independent groups in the field. To meet these new challenges, Forward Reconnaissance teams were suggested; in essence, technical advisors to the "T" Force commanders of each Army Group. When unexpected Black or Grey List "Targets" were encountered, newly discovered facilities, underground shelters, or material, those not on their original Target List, the teams communicated their needs to the "T" Force commander. CIOS c/o SHAEF (Rear), "CIOS Forward Reconnaissance Teams," February, 1945, typed documented, apparent in-house document. NARA.

[378] The CAFT leaders were issued a statement of purpose. It detailed their responsibilities, familiarizing them with the chain of command. It further pointed out that "British civilian personnel held an honorary commission and wear the uniform appropriate to their rank, arm, and service. US civilian CAFT personnel will wear officer uniform. These US uniforms will bear all insignia except that of rank." CIOS/118/8/S Instructions To CIOS Consolidated Advance Field Team Leaders, March 14, 1945. NARA.

[379] The Memorandum, "Air Technical Intelligence (Investigation of German Air Force Equipment including Radar and Crashed Enemy Aircraft)," outlining the specifics of a new Air Intelligence unit was issued on March 18. Information was then passed to "Operational Intelligence in the field, Air Ministry and the War Department;" ensuring "accurate and up to date intelligence on enemy aircraft for evaluation and dissemination in other theaters of war and for the benefit of Research and Design departments." The new ATI unit examined "all crashed and captured enemy aircraft, airfields, and installations." Flak weapons were allocated to other ATI teams, and this fit well into the Air Ministry's investigation of the unconventional aircraft phenomenon since the Air Ministry felt Bomber Command crews were encountering some type of flak rocket. Since the team's composition was a mix of personnel from USSTAF and the Air Ministry's AI2(g), all information was shared. The close liaison between the Americans and British ensured both parties got what they needed, including the capture of "any new type of Radar or aeronautical equipment"; the first specimen went to Air Ministry and the second specimen to Wright Field. SHAEF Policy, Memorandum Number 15: Air Technical Intelligence (Investigation of German Air Force Equipment including Radar and Crashed Enemy Aircraft), March 18, 1945. NARA.

[380] 416th NFS Daily Operational Report, March 18, 1945. NARA.

[381] 64th Fighter Wing, Mission Report: 415th NFS, 19/20 March 1945. NARA.

[382] Operational Flash Report from 422nd NFS to Commanding General, IX Tactical Air Command, March 18/19, 1945; Operational Flash Report from 422nd NFS to Commanding General, IX Tactical Air Command, March 19/20, 1945; 422nd NFS Operational Flash Report No. 5 to Commanding General, IX Tactical Air Command. 20/21 March 1945. NARA.

[383] Operational Research Section Bomber Command, Report No 135, Report On Losses and Interceptions of Bomber Command Aircraft, February, 1945, March 22, 1945. NARA.

[384] 414th NFS Daily Operations Report, March 23, 1945. NARA.

[385] 64th Fighter Wing Mission Report: 415th NFS, 23/24 March 1945. NARA.

Chapter 16: The Pacific Balls of Fire
[386] *The Second World War: A Complete History*, Revised Edition, by Martin Gilbert, An Owl Book, Henry Holt and Company, 1989, P.562.

[387] Report by Stephen Pratt, Chief Field Investigator, MUFON, Southern Vermont. Report provided by Barry Greenwood. Cpl. Pratt's sighting was by no means a hush-hush affair; thousands of witnesses observed the object that day. A couple of years after the war, on two occasions, he recalls seeing a magazine article and listening to a television talk show program, both of which described the incident. There exists no paper trail.

[388] Headquarters 14th Antiaircraft Command, Weekly Intelligence Summary, No. 67, March 24, 1945. NARA.

[389] Headquarters Allied Air Forces, SWPA Intelligence Summary No. 262, March 11, 1945; as contained within Weekly Intelligence Summary, No.67, Headquarters, 14th Antiaircraft Command, March 24, 1945. NARA.

[390] Headquarters XXI Bomber Command, Tactical Mission Report Mission No. 45, March 24, 1945. NARA.

[391] National Investigations Committee On Aerial Phenomena (NICAP) Report On Unidentified Flying Objects, filed by John G. Norris on July 19, 1965. Document provided by Jan Aldrich.

[392] Jet-propelled aircraft were not confirmed to exist. A lone AR-234 was photographed, but there seemed to be nothing else in the area. There was, however, much information about this strategic area being supplied with jets, but the best intelligence gathered by the end of March indicated that jet activity existed of only "a small reconnaissance or bomber unit." Mediterranean Allied Strategic Air Force Weekly Intelligence Summary, No. 13, Office of Assistant Chief of Staff, A-2, 2 April 1945.

[393] Lippisch had for years been associated with two other prominent glider experts, the Horten Brothers. According to the prisoner, who was a manager of the wind tunnel section at the Vienna Aircraft Research Establishment (L.F.W.), the Delta series aircraft prototypes were to be flown in March. There were four aircraft in the Delta series: a glider; a jet-propulsion version; and two "coal-fueled" types, the P-11 and P-12. ADI (K) Report No. 250/1945, 26 March 1945. NARA.

[394] *The Second World War: A Complete History*, Revised Edition, by Martin Gilbert, An Owl Book, Henry Holt and Company, 1989, pp. 650-655.

[395] Air Intelligence Report, Vol. 1, No. 4, 29 March, 1945, XXI Bomber Command, Twentieth Air Force. NARA.

[396] Headquarters XXI Bomber Command, Tactical Mission Report, Mission No. 45, March 30 and April 1, 1945. NARA.

[397] Consolidated Mission Report, Tactical Narrative, Headquarters 73rd Bombardment Wing, April 3-4, 1945; Supplement To Preliminary Mission Report, 73rd Bomb Wing, March 4, 1945. NARA.

[398] Extract of Teletype Conference Between Washington and Guam, Incoming Message, Subject: Supplement To Preliminary Mission Report, Modeler One April 3, from Deputy Commander, Twentieth Air Force, Pacific Ocean Area, to Commanding General Twentieth Air Force, 4 April 1945. NARA.

[399] *Project Identification: The First Scientific Study of the UFO Phenomenon*, Dr. Harley D. Rutledge, Prentice Hall, 1981, p. 250.

[400] The piloted bombs had a wing width of 14 inches and 16 feet in length, with a body diameter of three feet. The body of the rocket was constructed of wood and metal. A warhead was placed in the nose and guided in by a pilot, who looked out a small bubble type canopy. The team reported that the rocket bombs were designed to be carried under a bomber or transport plane, and once released, powered by a rocket. Letter from Headquarters Tenth Army, Office of the AC of S, G-2 to Commanding General, Army Air Forces, Attention Chief of Air Staff Intelligence, subject: Japanese rocket propelled, piloted flying bomb, 6 April 1945. NARA.

[401] Intelligence memorandum by Air Intelligence Branch, Headquarters Army Air Forces, Pacific Ocean Areas, Office of the Director of Intelligence, April 7, 1945. NARA.

[402] War Department Incoming Classified Message from Commanding General, U.S. Army Forces, Pacific Ocean Areas, to War Department, CG, U.S. Army Forces India Burma Theater, New Delhi, India; Commander In Chief Southwest Pacific Area, Manila, Philippines; CG, U.S. Army Forces, China Theater, Chunking, China; CG, 20th [XX] Bomber Command, Kharagpur, India; CG, South Pacific Base Command, Noumea, New Caledonia, April 7, 1945. NARA.; "Enemy Air Information" from Annex #6 to G-2, USPOA Periodic Report, No. 67, April 7, 1945. NARA.

[403] AA Command Intelligence Review, No. 232, 7 April 1945; as included in Military Intelligence Division WDGS, Military Attaché Report, 11 April 1945. NARA.

[404] *Weekly Air Intelligence Digest*, Headquarters XX Bomber Command, April 7, 1945. NARA.

[405] Incoming Message, Subject: Final Mission Report Eradicate 7, Mission 59, 7 April 45, from XXI Bomber Command to Commanding General Twentieth Air Force. NARA.

[406] The Incoming Message Log contains extracts of pertinent Army Air Force intelligence matters, and included other combined allied intelligence. Secret In-Log, Intelligence

Briefs to the Commanding General Army Air Forces, April 8, 1945. NARA.

Chapter 17: "Circles of Light"

[407] The memorandum provided the latest information on Japanese antiaircraft weapons and defensive measures. It mentioned that though the use of experimental ground-to-air rockets was suspected, these reports were "unconfirmed by photographs, captured equipment, documents, or known damage" to allied aircraft. Flak Intelligence Memorandum Number 4, United States Pacific Fleet and Pacific Ocean Areas, 11 April, 1945, as reprinted in the "United States Strategic Air Forces In Europe, Air Intelligence Summary" No. 79, Week Ending 20 May, 1945. NARA.

[408] Twentieth Air Force, XXI Bomber Command, Air Intelligence Report, Vol. 1, No. 8, 26 April 1945. NARA.

[409] Mission Report No. 11-327, 2 May, 1945, Headquarters VII Bomber Command, May 8, 1945. NARA.

[410] War Department Incoming Classified Message from Deputy Commander, Twentieth Air Force, to War Department, Commanding General, Army Air Forces, Pacific Ocean Areas, Administrative, Hickam Field, TH Radio Lualualei, 4 May 1945. NARA.

[411] "Planes or Star??" Air Intelligence Memorandum No. 4, Air Intelligence Branch, Director of Intelligence, Headquarters Army Air Forces, Pacific Ocean Areas, Office of the Director of Intelligence, 8 May, 1945. NARA.

[412] Extract of Teletype Conference Between Washington and Guam, Incoming Message, subject: Enemy Fighter Reaction Mission No.67, from LeMay, Commanding General XXI Bomber Command to Commanding General Twentieth Air Force, May 10, 1945. NARA.

[413] Headquarters Seventh Air Force, Central Pacific Area, AC of S, A-2, Intelligence Summary No. 15, Vol. 2, issued May 12. NARA.

[414] Headquarters 58th Bombardment Wing, Mission Information, 16 May, 1945 Seth S. Terry, Lt. Col., Air Corps, A/C of S, A-2; Tactical Mission Report, Mission No. 176, Headquarters XXI Bomber Command, APO 234, 8 July 1945, Subject: Report of Operations 16-17 May 1945, to the Commanding General, Twentieth Air Force, Washington D.C. NARA.

[415] Letter from General Carl Spaatz, Commanding General, United States Strategic Air Forces in Europe, APO 633, US Army, to Dr. Edward Bowles, Expert Consultant to the Secretary of War, Office Of The Secretary Of War, 3 May 1945. NARA.

[416] Paraphrase of Message to Kenney from Bowles, 28 April 1945, attached to letter from John E. Buchard, Acting Director, OSRD, to Dr. L.A. DuBridge, Director, Radiation Laboratory, Massachusetts Institute of Technology, May 16, 1945. NARA.

[417] Fehler had determined that it was futile to continue with their mission. He knew the war was over for them; why risk such imminent death, reasoning it would be far better to

fall into the hands of the Americans or British than to end up on the bottom of the sea floor. *Germany's Last Mission to Japan: The Failed Voyage of U-234*, by Joseph Mark Scalia, Naval Institute Press, 2000, pp. 54-64.

[418] One item on board that captures the imagination was the 1,235 pounds of "highly radioactive" uranium oxide contained in ten gold-lined containers. *Germany's Last Mission to Japan: The Failed Voyage of U-234*, by Joseph Mark Scalia, Naval Institute Press, 2000, p. 35 & 72.

[419] Ibid. p.70.

[420] He was "well-informed on past exchanges of technical information between Germany and Japan." General Kessler was also sent to establish a "naval air arm for Germany in Singapore"; once completed, he would return to Germany and set up and command the same organization.OP-16-Z Memorandum, to Op-16- PT, Subject: Passengers o U-234, now prisoners of war, available for interrogation, 29 May 1945. NARA.

[421] *Germany's Last Mission to Japan: The Failed Voyage of U-234*, by Joseph Mark Scalia, Naval Institute Press, 2000, p. 86.

[422] OP-16-Z Memorandum, to Op-16- PT, Subject: Passengers o U-234, now prisoners of war, available for interrogation, 29 May 1945. NARA.

[423] *Germany's Last Mission to Japan: The Failed Voyage of U-234*, by Joseph Mark Scalia, Naval Institute Press, 2000, p. 102.

[424] In Japan, his mission was to teach tactical anti-aircraft defenses OP-16-Z Memorandum, to Op-16- PT, Subject: Passengers o U-234, now prisoners of war, available for interrogation, 29 May 1945. NARA.

[425] It was learned that the Japanese were going to increase moral by stating that they had a new weapon, one that "involved an 'atomic discharge' that would paralyze the enemy aircraft." One of the ways it might make its appearance was "in the form of 'a colored ball of sort shot in the air.'" *Germany's Last Mission To Japan: The Failed Voyage of U-234*, by Joseph Mark Scalia, Naval Institute Press, 2000, pp. 112-113.

[426] Report of Interrogation: Oberst Fritz Von Sandrart, May 25, 1945. NARA.

[427] Report of Interrogation: August Bringewald, May 25, 1945. NARA.

Chapter 18: The Secrets Flood In
[428] Interrogation: Reich Marshal Hermann Goering at Ritter Schuleugsburg, 1700 to 1900 hours, 10 May 1945. NARA.

[429] *American Raiders: The Race To Capture The Luftwaffe's Secrets*, by Wolfgang W. E. Samuel, University Press of Mississippi, 2004, p. 127

[430] The Horten brothers' Ho-9, a sound and proven aircraft, was being modified with two jet-propelled engines and designated as Ho 18-A, the "Amerika Bomber." *The Horten*

Brothers and Their All-Wing Aircraft, by David Myhra, Schiffer Press, 1998, pp. 217-229.

[431] Arnold requested that USSTAF officers, 1st Lt. Chester N. Hasert, Captain Robert W. Bratt, and Captain Anthony F. Dernbach interrogate the Horten brothers. Secret Message to Spaatz for Kneer, attention Director Technical Services from Hodges, signed Arnold, 19 May 1945. NARA.

[432] Colonel Putt, like Colonel Watson, had come to Europe from Wright Field. Instead of actually flying aircraft, Putt was with the Aircraft Projects Branch; his concern was making sure the AAF men were provided the best possible aircraft. *American Raiders: The Race to Capture the Luftwaffe's Secrets*, by Wolfgang W. E. Samuel, University Press of Mississippi, 2004, pp. 107-110.

[433] The Goering research center was composed of six separate institutes; Colonel Putt reported they "were equipped with 'large quantities of the finest and most superb instruments and test equipment.'" *American Raiders: The Race to Capture the Luftwaffe's Secrets*, by Wolfgang W. E. Samuel, University Press of Mississippi, 2004, pp. 107-110.

[434] One of the most advanced tunnels was built underground. Investigators reported that research using the wind tunnels were "believed to be far more extensive than anything" undertaken in the United States. *American Raiders: The Race to Capture the Luftwaffe's Secrets*, by Wolfgang W. E. Samuel, University Press of Mississippi, 2004, pp. 107-110.

[435] On May 15, a CIOS/CAFT team moved into the Bavarian town of Kochel. They had uncovered another wind tunnel that was "superior" to the ones Colonel Putt's team was investigating at Volkenrode. *American Raiders: The Race to Capture the Luftwaffe's Secrets*, by Wolfgang W. E. Samuel, University Press of Mississippi, 2004, pp. 153-157.

[436] *American Raiders: The Race to Capture the Luftwaffe's Secrets*, by Wolfgang W. E. Samuel, University Press of Mississippi, 2004, pp. 108.

[437] Ibid., p.122.

[438] Ibid., p.222.

[439] Not mentioned in Wing Commander H.F. King's report: Ho-9 was the design that evolved into the "Amerika Bomber." AI2 (g) Report No. 2342, Ho 9 Tail-less Jet Propelled Fighter, AI2 (g), D. of I. (R), signed H.F. King, Wing Commander, 5 May 1945. NARA.

[440] CIOS Progress Report, June 4, 1945, c/o G-2 Division SHAEF, (Rear). NARA

[441] Combined Intelligence Objectives Sub-Committee, Evaluation Report 51, Interrogation of Professor Osenberg, 2 June 1945. NARA.

[442] The information reached the chief of Ordnance Technical Intelligence, Colonel Holger Toftoy. He in turn passed the exciting news to Colonel Trichel, head of the Rocket Branch, located in the Pentagon. *Crossbow And Overcast* by James McGovern William Morrow and Company, 1964, pp. 118-123.

[443] Memorandum, Report on Examination of Mittelwerke Target, to Commander S.P. Johnson, USNR, from Colonel Peter Beasley, 5 June 1945. NARA.

[444] *Crossbow and Overcast* by James McGovern, William Morrow and Company, 1964, pp. 166-168.

[445] Memorandum: Location of Peenumunde Documents, to G-2, SIAS, from H.P. Robertson, Expert Consultant, Scientific Advisory Section, G-2, 15 May 1945. NARA.

[446] *Crossbow and Overcast* by James McGovern, William Morrow and Company, 1964, pp. 168-175.

[447] Memorandum, Report on Examination of Mittelwerke Target, to Commander S.P. Johnson, USNR, from Colonel Peter Beasley, 5 June 1945. NARA.

[448] CIOS Progress Report, June 4, 1945, c/o G-2 Division SHAEF, (Rear). NARA.

[449] Memorandum GBI/SS/322-17, Subject: Establishment of Field Intelligence Agency, Technical (FIAT) of G-2, Supreme Headquarters, AEF, May 31, 1945. NARA.

[450] Memorandum GBI/SS/322-17, Subject: Establishment of Field Intelligence Agency, Technical (FIAT) of G-2, Supreme Headquarters, AEF, May 31, 1945. NARA.

Chapter 19: Multiple Choice

[451] Headquarters, Ninth Air Force, Director of Intelligence, Intelligence Summary No. 133, 21 May 1945. NARA.

[452] Headquarters XXI Bomber Command, APO 234, Report of Operations, 25 May 1945, to the Commanding General, Twentieth Air Force, Washington 25, D.C., 14 July 1945. NARA.

[453] Incoming Message, Subject: Intermediate Report on Balls of Fire and Bakas, Missions 181 and 183, from Commanding General, twenty-First Bomb Command to Commanding General Twentieth Air Force, 30 May 1945, NARA. The following day Washington received an updated report about the two Tokyo missions, which included numerous sightings of Bakas and Balls of Fire; and again, each sighting was placed under the XXI Bomber Command's new classification headings: Flares, Rockets, and Midget Aircraft. Incoming Message, Subject: "Further Report on Missions 181 and 183," from Commanding General XXI Bomber Command to Commanding General Twentieth Air Force, May 31, 1945. NARA.

[454] *Project Identification: The First Scientific Study of the UFO Phenomenon*, Dr. Harley D. Rutledge, Prentice Hall, 1981, pp. 250-251.

[455] Memorandum from Brigadier General D.R. Hutchinson, Chief of Air Staff, Headquarters Far East Air Forces, to Commanders of all FEAF units down to and including group level, Subject: Advisory Specialist Group, June 8, 1945. NARA.

[456] Air Intelligence Report, Vol. 1, No. 14, 9 June, 1945, XXI Bomber Command. NARA.

[457] Headquarters XXI Bomber Command Tactical Mission Report, June 17/18, 1945. NARA.

[458] Headquarters XXI Bomber Command, Subject: Report of Attacks on Toyohashi, Fukuoka, and Shizuoka, 19/20 June, 1945. NARA.

Chapter 20: The Skies Stay Busy

[459] TAIC Secret Brief No. 3, Possible Japanese Jet and Rocket Development, Technical Air Intelligence Center, U S Naval AIR Station, Anacostia, (20), D.C., July 1, 1945. NARA.

[460] Tactical Mission Report: Targets on the Islands of Kyushu and Honshu, Japan, 1/2 July, 1945, from A-2 Section, XXI Bomber Command to Commanding General, Twentieth Air Force. NARA.

[461] Air Operations Memorandum, 88, reprinted by Air Intelligence Technical Group, Division of Naval Intelligence, Office of the Chief of Naval Operations, Navy Department, Washington, D.C., 6 July 1945. NARA.

[462] Air Operations Memorandum, 86, reprinted by Air Intelligence Technical Group, Division of Naval Intelligence, Office of the Chief of Naval Operations, Navy Department, Washington, D.C., 22 June 1945. NARA.

[463] Combat Information Center Intelligence Report, Office of the Chief of Naval Operations, July 1945. NARA.

[464] Intervention at Nansei Shoto, by James Dawson, unpublished, approximately 1951; article by unknown author and date; supplied by Jan Aldrich.

[465] http://www.ibiblio.org/hyperwar/AAF/Hansell/Hansell-6.html; p. 210.

[466] Letter dated 11-8-75; author and recipient unknown. Document supplied by Richard Hall.

[467] Tactical Mission Report: Report of Attacks on 4 Cities and 1 Precision Target on Honshu on 12/13 July, 1945, from A-2 Section, XXI Bomber Command to Commanding General, Twentieth Air Force. NARA.

[468] Telephone interview by Dr. James McDonald with Dr. David T. Griggs, April 10, 1969; provided by Jan Aldrich, respected UFO researcher/ historian and internet site coordinator for Project 1947, a premier source of UFO historical documents and writings. Since Dr. McDonald's handwriting is very difficult to read, Richard Hall supplied transcription of most of his telephone notes.

[469] "UFO Sighting Over Nuclear Reactor, Hanford, Washington, July, 1945," composed by Walt Andrus and Rolan D. Powell, http://www.niccap.dabsol.co.uk/hanford.htm. No

sighting reports have been located so far.

[470] Report #49, Carl Feindt's http://www.waterufo.net.

[471] Personal correspondence; William Mandel to Dr. J. Allen Hynek, February 10, 1967; provided by Jan Aldrich.

[472] *The Second World War: A Complete History*, Revised Edition, by Martin Gilbert, An Owl Book, Henry Holt and Company, 1989, pp. 712-717.

[473] SECRET War Department Classified Message Center, Outgoing Classified Message, Teletype Conference Between Major General E.R. Quesada and Colonel J.F. Olive, August 14, 1945. NARA.

[474] *The Second World War: A Complete History*, Revised Edition, by Martin Gilbert, An Owl Book, Henry Holt and Company, 1989, pp. 712-714.

[475] *Inside Saucer Post... 3-0 Blue*, CRIFO (Civilian Research, Interplanetary Flying Objects) views the status quo: a summary report, by Leonard Stringfield, 1957, pp. 7-8; *Situation Red: The UFO Siege, An Update On Strange And Frequently Frightening Encounters*, by Leonard H. Stringfield, Doubleday and Company, 1977, pp. 9-10; and personal telephone interview between Leonard Stringfield and Keith Chester, February 11, 1991. Telephone conversation with Dell Stringfield, June 17, 2004 and January 16, 2005.

Chapter 21: Dr. Griggs in Japan

[476] SECRET War Department Classified Message Center Outgoing Classified Message, Teletype Conference Between Major General E.R. Quesada and Colonel J.F. Olive, August 14, 1945. NARA.

[477] Memo-Telephone Call; from Colonel Lane to Dr. Waterman, August 13, 1945. NARA.

[478] Telephone interview between Dr. James McDonald and Dr. David T. Griggs, April 10, 1969; provided by Jan Aldrich.

[479] Letter from Dr. Karl T. Compton, Director, Pacific Branch, OSRD, to Dr. Vannevar Bush, Director, OSRD and Dr. Alan Waterman, Chief, Office of Field Service, OSRD, 31 August 1945. NARA.

[480] Telephone interview between Dr. James McDonald and Dr. David T. Griggs, April 10, 1969; provided by Jan Aldrich.

[481] *USS Beaver* (ID # 2302, later named: AS-5 and ARG-19), 1918-1950. http://www.history.navy.mil/photos/sh-usn/usnsh-b/as5.htm.

[482] Knowing nothing at the time, not even about foo fighters, it was not until after the war that Reynolds realized he had witnessed a UFO. Telephone interview, October 15 and 16, 2006, George M. Reynolds MUFON Maryland State Sectional Director.

[483] *The Hunt For Zero Point: Inside The Classified World Of Antigravity Technology*, by Nick Cook, Broadway Books, 2001, pp. 68-69.

[484] Telephone interview: between Dr. James McDonald and Dr. David T. Griggs, April 10, 1969. Document provided by Jan Aldrich

[485] *The USAF Scientific Advisory Board: Its First Twenty Years, 1944-1964*, by Thomas A. Sturm; Office of Air Force History, United States Air Force, 1986, pp. 8-10.

[486] "The Foo Fighter Mystery" by Jo Chamberlain, *American Legion Magazine*, December 1945. Article supplied by Anderson Henshaw.

Chapter 22: And So...
[487] *The Flying Saucers Are Real*, by Donald Keyhoe, Fawcett Publications, New York, 1950: pp.30-36. http://www.nicap.org/fsar/fsar-chapters.htm.

[488] National Archives document to unknown recipient from Air Force staff member signing for W.W. Ottinger, Lt. Colonel, USAF, Executive, Evaluation Division, Directorate of Intelligence, 23 April 1952. Document supplied by Barry Greenwood.

[489] The so-called "Massey Project" was "instigated to some extent by the reports of a spy who was in reality a double agent, working under the direction of the Mayor of Cologne." Edwards is the first researcher to discuss the "Schweinfurt Discs." *Above Top Secret: The Worldwide UFO Cover-up*, by Timothy Good, William Morrow and Company, 1988, p. 28.

[490] Letter: from Air Marshall Sir Victor Goddard, *Flying Saucers Review*, No. 1, Vol. 24, 1978, 30-31; *Out of the Shadows: UFOs, the Establishment & The Cover-Up*, Dr. David Clarke & Andy Roberts, Piatkus Limited, 2002, pg. 21.

[491] Churchill Archives Center, R.V. Jones Papers, RVJO D145: Letter from R.V. Jones to Hadrian Jeffs, 22 January 1996. *Out of the Shadows: UFOs, the Establishment & The Cover-Up*, Dr. David Clarke & Andy Roberts, Piatkus Limited, 2002, pg. 21.

[492] "A Die-Hard Issue: CIA's Role in the Study of UFOs, 1947-90," by Gerald K. Haines, *Studies In Intelligence*, Vol.01, No. 1, 1997, endnote 4. In 1997, CIA historian, Gerald K. Haines, penned the in-house publication. He referenced David Jacobs' *The UFO Controversy in America*.

[493] Established in early May 1943, four to five thousand technical reports were generated month until late August of 1944 when France was liberated. Office of Strategic Services: 'Technical Section, SI – History," 9 February 1945, NARA.

[494] "Memorial Tribute For Luis W. Alvarez," by Richard L. Garwin, published in *Memorial Tributes*, National Academy Press, Washington, DC, 1992, http://www.fas.org/RLG/alvarez.htm.

[495] Already a well-known, well respected and important UFO author/researcher.

[496] Telephone interview between Dr. David T. Griggs and Dr. James McDonald, April

10, 1969; provided by Jan Aldrich. Griggs' military affiliation after the war may have contributed to his reluctance to speak, since he carried a postwar security clearance. Griggs was a consultant for the RAND Company. When General Arnold approached Dr. Von Karman in November of 1944 to assemble the Army Air Force Scientific Advisory Group, the genesis of another project was born. A group of civilian scientists and engineers, working independently of the Scientific Advisory Group, was organized and became known as Project RAND; commonly referred to as Research and Development. RAND represented the Douglas Aircraft Company's finest. The talented scientists were presented with all the latest information regarding warfare technology and were told to study and research aerial warfare with the "object of recommending to the Air Force preferred methods, techniques, and instrumentalities for this purpose." *The Wizards of Armegeddon, by Fred Kaplan, Simon and Schuster, 1983, pp. 51-59*

[497] In the 1950s Major Donald E. Keyhoe collected "hundreds" of foo fighter sighting reports by both Allied and Axis pilots; *UFOs and the National Security State: Chronology of a Cover-Up, 1941-1973*, by Richard Dolan, Hampton Roads Publishing Company, 2002, p.7.

Epilogue: Postwar Thoughts
[498] Tape recording provided by UFO historian and author Wendy Connors.

[499] Letter correspondence: between William Mandel and Dr. J. Allen Hynek, February 10, 1967. Document provided by Jan Aldrich.

[500] "Joe Thompson and the Foo Fighters," by Max York, *The Nashville Tennessean Magazine*, 30 October 1966. Article supplied by Jan Aldrich.

[501] Personal telephone interview: between Harold Augspurger, November 29, 2003.

[502] Telephone interview: between Warren Barber and Keith Chester, November 2003.

[503] *Aerial Intelligence Of The Eighth Air Force*, by George Sesler, Taylor Publishing Company, 1996, p. 151; provided by Warren Barber.

[504] Telephone interview: between Mrs. Dell Stringfield and Keith Chester, June 17, 2004.

Appendix: Dr. Goudsmit and ALSOS
[505] *The Second World War: A Complete History*, Revised Edition, by Martin Gilbert, An Owl Book, Henry Holt and Company, 1989, pp. 20-21.

[506] *The Alsos Mission*, by Boris T. Pash, Award House, 1969, pp. 9-14

[507] Alsos Mission Report, 4 March 1944, by Major William P. Allis, AUS, Dr. James B. Fisk, OSRD, Dr. John R. Johnson, OSRD, Lt. Commander Bruce S. Old, USNR, and Lt. Colonel Boris T. Pash, M.I. Commanding. NARA.

[508] Memorandum from Major General Clayton Bissell, A.C. of S., G-2, for Chief of Staff, Mission Organized in MID for the Collection of Scientific Intelligence, May 11, 1944. NARA

509 *The ALSOS Mission*, Colonel Boris T. Pash, AUS Ret., Award House, New York, 1969, pp. 34-35.

510 Memorandum from Major General Clayton Bissell, A.C. of S., G-2, for Chief of Staff, Mission Organized in MID for the Collection of Scientific Intelligence, May 11, 1944. NARA.

511 Final Report of "S" Force Operations, Headquarters "S" Force, C/O HQ. Fifth Army, A.P.O #464, U.S. Army, to Commanding General, Rome Area, 17 June, 1944. NARA. Colonel Pash made arrangements with authorities in Washington for Major Richard Ham to be placed in charge of the Rome operation. There was no problem and Colonel Pash was off to London to resume his new post as Commander of the European ALSOS Mission. *The ALSOS Mission*, by Colonel T. Pash, AUS Ret., Award House, New York, 1969, pp. 30-36.

512 *The ALSOS Mission*, by Colonel Boris T. Pash, AUS Ret., Award House, New York, 1969, p. 74.

513 War Department General Staff/Special Staff Files: Dr. Samuel A. Goudsmit, no date. NARA.

514 Goudsmit pointed out that in the event of Germany's collapse, the ALSOS Mission would be split into four groups: "Group I, covering North West Germany; Group II Central West Germany; Group III, South West Germany; and Group IV, High Priority Targets." Memorandum, Subject: ALSOS Organization for Operations In Germany, from Dr. S.A. Goudsmit, Scientific Chief, to Lt. Colonel Boris T. Pash, Chief, ALSOS Mission, MIS, G-2 Section, HQ., ETOUSA, APO 887, US Army, 29 October 1944. NARA.

515 Memorandum: Policies And Procedures For ALSOS Scientific Personnel, by Dr. S.A. Goudsmit, no date. NARA.

516 *The ALSOS Mission*, by Boris T. Pash, Award house, 1969, pp. 179-200.

517 *A Series in the History of Modern Physics: 1800-1950, Vol. 1- "Alsos,"* by Dr. S.A. Goudsmit (1947). Tomash Publishers, 1983, pp 87-88.

518 They were to continue capturing all the atomic scientists and facilities. The find at Stadtilm had proven so significant, that General Groves informed General Marshall that the discovery "would seem to remove definitely any possibility of the Germans making use of an atomic bomb in this war." *The ALSOS Mission*, by Boris T. Pash, Award house, 1969, pp. 179-200

519 "SECRET" War Department, War Department General Staff, Military Division, G-2, Memorandum For The Assistant Chief Of Air Staff, Intelligence, AAF: Subject: AAF Representation on the Alsos Mission, from Major General Clayton Bissell, Assistant Chief of Staff, G-2, 23 March 1945. NARA.

520 War Department General Staff/Special Staff ALSOS files. No date. NARA.

Documents

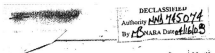

BRITISH SECRET
U.S. CONFIDENTIAL

CONSOLIDATED F.L.O. REPORT 21 to 26 May 43)

No. 161

A note on the abandonment of "Deterrent Fire" is published in an appendix to this report.

DAY OPERATIONS

WILHELMSHAVEN (21 May) (USA)

In this attack, which was carried out by five groups from the NORTH EAST, it was noticeable that the defences concentrated accurate and intense fire upon one group, the remainder receiving comparatively little attention. All the fire was predictor-control "seen".

ZEEBRUGGE (23 May). Nothing of interest to report.

ABBEVILLE/DRUCAT A/F (26 May). 7-8/10th cloud at 7,000 feet. Poor visibility.

This attack presented a great contrast to the last occasion, when the defences were completely inactive. Moderate heavy Flak fire was encountered at 11,000-12,000 feet and was described as being in bursts of two; the standard of accuracy was high, especially in view of the cloudy conditions.

NIGHT OPERATIONS

DORTMUND (23/24 May). No cloud, half moon. Good visibility. Some haze and smoke.

Aircraft heights varied from 8,500 to 24,000 feet, the defences generally, though not always, concentrating on those flying at the lower levels. A number of sightings of enemy fighters were reported, these taking place at heights of 18,000 feet and upwards. Several crews report a "lane", possibly left for fighters, running NORTH to SOUTH into the target area. Although the volume of Flak fire was considerable, crews on the whole found the defences less formidable than might have been expected at a well-defended target of this kind.

The main effort of the heavy guns was predictor control "seen"; a number of particularly accurate engagements were reported at heights around 16,000 feet. Barrage fire at about 15,000-17,000 feet towards the end of the attack and occasional "unseen" predictor control fire were also reported.

Intermittent light Flak fire, sometimes intense and accurate, was directed into the searchlight "cones", mainly from the western side of the town.

Up to 100 searchlights were estimated to have been in action, mainly to the NORTH and WEST. Many illuminations were obtained, though some deterioration in the standard of control was noticeable towards the end of the attack. At times up to six "cones" were formed and it was estimated that at no time during the attack were less than three aircraft simultaneously illuminated.

Phenomena

During this operation a large number of reports was received of so-called "rockets" which were observed not only in the approaches to the RUHR and the target area, but also over HOLLAND. In general these phenomena appear to have been similar to the "meteor" projectiles described in Consolidated F.L.O. Report No. 159, except that on this occasion many were said to have been seen flying at lower altitudes (some quite close to the ground) and mainly in a horizontal direction.

INCLOSURE 1 TO REPORT No. 27422
MILITARY ATTACHE, LONDON

CONFIDENTIAL
(EQUALS BRITISH SECRET)

SECRET

HEADQUARTERS   D-A-3
AAF STATION NO. 106
Office of the Intelligence Officer

APO   634,
8 February, 1944.

SUBJECT: Unusual Tactics of E/A or AA Gun Fire.

TO   : A-2 Section, 41st Combat Bombardment Wing, APO 634.

1. No attacks made on our formation today.

2. Ball like object, appeared silvery, hung in air at 30,000 feet. No chute was observed to be attached to the object, and it remained under observation for approximately fifteen (15) minutes by the crew while in the target area. The crew did not see the object fired from the ground.

W. E. DOLAN,
Major, Air Corps,
Station S-2 Officer.

6535 (R) Phenomena

GERMANY

Southwest of St. Quentin three silver objects about 30 ft. long were seen 1,000 ft. below and 600 yds astern of the observers. They were described as resembling Zeppelins and, although moving in unison independently of the wind, were apparently not interconnected. Similar phenomena were described in Consolidated FLO report No. 205 and although on this occasion a closer view was obtained there is no explanation at present of the purpose they may serve.

SOURCE: MA London - 66474 - 9 Mar 1944 - filed 9815 Spec. Binder.

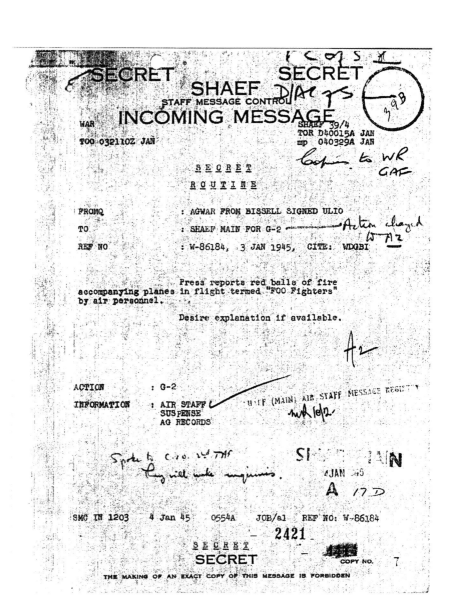

SECRET SHAEF SECRET

STAFF MESSAGE CONTROL

INCOMING MESSAGE

WAR

TOO 032110Z JAN

SHAEF 39/4
TOR D40015A JAN
mp 040329A JAN

S E C R E T

R O U T I N E

FROMQ : AGWAR FROM BISSELL SIGNED ULIO

TO : SHAEF MAIN FOR G-2

REF NO : W-86184, 3 JAN 1945, CITE: WDQBI

Press reports red balls of fire accompanying planes in flight termed "FOO Fighters" by air personnel.

Desire explanation if available.

ACTION : G-2

INFORMATION : AIR STAFF
SUSPENSE
AG RECORDS

SMC IN 1203   4 Jan 45   0554A   JOB/al   REF NO: W-86184

- 2421

S E C R E T

SECRET

COPY NO. 7

THE MAKING OF AN EXACT COPY OF THIS MESSAGE IS FORBIDDEN

1st W/Ind.   D-W-2

HEADQUARTERS XII TACTICAL AIR COMMAND, APO #374, U.S. Army, 23 January 1945.

TO: S-2, 415 Night Fighter Squadron.

Forwarded for compliance with paragraph 2 of 1st Ind.

LEAVITT CORNING, JR.,
Lt. Colonel, G. S. C.,
A/C of S, A-2.

2nd. W/Ind.

415th. NIGHT FIGHTER SQUADRON, APO #374, U. S. Army, 30 January 1945.

TO: AC of S A-2 XII Tactical Air Command, APO 374, U. S. Army.

1. In compliance with paragraph 2 of 1st. Ind., the following extracts from the Sortie Reports of various pilots who have encountered the Night Phenomenon are submitted for your information.

Night of 14-15 December 1944 - "In vicinity of Erstein (V-9381) flying at 1000 ft. observed large red light at 2000 ft. going East at 12:40 hrs. Travelling at approximately 200 MPH"

Night of 16-17 December 1944 - "20 miles North of Breisach (W-0173) at 800 ft. observed 5 or 6 flashing red and green lights in "T" shape. Thought they were flak. About 10 minutes later saw the same lights much closer and behind me. We turned port and Starboard and the lights followed. They closed in to about 8 O'clock and 1000 ft. and remained in that position for several minutes and then disappeared."

Night of 22-23 December 1944 - "Patrolling at Angels 10 from Sarrebourg to Strasbourg North and South of highway. At 06:00 hrs. saw two lights coming towards A/C from the ground. Upon reaching altitude of plane, they leveled off and stayed on my tail for approximately 2 minutes. Lights appeared to be a large orange glow. After staying with A/C for approximately 2 minutes, they would peel off and turn away, fly along level for a few minutes and then go out. They appeared to be under perfect control at all times. Lights were seen somewhere in vicinity of Hagenau."

2406   4896

Incl #1

2 nd. W/Ind., 415th. Night Fighter Squadron 30 January 1945 con't.

Night of 23-24 December 1944 - "Observed reddish colored flames at considerable distance and at approximately 10,000 ft."

Night of 23-24 December 1944 - "Approximately 10 miles South of Point X (Q6745) noticed to NE approximately 5 miles a glowing red object shooting straight up. Changed suddenly to plane view of A/C doing a wing over and going into a dive and disappearing."

Night of 26-27 December 1944 - "At 01:45 hrs. saw two yellow streaks of flame flying at same level at approximately 3000 ft. off port side. We also saw red balls of fire that stayed up for 10 seconds approximately 45 miles away. After seeing yellow streaks, made starboard vector lost altitude and streaks disappeared from view. Called GCI Blunder and asked if any E/A were in vicinity. They answered No. Instructed to return to Angels 10. We felt what was thought to be prop wash; very distinct. Noticed several groups of lights off port while patrolling in vicinity of Q-9050 and R-1556 Lights made distinct lines somewhat like arrows."

Night of 26-27 December 1944 - "While on vector 090 near V-7050 during patrol we observed airborne white lights. They were staggered evenly vertically and we could see from 1 to 4 swing at once. They appeared stationary at 10,000 ft."

Night of 26-27 December 1944 - "Observed light at same altitude while in vicinity of Worms Observer saw light come within 100 ft. Peeled off and took evasive action but light continued to follow for 5 minutes. Light then pulled up rapidly and went out of sight."

Night of 27-28 December 1944 - "While on North heading in patrol area noticed in vicinity of Q-1378 lights suspended in air moving slowly and would then disappear. Were orange in color. Lights appeared singly and in pairs. Observed these lights four or five times during period."

Night of 27-28 December 1944 - "Eight miles NE of Luneville at 19:10 hrs. saw three sets of three lights (red and white) one on starboard and one on port from 1000 ft. to 2000 ft. to rear and closing in at Angels 10. Pulled up to Angels 8 and lights went out. Called Churchman to see if there was anything in area. Received a negative reply."

Night of 30-31 December 1944 - "Saw a group of lights flying through the air 30 or 40 miles East of base while flying at Angels 9 - 10."

Night of 1-2 January 1945 - "Saw Foofighters North of Strasbourg and North of Saverne".

Night of 14-15 January 1945 - "Observed a large orange glow in sky approx. 5 ft. in diameter in vicinity of Ingweiller at 6000 ft. at 20:00 hrs."

2407

S-E-C-R-E-T

4497

S-E-C-R-E-T

2nd. W/Ind., 415th. Night Fighter Squadron, 30 January 1945 Con't.

Night of 29-30 January 1945 - "At about 00:10 hrs. sighted a Foofighter about half way between Weissembourg and Landau. Foofighter was off to the starboard and rear at Angels 2. Lights were amber and one was 20 - 50 ft. above the other and of about 30 seconds duration. Foofighter was about 1000 ft. away and following. The lights were about a foot in diameter. Lights disappeared when Travel 34 turned into them."

2. In every case where pilot called GCI Control and asked if there was a Bogey A/C in the area he received a negative answer.

F. B. RINGWALD,
Captain, A. C.,
Intelligence Officer.

* Foofighters is the name given these phenomenon by combat crews of this Squadron.

S-E-C-R-E-T

2nd Ind.

HEADQUARTERS XII TACTICAL AIR COMMAND (ADV), APO #374, U.S. Army,
4 February 1945.

TO: Commanding General, First Tactical Air Force (Prov) APO 374,
U.S. Army. Attn: A/C of S, A-2.

Attention is invited to 2nd W/Ind.

LEAVITT CORNING, JR.,
Lt. Colonel, G. S. C.,
A/C of S, A-2.

3rd Ind.   D-Y-1
HEADQUARTERS, FIRST TACTICAL AIR FORCE (PROV), APO 374, U S Army, 5 February 1945.

TO: Chief Intelligence Officer, Air Staff SHAEF, APO 757.

1. Forwarded for your information.

2. This headquarters has no further information or explanation in connection
with these phenomena.

3. It is believed that further investigation is warranted. Since appropriate
technical personnel are not available within the First Tactical Air Force, the matter
is forwarded for such further investigation as may be advisable.

C. A. YOUNG,
Colonel, AC,
AC of S, A-2

1 Incl.
#1 - 1st & 2nd W/Ind, 23 Jan 45
and 30 Jan 45.

2404

- 2 -

AIR STAFF
SUPREME HEADQUARTERS
ALLIED EXPEDITIONARY FORCE.

SECRET.

REF: SHAEF AIR/TS.37153/A-2.   11 February 1945.

SUBJECT: Night Phenomena.

TO: Headquarters, U.S.S.T.A.F
       (For attention of Chief Technical Intelligence
       Officer, Col. Bradley).

1.   Attached are copies of papers received from the First
Tac. Air Force (Prov). From the number of reports quoted in
the 2nd W/Ind from the 415th Night Fighter Squadron, it would
seem that there must be something more than mere imagination
behind the matter, and in view of the fact that pilots and crews
are becoming slightly worried by them, it is considered that
everything possible should be done to get to the root of the
matter.

2.   Copies of the reports have been sent to the Air Ministry
for their consideration, and the Scientific Investigation
Division of this Headquarters (Mr. Robertson) has also been asked
to consider the problem.

3.   In the meantime, it is suggested that it might be as well
for an Air Technical Intelligence Officer to visit the Unit
concerned and obtain reports and impressions at first hand from
aircrew personnel.

         For the Deputy Supreme Commander,

                    C.M. GRIERSON,
                    Air Commodore,
                    A.C. of S., A-2,
                    Air Staff, SHAEF.

    - 2402

    - 4891

FILE COPY
47A

AIR STAFF
SUPREME HEADQUARTERS
ALLIED EXPEDITIONARY FORCE

REF:- 3715 0

11 February 1945.

TO:- First Tactical Air Force (Prov.), APO 374, U.S. ARMY.

1. Reference to your 3rd Indorsement on the subject of night phenomenon originated by the 415th Night Fighter Squadron, there is no information at this Headquarters which might explain the nature and cause of the lights and other phenomena described by the pilots of this Squadron.

2. The matter is, therefore, being referred to the Air Ministry in order to find out whether any further information can be obtained from that source. It is also hoped to make arrangements for an Air Technical Intelligence Officer from USSTAF to visit the Unit concerned.

For the Deputy Supreme Commander,

C. J. Graham,
Air Commodore,
A.C. of S., A-2.

— 2403

— 4382

T{

A/Cmdr. Grierson,
A.C. of S. A-2
Air Staff S.H.A.

(62A)

From : Air Ministry, D.D.I.2.

Date : 13th March 1945

STAFF. F b

Ref : 111/45/DDI2

15 MAR 1945

6C A 37/63

BALLS OF FIRE - RED.

      The papers dealing with
the above subject which you enclosed with your memo SHAEF Air/
TS.37153/A2 dated 11th February,
have been carefully examined and
discussed with the various other
Departments concerned.

      Bomber Command crews have
for some time been reporting similar phenonema. A few of the
alleged aircraft may have been Me.
262 and for the rest, flak rockets
are suggested as the most likely
explanation.

      The whole affair is
still something of a mystery and
the evidence is very sketchy and
varied so that no definite and
satisfactory explanation can yet
be given.

2355

E. D. M. Hopkins
Group Captain

SECRET.

AIR STAFF
SUPREME HEADQUARTERS
ALLIED EXPEDITIONARY FORCE
(FORWARD)

REF:- SHAEF/A/TS.37153/A.2.   18 March 1945.

SUB:- Night Phenomena.

To:- First Tactical Air Force (Prov.), APO 374, US ARMY.

　　　1.　　With reference to reports forwarded from the XIIth Tactical Air Command through your Headquarters on the subject of night phenomena (foofighter), and further to this Headquarters' letter of even reference dated 11 February, a reply has now been received from the Air Ministry who say that Bomber Command crews have for some time been reporting similar phenomena.

　　　2.　　The Air Ministry view is that a few of the alleged aircraft may have been Me.262's and for the rest, flak rockets are suggested as the most likely explanation.

　　　3.　　It is regretted that no further, or more definite, information can be given.

　　　　　　　　　For the Deputy Supreme Commander,

　　　　　　　　　　　　　　C.M. GRIERSON
　　　　　　　　　　　　　　Air Commodore,
　　　　　　　　　　　　　　A.C. of S., A-2.

　　　　　　　　　　　2354

FILE COPY

CONFIDENTIAL IVI

log

Chief of Staff	
Deputy C. of S. P & A	
Deputy C. of S. Opr.	
Deputy C. of S. T.M.& E.	
A. G.	

From: Deputy Commander, 20th Air Force, Guam

To: War Department
CG, Army Air Forces, Pacific Ocean Areas,
Administrative, Hickam Field, TH
Radio Lualualei

2250   4 May 1945

Nbr 2250, from DEPCOMAF 20 POA to CINCPOA Adv,
CINCPOA Pearl, COMAF 20, BOMCOM 21 USA COMGENAAFPOA Admin,
COMGENAAF, attention A-2.

Following phenomenon observed by B 24 of 11th Bomb
on return from snooper mission to Truk morning 3rd May
Eastern longitude date: while still over Truk Lagoon two red
circles of light approached plane from below one on right
one on left. One on left turned back after one and one
half hours. One on right continued to about ten miles
from Guam. stayed on right side throughout sometimes
ahead sometimes behind or alongside. Always about 12 to
1500 yards distant until day break when it climbed to 15,000
feet and stayed in sun.

Our plane at 0745K came down from 8,300 feet through
undercast and lost contact. During trip light observed to
change to orange, gradually grew bright yellow or white like
electric light or phosphorus glow, then go out for second or
two, then came gradually back as orange color at regular
intervals. Light appeared about one foot diameter. changes
in color did not follow pattern of acceleration and deceleration.

CM-IN-3605 (4 May 45)

CONFIDENTIAL

A-3 (retd) ok
A-4
Comm 12
COPY NO.

THE MAKING OF AN EXACT COPY OF THIS MESSAGE IS FORBIDDEN

CONFIDENTIAL IVI

Page 2

From: Deputy Commander, 20th Air Force, Guam

Nr: 2250   4 May 1945

Light followed B 24 in dives from 11,000 to 3,000 feet sharp course changes and brief cloud covered intervals. Did not resemble exhaust plume. When turned into kept same relative position and distance. During night high cirrus clouds masked moonlight to considerable extent and no part of object except light observed until day break.

At day break light changed to steady white glow and possible wing shape and silver color observed but no details due to distance and sun glare.

Above facts based on careful interrogation of entire crew. Guam radar showed no hostile bodies at time involved. Can you suggest possible explanations.

End.

ACTION: 20th Air Force

CM-IN-3605 (4 May 45)   DTG 040651Z   da

CONFIDENTIAL   12

COPY No.
THE MAKING OF AN EXACT COPY OF THIS MESSAGE IS FORBIDDEN

Sighting Index

Date	Location	Description	Page #
Oct. 11, 1931	WV, United States	"flaming, one-hundred foot blimp"	6
Dec. 29, 1932	NJ, United States	"airplane"	6
July 5, 1933	Sussex, England	Gigantic "light"	6-7
Sometime between Aug.-Dec. 1933 (two week period)	East Coast United States and Britain	Mysterious aircraft	7
Dec. 24, 1933	Kalix, Sweden	"beam of light" coming from "machine"	7
Dec. 30, 1933	Sweden	"Low-flying aeroplane"	7
Feb. 3, 1934	Sweden, Northern Finland, Norway	"Ghost aviators" (as reported by the New York Times)	8
Apr. 1, 1934	Oslo, Norway	"very large aeroplane" with eight propellers	8
Nov. 24, 1935	Palestine, Texas	"Bright shaft of light"	10
Dec. 1935	Brazil, South America	"Snake-like shafts of light" hanging motionless in sky	10
Jan. 1, 1937	NC, United States	30-40 foot in diameter object, no propellers, gun metal color	10-11

Feb. 11, 1937	Kvalsik, Norway	"Large aeroplane" with red and green glowing lights	11
July 20, 1937	London, England	Light (Nicknamed Ghost Flier)	11
July 22, 1937	500 miles off US coast	Lights of alleged "aircraft"	11
Late 1937	German/polish border	Objects described as "coffins" and "swords"	11
February 8, 1938	England	"'things like glowing spheres' that were 'floating in the British sky'"	11-12
Summer 1938	MA, United States	"silvery" object with rectangular portholes	12
July, 1939	PA, United States	"resembled a modern day jet airliner without wings"; "weird glow"	12
September 1941	Between African mainland of Mozambique and Island of Madagascar	"strange globe glowing with greenish light about half the size of full moon."	17
Early Dec. 1941	GA, United States	Light moving in counter-clockwise circles	17-18
Dec. 22, 1941	NY, United States	"round sharply outlined object" with "bright aluminum or chrome finish"	18
Feb. 26, 1942	CA, United States (Known as Battle of Los Angeles)	Multiple sightings: "triangular grouping" of "glowing objects"; "luminous white dots"; "bright red spots of light"; "silver dot"; "like a moving star"	19-22
February 27, 1942	Timor Sea	"large disc;" departed location at 3,500 miles per hour	23

Spring 1942	KY, United States	"powerful searchlight" shining down, emanating from unidentifiable object; sometimes remained motionless	23
Spring 1942	IL, United States	Light grey, "sharply defined rectangle;" grey in color	23
June 25, 1942	Holland	Shining copper "object," like setting sun, the size of a full moon	23-25
Aug. 5, 1942	Solomon Islands	"silver-shaped cigar" with "round dome" on top; approximately ninety-feet in diameter	27
Aug. 11/12, 1942	Near Aachen, Germany	"a phenomenon described as a bright white light"	29-30
Aug. 12, 1942	Solomon Islands	"formation of silvery objects directly overhead," numbering close to 150; "mighty roaring sound"	28
Aug. 17/18, 1942	Osnabruk, Germany	"...a rocket with a long white tail of light..."	30
Mid Aug. 1942	Tula Region, near Moscow, Russia	"huge cigar-shaped object something like a Zeppelin, but much bulkier and rounder at the front"; "aluminum hued color"	30-31
Summer 1942	Tasman Peninsula, Bass Strait between Island of Tasmania and Australia	"...a singular airfoil of glistening bronze color;" domed upper surface; possible crewmember, "Cheshire cat" emblem on dome	29

Nov. 28/29, 1942	Turin, Italy	"object…two to three hundred feet in length…500 mph…. four red lights spaced at equal distances along its body"	34-35
November 1942	Bay of Biscay, England	"Thing," massive in size; no wings; electronic interference	35-36
December 1942	French coast, over mouth of Somme River	Two amber and orange lights, flying in unison; not aircraft	36
Mar. 13, 1943	Naples, Italy	"roman candle" lights; "bright very large red light" that "looked like a huge irregular mass of neon…"	38
May 12/13, 1943	Duisburg, Germany	"meteor"; "object was reddish-orange in color"; "emitted a burst giving off a green star"	39
May 23/24, 1943	Dortmund, Germany	Large number of so-called "rockets"	39-40
May 27/28, 1943	Essen, Germany	Cylindrical object, silvery-gold in color, with several portholes evenly spaced along its side; motionless until speeding away at several thousand miles per hour	40-41
May 1943	English Channel	Large, stationary "orange balloon on or near the sea"	41
Sept. 6, 1943	Stuttgart, Germany	"objects resmbling silver discs"	43
Oct. 24, 1943	Schweinfurt, Germany	"silver-colored discs"	46
Dec. 11, 1943	Edmen, Germany	"unidentified object"; "size of thunderbolt aircraft"; "streak-like vapor trail"	51
Dec. 14, 1943	Naples, Italy	Small round bright "light"	52

1943 (date unknown)	CA, United States	"object...international orange in color... elliptical shape;" wobbled in "unstable manner;" no wings, jet exhaust, smoke, or vapor trails	51
Jan. 2/3, 1944	Halberstadt, Germany	"two rockets"; "altered course"; "fiery head and blazing stern"	54
Jan. 5, 1943	Keil, Germany	"black plate-sized discs"	55
Jan. 28, 1944	Somewhere over France	"airborne red light"	56
Jan.29, 1944	Location unknown	"red ball"; "yellow/red flames" followed aircraft through evasive action	56
Feb. 4, 1944	Frankfurt, Germany	Two sightings: "stationary object of tear-drop shape, resembling a balloon"; "shiny silver ball" looking like a "very bright weather balloon with a metal sheen"	59
Feb. 4, 1944	Dutch coast	"one long black stationary object, similar to a small flak burst floating..."	59
Feb. 8, 1944	Frankfurt, Germany	"silver-colored ball-like object" hanging stationary	59
Feb. 19/20, 1944	Leipzig-Berlin area, Germany	Two objects: "glowing" balls; "'snake-like' motion"	59-60
Feb. 19/20, 1944	Coblence and Aachen, Germany	"silvery cigar-shaped object like an airship"; "appeared to be a line of windows along the bottom of the object"	60
Feb. 24/25, 1944	St. Quentin, France	"three silver objects ...resembling zeppelins... moving independently of the wind...not interconnected"	60

April 11, 1944	location unknown, probably Germany	rojectiles resembling glider-bombs; "a large orange glow... smoke trail"	66
April 25, 1944	France	Black tear-dropped craft; "probable" Me-163	63
April 26, 1944	Essen, Germany	"things"; "four orange glows"; "short stubby wings"; "football" size; looking like "large oranges"	64-65
June 6, 1944	Normandy Coast, France	"dark ellipsoidal object...blunted on each end like sausage"	67
June 1944	Normandy, France	"luminescent" discus-shaped object	67-68
June/July 1944	Normandy, France	"spheres" approximately the "size of a football"	70
July 1944	Normandy, France	"targets flying at extremely high altitudes"	81
Aug. 1, 1944	Ploesti, Rumania	"yellow object" traveling "several times the speed of an aircraft"	71
Aug. 10/11, 1944	Palembang, Sumatra	"reddish-orange" balls, about the size of a baseball; "spherical object, probably 5 or 6 feet in diameter, of a very bright and intense red or orange in color"	71-74
August 12, 1944	Pelice, Southern France	"enormous disc;" circular lights (changing from bright yellow to white) "like portholes in a ship;" motionless	75
August 13, 1944	Kaoe Bay, Indonesia	"Very brilliant light appearing to hover in air for at least five minutes"	76

August 1944	Between St. Lo and Vire, France	"cherry-red light;" size of a large star; sat "motionless" in sky before disappearing into clouds	79-80
Summer 1944	Italy	"egg-shaped, metallically glistening motionless object"	78
September 1944	Unknown Japanese island	"white object... egg-shaped... very brilliant"	76
Late September 1944	Dover, England	Solid black cylindrical-shaped; red glow emitting from rear	81-82
September 1944	England	"bright spherical object... like a rolling ball..."	83
September 1944	Antwerp, Belgium	"glowing" globe," "cloudy gas with a light inside"; "...three to four feet in diameter..."	82-83
Fall 1944	Holland	"light" movig high in night sky	84
Oct. 16, 1944	Formosa, Taiwan	"small black dot;" hanging stationary	78
Oct. 20, 1944	Po Valley, Italy	"red light" – appearance of an aircraft light	84
Oct. 20, 1944	N. Florence, Italy	"two orange balls diving into the hills"	84
Oct. 25, 1944	Omura, Japan	Multiple sightings of "possible" balloons	78
Oct. 29, 1944	Munich, Germany	"light blue colored ball of fire approximately three feet in diameter"	85-86
Oct. 30/31, 1944	Cologne, Germany	A "ball of fire"; "circular, pale orange, clean edged light..."	86

Nov. 5, 1944	Singapore, Malaya	"a long purple-blue parabolic trail"	77-78
Nov. 5/6, 1944	Aachen/Bonn, Aachen/ Cologne, Germany	Possible jet; "single light"; "5 free lance visuals on jets, no A.I. or G.C.I. contacts; "several flares similar to jets"	86-87
Nov. 22, 1944	Germany	Spherical object, fluctuating in brightness, pyrotechnic pink in color, changing speeds "violently," "swift" and "jerking" movements	89
Nov. 24, 1944	Northern Italy	"round amber light," "luminous orange-yellow," blinding light; felt "unbearable" heat	89-93
Nov. 26, 1944	Mannheim, Germany	"red light" that "disappeared in long red streak"	93-94
Late November 1944	Strasbourg, Germany	Eight to ten lights in a row, glowing orange, and moving at terrific speed	95
Late November 1944	Lingayen Gulf, Philippines	"bright green 'globe'"	95-96
Dec. 2, 1944	Villafranca, Ghedi Airdrome area, Italy	"a steady, seemingly hanging light"	96
Dec. 5, 1944	Rhine River area, Germany	Alleged aircraft that "climbed out of range in nothing flat"	96
Dec. 14/15, 1944	Erstein, Germany	"brilliant red light... appeared to be 4 or 5 times larger than a star going 200 mph"	96, 130
December 1944	Germany	Amorphous reddish-glow that at times appeared cigar-shaped	97-98

Dec. 17, 1944	Breisach, Germany	"5 or 6 flashing red and green lights in 'T' shape"	100, 130
Dec. 22/23, 1944	Hagenau, Germany	Multiple sightings: Two lights that "appeared to be a large orange glow" coming from ground - followed plane - "appeared to be under perfect control"	102, 130
Dec. 23/24, 1944	Germany	"red streak in sky"	103, 130
Dec. 23/24 1944	Germany	"glowing red object shooting straight up"; appeared to be aircraft "doing a wing-over and going into a dive and disappearing"	103, 130
December (between 16-24) 1944	Germany	Amorphous reddish-glow that at times appeared cigar-shaped	97-98
Dec. 26/27, 1944	Germany	Multiple sightings: "red balls of fire;" "two yellow streaks of flame...disappeared from view;" the crew thought they felt "prop wash;" a group of lights that "made distinct lines, somewhat like arrows;" row of vertical white lights	103, 131
Dec. 26/27, 1944	Worms, Germany	Circular, "fiery ball"; "triangle of ovals" – three circular, reddish-blue in color, vivid lights, looking like flames, in a tight inverted triangle formation	104-106, 131
December 27, 1944	Luneville, France	"two sets of three red and white lights"	107-108, 131

Dec. 27, 1944	France	Orange lights, singly and in pairs, suspended in air, "moving slowly" before disappearing	108
Dec. 28, 1944	Neuwied / Koblenz Germany	"a green ball about six inches in diameter"; "motionless and did not appear to have anything supporting it"	108
Dec. 28, 1944	Ardennes, Belgium	Large white light"; no radar contact; "went straight up at a tremendous speed"; disappeared	108-110
December 1944	Between Strasbourg and Mannheim, Germany	Bright "fuzzy round" ball, twice the size of "full moon"; "yellow, white, red tint" that was "not solid color"; no radar return	118-119
December 1944	Between Frankfurt and Karlsrhue, Germany	Three to four very bright balls, completely illuminated – red, yellow, white and blue in color; size of tennis ball at arm's length	119
December 1944	Somewhere between eastern France and Western Germany	String of lights, twelve to fifteen in number, orange to yellow in color, approximately four feet in diameter, stretching twice the length of crew's aircraft; no radar contact	120
Jan. 1, 1945	Ardennes, Belgium	"pair of fog lights"; "bright yellowish orange"; flying in "tandem'; three feet in diameter	114-117
Jan.1/2, 1945	North of Strasbourg, France	"Foo fighters"	131
Jan. 10, 1945	Iwo Jima, Japan	"an amber light pass parallel and at same altitude"	125

Jan. 14/15, 1945	Ingweiller, Germany	"a large orange glow in sky approx. 5 ft. in diameter"	131
Jan. 18, 1945	Oyster River, near Vancouver Island, Canada	"large silvery cylinder or balloon" that "appeared to discharge another balloon or object," each traveling in separate directions	132
Jan. 29, 1945	Between Wissembourg and Landau, Germany	Two amber colored lights about "one foot in diameter"	129, 131
February 2, 1945	Colmar, France	Unusual "green light... moving rapidly"	133
Feb. 8, 1945	Near Strasbourg, France	"yellow light"	133
Feb. 9/10, 1945	Riegel, Germany	"very bright light moving slowly"	133
Feb. 13/14, 1945	Between Rastatt and Bishwiller, Germany	Two sets of lights; separated after being attacked and then returned to original position	136
Feb. 14/15, 1945	Freiburg, Germany	"string of lights...(1 red one in center, 4 white ones on each side) blinking off and on"	136
Feb. 15/16, 1945	Pisa, Italy	Multiple sightings: "flare"; "flare" that "seemed to spiral";	136
Feb. 15/16, 1945	Viareggio, Italy	Alleged jet; multiple spurts of "flame"; no radar return	136
Feb. 16, 1945	La Spezia, Italy	Possible jet: dropped what looked like "white flares"; no radar contact	136-137
Feb. 17, 1945	Central Po Valley, Italy	"observed two very bright lights" appear directly in front of aircraft; fired upon without result	137

Feb. 17, 1945	Massa and Central Po Valley	"red ball of fire" that "did not appear to be Jet A/C"	137
Feb. 17/18. 1945	La Spezia, Italy	Multiple sightings:(1)"blinking light"; (2) "reddish white light going off and on in spurts," faded out during chase; (3) light, a "glow" alternating between "weak and bright" was chased several times, never caught	138-139
Feb. 21, 1945	Po Valley, Italy	Alleged flares; "cluster of 11 or more colored flares" that remained motionless; "cluster of 15 orange balls of fire"	139-140
Feb. 21, 1945	Piacenza, Italy	"two large red balls of fire"; hovering	140
Feb. 22, 1945	Near Leghorn, Italy	Three lights red-orange in color that "did not appear to be flares"	141
Feb. 27, 1945	Bologna, Italy	Chased "three lights" in "shape of triangle" observed; no radar contact	141-142
February, 1945	Chemnitz, Germany	"flying wing, giving off a yellowish-red intermittent glow"	149
March 1945	NM, United States	Object "aluminum" colored, "12 to 14" feet off ground, "motionless," "swept away like dragonfly"	142-143
Mar. 3, 1945	Misburg, Germany	Two "balloon-like silver balls"	143
Mar. 5, 1945	Either Holland or Northern Germany	Two sightings: (1) "large orange ball" hanging in air; (2) "similar ball" that was "moving horizontally at same altitude"	145

Mar. 9, 1945	North Friesian Islands	Three lights; "had the appearance of white flares dropped in air"; called "foo fighters"	145-146
Mar. 13, 1945	Bologna, Italy	Two sightings: (1) "100 hundred balls of orange fire"; (2) two "balls of foo fire"	147
Mar. 18, 1945	Florence, Italy	Chased "light," no radar contact, then "light disappeared"	148
Mar. 19/20, 1945	Speyer, Germany	"saw 2 'Foo fighters'"; one "orange" and one "green" ball	148
Mar. 23, 1945	Bergamo/Ghedi, Italy	"2 balls of foo fire"	150
Mar. 23, 1945	Germersheim, Germany	"stationary airborne object"	150
Mid-Mar. 1945	New Guinea	Object, "silver in color," "very shiny... much larger than the brightest star;" unaffected by gunfire; departed upward "at a fantastic rate of speed"	151-152
Mar. 24, 1945	Nagoya, Japan	Multiple sightings: "yellow ball of fire about 6 inches in diameter"; "orange and red flashes; "six white balls of fire"; grayish ball of fire about size of soccer ball; "red ball of fire"	152-153
Mar. 25, 1945	Between Mannheim and Darmstadt, Germany	Six or seven circular, yellowish-orange objects, solid color, and brightness; apparently individually controlled	153-154

Apr. 3/4, 1945	Honshu, Japan	Multiple "balls of fire" sightings: "size of basketball"; "streamer of light behind the ball of fire"; ball of fire emitting a "steady phosphorescent glow"; "wing in connection with ball of fire…"; "amber-colored" searchlight; "stream of fire emanating from object," twelve inches in diameter, followed through evasive action	157-158
April 7, 1945	North Sea	A wingless object, able to stop in mid-flight and travel thousands of miles per hour	158-159
April 7, 1945	Nagoya, Japan	"ball of fire" changing colors; "orange to red"	161
May 2, 1945	Fala Island, Truk Atoll	Two "airborne objects… red circles of light… changing from a cherry-red to orange" to a "white light" and then cherry-red again; followed for over an hour; no radar return	163
May 14, 1945	Nagoya, Japan	"red or 'flame-colored' light," constant position, "same size as B-29 landing light"	166
June 18, 1945	Japan	A "fluctuating light round in shape that changed from bright red, to dim orange".	180
June 19, 1945	Japan	B-29 followed by "strong white light"	180
June 19, 1945	Fukuoka, Japan	"one bright 'ball of fire'; no fuselage or any wings	180

July 2, 1945	Japan	Several "balls of fire... much larger than supercharger glow, but of somewhat the same color"	182-183
July 7, 1945	Sasebo, Japan	Foo fighter; "a big ball of fuzzy orange-red light"; B-29 fired on object, appearing to hit with no affect	186
July 12, 1945	Honshu, Japan	"Light Phenomenon." Spotted "enemy aircraft" apparently trailed by "large orange light traveling" with it "at same speed"	186-187
Mid-July 1945	WA, United States	Object was "very bright" and had "saucer-like appearance"; "…was the size of three aircraft carriers, side-by side, oval shaped, very streamlined like a stretched-out egg and, and pinkish in color;" hovered in "fixed position and then went straight-up and "disappeared"	188
Summer 1945	Aleutian Islands	Crew saw "large round object" emerging from sea; 150-200 feet in diameter; object circled ship; three white flashes observed in direction object departed	188-189
August 1945	Okinawa, Japan	"cigar-shaped, metallic, and without markings or visible openings," and "35 to 50 feet in length"	189-190

Aug. 28, 1945	Between Ie Shima and Iwo Jima, Japan	"three teardrop-shaped objects," "brilliant white, like burning magnesium," "about the size of a dime held at arm's length," flying in "tight formation," and seemed "intelligently controlled"	191-193
September 1945	Buckner Bay, Okinawa, Japan	A stationary "bluish-white" light, "about the size of a dime at arm's length," move and then return to original position	195-196

Index

Bringewald, Franz   168-169
Brink, Rodney L.   21
British:
  AI2(a)(Air Ministry Intelligence)   30,
    57, 63-64, 81, 129
  AI2(g) (Air Technical Intelligence) 68,
    81, 172
  Air Intelligence Branch (AII (c))   15
  Air Ministry   11, 14-16, 25-26, 32,
    49, 63, 68, 80, 88, 134, 141, 147, 154,
    202-203, 214-215
  Air-Officer-In-Charge (AOC)   34,
    57
  Anti-Aircraft Command   45
  Assistant Director of Intelligence   16
  (Science) - (also see R.V. Jones)
  Crossbow Committee   51, 56, 58, 63,
    69, 80, 204
  Crossbow operation   51, 53, 55, 58,
    69-70, 97, 124, 204
  Intelligence   34, 50, 65, 147
  Interdepartmental Radiolocation
    Committee   70
  MI6   15
  MI14 (E)   32, 34, 37-38
  MI14(E) Phenomena Report   36-37
  MI14(E) rocket phenomena
    investigation   34, 36-37
  Ministry of Aircraft Production   16
  Naval Intelligence   213
  Psychological Warfare Branch
    (PWB)   50
  Royal Aircraft Establishment
    (RAE)   172
  Royal Air Force (RAF)   6, 15-17, 23-
    24, 29-30, 32, 34, 36-41, 45, 47 52,
    54, 56-57, 64, 75, 81, 86, 88-89, 93,
    112-113, 115-116, 124-125, 129, 144,
    149, 168-169, 182, 187, 202-203
  Bomber Command (BC)   15-16, 25-
    26, 32, 34-35, 37, 39-40, 57-59, 106,
    147, 202-203
  Operational Research Section
  (ORS)   32, 34, 106-107, 149, 152
  Fighter Command   30
  Photo Intelligence Section   36
  Secret Intelligence Service (SIS)   15
  Special Air Service (SAS)   50, 67, 214
  War Office   34, 57, 59, 202

Bruce, P. Kendall   95
Buck Rogers   1, 13, 34, 42, 100, 125,
  152, 155
Buscio, Chester L.   103-104
Bush, Vannevar   161, 213-214
Butterfield, C.E.   120-122

Cammell, Gordon. W.   41
Cameron, James   50, 67, 214
Camp Dustbin   173-174
Carlson, L.H.   55
Chamberlain, Jo   197-
Chester, Keith   vii, 208-209, 275, 278
Christian, K.C.   151-152
Christian Science Monitor   21
Churchill, Winston S.   41, 49, 51, 53,
  55, 59, 69, 212
Clairidge, Ronald   75
Clark, Ed   138
Clark, Jerome   vii
Cockcroft, Gordon N.   40-41, 171, 211
Columbia Broadcasting System
  (CBS)   13
Collins, Paul T.   20-21
Continental Crossbow Collation
  Section   97
Continental Crossbow Intelligence
  Section   97
Corning, Leavitt Jr.   127
Crawford, Robert S.   189

Davis, Harold O.   119, 138
Davis, Henry C.   21
Dawson, James   185-186
Dehority, James   92
Devers, Jacob L.   49
Dickey, E.E.   142-143
Dirigible   6, 21, 61, 79
"Disc": 23
  "Plate-sized"   55
  Shaped aircraft   47
  Shaped object   18, 45, 47
  "Silvery-colored"   43-46
  "Silvery Colored..." report   43
Donovan, William J.   17, 23, 81
Doolittle, James H.   55, 70, 140, 166,
  204

LeMay, Curtis (cont.)
176, 178-179, 182
Life   206
Lights   6, 11, 18-20, 24-25, 29-30,
34-36, 38-39, 41, 44, 52, 56, 73, 75-76,
79, 82-84, 86-87, 91, 94-96, 100, 102-
105, 107-1110, 113, 115-121, 124-125,
127, 129-131, 133, 136-139, 141-142,
145-146, 148-149, 153-154, 157-160,
163-166, 180, 186-187, 189, 195, 198-
199, 203
   Beams   7
   Blinding   91-92
   "Circles of   164, 177-180, 187, 197
   Gigantic   7, 93
   Glowing   11, 14, 17, 60, 102
   "Roman Candle"   38-39
   Shafts   10, 14
   "Snake-like"   10
   Sword-shaped   14
   Triangle of   20, 105-106
   Unearthly   91
Lincoln and Welland Regiment   83
Lingayen Gulf (Philippines)   95
Lippisch, Alexander   155, 171
"Loch Ness Monster of Edmen"   52
London (England)   11, 17, 25, 54, 58,
63, 70, 80-81, 122, 144
Loomis, A.L.   56
Lott, Floyd   104-106 (picture), 113
Lovett, Robert A.   41, 174
Lumsden, B.C.   36

Malaya (Singapore)   78
Mandel, William A.   189-190, 206
Manhattan Project   212
Mars   13-14
Marshall, George C.   22-23
Martin, Kenneth L.   19
Massey Project   202
McClanahan, Finis D.   116, 145
McCoy, Howard   80, 215
McDonald, George   80, 122, 196
McDonald, James   204
McFalls, David L.   103
Mediterranean Allied Air Force
   (MAAF)   61, 126, 143-144

Mediterranean Allied Coastal Air Force
   (MACAF)   56
Meiers, Donald J.   93-95, 117
Men from Washington (Foo fighter
   investigation)   134-135, 140, 200
Menzel, Erich   168
Meteor   1, 13, 30, 39-40, 83, 169, 199
"Meteor projectiles"   37, 39-41, 60
Military Units (numbers)
   American and Allied:
      1st Marine Division   28
      2nd Bomb Group   90
      3 Group   32, 34
      4th Interceptor Command   19
      5 Group   32, 34-35, 51, 57-60, 89,
         112, 124, 202
      5th Wing   89-90
      6th Ferry Group   51
      6th Allied Army Group   147, 215
      6 Squadron   106
      9 Squadron   89
      11th Bomb Group   125, 163
      12th Allied Army Group   99, 147
      17th Bomb Group   55
      21st Allied Army Group   147
      23 Squadron   56
      25th Bomb Group   114, 116,
         145-146
      37th Coastal Artillery Brigade   19,
         21-22
      38th Regiment   78
      40th Bomb Group   77
      40th Combat Wing   55
      41st Combat Wing   59, 143
      42nd Bomb Group   125
      44th Armored Infantry
         Battalion   153
      49 Squadron   56
      58th Bombardment Wing   166
      61 Squadron   34
      64th Fighter Wing   93, 100, 104,
         106,110, 127, 135
      73rd Bombardment Wing   146, 157
      78th Coastal Artillery   21
      78 Squadron   149
      92nd Bomb Group   59
      109th Tactical Reconnaissance
         Squadron   207
      115 Squadron   52

Printed in the United Kingdom
by Lightning Source UK Ltd.
124265UK00002B/333/A